Drifting: Architecture and Migrancy

To dwell in these globalizing times requires us to negotiate increasingly palpable flows – of capital, ideas, images, goods, technology and people. Such flows seem to pressurize, breach and sometimes even disaggregrate the places we always imagined to be distinctive and stable. This book is focused on the interaction of two elements within this contemporary situation. The first is the idea of a place we imagine to be distinctive and stable. This idea is explored through architecture, the institution that in the West has claimed the responsibility for imagining and producing places along these lines. The second element is a particular kind of global flow, namely the human flows of immigrants, refugees, exiles, guestworkers and other migrant groups. This book carefully inspects the intersections between architectures of place and flows of migrancy. It does so without seeking to defend the idea of place, nor lament its disaggregation. Rather this book is an exploration of the often complex and unorthodox modes of dwelling that are emerging precisely from within the ruins of the idea of place.

The book is animated empirically by a set of overlapping and intersecting trajectories that shift from Hong Kong to Canada, Australia and Germany; from Southern Europe to Australia; from Britain to India, Canada and New Zealand; from Southeast Asia, to the Pacific Islands, to New Zealand; and from Latin America and East Asia to the United States. But each geographical context discussed represents only one point within a wider pattern of movement that implicates other localities, and so signals the very undoing of a unified geographical logic.

Stephen Cairns is a Senior Lecturer at the University of Edinburgh where he teaches and researches on architectural design and theory.

THE ARCHI*TEXT* SERIES

Edited by Thomas A. Markus and Anthony D. King

Architectural discourse has traditionally represented buildings as art objects or technical objects. Yet buildings are also social objects in that they are invested with social meaning and shape social relations. Recognizing these assumptions, the Archi*text* series aims to bring together recent debates in social and cultural theory and the study and practice of architecture and urban design. Critical, comparative and interdisciplinary, the books in the series will, by theorizing architecture, bring the space of the built environment centrally into the social sciences and humanities, as well as bringing the theoretical insights of the latter into the discourses of architecture and urban design. Particular attention will be paid to issues of gender, race, sexuality and the body, to questions of identity and place, to the cultural politics of representation and language, and to the global and postcolonial contexts in which these are addressed.

Already published:

Framing Places
Mediating power in built form
Kim Dovey

Gender Space Architecture
An interdisciplinary introduction
Edited by Jane Rendell, Barbara Penner and Iain Borden

Behind the Postcolonial
Architecture, urban space and political cultures in Indonesia
Abidin Kusno

The Architecture of Oppression
The SS, forced labor and the Nazi monumental building economy
Paul Jaskot

Words between the Spaces
Building and language
Thomas A. Markus and Deborah Cameron

Embodied Utopias
Gender, social change and the modern metropolis
Rebeccah Zorach, Lise Sanders and Amy Bingaman

Writing Spaces
Discourses of architecture, urbanism, and the built environment, 1960–2000
C. Greig Crysler

Drifting: Architecture and Migrancy
Edited by Stephen Cairns

Forthcoming titles:

Beyond Description
Space historicity Singapore
Edited by Ryan Bishop, John Phillips and Wei-Wei Yeo

Moderns Abroad
Architecture, cities and Italian imperialism
Mia Fuller

Spaces of Global Cultures
Anthony D. King

Edited by

Stephen Cairns

Drifting: Architecture and Migrancy

LONDON AND NEW YORK

First published 2004
by Routledge
11 New Fetter Lane, London EC4P 4EE

Simultaneously published in the USA and Canada
by Routledge
29 West 35th Street, New York, NY 10001

Routledge is an imprint of the Taylor and Francis Group

Typeset in Frutiger by
Florence Production Ltd, Stoodleigh, Devon
Printed and bound in Great Britain by
TJ International Ltd, Padstow, Cornwall

British Library Cataloguing in Publication Data
A catalogue record for this book is available from the British Library

Library of Congress Cataloging in Publication Data
A catalog record has been requested

ISBN 0–415–28360–4 (hbk)
ISBN 0–415–28361–2 (pbk)

Contents

Illustrations

FIGURES

TABLE

Contributors

Ackbar Abbas is Chair/Professor of Comparative Literature and Co-Director of the Center for the Study of Globalization and Cultures (CSGC), both at the University of Hong Kong. He is author of *Hong Kong: culture and the politics of disappearance* (University of Minnesota Press, 1997) and numerous academic essays.

Mike Austin is Professor of Architecture at the School of Architecture at Unitec Institute of Technology, Auckland, New Zealand, where he teaches theory and design.

Stephen Cairns is Senior Lecturer at the University of Edinburgh where he teaches and researches on architectural design and theory.

Paul Carter is a Professorial Research Fellow attached to the Australian Centre, the University of Melbourne. His most recent book is *Repressed Spaces: the poetics of agoraphobia* (Reaktion Books, 2002).

Mike Davis writes widely on contemporary urbanism. His most recent publications include *Ecology of Fear: Los Angeles and the imagination of disaster* (Picador, 1999) and *Magical Urbanism: Latinos reinvent the US city* (Verso, 2000).

Andrew Dawson is Senior Lecturer in Social Anthropology at the Universities of Melbourne and Hull. He has published extensively on migrancy and identity, including the volumes *Migrants of Identity* (with N. Rapport) and *After Writing Culture* (with A. James and J. Hockey).

Jacques Derrida is Director of Studies at the Ecole des Hautes Etudes en Sciences Sociales, Paris, and Professor of Humanities at the University of California, Irvine. He is the author of over 50 books on philosophy, literature and the humanities.

Catherine Ingraham is Chair/Professor of Graduate Studies in Architecture and Urban Design at Pratt Institute in New York City. She is the author of

Architecture and the Burdens of Linearity (Yale University Press, 1998) and has written and lectured extensively on architectural theory and history.

Jane M. Jacobs is a Reader in Geography with the School of GeoSciences, the University of Edinburgh. Her most recent books include, with Ken Gelder, *Uncanny Australia: sacredness and identity in a postcolonial nation* (Melbourne University Press, 1998) and, co-edited with Ruth Fincher, *Cities of Difference* (Guilford, 1998).

Mark Johnson is Senior Lecturer in Social Anthropology at the University of Hull.

Mirjana Lozanovska is Senior Lecturer in the School of Architecture and Building, at Deakin University. She has published academic essays on migration, war and architecture.

Katharyne Mitchell is an Associate Professor in the Department of Geography at the University of Washington in Seattle. She is interested in questions of transnational migration, urban development and cultural politics in the Pacific Rim, and has a forthcoming book entitled *Transnationalism and the Politics of Space* (Temple).

Brian Morris teaches in the School of Applied Communication at RMIT University, Melbourne. His publications and current research addresses the role of media and communications technologies in the formation of urban cultures and everyday experience.

Mark Rakatansky is an architect, artist and writer; he is Principal of Mark Rakatansky Studio located in Brooklyn, New York. He teaches design and theory at Columbia University,

Ella Shohat is Professor of Cultural Studies at the departments of Art & Public Policy, Middle Eastern Studies and Comparative Literature, New York University. She has lectured and published extensively on the intersection of post/colonialism, multiculturalism and gender. Her most recent book is the co-edited *Multiculturalism, Postcoloniality, and Transnational Media* (Rutgers, 2003).

Sarah Treadwell is a Senior Lecturer at the School of Architecture, University of Auckland, where she teaches architectural design and architectural drawing. She has published essays on representations of architecture in New Zealand and the South Pacific.

Preface

This collection began its life as a conference held in Melbourne in 1997. This conference – with its rather intricate title *Building Dwelling Drifting: migrancy and the limits of architecture* – was the third in a series of four (to date) organized by members of the 'Other Connections' group. It was preceded by conferences in Singapore (1993) and Chandigarh (1995), and was followed by another in Beirut (1999). The intellectual agenda of the group was unique in the field of architecture for its interest in postcolonial criticism as a means of provincializing and displacing dominant Western conceptions of architecture and urbanism. Each conference in the series was committed to a situated discussion of particular postcolonial questions. So by staging the third conference in Melbourne, arguably one of the world's most multicultural cities, migrancy presented itself as a kind of ready-made postcolonial theme. This collection's origins, then, were quite circumstantial. The catalyst that allowed the (sprawling and diffuse) possibilities of those circumstantial beginnings to be galvanized into this book form was, ultimately, a particular group of eight papers delivered at the conference (Abbas, Austin, Carter, Ingraham, Jacobs, Lozanovska, Rakatansky and Treadwell) – although such was the richness of the papers not included here that various alternative (historical or geographical) formulations on the general theme might have been developed. A further two chapters have been written for this collection (Cairns and Morris), while five chapters (Davis, Dawson and Johnson, Derrida, Mitchell and Shohat) have been taken from existing publications to flesh out under-represented thematic or theoretical perspectives in the collection.

Many individuals were involved in the organization of the original conference. Thanks first to my co-convenor, Philip Goad, for his collaboration in organizing it, to Mirjana Lozanovska for her assistance in thinking through its themes and to Mathilde Lochert and Hilary Ericksen for their help in running it. I am grateful for the financial and in-kind assistance contributed by the Faculty of Architecture Building and Planning at the University of Melbourne, and to the many members of Melbourne's architectural community who supported the event. Subsequently, many others supported the development of this book project. Tony King made important suggestions on the original conference and, subsequently, he and Tom Markus read and commented on the book manuscript; I am grateful to both for their efforts. Thanks to Paul Carter, Catherine Ingraham, Mark Rakatansky and Paul Walker for their guidance and suggestions on the intellectual shape of the project. In particular, I want to acknowledge a special debt to Jane Jacobs for her support of this project from the very beginning. Finally, I want to acknowledge the patience and commitment of the contributors as this collection has made its, sometimes circuitous, way to publication.

The following are the sources for Chapters 2, 6, 7, 8, 13 and 15 respectively:

Derrida, J. (2001) 'On cosmopolitanism', in J. Derrida *On Cosmopolitanism and Forgiveness*, trans. M. Dooley and R. Kearney, London: Routledge. Republished with permission from Routledge and Editions Galilée.

Dawson, A. and Johnson, M. (2001) 'Migration, exile and landscapes of the imagination', in B. Bender and M. Winer (eds) *Contested Landscapes: movement, exile and place*, Oxford: Berg. Republished with permission from the authors.

Abbas, A. (1998) 'Building Hong Kong: from migrancy to disappearance', *Postcolonial Studies: Culture, Politics, Economy* 1 (2): 185–99. Republished with permission from the Institute of Postcolonial Studies.

Mitchell, K. (1997) 'Conflicting geographies of democracy and the public sphere in Vancouver BC', *Transactions of the Institute of British Geographers*, NS 22: 162–79. Republished with permission of the Royal Geographical Society.

Davis, M. (2000) 'La Frontera's Siamese twins', in M. Davis, *Magical Urbanism: Latinos reinvent the US city*, London: Verso. Republished with permission from Verso.

Shohat, E. (1999) 'By the bitstream of Babylon: cyberfrontiers and diasporic vistas', in H. Naficy (ed.) *Home, Exile, Homeland: film, media, and the politics of place*, London: Routledge. Republished with permission from Routledge.

Cover image: Navigation chart from the Marshall Islands, Micronesia. From *National Geographic*, December 1974.

Stephen Cairns

Introduction

Stephen Cairns

RESIDUAL SCRIPTS

Architecture/migrancy. What is it to bring these terms together in this way? The two terms activate opposite meanings, one being associated with the groundedness of buildings, the constitution of places, and the delimitation of territories, the other with uprootedness, mobility, and the transience of individuals and groups of people. Yet, so neat is the opposition between the terms, that in Western thought they were often brought together as counterparts within a more general binary relation. This binary relation privileged such principles as settlement, stability, and permanence over those of movement, flux, and fluidity. Migrancy, in its various enforced and voluntary forms was aligned with the suspect qualities of movement, and so came to be considered to be the unfortunate exception to a more general principle of settlement. Within this logic, the migrant was ascribed kinship with the nomad, the Scythian, the gypsy, the wild man, and other figures that haunted the imagination of the settled citizen.

Yet, however closely identified migrants were with nomadic styles of mobility, their aspirations were oriented towards stability and settlement. Migrancy, for migrant and host alike, traditionally carried with it the expectation that its flows would be controlled and managed. Migrancy was shaped by expectations that immigrants would be accommodated, and eventually settled, into the modes of living of host territories. In this sense, the migrant was not the same as the nomad, and carried quite different threats to the principle of settlement. For Deleuze and Guattari (1986: 52), the figure of the nomad is 'the Deterritorialized *par excellence*', meaning that it always existed outside of, and in contradistinction to, the ordered and secure space of territory – the 'points, paths, or land' of the city, the province, or the nation. In contrast, the figure of 'the migrant', they observe, undergoes 'reterritorialization' following a periodic deterritorialization. The figure of the migrant moved, but often in pursuit of, or in the service of, territory – labour markets, population goals, nation building, empire. The migrant, then, cannot be scripted as the other to the settled citizen in any simple way. However rootless and deterritorialized s/he might appear, unlike the nomad, the migrant's aim/destiny was precisely to reterritorialize – to settle, to make a home, to become a citizen in a new place. Migrancy, understood in this way, was guided by a teleology that openly anticipated the transformation of migrant to citizen. But we also know that the sequence of movement and settlement that characterized migrancy was seen to have a range of unsettling effects: jeopardizing social cohesion; straining housing and servicing infrastructure; disrupting sense of home and belonging; inducing social resentment and racism. And herein lay the 'threat' to the territorial logics of nation and metropolis. The expectation that migrants would enter into national and metropolitan spaces, meant that they had the capacity to smuggle into those spaces specific effects of unsettlement that in the hands of the nomad, the gypsy, the Scythian, or the wild man would remain more safely at a distance.

Architecture was explicitly scripted into this conventional understanding of migrancy. Its capacities for grounding, delimiting, and accommodating were readily and routinely put to work in the material, social, cultural, and emotional reterritorialization of uprooted migrants. Historically, such reterritorialization took various architectural forms, ranging from the establishment of enclaves clearly segregated from host communities, to the construction of individual dwellings distributed among host communities in the name of assimilation. In between the extremes of segregation and assimilation were diverse adaptive, syncretic, and hybridized modes of architectural reterritorialization. While there are many examples of these diverse architectural modes – some of which I will discuss in Chapter 1 – the teleological drive of the conventional migrancy script meant that the pressure to assimilate was always felt. The pressure to assimilate assumes, what Ingraham (in this volume) has called, an isomorphic relation between various dimensions of national and metropolitan space. This isomorphism seeks to produce clear correspondences between social space and architectural space, such that social life might be registered in a legible and secure way with the architectural and urban forms that frame it. Derrida usefully encapsulates the more general motivations of such a process under the heading 'ontopology'. By ontopology, he means 'an axiomatics linking indissociably the ontological value of present-being [*on*] to its *situation*, to the stable and presentable determination of a locality, the *topos* of territory, native soil, city, body in general' (Derrida 1994: 80).[1] The ideology and practice of assimilationism assumed a prior ontopological link between being and territory such that proper being (well being) required territory. Architecture, in this schema, functioned as a specific isomorphic technology and imaginary that produced the necessary correspondences to confirm this link. In doing so, it carried with it the expectation that, however many generations it took, the signs of a migrant's origins would be reshaped – morphed – according to the cultural norms and forms that operated within their host society.

ACCOUNTING FOR MIGRANCY

Architecture is, then, foundationally implicated in '(re)solving' the 'threat' and 'problem' of migrancy as it was conventionally understood. But we now live in, what sociologists Stephen Castles and Mark Miller (1993) have called, 'the age of migration', an age in which the long-standing themes of the conventional migrancy script are being challenged. Architecture's place in that conventional script can no longer be taken for granted, so it seems both timely and compelling to consider the current contours and future prospects of that relationship.

Since the Second World War, migrancy has rapidly become more global in its scope and scale, such that now, in the first years of the twenty-first century, it involves more diverse points of origin, destinations, trajectories, and forms of mobility than at any time in history (Castles 2000; Castles and Miller 1993; Papastergiadis 2000; Pries 1999; Rapport and Dawson 1998). It is impossible not to notice that to dwell in these times requires negotiation of increasingly forceful flows – of capital, ideas, images, goods, technology, and people. Contemporary migrancy, involving the movements of immigrants and emigrants, guestworkers, refugees, asylum-seekers, exiles, and other diasporic groups, is thoroughly caught up in these global flows. As a consequence, its effects are more troubling, intensely felt and widespread than ever before. Yet, these effects, for all their ubiquity and troublesome character, are strangely difficult to account for empirically. The enduring resonance of migrancy's residual script – in particular its teleological, isomorphic, and ontopological themes, as outlined above – contributes fundamentally to this difficulty. But before exploring this issue further, I will attempt to sketch, however inadequately, the empirical dimensions of contemporary migrancy.

Statistically speaking, there are more people undertaking migratory journeys around the world today than ever before. A direct comparison of the scale and scope of contemporary and historical migrancy is difficult to make, but the following figures offer a useful guide: the number of slaves in the Americas between 1800 and 1860 rose from 3 million to 6 million; indentured labour used in 40 countries by all the colonial powers increased from 12 to 37 million workers between 1834 and 1941; between 1800 and 1930, triggered in part by the labour requirements of industrialization, 40 million Europeans emigrated permanently to the Americas and other New World destinations (Castles and Miller 1993: 48–51); and from 1933 to the outbreak of the Second World War, some 100,000 individuals, fleeing the rise of National Socialism in Germany, arrived in the US (around 10,000 of whom were academics, intellectuals, artists, and writers) (Jay 1998: 326). Compare these historical figures with those of the present. In 2000 alone, 850,000 legal immigrants arrived in the US (OECD 2001) – of these, 42,000 were from India, demonstrating the significant shift in quantity and source of migrants that has taken place since the War. United Nations estimates suggest that the number of international migrants rose from 75 million in 1965, to 120 million in 1990, to 140 million in 2000, an average growth rate of 1.9 per cent per annum. These figures show that contemporary migration far eclipses the movements associated with colonialism, industrialization, the Second World War, or, indeed, the immediate post-war period.

Despite the enormous numbers involved, migration can still appear to be a minor phenomenon in statistical terms. Castles and Miller (1993) estimate that international migrants constitute only 2–4 per cent of the world's population, suggesting that despite the evident scale of current migration, the majority of the world's population is still relatively sedentary. The profound turbulence widely imputed to contemporary migration seems out of step with the statistical realities, such that the global 'flow' of migrants is, relatively speaking, but a trickle.

To gain a better sense of migrancy's global reach and the intensive nature of its effects on contemporary life, figures such as these require substantial qualification. First, contemporary migratory movement has such diverse scales and trajectories it is likely, as official United Nations monitors suggest, that available figures represent lower-end estimates only (UN 2002a: 2). Second, and more importantly, contemporary migration is concentrated in very particular ways and in specific places. While migrants make up only 1.6 per cent of the population in developing countries, they constitute on average 4.5 per cent of the population in developed countries (UN 2002a: 5). This concentration of migrants in the developed world becomes even more evident in particular national contexts. For instance, 23.6 per cent of the population in Australia is foreign born, as is 17.4 per cent in Canada, 11.8 per cent in Sweden, and 10.3 per cent in the US (OECD 2001). Indeed, over the past decade most population growth in developed nations (56 per cent) has been driven not by birth rates but by immigration (UN 2000a: 9). Furthermore, immigrants to the countries of the developed world overwhelmingly concentrate in urban areas.[2] The United Nations expects 'virtually all the population growth [. . .] during 2000–2030 [to] be concentrated in the urban areas of the world' (UN 1999: 1). As fertility rates in developed countries are predicted to continue to fall, the pattern of concentration of immigrants in urban areas can only become more intensive in character.

Two supplementary points might be made about this situation, both of which underscore the intensified character of contemporary migrancy. First, the United Nations and OECD (Organization for Economic Co-operation and Development) studies upon which these observations are made, primarily record unidirectional population movements from countries in the non-West to those in the West. This underestimates circulatory and shuttling journeys to and from the West, as well as the large population movements that take place between non-Western nations and regions. Furthermore, the crude nature of these measures ignores the profound non-linearity of those itineraries whose ultimate destination is the West. For instance, by far the greatest proportion of international migration takes place between countries in the Southern Hemisphere (in Africa, parts of Asia and the Middle East, and South America), yet this goes largely unreported (OECD 2001). Second, the primary focus of much official inter-governmental analysis of human mobility is on permanent migration and, specifically, the dimension of immigration – i.e. the process of arrival and settlement in a new country. Usually under-represented in these official studies are the effects of emigration – i.e. departure – on places outside the West, as well as the scale and scope of various illegal and temporary migrations (see Lozanovska, this volume, on the reciprocities involved in migrancy's points of departure and arrival).

THE UNACCOUNTABILITY OF MIGRANCY

When we start to qualify in this way, even the most gross of migration statistics, it is possible to see why the numerical and the felt dimensions of contemporary migrancy do not seem to correspond. Despite the fact that statistics on contemporary migrancy abound, it remains a stubbornly unaccountable phenomenon within a wide range of political, cultural and academic discourses. The relation between migrancy's affectual and statistical dimensions can appear, by turns, wildly exaggerated and strangely understated. This unevenness is discernible, for instance, when recent treatments of migrancy in both Western national politics and in the social sciences are compared.

The political discourse of most Western nations in recent years indicates an increasing wariness of immigration. The United Nations reports that by 1996, 60 per cent of governments in developed nations, responding to the shifting 'mood of the national electorate', had initiated laws explicitly aimed at lowering levels of immigration. This compares to 18 per cent of countries that had such policies in 1976 (UN 2002b). This widespread adoption of immigration controls has come about despite the documented need most of these same nations have for net immigration in order to sustain population growth and to supplement specific sectors of the labour market. Yet, when we turn to the social sciences, where we might expect such a prominent social phenomenon as international migrancy to be given disinterested treatment, we find that it is consistently under-represented. As Castles and Miller (1993: 43) suggest, migrancy constitutes a 'blind spot' in the traditional scope of the social sciences. They argue that in the last decades of the twentieth century, social science became so integrated into the policy research machinery of national governments throughout the Western world that its capacity to theorize socio-spatial formations was constrained by the framework of the nation state. This framework privileges links between birth and national territory, man and citizenship (Agamben 1998: 134). In the terms of the International Court of Justice, traditional citizenship and nationality requirements are predicated on evidence of a tangible 'genuine link' and 'true bond of attachment' and 'reciprocity of rights and duties' between an individual and a nation state (Preuss 1998: 309). We might note that this represents another manifestation of the ontopology that underscores the circumstances of migrancy. Social science's allegiance to the nation state, predetermines that the migrant is understood as the subject (and object) for improvement within the parameters of those ideologies – a point that has important consequences for architecture, and which I will explore in Chapter 1. As Castles and Miller go on to suggest, social science's 'blindness' in this context is constituted around its inability to register the mobile, transactive, and transnational processes entailed in contemporary migrancy.

This brief comparison suggests that political and academic discourses about migrancy are out of kilter with each other, precisely when they have become more thoroughly integrated. At the heart of this imbalance is the intensification of the residual threat migrancy poses to the ontopology of settlement. This threat has far-reaching consequences for migrant and host communities alike. For the migrant, departure and arrival was once imagined to be a more-or-less singular act in which one integrated locality (an old 'home') was cleanly substituted for another (a new 'home'). But departure is now rarely met with a symmetrical point of arrival. Instead, departure opens onto a diasporic network of fragmented spaces that are dispersed across national boundaries, through which individuals find work, do business, engage in study, conduct friendships, and sustain families intermittently. Migrants, having loyalties to multiple contexts, come to be bi- or pluri-located. Host communities find that long-established patterns of defensiveness, now more than ever, are shot through with desires for the real and imagined benefits migrants bring – labour, investment capital, consumption capacities, skills, culture, cuisine, . . . What was once simply a singular metropolitan destination, is now increasingly implicated in this networked and less accountable form of migrant space. In this more complex structure of mobility, social space and architectural space do not so neatly correspond as the ontopological and assimilationist models would have it. Seemingly desedimented, these spaces can be stacked thick and stretched thin to produce startling and hitherto inconceivable patterns of dwelling (Pries 1999: 5).

Contemporary migrants sustain 'true' and 'genuine' bonds of attachment to more than one place by intensifying modes of transit between them. This poses direct challenges to the exclusivity of the loyalty and commitment between citizen and territory upon which the nation state is founded. The fragmented and distended nature of migrant space can only be registered partially in statistical analyses. In turn, this partiality is refracted through political and academic discourses in quite different ways – an exaggerated sensitivity towards the perceived threats to national and metropolitan ontopology in the case of the state, and an historical 'blindness' to the transnational movements and transactive mobilities in the case of social science scholarship.

MULTICULTURALISM

Historical patterns of migrancy have rarely conformed to the assimilationist orthodoxy. Rather, they have always carried dislocating effects that run counter to or undermine assimilation. As Derrida suggests, the process of dislocation is 'just as "archaic" as the archaism [of the ontopology] that it has always dislodged' (Derrida 1994: 80). But the nonconforming effects of migrant flows today are so palpable and widespread that the conventional migrancy script has lost its explanatory power and political effectiveness – even if its assimilationist themes may have gained renewed currency within the rhetorics of xenophobia and nationalism. This more openly diverse and mobile social field has been codified through multiculturalism. Under this logic, the expectation that immigrants would simply arrive, settle, and assimilate, has been tempered by an assumption that immigrants might settle in their new destinations in ways that openly acknowledge and express their own cultural origins, even in ways that sustain links to their places of origins. Under a multicultural conception of national or metropolitan life, the split loyalties that accompanied migrant dislocation are given public expression. Architecture and migrancy accommodate each other in an altered way in this context. Architectural reterritorialization takes place not according to the dominant territorial logic of the host, or according to some universally assumed principle of settlement. Rather, it is expected to articulate the diverse styles of settlement that distinctive immigrant cultures bring. This entails the reinterpretation of national principles of settlement (which are often also assumed to be universal) according to culturally relativist criteria which recognize and value difference. Such criteria might be represented, for instance, in the new appreciation for the architectures of ethnic enclaves – with their exotic restaurants, emporia, religious shrines, and cultural festivals – found in most Western cities. Under the logic of multiculturalism, national and metropolitan citizens take comfort in the image of a reconstituted architecture of places, regions and territories. These are places that have been rearranged and disturbed perhaps, but they are also places that are understood to have been culturally enriched and enlivened, and are consequently celebrated.

However liberalized and diversified the conceptions of space and place delivered by multiculturalism have become, there remains a sense, for migrant and host alike, that the flows of migrancy are still not adequately accommodated. The flows continue to pressurize, routinely breach, and sometimes disaggregate national and metropolitan spaces. In this context, multiculturalist architectural reterritorializations quickly become reinstatements of older ontopologies in liberal guise. Rather than acting as an open acknowledgement of difference, architecture so deployed operates as a defensive mechanism. It temporarily assuages metropolitan fears about succumbing to the pressures of migrancy or about the disaggregation of place that is bound to follow.[3] As such, multiculturalism conceals and manages a more profound and unsettling shift in which migrancy threatens to break with its conventional role altogether and become immanent to the condition of dwelling, not so much the unfortunate exception to proper, settled modes of dwelling, as a predicate to the rule of how we dwell now. If contemporary dwelling is co-constituted with migrancy, then this sets challenges for architecture's traditional investment in statics, foundations, groundedness, and stability. These challenges are more demanding and consequential than either the assimilationist or multiculturalist scripts allow. As Ackbar Abbas succinctly puts it in his essay to follow, 'migrancy means [. . .] not only changing places; it also means changing the nature of places'.

The preceding discussion has suggested that the need to accommodate architecture to migrancy can be discerned in multiculturalist responses to migrancy, as much as to assimilationist ones. This book does not, then, seek to firmly articulate 'architecture' and 'migrancy' in order to disclose yet further iterations of the ontopological ideology that nourishes that need. To do this would be to foreclose on the prominent and unsettling effects that contemporary migrancy generates in terms of the relations between social space and architectural space. Instead, this book seeks to deploy architecture/migrancy as a tentative pairing whose mode of articulation has been, for the moment, left open so that particular disturbances can surface. Such disturbances coalesce into strange affectual landscapes that appear, by turns, paranoiac and exhilarating, melancholic and enthusiastic. As such, this book inspects the affiliations and tensions between architectures of place and dynamics of contemporary migrancy. It does so without seeking to defend the idea of place, or lament its disintegration. Rather, it seeks to explore the often complex and unorthodox modes of dwelling that are emerging precisely from within its ruins.

THE CHAPTERS

The chapters that follow explore the possibilities of the architecture/migrancy association through diverse disciplinary points of view. These include architecture (Cairns, Ingraham, Rakatansky, Lozanovska, Treadwell, Austin), urban geography (Mitchell, Jacobs), cultural studies (Abbas, Morris), cinema studies (Shohat), anthropology (Dawson and Johnson), and what might be called a philosophically inflected postcolonialism (Derrida, Carter). Each of these disciplinary perspectives activate quite distinctive epistemological and methodological heritages that come to be expressed through particular objects of analysis and conceptual vocabularies, privileged rhetorical tropes and turns of phrase. This disciplinary diversity compromises any harmonious and coherent approach to the topic. But what coherence is lost is more than recouped through the associative, exploratory, and open-ended working ethos the contributing authors are prepared to risk. This ethos is most clearly manifest in the sensitivity the authors have to the unorthodox and uneven ways in which material and representational conditions interact in the context of migrancy. As a consequence, these conditions are held in tension throughout this collection, without necessarily being resolved in favour of one or the other as they tend to be within more tightly integrated disciplinary discourses.

The diversity of disciplinary approaches is compounded by the wide range of empirical material that is tackled in the book – from particular geographical contexts to different cultural forms such as architecture and film. The chapters are not strictly distinguished between those that have theoretical or empirical motivations, rather, the emphases of each differs according to its own disciplinary and philosophical investments. Nonetheless, a rough empirical focus comes into view as the book unfolds. The earlier chapters elaborate the central problematic of this collection. In particular, architecture is considered in terms of the wider ethical and political principles – such as hospitality and courtesy – which underpin contemporary representations of migrancy. Empirical material from Europe, the US, and Australia feature here. The chapters in the latter parts of the collection explore these themes within (and between) more specific geographical contexts. These contexts tend to coalesce around, across, and in the Pacific – Vietnam, Hong Kong, Canada, the US, Mexico, Australia, New Zealand, and the Pacific Islands. The Pacific Rim is privileged in this book because it is a space that is often said to be at the vanguard of late modern globalization, where complex tensions are staged between the new economies of East Asia and the settler nations of Canada, the US, Australia, and New Zealand (Connery 1996; Watters and McGee 1997). These tensions produce difficulties for the narrative of the nation state, and herald conditions that no longer conform to the geo-political norms of the Old World. At the same time, the studies in this book show how difficult it is to discuss migrancy within a single geographical framework, whether it is 'East Asia', 'the Pacific Rim' or 'Europe'. The book follows overlapping and intersecting movements that lead us from Hong Kong to Canada, Australia and Germany; from Southern Europe to Australia; from Britain to India, Canada and New Zealand; from Southeast Asia, to the Pacific Islands, to New Zealand; and from Latin America and East Asia to the US. Each geographical context discussed in the chapters that follow represents only one point within a wider pattern of movement that implicates other localities, and so signals the very undoing of a unified geographical logic.

The collection begins with my own (Chapter 1) elaboration of some of the central issues discussed in this 'Introduction'. This extended introduction is followed by Jacques Derrida's essay 'On cosmopolitanism' (Chapter 2) which calls for the reinvigoration of the idea of the 'city of refuge' in a time when the very idea of refuge and asylum has come to seem anachronistic. For Derrida, the nation state has so entrenched and naturalized the concept of state sovereignty that it 'should no longer be the ultimate horizon for cities of refuge'. To imagine, now, in the early twenty-first century, a state of refuge that did not involve repatriation or assimilation necessarily requires us to think beyond the framework of the state, and think again about the idea of the city. Derrida argues that it is the city, and not the state, which offers the greatest potential for embodying the kind of hospitality that is required in the age of migration. For Derrida, hospitality necessarily implicates the architecture of 'the residence, one's home, the familiar place of dwelling' as it does the city itself. His chapter explores the history of the idea of the city of refuge through three distinct, but related, traditions: Hebraic and Medieval, and Classical/Enlightenment. It calls for 'a genuine innovation', 'experimentation', and the 'invention' of new forms of solidarity that extend this history.

Catherine Ingraham's 'Architecture as evidence' (Chapter 3), dwells on the intersections between architectural and legal discourses as they pertain to the definition of property. The broader themes of hospitality and the city, as they are elaborated in Derrida's chapter, are given more specific architectural consideration here through the related concepts of courtesy, security, and property. Ingraham argues that the term 'property', particularly through its cognate 'proper', is a fundamental precept in the conception of civility and liberty in the West, and that architecture has always been instrumental in the formation of larger systems of intelligibility in the West. Architecture, in this context, is shown to function as a kind of concealed (or all-too-apparent) 'evidence' that underwrites wider principles of social propriety, liberty, and civility. Ingraham proceeds to scrutinize architecture for evidence of the particular kinds of disturbance that migrancy activates in the West. She suggests that an ethical architectural practice attuned to the demands of hospitality is necessarily one that is prepared to risk the consequences of reading in an evidentiary way.

Paul Carter's critique of the 'cult of placism' in his 'Mythforms: techniques of migrant place-making' (Chapter 4), might be read as an attack on the isomorphic tendencies of multiculturalism. Carter takes up some of the challenges posed by Derrida and Ingraham by explicitly addressing design practice, in particular the practice of line-making. Carter identifies a multiculturalist design orthodoxy that is itself invested in an ideology of non-design. This orthodoxy openly acknowledges the figure of the migrant, but only insofar as s/he might be represented as a culturalist caricature. Carter unstitches the linear design logics that give (architectural and urban) form to this orthodoxy, and, developing a hint from Elias Canetti that pictures 'migration as a group of people walking in single-file', he elaborates an ethos of tracking and tracing rather than line drawing. Carter's central innovation here is his diagnosis of the subtle kinetic possibilities and the finely balanced semiotic weight that a track – as opposed to a (Cartesian) line – might carry. This particular tracing/tracking practice gives rise to an intermittent, labyrinthine, non-monumental, non-linear, and non-teleological mode of spatial production.

The philosophical questions of hospitality, courtesy, and security, as explored in Chapters 2 and 3, and their possible modes of spatialization as diagnosed by Carter, are further entangled with architecture's peculiar disciplinary investments in Chapter 5, 'Why architecture is neither here nor there'. Here, Mark Rakatansky begins with the general observation that architectural design practice quite routinely oscillates between specific (the here) and general (the there) registers. This observation allows us, he suggests, to think of architecture performatively, that is, as a practice that is enmeshed, enfolded, in a field of 'non-localized relations', rather than being rooted in the idea of some essential place or in a particular set of contextual contingencies. Rakatansky, resonating with Carter's critique of placism, argues that this (often unacknowledged) feature of architectural practice renders it useful for considering the phenomenon of migrancy. Rakatansky pays particular attention here to the way migrancy has been theorized in postcolonial theory through such tropes as hybridity, mimicry, and ambivalence. He goes on to examine this postcolonial terminology with reference to the work of Japanese architect Shigeru Ban, particularly his designs for emergency shelters for Rwanda and Japan.

Andrew Dawson and Mark Johnson take up the themes of generality and specificity through an anthropological framework. Their chapter, 'Migration, exile and landscapes of the imagination' (Chapter 6), explores the convolution of a migrant's actual and imagined movements. They extend James Clifford's well-known pairing of 'roots and routes', to show that fixity and travel are rarely stable and distinctive categories in migrancy, but that they usually collapse into each other. As a consequence, places that appear to be most fixed in social, material, and architectural terms can support highly mobile or fluid collective imaginaries, while more fluid and transient places, whose architectures may be more lightweight and fragile, can sustain more grounded and fixed imaginaries. These observations are worked out through two ethnographic studies – one focused on proposals for a community museum in a mining town in Northeast England, and the other on a tourist town in central Vietnam. Through these fine-grained studies, Dawson and Johnson 'disrupt this oppositional logic of either roots or routes', and suggest 'a more complex relation of both/and', a condition they dub 'ex/isled'.

Ackbar Abbas works with a related theme in the context of Hong Kong. His essay, 'Building Hong Kong: from migrancy to disappearance' (Chapter 7), diagnoses in that city a ubiquitous atmospherics of migrancy that is governed by an imagined, rather than an actual, transnational movement. This atmospherics has very particular effects on urban and architectural forms in the city. Drawing on the work of Paul Virilio, Abbas suggests that there is a condition of 'disappearance' at work in Hong Kong – ironically most palpable at the point of its 'appearance' as a postcolonial entity in the 1997 'handover'. This condition, he suggests, renders architectural and urban embodiments of historical memory and origin as strangely anachronistic. Abbas develops these observations by suggesting that contemporary film in Hong Kong is one cultural form that has come to grips with this fluid condition most successfully. He points to the absence of sentimentality in the imaginative configuring of history, origin, memory, and architectural place in these films. In this, he argues, are clues as to how an 'architecture of disappearance' might be produced.

Where Abbas scrutinizes the architectures of a Hong Kong within the grip of an atmospherics of migrancy-in-place, in Chapter 8 we follow the fortunes of a particular group of Hong Kong emigrants who do leave the country to settle elsewhere. In her essay 'Conflicting landscapes of dwelling and democracy in Canada', urban geographer, Katharyne Mitchell, explores the consequences of the flight of wealthy middle-class emigrants from Hong Kong to Vancouver following the 'handover'. Her chapter focuses on the conflicts that have arisen over the so-called 'monster' houses built in Vancouver by migrants from Hong Kong (and Taiwan), and examines how these architectures became a condensation point for wider discussions on the urban consequences of rapid economic change. Mitchell shows how the construction of these houses, and the controversial land-use decisions associated with them, spurred a rethinking of democracy and the public sphere in Vancouver. Deploying the work of Habermas and Bourdieu, she places aesthetic and architectural questions into contact with wider planning, economic, and political processes in very direct and intimate ways.

In Chapter 9, 'Too many houses for a home: narrating the house in the Chinese diaspora', Jane M. Jacobs follows another outbound migrant journey from Hong Kong, this time to Germany and Australia. Jacobs explores the ways in which the idea of home is reconstituted in diverse diasporic contexts in both emotional and architectural ways. She elaborates this theme through the diasporic experiences of a single Chinese family as depicted in the feature film, *Floating Life* (Clara Law 1995). Jacobs deploys Freud's account of the uncanny in this context to demonstrate the ways in which the very ordinariness of these migrants' homes come to simultaneously carry extraordinary effects. The uncanniness of this migrant experience is analysed through the new vocabulary of diasporic life – 'sojourner', 'astronaut family', 'parachute children', and 'empty wife' – as it comes into touch with particular domestic architectural technologies, materials, and spaces. Jacobs scrutinizes specific everyday elements of the migrant homes depicted in the film, such as stairs, passages, living rooms, kitchens, gardens, to chart a complex emotional terrain that swings between enthusiasm, optimism, pathos, and paranoia.

Mirjana Lozanovska's 'Emigration/immigration: maps, myths and origins' (Chapter 10) deals directly with the asymmetrical relations between migrancy's points of departure and arrival. Her chapter elaborates themes we have already encountered in the chapters by Abbas, Jacobs, and Carter. Lozanovska focuses on a migrant route that links parts of Southern Europe and Australia, a route first established in the post-war period under the racist 'White Australia' immigration policy. Lozanovska examines the ways in which the 'em' and the 'imm' of migration suggest dependent and asymmetrical sites where real and imaginary identities are located, projected, memorialized, and exchanged. This dependence can be represented simply: to say that 'we are here' (in Melbourne), at the site of immigration, is to acknowledge that that 'they are there' (in Zavoj), at the site of emigration. Lozanovska argues that migrancy's departure-and-arrival dynamic poses particular temporal and narrative difficulties for architectural scholarship, and, in particular, for the formal representation of space and built form. This difficulty, she suggests, produces a kind of 'abject geometry' of migrancy in which fantastical projections, desires are registered within the conventions of planimetric representation.

New Zealand and Australia were both settled in the colonial era by migrant populations from Britain. Although their subsequent histories of migration are quite distinctive, they share a common Anglo-settler heritage. Sarah Treadwell's 'Earthquake weather' (Chapter 11) is focused on the passage and the disturbing moment of arrival in the colonial settler journey to New Zealand. Treadwell suggests that for colonial settlers, the strangeness of New Zealand's geological, meteorological, and topographical dimensions became conflated with the cross-cultural strangeness of their encounters with native Maori inhabitants. This inaugural settler experience posed challenges to the European architectural logics that settlers brought with them. The multiply strange conditions of New Zealand meant that European notions of architecture, homeliness, and security had to be radically reconfigured. This chapter explores these reconfigurations through the many journal accounts that settlers wrote. Through this history, Treadwell suggests that those inaugural challenges that settlers faced continue to ripple through the social and built fabric in New Zealand today. The chapter is guided theoretically by Julia Kristeva's notion of foreignness within, and by her characterization of foreignness as a type of perpetual motion.

Mike Austin's 'Pacific island migration' (Chapter 12) could be read as a parallel chapter in the history of architecture and migrancy in the South Pacific. Where Treadwell explores settlement in relation to European conceptions of architecture – obsessed with foundational and terrestrial logics – Austin leads us into the Pacific where architecture has to be considered in an altogether more fluid, flexible, supple, even aquatic way. Ever since it entered into the European imagination, the Pacific has been conceived as a space of transit between remote island destinations. This topographical condition, Austin argues, has meant that land-based architectural propositions do not necessarily apply in the Pacific. His discussion on the historical journeys that have criss-crossed the Pacific, is brought to bear on migrancy in the present day as large numbers of people move from the Pacific islands towards the urban centres of New Zealand. Austin explores the significance of the role of boats in the architecture of the Pacific, and argues that this 'typological' heritage can inform contemporary debates about appropriate architectures for Pacific migrants in such urban settings.

Chapter 13 transports us from the South Pacific to the eastern edge of the Pacific, to Southern California. Here, the older patterns of settler migration from inland US are now intersected with population movements from the South (Mexico and Latin America) and from the West, across the Pacific (Hong Kong, Japan, Korea, Taiwan, and Vietnam). In this chapter, 'La Frontera's Siamese twins', Mike Davis focuses on the infrastructures of the border between the US and Mexico at San Diego/Tijuana. Davis presents a kind of report from the front line where the 'line' itself is a convoluted geometrical entity. This border line functions as a kind of 'dam and sieve': both a barrier that establishes a reservoir for cheap labour that can be tapped on demand, and a porous membrane that allows migrant labour to cross into Southern California and Nevada to service their postindustrial economies. This, Davis argues, has transmogrified a space that was once famous for its sharp juxtaposition of first and third worlds into one characterized by an 'magical realist' interpenetration of 'national temporalities, settlement forms and ecologies'.

In 'Screening Los Angeles: architecture, migrancy and mobility' (Chapter 14), Brian Morris takes us to Los Angeles. Here, the materialities of the borderland migrancy that Davis examines are cloaked, embedded and transformed within the heightened representational milieu of the metropolis. Los Angeles is usefully understood, Morris suggests, as being constituted by an 'architecture of screens' – car windscreens, domestic windows, cinema screens, computer screens. This image suggests a city that is partially and intermittently 'dematerialized', whose spaces are constituted through flickering regimes of in/visibility and im/materiality. This analysis, as it pertains to migrancy in LA, is explored through Wim Wenders' film, *The End of Violence*. Morris argues that this film uniquely charts a range of spaces that have been rendered invisible to the technologized gaze of the state, and that these are directly implicated in the daily practices of the film's migrant characters. Morris shows that these invisible spaces do not simply represent a parallel urban realm that is the exclusive preserve of migrants, but that they are imbricated within the official metropolitan spaces of LA in complex and surprising ways.

Ella Shohat takes up the architecture of screens that Morris thematizes in LA, in a more global way in the final chapter of this collection. Her essay, 'By the bitstream of Babylon: cyberfrontiers and diasporic vistas' (Chapter 15), offers a careful assessment of the possibilities for the formation of digitally mediated global migrant communities. Like Morris, she argues that the spectacular qualities of contemporary representational media do not inevitably lead to the dematerialization of locality. Rather, she critiques the 'futurist euphorics' of the cyberdiscourse – as found, for instance, in the architectural writings of William Mitchell – on urban and geographical space. Shohat is interested in the political implications of this cyberdiscourse as it pertains to the formation of global diasporic communities. She reads the cyberdiscourse against immigrant struggles for land and labour, and argues that the material and the virtual must be understood as being complexly and mutually overdetermining. Shohat holds out a 'qualified optimism' for the possibilities of migrant cyberspaces, in which '[t]he digital undermining of territoriality' can simultaneously engender 'the virtual reterritorialization of immigrants and refugees'.

NOTES

1 See Homi Bhabha (1996) for a wider postcolonial treatment of this idea.

2 The primacy of initial labour markets in urban areas are important, but not determining factors, in migration patterns. As Castles and Miller (1993: 20–1) have suggested, much twentieth-century migration has followed the contours of uneven development. Developing countries, whose capital investment and production levels were comparatively low, and whose labour surpluses high, provided ready supplies of unskilled labour to the expanding economies of the industrialized developed world. Patterns of global migration in this context are underscored by a complex range of factors that include the 'push-pull' of economic imperatives, historical ties, and cultural associations, and by national and international programmes that encourage and regulate various forms of temporary and permanent migration.

3 Recent critiques of multiculturalism, such as those articulated by Slavoj Zizek (1997) and Ghassan Hage (1998), draw attention to the domesticating consequences certain kinds of multiculturalism have on immigrant communities. 'Liberal "tolerance" condones the folklorist Other deprived of its substance – like the multitude of "ethnic cuisines" in a contemporary megalopolis; however, any "real" Other is instantly denounced for its "fundamentalism"' (Žižek 1997: 37). According to this line of argument, these new, celebratory effects of multiculturalism, in fact, sustain older teleological and assimilationist structures, and cannot come to terms with the more radical kind of fragmentation, stretching, and desedimentation associated with globalized migrancy.

REFERENCES

Agamben, G. (1998) *Homo Sacer: sovereign power and bare life*, trans. D. Heller-Roazen, Stanford: Stanford University Press.

Bhabha, H. (1996) 'Day by day . . . with Frantz Fanon', in A. Read (ed.), *The Fact of Blackness: Frantz Fanon and visual representation*, Seattle: Bay Press.

Castles, S. (2000) *Ethnicity and Globalization*, London: Sage.

Castles, S. and Miller, M.J. (1993) *The Age of Migration: international population movements in the modern world*, Hampshire and London: Macmillan.

Connery, C.L. (1996) 'The oceanic feeling and the regional imaginary', in R. Wilson and W. Dissanayake (eds) *Global/Local: cultural production and the transnational imaginary*, Durham and London: Duke University Press.

Deleuze, G. and Guattari, F. (1986) *Nomadology*, New York: Semiotext(e).

Derrida, J. (1994) *Specters of Marx: the state of the debt, the work of mourning, and the new international*, London: Routledge.

Freud, S. (1991) *Introductory Lectures on Psychoanalysis*, trans. J. Strachey, London: Penguin.

Hage, G. (1998) *White Nation: fantasies of white supremacy in a multicultural society*, Sydney: Pluto Press.

Jay, M. (1998) 'The German migration: is there a figure in the carpet?', in S. Barron (ed.) *Exiles + Emigrés*, Los Angeles, Los Angeles County Museum of Art: Harry N. Abrams.

OECD [Organization for Economic Co-operation and Development] (2001) *Trends in International Migration: annual report*, Paris: OECD Publications.

Papastergiadis, Nikos (2000) *The Turbulence of Migration: globalization, deterritorialization, and hybridity*, Cambridge: Polity Press.

Preuss, Ulrich K. (1998) 'Migration: a challenge to modern citizenship', *Constellations* 4 (3): 307–19.

Pries, Ludger (1999) 'New migration in transnational spaces', in L. Pries (ed.) *Migration and Transnational Social Spaces*, Aldershot: Ashgate.

Rapport, N. and Dawson, A. (eds) (1998) *Migrants of Identity: perceptions of home in a world of movement*, Oxford: Berg.

UN Secretariat, Population Division, Department of Economic and Social Affairs (1999) 'World urbanization prospects: the 1999 revision'.

UN Secretariat, Population Division, Department of Economic and Social Affairs (2001) *World Population Prospects: the 2000 revision, volume III: analytical report*, 'International migration', ST/ESA/SER.A/200.

UN Secretariat, Population Division, Department of Economic and Social Affairs (2002a) 'Measuring international migration: many questions, few answers', UN/POP/MIG/2002/BP1.

UN Secretariat, Population Division, Department of Economic and Social Affairs (2002b) 'International migration: explicit policies, uncertain consequences', UN/POP/MIG/2002/BP2.

Watters, R.F. and McGee, T.G. (eds) (1997) *Asia-Pacific: new geographies of the Pacific Rim*, Wellington: Victoria University Press.

Žižek, S. (1997) 'Multiculturalism, or, the cultural logic of multinational capitalism', *New Left Review*, September/October: 28–51.

Chapter 1: Drifting

Architecture/migrancy

Stephen Cairns

ASSOCIATION EXPERIMENTS

The aims of this book demand that we simultaneously acknowledge the scope of the well-entrenched orthodoxies of assimilationism and multiculturalism, and disturb the horizons of expectation they set in place. How might this doubly oriented approach be pursued? In traditional association experiments, randomly chosen stimuli, such as words, are placed in particular proximity in order to trigger diverse, and often unrelated, associations, impressions, connotations and mental images. For Freud, the significance of such outcomes was that they can belie the arbitrariness of the stimuli that provoked them. The associations and images thrown-up in this process were, he argued, not arbitrary, but 'always strictly determined by important internal attitudes of mind' (Freud 1991: 136). As such, any investigation of the determining capacities of those internal, unconscious attitudes can only be inhibited by logical styles of thinking – after all, such styles of thinking *presuppose* the elimination of arbitrariness. Arbitrarily chosen words are deployed in such experiments precisely for their capacity to loosen the inhibiting effects of logical thinking.

My intention in this chapter is to pose 'Architecture/migrancy' as a pairing that enables the doubly oriented approach that this book's themes require. 'Architecture' and 'migrancy' are not arbitrarily chosen words of course. But, to invoke them as if they were, and to associate them crudely, without conjunctions, allows us to provisionally suspend the horizons of expectation that assimilationist and multiculturalist ideologies have already established in relation to them. To adopt this naïve posture, however *faux*, is to induce a momentary relaxation of our critical faculties enabling a wider range of possible effects to surface. When 'architecture' and 'migrancy' are juxtaposed, without predetermined articulation, we can expect an unwieldy stream of associations to present themselves, from the obvious to the cryptic, the significant to the trivial, the reliable to the anecdotal, the threatening to the comforting. Sifting through these outcomes allows us to inspect the means by which these terms come to be mediated within the 'internal attitudes', not simply of 'the mind', but also of the various pragmatic and disciplinary discussions that circulate around architecture and the city. The association experiment allows us to explore the shifting interval between the terms, and the kinds of slippages that occur when the most common-sense and obvious associations have been exhausted. It enables a primitive style of thinking whose primary usefulness, as Freud warned, lies less in its refinement of well-worn intellectual trajectories than in the novel, often disturbing and provocative, lines of inquiry solicited.

ARCHITECTURE-BY-MIGRANTS

One of the first images to surface from the architecture/migrancy association is that of the adaptations carried out by migrants on the architectures of their 'destinations'. Such transformations are evident throughout many contemporary cities: Mexican and Salvadorian makeovers of suburban bungalows in Los Angeles; Cuban Catholic shrines in Miami's Little Havana; Vietnamese market gardens in inner-city Melbourne; Bangladeshi mosques within the Georgian urban fabric of London's East End; and hyper-real Hindu temples in the outskirts of Toronto. Perhaps the most prominent example of such architectures is the Chinatown, with its restaurants, emporia, laundries, ancestor shrines, sweatshops and other associated architectural clichés (Lin 1998: ix) – so ubiquitous that they are now stock elements of any multiculturally inclined urban planning strategy and municipal tourist promotion campaign seeking to capitalize on local marks of distinction. Such architectures form the infrastructure of what sociologist Michel Laguerre (2000: 11) refers to as the contemporary 'ethnopolis'. The ethnopolis takes shape as permanent immigrants from relatively coherent ethnic backgrounds concentrate, through complex processes of choice and constraint, within particular sectors of the city. Such concentrations are made visible within the urban fabric by different and even exotic architectural forms, styles and motifs and their interaction with equally novel everyday modes of living. The identification of such ethnic enclaves through diminutives such as Little Italy, Little Saigon, Little Taipei, etc. seems to articulate homeland nostalgias. But these identifications were often applied, in the first instance, by municipal authorities seeking to regulate foreign populations, and were repeatedly resisted by the migrant inhabitants themselves. The ethnopolis operates as an 'urban portal' that opens onto larger diasporic networks of association. It is an urban form that both attracts migrant groups and disperses them to national hinter-lands and beyond to further international locations (Laguerre 2000: 20). This larger global network, with its nodes, portals and circuitry, is what Arjun Appadurai (1990) has called an 'ethno-scape'.

Migrancy can also take more privileged and less evidently 'ethnicized' forms than those that are normally associated with shaping the ethnopolis. We might think, in the first instance, of the international shuttling of Western employees of transnational corporations and diplomatic personnel as one such (hyper-)privileged form of migrancy. Such movement is associated with another kind of urban enclave, one that services the wider housing, work, education and leisure needs of communities defined as 'expatriate' as opposed to 'ethnic'. Enclaves of this kind are dotted throughout the capitals of the developing world, and are characterized by their coffee shops, maid-employment bureaux, international schools, florists, supermarkets and sports clubs. Unlike the urban ethnic enclave which articulates difference, these architectures of migrancy often self-consciously embody a unified taste culture that is explicitly 'international' in character.[1] So distinct are they from the ethnically coded enclave, that we might label them collectively as 'expat-towns', in contradistinction to 'Chinatowns'. The broader significance of the expat-town lies in its function as beach-head for the dissemination of international taste cultures – including architectural styles, fashions and technologies – into local middle-class life. Together, the expat-town and the ethnopolis encapsulate a more abstract distinction between generic (international, universal, modern) and cultural (ethnic, exotic, differentiating) values within a global urban aesthetics. Of course, the apparently polar conditions of the expat-town and Chinatown reflect a colonial structure of mobility. These days it is not just a Western middle class that is on the move. The emergent middle-classes of the non-West include highly skilled, white collar personnel in the business and service sectors who routinely shuttle between international localities. The taste cultures that emerge from this new kind of middle-class migrancy find architectural expression in such complex and (to mainstream taste) exaggerated stylistic amalgams as Khmer postmodernism, Javanese moderne, and, in India, where this phenomenon has been particularly well thematized, Punjabi Baroque, Tamil Tiffany and Chandni Chowk Chippendale (see Bhatia 1994).

As I have suggested, the expat-town and the ethnopolis (and their hybrids) have well-known historical dimensions that can be traced along the trajectories of colonialism. Settler colonialism implicated a specific form of migrancy that involved the permanent settling of European populations in New World territories. This form of migrancy was underwritten by utilitarian land-tenure ideologies that deemed territories without the marks of agriculture or permanent occupation to be 'under-populated' or simply 'empty' and hence available for settlement. This ideological sanction is registered in a particular settler toponymy. Throughout settler territories we find images of homelands and hometowns projected directly onto the landscape through the naming of towns, regions and nations – New York, New England, New South Wales, New Caledonia, New Zealand.[2]

Not all colonial migrancy carried the expectation of permanent settlement of 'empty' lands. Another, periodic, form of migrancy was associated with the careers of those individuals who were in the service of empire as administrators, clergy, soldiers or traders rather than as settlers. These migrants followed a pattern of movement consisting of long-term residencies in the colonies broken by shorter sabbaticals usually taken in their country of origin in Europe. This colonial form of migrancy delivered the manpower necessary to sustain an extractive colonialism (as distinct from a settler colonialism) that entailed the subjugation, control and administration of foreign territories and populations for the express purpose of generating wealth for the colonial power. Such movement is implicated in a complex politics of cultural production in which architecture was particularly prominent. In the hands of colonial architects (and their clients in governmental, cultural and economic institutions) European architectural styles found expression in unusually diverse ways that ranged from the rigidly conventional to the highly unorthodox, from the literal transplantation to the hybrid. Throughout such cities as Mumbai, Calcutta and Trivandrum, Macau and Kowloon, Hanoi and Phnom Phen, Malacca, Singapore, Kuala Lumpur, Jakarta and Bandung, are found surprisingly faithful architectural reproductions in Classical, Gothic, Art Deco styles. What is surprising to the Western eyes that come to see these exported architectures is the out-of-placeness that is registered in, for instance, lichen-drenched Doric columns, bamboo sunshades attached to pointed-arched windows, or blinding tropical light reflected from white, smooth-plastered facades. But those cities also contain composite architectures in such styles as Hindu-Javanese Neo-classicism, Indo-European Arts-and-Crafts, Indo-Chinese Beaux-Arts, Mughal Gothic, Soviet-Vietnamese Monumentalism, and Tropical Art Deco. In turn, historians of Chinoiserie and Orientalism point to a (not at all symmetrical) counter-flow that can be discerned in the various forms, patterns and colourings from Mughal, Chinese, Egyptian, Arabic origins that from the eighteenth century began to mingle in various measures with Neo-classical and Gothic Revival architectures in such unlikely places as Cheshire, Kew, Liverpool, Brighton and Glasgow (Honour 1961; Connor 1979; MacKenzie 1995: 71).

The mobility of architectural forms in the context of migrancy is also registered less formally, but no less importantly, through vernacular forms such as the bungalow, the warehouse and the barracks. Peter Scriver (1994) has detailed examples of these kinds of architectures as instituted by the British Public Works Department throughout colonial India. The bungalow's hybrid origins in colonial India, and its diverse geographical (India, Britain, North America, Africa) and economic/historical (colonialism, industrialization, globalization) fortunes have been tracked by Anthony King (1984).

This account of colonial architectural hybridity suggests a much older and longer history involving the traffic of people, goods and architectures throughout ancient imperial spheres of influence – Greek settlements around the Mediterranean, Roman settlements throughout Europe, Chinese ones in Southeast Asia. Beyond that is the substantial archaeological evidence of prehistorical entanglements of human movement and settlement. This historical charting would be an endless task, and my purpose here is not to engage in such comprehensive accounting. Rather, I would like to reflect briefly on the kinds of associate images that have already played across the architecture/migrancy pairing.

These first images – ethnopolis, expat-town, various colonial hybrids – all implicate a strong sense of migrant agency. We come to see such a diverse set of architectures as sharing certain formal attributes characterized by an out-of-placeness, hybridity and exoticism because they appear to be the 'outcome' of specific kinds of migrant activity. The evident differences between the modest and populist forms of the ethnopolis, the self-consciously international architectures of the expat-town, and those grander architectures associated with a state-sponsored colonial power, are momentarily transcended by the agency that is ascribed to diverse population groups on the move. The architecture/migrancy pairing becomes cleanly articulated here as an architecture-by-migrants, releasing a celebratory and optimistic aesthetics of possibility uniquely suited to the goals of multiculturalism. In this form, migrancy delivers to architecture, unorthodox stylistic expressions, mannerist compositions, baroque ornamental excesses, pragmatic bricoleur aesthetics, and an everyday semiotics of the exotic.

Yet, it should be clear that people on the move are not uniformly in control of their destinations or, indeed, their destinies. Those who are swept up into the trajectories of modern mobility are highly diverse groups and individuals with various class, race and culture affiliations. Their itineraries are charted not simply by choice, but by powerful economic circuits involving the traffic of raw materials, manufactured goods, produce, technology, capital, know-how and information. Traders, prospectors, soldiers and administrators travelled to the colonies, slaves and, later, indentured labourers were shunted from one colony to another. Indigenous colonial civil servants went to Europe and, from the latter part of the twentieth century, diverse groups, from skilled professionals to manual labourers and domestic servants, to refugees and asylum-seekers, shuttle around distinctive regional and international circuits. To reduce the play between architecture and migrancy to the formulation of an architecture-by-migrants distils a fantasy of a mobile agency from a complex structure in which agency is anything but complete. This is no more so than in the case of those migrants who come to be overdetermined by the category 'ethnic'. The ethnicized and exoticized products of an architecture-by-migrants fills a long-standing slot within the structure of architectural theory. In the past this position might have been filled by examples of pre-modern built environments, what in the post-war period was often called an 'architecture without architects' (Rudofsky 1964). It is possible to generalize the function of this slot in architectural theory as being the intellectual space that orchestrates otherness in order to furnish the discipline with stimulating architectural effects. The idea of an architecture-without-architects fulfilled this function by presenting vernacular built forms as pure and unsullied anthropological ideals. Apparently untouched by modernity, these forms could then serve as correctives for its excesses. The idea of an architecture-by-migrants works in a similar way, even though it substitutes anthropological purities with creolized and hybridized architectural effects. These are effects that are still offered 'from below', effects that in their surprising and beguiling qualities serve to nourish formally constituted architectural discourse in moments of creative drought.

This nourishing function as it is motorized by migrancy operated in colonial history via different mechanisms. John MacKenzie, writing on eighteenth- and nineteenth-century English architecture argues that the influx of Oriental motifs functioned to enliven a dull, limited and confused Western architectural discourse. Oriental garden design in particular 'represented a liberation from the formalism of Palladianism, the heavy luxuriance of the baroque, the rigidities of the formal garden or the extensive pseudo-wildness of its landscaped successor' (MacKenzie 1995: 76). In this way, the Orient offered 'relief' of a formal kind from 'the rigidities of classical rules' (MacKenzie 1995: 76). As colonialism came to be more formalized in the later part of the nineteenth, and early twentieth centuries, the colonies themselves came to be conceived as spaces for off-shore architectural and urban experimentation whose results, once assessed and properly refined, were exported back to Europe, enriching its well-worn architectural orthodoxies. In the early twentieth century, for instance, specific French-speaking colonial spaces (Indochina, Madagascar and, in particular, Morocco), were seen as 'laboratories', and were routinely described as '*champs d'experience*' – experimental terrains (Wright 1991: 12).

Perhaps the instance where architecture/migrancy is most comfortably resolved is the case of the museum of immigration. In one sense, a museum of immigration houses and displays an array of everyday examples of architectures-by-migrants: from personal effects, to the paraphernalia of travel such as suitcases and trunks, to migrant dwellings. The best known of these museums is the Ellis Island Immigration Museum in New York harbour (see Catherine Ingraham, this volume, on the 'evidentiary' status of this architecture), but more modest versions, including discrete exhibitions devoted to immigration, are found in almost every settler nation whose growth has depended upon immigration – Canada, South Africa, Brazil, Argentina, New Zealand and Australia. In the case of the museum of immigration, the architecture accommodates migrancy monumentally and publicly in order to serve a larger nation-building project. By way of such architecture, the fragmented drama of mass mobility finds a proper home within a coherent story of a new nation. The museum of immigration offers an example of an institutional architecture that assimilates the immigrant into an idea of national citizenry. The proliferation of these museums stands in contrast to the scarcity of museums of emigration that record, commemorate and celebrate the mass departure of particular populations.[3] Permanent emigration is, for the most part, a kind of betrayal. If one is forced to move, then one is failed by the nation. If one chooses to move, then one betrays the nation. In such a context, this rupture between nation and emigration produces an improbable terrain for any kind of monumental architectural expression. Yet, in other models of emigration – most notably temporary labour migration – new and vital connections between outbound movement and architecture are spawned. In fact, state-sanctioned remittance schemes, by which departed workers send money back to their home villages or to the national government, often provide the financial basis for a range of less monumental architectural interventions in rural villages and towns, ranging from the improvement of water reticulation infrastructure, to the construction of vernacular architectures that, in turn, sustain romantic images of an ideal homeland condition for those at home and abroad.

ARCHITECTURE-FOR-MIGRANTS

Migrancy is a term that cannot help but carry with it connotations of traumatic displacement. As a consequence, the celebratory mood that accompanies an architecture-by-migrants is easily punctured by the dismal one that often surrounds an architecture-for-migrants. An architecture-for-migrants is characterized, as Gert Mattenklott (1994) puts it in his editorial for a *Daidalos* special issue on 'cultures of migration', by the 'tediously administrative misery to be found in Nissen huts, shantytowns and refugee camps, in paper-lined car wrecks and cardboard boxes with peepholes, or the suffering of shopping-cart existences and metro-shaft dwellers'. Having identified a specific sub-architectural genre, Mattenklott (1994: 23) immediately advises that '[s]uch sights should not be reduplicated on high gloss paper', such as the pages of architectural journals, including his own.[4] This squeamishness is a consequence of a desire not to conflate these marginal architectures with the positive aesthetics so often constituted around the idea of an architecture-by-migrants. The matter of what is suitable to be represented on high gloss paper turns on a distinction between architectures that can and cannot embody signs of 'culture' and, with that, migrant agency. The marginal architectures of Nissen huts, shantytowns and refugee camps take the form of an architecture-for-migrants because of the diminished agency ascribed to its migrant inhabitants. But the deceptive nature of this ascription needs to be noted, as it can only be made by overlooking the agency that is routinely exercised by migrants in the provision of their own shelter in circumstances of disaster or poverty.

The situation in which this assumed diminished agency becomes most thoroughly embedded in the public imagination is that of the provision of emergency housing and disaster relief structures. These are structures designed to respond to the immediate aftermath of a mass displacement enforced by either natural disaster or war. Such traumatic moments represent one obvious catalyst for longer, more distant and permanent emigratory journeys. Emergency shelters of this kind are developed and provided by various governmental and intergovernmental agencies, such as the United Nations' Office for the Coordination of Humanitarian Affairs, the World Bank, the OECD, as well as by non-governmental organizations such as the Red Cross/Crescent and Oxfam, and often in collaboration with their military or private sector partners from the building and engineering industries. The discourse of emergency housing and disaster alleviation is strictly disciplined by the nature of the disaster itself and its anticipated disruptive effects on human life. As a consequence, its architectures are coded in terms of economic, logistical, structural and material efficiencies. Conventionally, they are conceived and delivered via seemingly anonymous and large scale and bureaucratized operations. As a kind of bureaucratic vernacular, these architectures can be thought of as a different kind of architecture-without-architects, 'from above'.[5]

This seemingly anonymous field is, however, interlaced with name architects. The most prominent of these include technologically-inclined architects such as Buckminster Fuller (the Wichita house, 1946), Renzo Piano (mobile construction unit in Senegal, 1978) and Future Systems (air-deliverable disaster relief shelter, 1985) and, in a different vein, Alvar Aalto (interlockable mobile wooden post-disaster shelters, 1942) (Kronenburg 1995: 138). One celebrated architect to work in this field in recent times is Shigeru Ban (see Mark Rakatansky, this volume). His work, deploying paper tube structures in diverse disaster scenes in Rwanda, Japan and Cambodia, has been widely discussed in bureaucratic, professional and art contexts, and has received formal institutional support from the United Nations.[6] Whereas emergency housing provision is disciplined by its instrumental remit, in architecture there is a more casual and licentious consideration of this kind of accommodation. We immediately sense this when Ban insists that emergency housing, in order to attend to the migrant's 'psychological state', be 'beautiful'. Ban deliberately promotes an ambiguity between being 'moved' emotionally and being moved on. The mild shock this licentiousness generates is, in part, a consequence of finding aesthetic experience in proximity to that of the dismal. But it is also a reassuring sign of the proper functioning of the architect's agency, a sign that architecture's aesthetic capacities are being exercised even in these most challenging of situations.

Not surprisingly, for many of the specialist agencies that deal with disaster relief shelter, the involvement of architects smacks of opportunism. These agencies tend to be sceptical of the 'ingenuity and persistence of designers' (Davis 1978).[7] For architects, they say, this architecture-for-migrants becomes simply 'an opportunity for generating innovative designs [that are] impossible to implement' (Kreimer 1979: 362). Embedded in this argument is the assumption that the design parameters of disaster relief shelter – which involve seemingly direct relations between cause and effect, necessity and urgency – offer architects a socio-political cover for unfettered exercises in *exitenz minimum* 'discipline', functionalism, as well as a more general aesthetics of minimalism. By way of this moral cover, deeply held modernist attitudes are able to be (once again) unapologetically aired. Rem Koolhaas, albeit in another context of homelessness, captures architecture's undifferentiating enthusiasm for this architectural genre by acerbically observing that 'Bums are the ideal clients of modern architecture: in perpetual need of shelter and hygiene, real lovers of sun and the great outdoors, indifferent to architectural doctrine and to formal layout' (Koolhaas 1994: 249).[8] As the increasing popularity of this genre within contemporary architectural discourse suggests, it is the possibility for experimentation, and not the object of experimentation, that is the compelling and over-riding concern. For instance, a recent special issue of *Quaderns* (Gausa 1999) featured Ban's emergency paper log shelters alongside articles on refugee housing, informal urban shanties, modular demountable housing, camping, exhibition infrastructure, lighting installations, and the camouflaging of architectural form in the landscape. A similar range of topics can be found in such books as *Houses in Motion* (Kronenburg 1995), *Mobile: The art of portable architecture* (Siegal 2002), *Prefab* (Arieff and Burkhart 2002) and *PreFab: Prefabricated and moveable architecture* (Bahamon 2002) where architectures that 'migrate', often typified by emergency housing, are considered within a theoretical framework that spans the vernacular architectures (without architects) of 'nomadic tribes' and avant-garde projects such as Archigram's 'Walking city' and Coop Himmelb(l)au's pneumatic 'Cloud I'. In current architectural discourse then, an architecture-for-migrants, despite its 'administrative misery', sits without differentiation within this larger pool of opportunities for experimentation on mobility, ephemerality and '21st century nomad life' (Bahamon 2002). The particular admixture of optimism and enthusiasm that is evident in architecture's engagement with this material is nicely encapsulated in Arieff and Burkhart's catchphrase 'putting the "fab" back into "prefab"'.

Architecture-for-migrants also calls to mind, as Mattenklott (1994: 23) suggests, the burgeoning numbers of 'refugee camps' and 'detention centres'. These facilities are designed to control and deter the unauthorized travel of refugees and asylum-seekers across national borders – the detention centres at Sangatte, Whitehead and Woomera were the best known, before being replaced by smaller and more dispersed facilities.[9] Sustained points of contact between the discipline of architecture and the politicized policy discourse relating to detention centres have been rare to date.[10] Where contact has been broached, it has been resisted by architecture – I have already noted one such point of resistance in Mattenklott's injunction against reproducing architecture-for-migrants on high gloss paper. But this resistance is manifest in other interesting ways, as was recently shown in Australia.

Relative to other First World nations, Australia has a small number of asylum-seekers and what it calls 'illegal migrants' crossing its national boundary. Yet, under the guidance of a conservative government, it has instigated a range of tough policies that seek to stem the flow of asylum-seekers. A central aspect of these policies involves confining 'illegal migrants' in detention centres. It was in pursuit of this policy that Philip Ruddock, Australia's Minister for Immigration and Multicultural and Indigenous Affairs, solicited architectural assistance. Under pressure to arrest the flow of bad press the government had been receiving nationally and internationally on its asylum policy, the minister announced an architectural competition that sought new and innovative designs for detention facilities for asylum-seekers. Such designs were as much about public relations as client provision. In a press release announcing the short-listed architects, the minister suggested that the competition offered 'a great opportunity for the Government to advance the quality and style of detention facilities in Australia'. He added that 'it also provides an opportunity for architectural organisations participating in the design process to showcase their talents and potentially earn international recognition in an environment where the illegal movement of people around the world is a growing international problem' (DIMIA 2002). The image of detention centres that had become fixed in the public imagination was of serried Nissen huts in remote and barren outback locations encircled by razorwire-topped fences (see Mares 2002). The new designs would ensure these centres were seen as 'administrative' rather than 'corrective' facilities (DIMIA 2002). For this politician, the principles of 'good design', 'style' and 'advancing quality', would, in a quite pragmatic way, alleviate the negative effects that media images of detention centres had had for his government. Furthermore, this made good business sense for the architectural profession. Forecasting the movement of refugees and asylum-seekers to be a permanent feature of the geopolitical landscape of the twenty-first century, he framed this competition as a 'ground floor' business opportunity for Australian 'architectural organisations'. Architects, he suggests, can take a lead in this emerging niche in the international design market.

Glenn Murcutt, Australia's best known architect, in a particularly strong response to this attempt to associate architecture with this form of migrancy, was reportedly 'disgusted' and driven 'berserk' by government asylum policy. He announced that he 'wouldn't have a bar' of designing detention facilities in Australia (Murcutt cited in Farrelly 2002). The President of the Royal Australian Institute of Architects (RAIA), Graham Jahn, also articulated an objection to the Minister's competition, but did so within his narrower professional remit. In a press release titled 'Sentenced to detention', he warned Institute members off the competition on the grounds its regulations obliged all entrants, successful or not, to cede copyright of their work to the government for a token fee. Jahn argued that this requirement would impede architects' intellectual property rights, was 'exploitative', and would 'likely to lead to poor results' (Jahn cited in RAIA 2001). This response is ostensibly concerned with protecting architects' creative rights against the government's desire to appropriate them for its own political ends. But it is made with one eye on the 'great opportunity' signalled in the minister's overture, and the possibility that architects might indeed fulfil those ministerial objectives, both in Australia and internationally, is not altogether forsaken. This hedging response finds expression in a series of semantic slips that ask us to see the 'detention' and 'exploitation' of architects' creative rights as correlated in some way with the detention and exploitation of refugees and asylum-seekers. This slippage in the Institute's rhetoric brings architectural creativity into proximity with the conditions of migrancy but, in contrast to Ban's emergency housing where a similar relation is broached, in this case it appears merely glib. Murcutt's outright disgust better articulates the disciplinary norm. His position circumscribes architectural agency within an ethico-aesthetic principle that seeks to activate aesthetic effects by way of humanitarian ideals. Within that disciplinary norm, the humanitarianism of Ban's architectures of shelter seems irrefutable, while the Australian Government's invitation to design an architecture of 'administration' is ethically irretrievable. For an architect like Murcutt, a fundamental distinction between the two types of architecture-for-migrants can be drawn on these grounds. The conditions for the exercise of architectural agency in this case of incarceration are so attenuated that the only proper action for an architect is to refuse outright to engage with it as an architectural issue.

Thus far, I have outlined two conditions embodied in an architecture-for-migrants. These can be distinguished from each other by issues of humanitarianism and security, aesthetics and technique. It would seem that in the context of disaster relief shelter, architectural aesthetics are surplus to the base technical parameters. While in the context of detention centres and refugee camps, architectural aesthetics are required to supplement the insufficiencies of mere technique. But this distinction within an architecture-for-migrants, and architecture's curious negotiation of it, is misleading. The political pragmatism that motivates the construction of detention centres casts a different light on the humanitarian dimensions of disaster relief shelter. The architectures of both share a stripped-down, technological attitude, but one directed towards quite distinct ends: in one instance, shelter and, in the other, incarceration. Yet, the figure of the asylum-seeker is far from stable. Depending on where they are in their journey, they might be classed as homeless, in exile, an asylum-seeker or a refugee. For example, an occupant of UN-provided emergency shelter at one moment, may well be an occupant of a refugee camp or detention centre at another. As such, the humanitarian motivation that attaches to one architecture-for-migrants is always implicated in the less noble motives that seek to keep people in place by regulating who becomes a bona fide refugee and where they can go. In this light, both kinds of architecture-for-migrants function as different techniques within a singular geopolitical logic that is not only directed towards the protection of national borders, but also towards the projection of those borders far beyond their obvious geographical limits. An architecture-for-migrants in this sense is a 'forward defence' of national borders, borne out of a fear for the integrity of those borders.

The connotations that are stimulated by this exploration of architecture-for-migrants cannot offer conclusive evidence for architecture's place in this context. But they produce suggestive patterns of resistance and accession. Could it be that the discipline of architecture operates in this context to reaffirm a distinction between the categories of shelter and incarceration just as the geopolitical logic of global mobility threatens to collapse them together? If so, this reaffirmation is achieved through architecture's strategic deployment of its own creative agency – exercising it here, withholding it there. In doing so, architecture aligns with more general responses to current patterns of human mobility which tend to waver between the extremes of xeno-racist fear (see Sivanandan 2001) and humanitarian empathy. In the public imagination, the association of aesthetics with the architecture of incarceration can only be suspicious. The consensus seems to be that, where architecture-for-migrants is concerned, aesthetics are most safely deployed offshore in the context of disaster relief shelter. In this distant context, it plays out a kind of ambassadorial role within the framework of international aid. Here, at a safe geographical distance and securely framed by imperatives of need, architecture's complicity with the authoritative, distasteful functions of the state can be forgotten. A distinction between shelter and incarceration can be sustained, and architect's agency – asserted on the basis of a diminished migrant agency – remains in place.

ARCHITECTS-AS-MIGRANTS

The architecture/migration pairing also reminds us that architects themselves can be migrants. For example, one of the most significant episodes in twentieth-century architectural history – the mainstreaming of modernism in the form of the International Style – cannot be understood without a sense of a migratory dynamic and, specifically, a knowledge of the migration of modernist architects from Germany to diverse locations across the globe: most prominently the US, but also South America, South Africa, Israel, Australia and New Zealand. The period between 1933 and 1941 – dubbed architecture's 'emigration decade' (Moholy-Nagy 1965: 24) – saw the migration to the US of such Bauhaus figures as Walter Gropius and Marcel Breuer (Graduate School of Design at Harvard University), Mies van de Rohe and Ludwig Hilberseimer (Armour Institute of Technology), Josef Albers (Black Mountain College) and Laszlo Moholy-Nagy (New Bauhaus). The theme of migrancy has coloured this well-rehearsed narrative in particular ways.[11] Most simply, migrancy introduces an orderly and symmetrical geography of departure and arrival. In conjunction with existentialist themes of loss, dislocation, alienation, expectation, settlement and assimilation, migrancy provides a convenient and dramatic comparative framework for the assessment of this episode in architectural history. Such assessments usually turn on the ways in which the adversarial energy that migrant architects brought to architectural pedagogy and practice in the US was deployed within the gravitational pull of a prosperous cultural and social mainstream. Conventionally, this account has a melancholy resolution in which that energy was seen to be channelled into pragmatic ends or, as it is also argued, domesticated through aestheticized design sensibilities. We can say, borrowing from Martin Jay, that in this context the architect-as-migrant was effectively transformed from 'critical outsider to mainstream insider' (Jay 1998: 332). What gives this episode particular drama is that the relatively abstract tension between politics and aesthetics that structures it is cross-hatched with specific existentialist biographies plucked out of the mass migratory passage itself. Globally significant architectural themes come to be narrated through highly personal circumstances that carry all the poignancy, trauma and difficulty of migrant experiences.[12] This is a quality that Sibyl Moholy-Nagy hinted at when she spoke of the 'drama and farce of diaspora architecture' (Moholy-Nagy 1965: 24).

The existential atmosphere attached to the story of the International Style was all but shed in the post-war period as architectural work, as well as architects themselves, became less confined by national boundaries or customary international routes. Middle-class migrancy as a particular mode of movement became conflated with more intermittent forms of mobility – from business travel to tourism – that were enabled by a liberalizing global economy and wider accessibility to international travel. In this context, the architect-as-migrant is better understood as a member of a deterritorialized 'global intelligence corps': a professional sector, including, among others, architects, engineers, information technology specialists, which services transnational corporate institutions involved in the control and orchestration of productive assets on a global scale (Rimmer, cited in Olds 2001). The idea of a global intelligence corps more openly articulates the instrumental nature of much contemporary and global architectural work. Unlike the architects of the German diaspora, whose professional practices and migrant-mobility resonated so strongly, the movements of contemporary architects-on-the-move are altogether unexceptional. This condition reveals more starkly than ever the thorough entanglement of architecture with the movements of capital. This truth is frankly and unsentimentally admitted to in the series of graphs published in the first pages of Koolhaas and Mau's (1995) book *S,M,L,XL*. These graphs chart the annual distances travelled and the hours spent in transit by Koolhaas himself. They also plot the national origins of his office's work force. This statistical snap-shot renders a highly mobile, transnational workforce, operating as much in transit as in a single office location. Such a pattern is exaggerated further in the operations of architectural practices like Skidmore Owings and Merrill, which are geared more explicitly to servicing transnational corporations (see Olds 2001). The patterns of movement associated with this kind of architectural practice represent a migrancy stripped of existential angst and trauma, a migrancy normalized in the service of capital. This generation of architects-on-the-move join the ranks of white collar expatriates, business travellers and 'corporate nomads' discussed earlier.

ARCHITECTURE'S MIGRANCY

Architecture-by-migrants, architecture-for-migrants, and architects-as-migrants, discussed thus far, are three possible articulations of the architecture/migrancy pairing. Each conjunction, 'by', 'for', 'as', allows us to identify and thematize specific contemporary and historical conditions in which architecture and migrancy come into contact. But these preliminary investigations also give rise to other more provisional and fleeting qualities. So much so, that the linkages between architecture and migrancy do not appear to offer so much a set of fixed co-ordinates around which might be charted a new intellectual field, as draw attention to the stream of associations that continue to eddy around the terms in turbulent and unpredictable ways. This unpredictability suggests that migrancy's diverse symptoms will inevitably leak out from whatever association we seek to forge with the architectural term. How, then, might we be more responsive to the effects of this unpredictability. And, more precisely, does this responsiveness implicate architecture? Thus far, I have explored the architecture/migrancy pairing with a kind of 'mobile attention' – to borrow Freud's words again – that has drawn freely on the vocabularies of various disciplines, including social science, architecture and geography. This notional interdisciplinarity has the effect of placing architecture within wider social, economic, political and geographical processes. But within the more tightly circumscribed discourse of architecture, the interactions between social space and architectural space are understood to take place along quite distinctive lines. Within this discourse, what are otherwise quite everyday, even epiphenomenal, conditions such as foundations, thresholds, edges, wall, doors, roofs, fences, openings and closures, are invested with heightened material and conceptual significance. Where the power of architecture to authorize, constitute and maintain conventional relations of space and social identity is rapidly waning, these, and other such technologies of that authority, necessarily come into focus. In what follows, I want to reorient our attention towards architectural discourse more exclusively and, in particular, towards a set of significant moments in that discourse where the issues of social space – including its unruliness and unpredictability – are considered.

In the recent past, orthodox architectural discourse has been shaped by three quite distinctive positions in relation to the interaction between social and architectural space, these being: functionalism, neo-rationalism and a commitment to *genius loci* or spirit of place – what Paul Carter (in this volume) calls 'placism'. At their purest, these are mutually exclusive positions to take. The first, functionalism, reduces the social to the idea of function and insists on a strongly motivated interaction between it and architectural form. The second, neo-rationalism, claims a categorical divide between the social and the architectural in order to establish an interaction of relatively autonomous realms. The third, placism, explicitly activates an existentialist version of the social, and relates that to specific practices of place making. While each position has had its day, so to speak, and would rarely feature as a self-conscious rallying point within contemporary architectural debate, they remain latent and deeply influential within the everyday discourse and practice of architecture. Indeed, they are no longer active as distinctive and competing positions. Rather, they are manifest as vaguely, almost unconsciously, felt mutually complementary positions that come to be manifest in a familiar set of architectural truisms: a functional fit, and a sense of typological licence, and a sensitivity to the spirit of place. Architecture's recent engagement with social space, including its migrant forms, has usually occurred through one or other points within this range of positions.

Insofar as studying and theorizing migrancy can be taken to be a task of the social sciences, as it conventionally is, then architecture's relation to migrancy needs to be considered within the wider history of the social sciences. The history of its relationship to architecture has been of specific interest to architectural historian Manfredo Tafuri. He has shown that the parameters of this relationship were established as long ago as the eighteenth century when, during the Enlightenment, the general field of the social sciences first came into being. Although society has always implicated itself in architecture, for Tafuri, social concerns came to particular prominence in architectural thinking only after they were codified by the social sciences. Tafuri develops his argument by drawing on Michel Foucault's account of modernity, as set out in his *Order of Things* (1970), and it is helpful to restate some of the outlines of that account before returning to Tafuri. Foucault's account hinges on the emergence of a system of representation that was predicated on an arbitrary relation between signifier and signified. For Foucault, this system quickly displaced older – 'Classical', in his nomenclature – conceptions of representation in which words and things were meaningfully related in fixed and motivated ways through the authority of nature and God. A consequence of this displacement, was that Classical subject–object relations were reconfigured, such that relations between words and things came to be mediated, and given meaning, by a more active human subject encapsulated in the idea of 'man' or the 'sovereign subject'. Man was the agent of a new and radically open-ended epistemological architectonic, more capable than ever before of inquiring into, diagnosing, and so improving, the world of things. This sovereign subject charted new regions and objects of empirical inquiry that, most importantly and problematically, included man himself. Man's own mode of being in the world, including his social formations, became the foci for new social 'sciences'. This constituted man, in Foucault's words, as an 'empirico-transcendental doublet' (1970: 319), in which he is both the authorizing subject and the empirical object of his own inquiry. For Foucault, modernity's project of progress and improvement, and its associated atmosphere of optimism, is underpinned by this methodological sophistry. It induced what he dubbed 'the anthropological sleep' (1970: 340) in which man projected a simultaneously authoritative and self-deceiving dreamlike reality. For Foucault, the social sciences mark the very 'threshold of our modernity' (1970: 319) by inaugurating this problematic epistemology and a wider ideology of humanism.

Tafuri, developing Foucault's propositions, shows how architecture became enfolded within modernity's humanist project. He charts the way architecture moved from a state, in the sixteenth and seventeenth centuries, in which its codes were deemed natural – both 'practical and symbolic at the same time' – to a modern state, emerging in the eighteenth century, in which they came to be conventionally understood in relation to meaning-giving subjects. As Tafuri puts it, modern architecture emerged at the point when the discipline began to inquire into 'what makes architecture possible: that is, into its system of meanings as related to those who pose them' (Tafuri 1980: 80). Hereafter, architectural meaning was understood to be constituted in relation to 'those who pose them', in relation, that is, to the sovereign subjectivity of man, in increasing opposition to a naturally sanctioned or God given order.

In modern architecture, this relational condition was most thoroughly internalized in modernism itself, and particularly in functionalism, where man was manifest in the figure of 'the user' and in the idea of 'the public'. According to Tafuri, the new, rationalized, technologized architecture of modernism no longer found coherence in its own relation to fixed natural orders, but called on the 'user' to 'complete' its forms, and 'summoned the public to participate in its work of design' (Tafuri 1976: 101). In this analysis, Tafuri historicizes the relationship between the social and the architectural. In doing so he offers a way of seeing the architecture/migrancy pairing in a wider framework. His work reveals the discursive and institutional compact between the social sciences and architecture that enables, motivates and even wills the terms 'architecture' and 'migrancy' to come together.

Through Tafuri, we can picture the figure of the migrant in social science and the figure of the user in architecture as inter-generational siblings, both descendants from Enlightenment man, and both potential agents, and objects, of their own improvement, development and progress. We should not be surprised, then, to find an atmospherics of optimism and enthusiasm persistently enveloping migrancy in architectural discourse. As we have seen, this atmospherics is present in quite distinct circumstances: in an architecture-by-migrants where migrant agency is imagined to underwrite multiculturalist expressions of diversity, and in an architecture-for-migrants, where the provision of disaster relief shelter is understood as an opportunity for architectural experimentation and improvement of the migrant's lot. In the light of Tafuri's analysis, we could say that the association of architecture with migrancy necessarily triggers an atmosphere of optimism, enthusiasm and possibility because it is forged within the overarching epistemology of humanism as refracted through the cluster of ideologies associated with nationalism, territoriality and ontopology.

Modern architecture's indebtedness to humanism sets the scene for neo-rationalism and placism. Each position is focused, in quite different ways, on the possibility that architecture might be woken from its own anthropological sleep, and freed from the hold of humanism. In the case of neo-rationalism, Tafuri's scepticism of the happy association of the architectural and the social (scientific) is taken to new intensities such that the architecture/migrancy pairing appears to be disarticulated altogether. In the case of placism, the social is embraced ever more intimately, but in the name of an altogether more fragile, existential subject, as opposed to the empirico-transcendental subject of social science. Let me turn first to neo-rationalism.

Neo-rationalism came to prominence in architectural discourse in the 1970s and 1980s as a refreshing alternative to the modernist doctrine of functionalism. Explicitly informed by Tafuri's historical analysis, it was based on (re)asserting a relative autonomy between user and architecture (subject and object). The prominent neo-rationalist architect Aldo Rossi articulated this position most clearly and consistently in a wide range of built, drawn and written work. In his best known book, *The Architecture of the City* (1984), he argued that to seek the basis for architectural form within the social dimensions of modern life, however well-intentioned, produced a 'moralistic confusion' in architectural thinking. Rossi illustrates this confusion by referring to modernism's whole-hearted engagement with the early twentieth-century 'crisis in housing' (Rossi 1984: 158). In developing his argument, Rossi refers to Engels' (1936) book, *The Housing Question*, as an early example of this confusion. Engels' book focused on the widespread housing shortage in late nineteenth-century Germany. Significantly, for our concerns here, this shortage was triggered by the migration of agricultural workers to urban centres in the context of rapid industrialization. Rossi argued that 'to focus on the problem of housing in order to resolve the social problem', as Engels had done, was 'an error' (Rossi 1984: 155). This was to consider 'housing' as the mere allocation of resources (foundations, walls, doors, roofs) against a particular set of needs (shelter). For Rossi, another logic needed to prevail. He argued that architecture operates according to 'proper' typological 'laws' that accrete within their own history. These laws, he suggested, have a stability and permanence such that any architecture they inform should be – relative to functionalism, at least – indifferent to the various social formations that might be expected to accrue in and around it. In supporting this claim, Rossi pointed to the successive and quite distinctive functional adaptations of ancient buildings in various European towns such as Padua, Seville and Milan. Rossi called this condition 'distributive indifference', a condition in which typical architectural forms are understood to be indifferent to the distribution of distinctive social formations in space and time. For Rossi, architecture's return to its own typological laws would have potentially emancipatory effects on design practice, offering 'maximum distributive freedom and, in a more general sense, maximum functional freedom' (Rossi cited in Scolari 1998: 143). In short, architectural space is seen by Rossi to be relatively autonomous from social space. For Rossi, architecture best serves society by attending to its own typological logics in the first instance, and not by trying to meet the needs of social users in any direct or instrumental way.

By challenging the ongoing purchase of functionalism, and its allegiance to a broader anthropological undercurrent within architecture, the neo-rationalist stance uncoupled certain naturalized associations between specific 'users' and specific architectures. Such a displacement suggests that a neo-rationalist position has nothing 'positive' to offer a consideration of architecture and migrancy. Read in this way, we are urged to consider the 'problem of migrancy' to be a latter-day correlate of the 'problem of housing', that is, a tempting but ultimately mistaken concern for architectural practice. That is, when this central tenet of neo-rationalist architectural theory is brought to the subject matter of architecture and migrancy, it suggests, in the first instance, a categorical divide between the two terms. Rossi's imaginary is of a world in which society always transits through the portals and openings, across the thresholds and sills, in and around the walls, under the roofs and canopies of a relatively autonomous and indifferent architecture. In this world, the migrant – that most mobile of social categories – must then experience an even more attenuated and fleeting association with architecture.

Yet, in his influential discussion of Rossi's neo-rationalism, Massimo Scolari finds himself returning to the theme of migrancy. Scolari takes up Rossi's emphasis on architecture's typological laws and elaborates this by noting that architectural types themselves have particular '*migratory* possibilities in time and space' (Scolari 1998: 143; emphasis in the original). Indeed, for Scolari, architecture's ability to exhibit a distributive indifference depends, in part, on the migration of its types from one place (and time) to another. So, while Rossi argues for a certain architectural autonomy by pointing out how society transits through architecture, Scolari, in turn, suggests that architecture has the ability (and need) to transit through society. Such movement produces what Scolari calls an architectural 'estrangement', in which typical and familiar architectural configurations

– walls, openings, thresholds – are 'encountered' 'with a laconic astonishment', as if 'for the first time' (Scolari 1998: 143).

Rossi and Scolari's commitment to the principle of distributive indifference implies, in one way or another, a disarticulation of form and function. They see in this, new emancipatory architectural possibilities that are enabled by displacing architecture's inherited anthropocentrism, and breaking with the more familiar authority of the universal subject of humanism, as diagnosed by Tafuri. Yet, humanism's subject is not banished altogether from this new architectural vision. A trace of that subject is returned to architecture's story through the idea of migratory movement. Migrancy's particular style of mobility provides the transactive principle for architecture's self-reproduction. The trope of estrangement is particularly important in this regard, describing an architectural correlate of the ontological estrangement a migrant feels when arriving in a new city or country. This 'migrant mobility' is seen to throw up novel formal and architectonic combinations that can 'enrich' and give material form to a collective civic imagination. It is the experience of defamiliarization associated with migrancy that provides the conceptual basis for a reinvigorated architecture based on its own typological lexicon being redeployed in times, places and configurations other than those of their origins. Scolari's attempts to insulate architecture from society has side-effects of its own. It finds the social, through its limit case in migrancy, leaking back into an architecture apparently evacuated of immediate social effects.

In the 'Introduction' to this collection I outlined a residual script that embodies a general relationship in which the migrant stands for the unsettlement against which a preferred and ideal state of sedentary settlement is understood. Mobility, in this script, is conceived of as an aberrant state that functions, at best, as a side-effect of processes of re-settlement.[13] In this account, the marginal figure of the migrant stands in for the once privileged figure of the user, the sedentary citizen, and surreptitiously returns to architecture the core features of a traditional humanism. As Gianni Vattimo points out, these core features still 'centre around the freedom, choice, and unpredictability of behaviour' (Vattimo 1988: 34). The marginal social subject recuperated here is, as Vattimo might say, a 'weakened' one. As we have seen, the migrant operates with choice, yet his/her moves are also more heavily over-determined than most by the macro-economic structures of globalization. I want to advance this exploration by taking up certain possibilities that are suggested by concepts like the 'weakened subject'. I want to do so by turning to a thinker whose ideas about space, society and architecture established the grounds for another critical approach to the legacy of humanism in architecture – this leads us to the third, 'placist', tendency in the current everyday architectural orthodoxy I sketched above.

In his later work on space, place and being, Martin Heidegger mobilized a famous critique of the rationalization of human existence that had taken place under the authority of humanism. This critique was put into direct and sustained contact with architectural questions in his essay 'Building dwelling thinking' (1971b). In the hands of architectural critics such as Christian Norberg-Schulz, Heidegger's critique – particularly as it was elaborated in this essay – formed the basis of a place-making alternative to architectural modernism. In this essay, Heidegger focused the wider dimensions of his critique of rationality by drawing on another 'problem of housing', this being the one associated with the shortage of housing in the period following the Second World War, around 80 years after the German housing crisis that troubled Engels. He sought to challenge the modernist assumption that by relieving the housing shortage through the mere provision of housing, a deeper sense of homeliness, rootedness and belonging might be cultivated in postwar reconstruction. Addressing the problem of housing, in the material sense of providing shelter, continued to be an important task of postwar reconstruction, of course, but it did not, in itself, 'make home appear'. The appearance of 'home', in this existential sense, would require the severing of architecture's direct claims on the well being of social life. For Rossi, as we have seen, a similar assessment led to the strategic (re)assertion of a certain architectural autonomy. For Heidegger, on the contrary, it involved a reconsideration of the way subjectivity itself was implicated in architecture and in the processes of building.

For Heidegger, this project implied a distinct conception of the human subject. His conception of subjectivity (*Dasein*) sees the subject to be constituted relationally.[14] As such, Heidegger's subject conspicuously breaks with the self-confirming humanist (empirico-transcendental) subject that Foucault identified in his account of the rise of social science in the Enlightenment. Subjectivity, for Heidegger, is not simply given or assumed to be stable and fixed, as in the case of Enlightenment man, but may well be concealed. This suggests a more troubled and fragile subject whose full constitution involves disclosure through tending and coaxing, often by the very act of movement – 'throwness' or 'falling'. With diverse capacities for 'authentic' and 'inauthentic' expression, this, then, is a negotiated subjectivity that is always situated and particular. So construed, it is a subjectivity in which architecture is always implicit through its capacities to situate and particularize. For Heidegger, the processes of building and place-making are inextricably linked to the constitution of authentic subjectivity. This can be seen as a re-ontologizing of the question of housing, and an intensification of the more general bond between architecture and society, and is encapsulated in Heidegger's use of the term, 'dwelling'.

To exemplify this process, Heidegger invokes a number of architectural images, the most well known being a 200-year-old vernacular farmhouse in the Black Forest (1971b: 160). For Heidegger, it is the 'wide overhanging shingle roof', and its sheltering character, that is particularly important. With the advance of modernity and rationalization, and the expansion of metropolitan life, traditional forms of dwelling such as this farmhouse, and its sheltering character, come to be seen as anachronistic. Metropolitan life seemed to have banished the architectural values of the vernacular (such that they might only be found in the Black Forest). Heidegger asks us metropolitan citizens to 'learn to dwell' again. There is a widely held perception that Heidegger advocates a return to the nostalgic architectural values embodied in the vernacular farmhouse in order to achieve this. But his essay is not as straightforward as that. For Heidegger, learning to dwell in modernity is not a matter of reviving vernacular forms of architecture, forms that might express communion with the land in deeply resonant ways but, rather, takes the form of a kind of vigil, or a 'listening' to the silence of archaic forms. It is this convergence between building and dwelling that will lead to the manifestation of authentic subjectivity.

Of course, Heidegger's essay title has a third term of reference, this being 'thinking'. And it is the idea of 'thinking' that forges the link between 'building' and 'dwelling'. Thinking, for Heidegger, is activated by the act of listening, not to the bricks and mortar of ancient buildings, but to language itself. Heidegger illustrates this in the opening pages of his essay, where he presents an etymology of the term 'building [*bauen*]' that uncovers its deeper relationship to 'dwelling' (see Rakatansky, this volume for further discussion on this etymology). Heidegger asks us to recall the forgotten and 'withdrawn' meanings embedded in language, because it is language, not built form, that is 'the house of Being' (Heidegger 1971a: 132). Language is, for Heidegger, 'the master of man' (Heidegger 1971b: 146), and as such is the media within which can be found clues for authentic subjectivity. Indeed, Heidegger adds that it is man's 'subversion' of his relation to language – 'as though *he* was the shaper and master of language' – that stands at the core of his 'alienation'.

For architectural critics such as Norberg-Schulz, Heidegger's account of subjectivity constituted through building and dwelling, offers a powerful critique of the instrumentality of modernism's subject, 'the user'. For him, transcending the instrumentality of modernism in architectural thinking, involves embracing the very relational fragility of Heidegger's *Dasein*. In doing so, Norberg-Schulz puts Heidegger's more abstract insights into contact with more pragmatic architectural questions. This unleashes a set of tensions, none more interesting for our purposes, than when the issue of mobility comes to be considered. It is important to note that Heidegger's concept of dwelling readily incorporated mobility – he quite openly suggests, for instance, that a truck driver may be 'at home' on the road (1971b: 145). But when Heidegger's ideas are translated into architecture by Norberg-Schulz, the issue of mobility is not so easily absorbed. It is perhaps unsurprising that at the hands of an architect, for whom issues of foundation, place, limit, wall, enclosure, etc., are so much more urgent, Heidegger's concept of dwelling comes to be grounded. In an excessively material interpretation of Heidegger's notion of dwelling, Norberg-Schulz argues that 'Man, thus, finds himself when he *settles*, and his being-in-the-world is thereby determined' (1985: 13; emphasis in the original). This said, Norberg-Schulz readily accepts that mobility is a feature of society and that:

> man is also a wanderer. As *homo viator*, he is always on the way, which implies a possibility of choice. He chooses his place, and hence a certain kind of fellowship with other men. This dialectic of departure and return, of path and goal, is the essence of that existential 'spatiality' which is set into work by architecture.
>
> (Norberg-Schulz 1985: 13)

Norberg-Schulz's mobile subject remains, nonetheless, 'caught' by the place of his/her birth. It is this birth place that offers the central anchor for a subject taken up into a fluid dialectic of departure and return. Regardless of where we come to settle, one's birth place is always present and has a kind of 'permanence' (1985: 13). Here the fragility of the subject is palpable, seemingly involuntarily cast, or thrown, into a world in flux. The architectures of place – of settlement or of birth – provide security within this flux, and offer potential for disclosure of authentic subjectivity. As he says, '*We* have to have an open mind, and the *places* have to offer rich possibilities for identification' (Norberg-Schulz 1985: 12).

Norberg-Schulz's ostensibly Heideggerian critique of architectural modernism has at its heart, then, the idea of authentic subjectivity being disclosed in relation to a particular spirit of place (*genius loci*). Yet, to frame this core, grounding principle, Norberg-Schulz must invoke a migrant-like figure. Indeed, the figure of the rootless wanderer, who does not need to, and cannot, properly settle, haunts Norberg-Schulz's architectural vision. A certain shuttling, or 'dialectic' movement, between the places of birth and settlement is entertained, but it is clear that this is to be resisted by the overwhelmingly static architectural world that Norberg-Schulz conveys. Once again we see that familiar thematic of migrancy as being something that must be contained by being organized around the teleological and ontopological themes of settlement and assimilation.

In the preceding discussion, I have suggested that a general architectural unconscious might be plotted around three fundamentally incompatible theoretical positions implicating function, type and place. As we have seen, each position draws on a particular version of the conventional migrancy script. Migrancy, and its subject, is alternately embraced, disavowed and recuperated within these architectural positions. The crudeness of these relationships – recalling the conjunctions 'by', 'for' and 'as' – allows migrancy to be domesticated and put to work within a given architectural logic. This suggests that for architecture/migrancy to find a more nuanced expression, alternative modes of articulation are required. To suggest some points of departure for this, I want to return to the idea of thinking in Heidegger, in particular, to the way he deployed that term as a kind of transiting mechanism between 'building' and 'dwelling'.

DRIFTING

As many critics have argued, the etymology of 'building' that lies at the core of Heidegger's account of building and dwelling, and that grounds Norberg-Schulz's highly influential critique of modernism, is an idiosyncratic one. The literary critic, J. Hillis Miller, for instance, points out that Heidegger privileges a small range of languages in his thinking, such that he works in 'Greek, Latin, and sometimes, as in "The Thing", a word or two of English, but rarely French, Italian, or Spanish, much less Japanese, Chinese, or Hindi' (1995: 228). Yet, on the basis of this highly restricted family of languages, Miller continues, 'Heidegger blithely draws universal, apodictic conclusions' on the conditions for authentic dwelling – 'the secrets of dwelling in the sense of the proper way to build, dwell, and think on earth are hidden in the now-withdrawn primal meanings of common German words' (Miller 1995: 252). The universality claimed by Heidegger's thinking stands in stark contradiction to the localized languages in which it is conducted. For Miller, this contradiction lies at the heart of the, widely commented upon, problematic and dangerous ties between Heidegger's conception of dwelling and 'national aestheticism' and 'National Socialism' (Miller 1995: 252). This is precisely the kind of danger Derrida articulates through his concept of ontopology, in which the constitution of being is predicated on a particular territory, soil, region or nation. In this context, Heidegger's image of the Black Forest farmhouse is not so innocent or casual, but resonates with a more insular and defensive parochialism. Such a resonance is also present in Norberg-Schulz's architectural theory, where issues of localism, situatedness and particularity are advocated in a more pragmatic way.

To 'listen' to the polyglot languages of migrancy, on the other hand, reveals a wide range of different kinds of dwelling vigils. Not least, through such vigils the authority of a single language, or language family, as the medium for immemorial lessons on authentic dwelling, may be undone. Such vigilance is sure to weaken the claims of ontology and *Dasein* in the constitution of place and dwelling, but it does not necessarily eradicate them. The subject-who-builds, *Dasein*, can be the subject-who-builds-as-migrant, one whose loyalties to place are dispersed yet so often intensified by the turbulence of migrancy flows. For Derrida, the idea of the stability of place, nation and metropolis must be understood in terms of the 'archaic' instability of language. Derrida points out that it is the 'spacing' of language, the space between signifier and signified, that instigates this instability through the 'drift' of meaning. The meaning of national belonging, for instance, 'is rooted first of all in the memory or the anxiety of a displaced – or displaceable – population' (Derrida 1994: 81). The title of this book substitutes 'drifting' for Heideggerian 'thinking' in an attempt to activate such instability. But the 'drifting' that concerns this book, is not precisely as it is deployed by Derrida. Here it is intended to register both the drift of migrancy and that of the languages and meanings that come to constitute its fractured conditions. So, the drifting invoked in this collection lies at the intersection of migrancy and its diverse languages. This configuration allows us to sustain an account of architecture that relates to, and is formed in conjunction with, an account of subjectivity. But it avoids the danger of circumscribing architecture's engagement with migrancy by way of an authorizing subject – be it the migrant as 'user' or 'beneficiary'. Despite (mis)conceptions of Heidegger, the relational and situated subject bequeathed by him takes us away from those grounds, and towards a more deterritorialized social in which a productively weakened subject is entangled within more complex and multiple relations to place and locality. The authority of being situated – as it is instituted in Heidegger through the authority of specific languages and their assumed correspondence to particular territories – is put into doubt. This, in turn, unsettles that comfortable association between locatedness and architectural vernacularism. The term 'drifting', therefore, signifies a discomfort that arises when the bonds between proper being and place are denaturalized. As Vattimo puts it: '[a] subject which can no longer be thought of as a strong subject is indispensable if we are to deny the grandeur of the metaphysical *ontos on* to technology, its productions, its laws, and the world that it creates' (Vattimo 1988: 47). The relation between architecture and migrancy, can be sought in a formulation that simultaneously draws upon and unsettles modern conceptions of subjectivity and place: 'building dwelling drifting'.

DESIRING PLACES

As a way of concluding, I would like to give specificity to Vattimo's notion of a productively weakened subjectivity in relation to migrancy and architecture. The historian, Macolm Bull, deploying an argument that gives economistic push-pull models of migration psychical dimensions, suggests that migrancy is motivated by an introspective narcissism. Migrancy, for Bull, 'presupposes a capacity to see yourself somewhere else, and the capacity to see yourself depends on the surface in which you are looking' (2001). He develops this point by invoking Lacan's account of the mirror-stage in the process of subject formation, arguing that it 'provides a model for the dynamics of migration'. Applying this process to migrant-subjectivity, he draws our attention to the structure of desire that serves as a precondition for uneven development, and for the various movements of migrancy. Migrancy takes place in a world constituted by 'the smooth reflective surface of the host region, the lure of the image glimpsed within it, and the experience of alienation that frequently results' (Bull 2001). In this account, the act of migration is preceded by a polishing of the image of an imagined place of destination in order to see one's self reflected in it. In short, the migrant conjures his/her own self into being in that other place. As Bull quips, citing Thomas Friedman's (2000) account of globalization, 'the "wretched of the earth" want to go to Disney World – not the barricades'. This metaphorics implies that the migrant-subject is not so much the strong subject of revolutionary political action, as the enfeebled subject of mass tourism.

This suggests that the Heideggerian vigil, or 'listening' to the language of dwelling, might entail a psychical register in which different fantasies for proper dwelling are activated. Migration is much more than simply a technique of wish fulfilment. Lacan insists that '[t]he picture is a trap' (Lacan 1981: 92), and we might usefully apply this notion to the places of desire that 'pull' at people to move – be it Disney World, Hollywood, the West, etc. This concept elaborates the spatial predicament of the migrant, who is, if we apply Norberg-Schulz's conception, at once forever 'caught' by his/her place of birth, and 'trapped' by a place of desire. Norberg-Schulz's state of capture is, of course, read positively by him, offering anchored security in the life-long wanderings of the subject. In contrast, Lacan's entrapped subject is always marked by, what he describes as, a 'blind spot' or 'shadow'. This blind spot represents the mark of the subject's lack of control of its own conscious self.[15] We are, at this point, dealing with the Lacanian notion of gaze. For him, the structure of the gaze constitutes the subject as it 'annihilates' it, and the shadowy blind spot is a metaphor for this process. If we follow Lacan, here, then the migrant cannot simply find him/herself reflected in the surface images of their destination. The point where the subject expects to find such a self-confirming reflection is marked instead by a blind spot that their own subjective fragility projects. While architectural surfaces, such as those of a Disney World, seem to hold out the possibility of occupying another place, they are also reminders of the very impossibility of the (migrant) subject fully occupying that place. The migrant-subject (anthropological man, the user, or *Dasein*) in this account, is further weakened ('annihilated'), in that s/he is in place and out of place at the same time, entrapped between desire for self-confirmation and its impossibility. This subject position cannot serve as the basis for an instrumental social and political programme in architecture, as the strong subject of humanism has done. This deflates the grander claims for a migrant agency within a geopolitical sphere, and undoes the binaries that tend to establish themselves around the conjunctions 'by', 'for', 'as' and even 'contra', in the case of neo-rationalism. The agency is neither fully operative as choice and control, nor completely absent as in the case of victimization.

This oscillation around the subject-status of the migrant and the more general unaccountability of migrancy, is encapsulated by two recent films that feature migrant stories. Stephen Frears' *Dirty Pretty Things* (2002) concerns two migrants (a Turkish woman and Nigerian man) working illegally in low-paid service sector jobs in London. Frears' attitude towards the cinematic representation of these migrant characters and migrancy in general is openly provocative:

> It seemed to me that the characters deserved to have a glamorous film made about them. If I was a Turkish immigrant I would like to be played by Audrey Tautou [the

> film's female lead]. People want to be shown in a nice light. In my experience they don't want to be shown to be boring or miserable or victims. I always encourage everybody to be as glossy and Hollywood as possible.
>
> (Frears cited in Sweet 2002)

In contrast is the Ken Loach-directed *Bread and Roses* (2000), a film that follows the fortunes of illegal Mexican and Hispanic migrants in Los Angeles supporting themselves through various kinds of domestic work. Loach pays particular attention, via his trademark close-to-the-bone realism, to the migrants' advocacy for workers' rights and unionization. One of the film's stars is Rocio Saenz, herself once an illegal migrant and now leader of the (Service Employees International) Union portrayed in the film. When asked if she would swap her job in the Union for a career in the movies, she responded by saying that '[i]t would be OK if all films were like Ken Loach's and not Hollywood, but the union is where my blood is' (Saenz cited in Campbell 2001).

Reading between Frears' and Loach's positions, we can discern a mode of being that has the potential to be both in and out of place at the same time (see Jacobs, this volume, for a discussion of the uncanny dimensions of migrant modes of being). The placial dimensions of this mode of being are pluri-local, consisting of one's sense of origin, current location and possible destinations, as well as the imaginary spaces through which these 'sites' are mediated: Hollywood, Disney World and the barricades. This multipolar condition entangles the 'gritty' and the 'glossy', interpenetrating geographical spaces, representational means and subjective desires. It does not embody the production of place that unfolds in any traditional sense, and so cannot simply support either a celebration of migrant agency or a despairing at migrant victimization. The glossy granite surfaces of corporate foyers and hotel lobbies (of Los Angeles and London), polished – in both the Lacanian and everyday senses – by migrant workers, capture this form of place and emplacement. These films represent architectures that are shot through with a new kind of transactive movement of migrancy. These architectures are distinct from both the older transplanted and hybridized architectures associated with various forms of colonial migrancy, and deterritorialized forms of postmodern mobility. The architectures of contemporary migrancy disturb the narrative of 'enlivenment' and 'security' associated with the protection/projection of national borders. What results is an architecture that comes to be imbricated with the effects of a particular kind of movement that carries ongoing, multiple, intermittent and intensified investments in place.

NOTES

1 The burden of representing national culture in this international context rests more explicitly with what Loeffler (1998) has called the 'architecture of

diplomacy'. This curious architectural sub-genre, consisting of embassies and consulates, is exemplified by architectures that are designed to 'speak' loudly of national identity, and are hard-wired to 'listen in' to the political discourses of the host, all the while maintaining rigorous enclave conditions. See also Robin's (1992) *Enclaves of America*.

2 See Miller (1995: 3–5) for a more general discussion of toponymy. Paul Carter (1987) elaborates a politics of naming in the context of the white settlement of Australia, and Laguerre (2000: 6) does so in the context of the contemporary ethnopolis in the US.

3 The *Norsk Utvandrermuseum* (Norwegian Emigrant Museum) is one of the few museums to deal explicitly with emigration, and the relations migrants sustain with their places of origin.

4 Despite Mattenklott's editorial remarks, the diverse contents of this issue of *Daidalos* unfold in relatively untroubled ways, with projects from the most sophisticated (Mecannoo) to the most ephemeral (the gardens of the urban homeless) being juxtaposed in direct ways on the same 'high gloss paper'.

5 The majority of accommodation built in post-disaster situations (80 per cent) is, in fact, built by the victims of such disasters themselves (Davis 1978). So the image of a purpose-built architecture-for-migrants, for all its familiarity in the public imagination, is an idiosyncratic one. Also, more recently, this conventional, 'from-above' model of emergency shelter provision has been augmented by more responsive, grass-roots models that seek to promote principles of sustainable knowledge-transfer in the field of housing and construction.

6 Incidentally, Ban's first experiment with cardboard tubes was to house an exhibition of Aalto's work held in Tokyo in 1986.

7 In a recent interview, Ban candidly admits to the persistence required to have the architectural help he offered accepted in the aftermath of the Kobe earthquake. His involvement began with an approach to the priest of a congregation of Vietnamese refugees whose church had been destroyed by fire following the earthquake. 'I proposed to the priest to rebuild [the church] in papertube structure. [. . .] He said we don't need architecture to have a church. But I didn't give up. [. . .] [Eventually, he] specified that if I could raise money and build it by myself, [he] would like to have me build a community space. So I started simultaneously raising money, designing and finding student workers' (Ban, cited in Obrist 1999).

8 Koolhaas is referring to Le Corbusier's *Asile Flottant* project (1929). Comissioned by the Salvation Army, Le Corbusier retrofitted a disused barge permanently moored on the Left Bank of the Seine as an asylum for the homeless and destitute in Paris.

9 The Whitehead Detention Centre in Hong Kong accommodated Vietnamese boat-people, and was closed down prior to the handover in 1997. Sangatte

refugee camp, closed in 2002, was in northern France, just half a mile from the entrance to the Channel Tunnel, and the Woomera detention centre, closed in 2003, was in outback Australia, North of Adelaide. Since 2001, the Australian government has infamously elaborated this detention model by establishing detention facilities off-shore in Melanesia and the Pacific. Current policy in the UK involves the dispersal of detention centres throughout cities and towns in 'middle England'.

10 See Giorgio Agamben's (1998) account of the camp as the 'materialization' and spatialization of a 'state of exception'. He suggests that this incarceral mode of managing migrants is a permanent and constitutive feature of the modern nation state, and is a kind of 'hidden matrix' of contemporary geo-political space. In this analysis, the diverse range of camps established to contain refugees and asylum-seekers today share a structural form with the concentration camps established in Nazi Germany (Agamben 1998: 174).

11 The terms 'migrant' and 'refugee' are often used interchangeably in discussions of the German architectural diaspora. In either case, it should be noted that this was, in general, a highly privileged group whose members arrived in the US with support from major cultural institutions of the day, to lucrative academic posts and architectural commissions – indeed Gropius moved with the approval of the National Socialist regime in Germany (Schulze 1998: 226–8).

12 For instance, it is a staple of twentieth-century architectural history that figures such as Mies flourished in the corporate environment while Gropius thrived in the Ivy League atmosphere of Harvard; but less familiar is the idea that others, such as Breuer and Mendelsohn 'absolutely collapsed in their architectural imagination once they were no longer on native ground' (Moholy-Nagy 1965: 80) and struggled to come to terms with life in the new country.

13 The privileged values of this script are well entrenched in neo-rationalism, as we can see from Rossi's, rather anachronistic, assertion that 'a human being is not only an inhabitant of one country and one city, but of a highly precise and delimited place' (Rossi 1984: 162).

14 Heidegger was wary of deploying 'subjectivity', because of the subjectivism it implied. I will persist with the term here as part of my intention is, precisely, to discuss the 'weakening' of its subjective aura.

15 Lacan points out that 'some shadow' 'marks the fact of consciousness in Freud's very discourse' (Lacan 1981: 79). 'If I am anything in the picture,' Lacan says, 'it is always in the form of the screen, which I earlier called the stain, the spot' (Lacan 1981: 97).

REFERENCES

Agamben, G. (1998) *Homo Sacer: sovereign power and bare life*, trans. D. Heller-Roazen, Stanford: Stanford University Press.

Appadurai, A. (1990) 'Disjuncture and difference in the global cultural economy', *Theory, Culture and Society* 7 (203): 295–310.

Arieff, A. and Burkhart, B. (2002) *Prefab*, Salt Lake City: Gibbs M. Smith.

Bahamon, A. (ed.) (2002) *PreFab: prefabricated and moveable architecture*, New York: Hearst Books International.

Bhatia, G. (1994) *Punjabi Baroque, and Other Memories of Architecture*, New Delhi: Penguin.

Bull, M. (2001) 'Hate is the new love', *London Review of Books* 23 (2), 25 January.

Campbell, D. (2001) '"Why don't you just go home, you wetbacks?"', *The Guardian*, Friday 20 April.

Carter, P. (1987) *The Road to Botany Bay: an essay in spatial history*, London: Faber.

Connor, P. (1979) *Oriental Architecture in the West*, London: Thames and Hudson.

Davis, I. (1978) *Shelter After Disaster*, Oxford: Oxford Polytechnic Press.

Derrida, J. (1994) *Specters of Marx: the state of the debt, the work of mourning, and the new international*, trans. P. Kamuf, London: Routledge.

DIMIA (2002) 'Architects shortlisted for new permanent detention facilities design competition', Canberra: Government press release MPS 23/2002 http://www.minister.immi.gov.au/media_releases/media02/r02023.htm [accessed 29 November 2002].

Engels, F. (1936) *The Housing Question*, London: Lawrence and Wishart.

Farrelly, E. (2002) 'The moral of the storey', *Sydney Morning Herald*, 15 June: 8, Spectrum section.

Foucault, M. (1970) *The Order of Things: an archaeology of the human sciences*, London: Routledge.

Freud, S. (1991) *Introductory Lectures on Psychoanalysis*, trans. J. Strachey, London: Penguin.

Friedman, T. (2000) *The Lexus and the Olive Tree*, New York: Harper Collins.

Gausa, M. (ed.) (1999) *Flashes: fleeting time, precarious time (Quaderns 224)*, Barcelona: Actar.

Heidegger, M. (1971a) 'What are poets for?', in M. Heidegger, *Poetry, Language, Thought*, trans. A. Hofstadter, New York: Harper and Row.

Heidegger, M. (1971b) 'Building dwelling thinking', in M. Heidegger *Poetry, Language, Thought*, trans. A. Hofstadter, New York: Harper and Row.

Honour, H. (1961) *Chinoiserie: the vision of Cathay*, London: John Murray.

Jay, M. (1998) 'The German migration: is there a figure in the carpet?', in S. Barron (ed.) *Exiles + Emigrés*, Los Angeles, Los Angeles County Museum of Art: Harry N. Abrams.

King, A.D. (1984) *The Bungalow: the production of global culture*, London: Routledge and Kegan Paul.

Koolhaas, R. (1994) *Delirious New York: a retroactive manifesto for Manhattan*, New York: Monacelli Press.

Koolhaas, R. and Mau, B. (1995) *S,M,L,XL*, New York: Monacelli Press.

Kreimer, A. (1979) 'Emergency, temporary and permanent housing after disasters in developing countries', *Ekistics* 279 (November/December).

Kronenburg, R. (1995) *Houses in Motion: the genesis, history and development of the portable building*, London: Academy Editions.

Lacan, J. (1981) *The Four Fundamental Concepts of Psychoanalysis: the seminar of Jacques Lacan, Book XI*, New York: Norton.

Laguerre, M.S. (2000) *The Global Ethnopolis: Chinatown, Japantown, and Manilatown in American society*, New York: St Martin's Press.

Lin, J. (1998) *Reconstructing Chinatown: ethnic enclave, global change*, Minneapolis: University of Minnesota Press.

Loeffler, J.C. (1998) *The Architecture of Diplomacy: building America's embassies*, New York: Princeton Architectural Press.

MacKenzie, J.M. (1995) *Orientalism: history, theory and the arts*, Manchester: Manchester University Press.

Mares, P. (2002) *Borderline: Australia's response to refugees and asylum seekers in the wake of the Tampa*, Sydney: University of New South Wales Press.

Mattenklott, G. (1994) 'Editorial', *Daidalos* 54 (December): 22–3.

Miller, J.H. (1995) *Topographies*, Stanford: Stanford University Press.

Moholy-Nagy, S. (1965) 'The diaspora', *Journal of the Society of Architectural Historians* 24 (March): 24–5, 80–6.

Norberg-Schulz, C. (1985) *The Concept of Dwelling: on the way to figurative architecture*, New York: Electa/Rizzoli.

Obrist, H.-U. (1999) 'Hans-Ulrich Obrist interviews Shigeru Ban, Paris May 1999', Nettime e-list http://www.nettime.org/Lists-Archives/nettime-l-9908/msg00079.html [accessed 10 November 2002].

Olds, K. (2001) *Globalization and Urban Change: capital, culture and Pacific Rim mega-projects*, Oxford: Oxford University Press.

RAIA (2001) 'Sentenced to detention', Sydney: RAIA press release, 18 April 2001.

Robin, R.T. (1992) *Enclaves of America: the rhetoric of American political architecture abroad, 1900–1965*, Princeton, New Jersey: Princeton University Press.

Rossi, A. (1984) *The Architecture of the City*, trans. D. Ghirardo and J. Ockman, Cambridge, Massachusetts: MIT Press.

Rudofsky, B. (1964) *Architecture Without Architects: an introduction to nonpedigreed architecture*, New York: Museum of Modern Art/Doubleday.

Schulze, F. (1998) 'Changing the agenda: from German Bauhaus Modernism to U.S. Internationalism: Ludwig Mies van der Rohe, Walter Gropius, Marcel

Breuer', in S. Barron (ed.) *Exiles + Emigrés*, Los Angeles, Los Angeles County Museum of Art: Harry N. Abrams.

Scolari, M. (1998) 'The new architecture and the avant-garde', trans. S. Sartarelli, in K.M. Hays (ed.) *Architecture Theory Since 1968*, Cambridge, Massachusetts: MIT Press.

Scriver, P. (1994) *Rationalization, Standardization, and Control in Design: a cognitive historical study of architectural design and planning in the Public Works Department of British India, 1855–1901*, Delft: Publikatieburo Bouwkunde.

Siegal, J. (2002) *Mobile: the art of portable architecture*, New York: Princeton Architectural Press.

Sivanandan, A. (2001) 'Poverty is the new black', *Race & Class: A Journal for Black and Third World Liberation* 43 (2): 1–6.

Sweet, M. (2002) 'Asylum. With added glamour', *The Independent on Sunday*, 8 December: ArtsEtc. 7.

Tafuri, M. (1976) *Architecture and Utopia: design and capitalist development*, Cambridge, Massachusetts: MIT Press.

Tafuri, M. (1980) *Theories and History of Architecture*, London: Granada.

Vattimo, G. (1988) *The End of Modernity: nihilism and the hermeneutics in postmodern culture*, trans. J. Snyder, Cambridge: Polity Press.

Wright, G. (1991) *The Politics of Design in French Colonial Urbanism*, Chicago: Chicago University Press.

Chapter 2: On cosmopolitanism

Jacques Derrida

Where have we received the image of cosmopolitanism from? *And what is happening* to it? As for this citizen of the world, we do not know what the future holds in store for it. One must ask today whether we can still make a legitimate distinction between the two forms of the metropolis – the City and the State. Moreover, one is seeking to inquire if an International Parliament of Writers[1] can still, as its name seems to suggest, find inspiration in what has been called, for more than twenty centuries now, cosmopolitanism. For is it not the case that cosmopolitanism has something to do either with all the cities or with all the states of the world? At a time when the 'end of the city' resonates as though it were a verdict, at a time when this diagnosis or prognosis is held by many, how can we still dream of a novel status for the city, and thus for the 'cities of refuge', through a *renewal* of international law? Let us not anticipate a simple response to such a question. It will be necessary therefore to proceed otherwise, particularly if one is tempted to think, as I do, that 'The Charter for the Cities of Refuge' and 'The International Agency for Cities of Refuge' which appear on our programme must open themselves up to something more and other than merely banal articles in the literature on international law. They must, if they are to succeed in so doing, make an audacious call for a genuine innovation in the history of the right to asylum or the duty to hospitality.

The name 'cities of refuge' appears to be inscribed in gold letters at the very heart of the constitution of the International Parliament of Writers. Ever since our first meeting, we have been calling for the opening of such refuge cities across the world. That, in effect, very much resembles a new cosmo*politics*. We have undertaken to bring about the proclamation and institution of numerous and, above all, autonomous 'cities of refuge', each as independent from the other and from the state as possible, but, nevertheless, allied to each other according to forms of solidarity yet to be invented. This invention is our task; the theoretical or critical reflection it involves is indissociable from the practical initiatives we have already, out of a sense of urgency, initiated and implemented. Whether it be the foreigner in general, the immigrant, the exiled, the deported, the stateless or the displaced person (the task being as much to distinguish prudently between these categories as is possible), we would ask these new cities of refuge to reorient the politics of the state. We would ask them to transform and reform the modalities of membership by which the city (*cité*) belongs to the state, as in a developing Europe or in international juridical structures still dominated by the inviolable rule of state sovereignty – an intangible rule, or one at least supposed such, which is becoming increasingly precarious and problematic nonetheless. This should no longer be the ultimate horizon for cities of refuge. Is this possible?

In committing ourselves thus, in asking that metropolises and modest cities commit themselves in this way, in choosing for them the name of 'cities of refuge', we have doubtless meant more than one thing, as was the case for the name 'parliament'. In reviving the traditional meaning of an expression and in restoring a memorable heritage to its former dignity, we have been eager to propose simultaneously, beyond the old word, an original concept of hospitality, of the duty (*devoir*) of hospitality, and of the right (*droit*) to hospitality. What then would such a concept be? How might it be adapted to the pressing urgencies which summon and overwhelm us? How might it respond to unprecedented tragedies and injunctions which serve to constrain and hinder it?

I regret not having been present at the inauguration of this solemn meeting, but permit me, by way of saluting those here present, to evoke at least a vague outline of this new charter of hospitality and to sketch, albeit in an overly schematic way, its principal features. What in effect is the context in which we have proposed this new ethic or this new cosmo*politics* of the cities of refuge? Is it necessary to call to mind the violence which rages on a worldwide scale? Is it still necessary to highlight the fact that such crimes sometimes bear the signature of state organisations or of non-state organisations? Is it possible to enumerate the multiplicity of menaces, of acts of censorship (*censure*) or of terrorism, of persecutions and of enslavements in all their forms? The victims of these are innumerable and nearly always anonymous, but increasingly they are what one refers to as intellectuals, scholars, journalists, and writers – men and women capable of speaking out (*porter une parole*) – in a public domain that the new powers of telecommunication render increasingly formidable – to the police forces of all countries, to the religious, political, economic, and social forces of censorship and repression, whether they be state-sponsored or not. Let us not proffer an example, for there are too many; and to cite the best known would risk sending the anonymous others back into the darkness (*mal*) from which they find it hard to escape, a darkness which is truly the worst and the condition of all others. If we look to the city, rather than to the state, it is because we have given up hope that the state might create a new image for the city. This should be elaborated and inscribed in our Statutes one day. Whenever the state is neither the foremost author of, nor the foremost guarantor against the violence which forces refugees or exiles to flee, it is often powerless to ensure the protection and the liberty of its own citizens before a terrorist menace, whether or not it has a religious or nationalist alibi. This is a phenomenon with a long historical sequence, one which Hannah Arendt has called, in a text which we should closely scrutinise, 'The decline of the nation-state and the end of the rights of man' (Arendt 1967). Arendt proposes here, in particular, an analysis of the modern history of minorities, of those 'without a State', the *Heimatlosen*, of the stateless and homeless, and of deported and 'displaced persons'. She identifies *two great upheavals*, most notably between the two wars:

1 First, the progressive abolition, upon the arrival of hundreds of thousands of stateless people (*l'apatrides*), of a right to asylum which was 'the only right that had ever figured as a symbol of Human Rights in the domain of international relations'. Arendt recalls that this right has a 'sacred history', and that it remains 'the only modern vestige of the medieval principle of *quid est in territorio est de territorio*' (280). 'But,' continues Arendt, 'although the right to asylum had continued to exist in a world organised into nation states, and though it had even, in some individual cases, survived two world wars, it is still felt to be an anachronism and a principle incompatible with the international laws of the State.' At the time when Arendt was writing this, *c.*1950, she identified the absence in international charters of the right to asylum (for example in the Charter of the League of Nations). Things have doubtless evolved a little since then, as we shall see in a moment, but further transformations are still necessary.

2 The second upheaval (*choc*) in Europe was to follow a massive influx (*arrivée*) of refugees, which necessitated abandoning the classic recourse to repatriation or naturalisation. Indeed, we have still to create a satisfactory substitute for it. In describing at length the effects of these traumas, Arendt has perhaps identified one of our tasks and, at the very least, the background to our Charter and of our Statutes (*Statuts*). She does not speak of the city, but in the shadow of the two upheavals (*l'onde du double choc*) she describes and which she situates between the two wars, we must today pose new questions concerning the destiny of cities and the role which they might play in these unprecedented circumstances. How can the right to asylum be redefined and developed without repatriation and without naturalisation? Could the City, equipped with new rights and greater sovereignty, open up new horizons of possibility previously undreamt of by international state law? For let us not hesitate to declare our ultimate ambition, what gives meaning to our project: our plea is for what we have decided to call the 'city of refuge'. This is not to suggest that we ought to restore an essentially classical concept of the city by giving it new attributes and powers; neither would it be simply a matter of endowing the old subject we call 'the city' with new predicates. No, we are dreaming of another concept, of another set

of rights for the city, of another politics of the city. I am aware that this might appear utopian for a thousand reasons, but at the same time, as modest as it is, what we have already begun to do proves that something of this sort can, from now on, function – and this disjointed process cannot be dissociated from the turbulence which affects, over the lengthy duration of a process, the axioms of international law.

Is there thus any hope for cities exercising hospitality if we recognise with Arendt, as I feel we must, that nowadays international law is limited by treaties between sovereign states, and that not even a 'government of the world' would be capable of sorting things out? Arendt was writing of something the veracity of which still holds today:

> contrary to the best-intentioned humanitarian attempts to obtain new declarations of human rights from international organisations, it should be understood that this idea transcends the *present sphere of international law which still operates in terms of reciprocal agreements and treaties between sovereign states*; and, for the time being, a sphere that is above the nations does not exist. Furthermore, this dilemma would by no means be eliminated by the establishment of a 'world government'.
>
> (Arendt 1967: 285, emphasis added)

It would be necessary to expand upon and refine what she says of groups and individuals who, between the two wars, lost *all status* – not only their citizenship but even the title of 'stateless people'. We would also have to re-evaluate, in this regard, in Europe and elsewhere, the respective roles of States, Unions, Federations or State Confederations on the one hand, and of cities on the other. If the name and the identity of something like the city still has a meaning, could it, when dealing with the related questions of hospitality and refuge, elevate itself above nation-states or at least free itself from them (*s'affranchir*), in order to become, to coin a phrase in a new and novel way, a *free city* (*une ville franche*)? Under the exemption itself (*en général*), the statutes of immunity or exemption occasionally had attached to them, as in the case of the right to asylum, certain places (diplomatic or religious) to which one could retreat in order to escape from the threat of injustice.

Such might be the magnitude of our task, a theoretical task indissociable from its political implementation (*mise en œuvre*) – a task which is all the more imperative given that the situation is becoming ever more bleak with each passing day. As the figures show, the right to political asylum is less and less respected both in France and in Europe. Lately, there has been talk of a 'dark year for asylum seekers in France'.[2] Because of such understandable despondency, the number of applications for political asylum has been regularly diminishing. In fact, OFPRA (The French Office for the Protection of Refugees and the Stateless) toughened its criteria and spectacularly reduced the number of refugees afforded asylum status. The number of those whose application for asylum has, I might add, continued to rise throughout the 1980s and since the beginning of the 1990s.

Since the Revolution, France has had a certain tendency to portray itself as being more open to political refugees in contradistinction to other European countries, but the motives behind such a policy of opening up to the foreigner have, however, never been 'ethical' *stricto sensu* – in the sense of the moral law or the law of the land (*séjour*) – (*ethos*), or, indeed, the law of hospitality. The comparative drop in the birth rate in France since the middle of the eighteenth century has generally permitted her to be more liberal in matters of immigration for obvious economic reasons: when the economy is doing well, and workers are needed, one tends not to be overly particular when trying to sort out political and economic motivations. This was especially true in the 1960s, when an economic boom resulted in a greater need for immigrant workers. It is also worth noting that the right to asylum has only recently become a specifically juridical concept (*définitionelle*) and a positive juridical concept, despite the fact that its spirit was already present in the French Constitution. The Constitution of 1946 granted the right to asylum only to those characterised as persons persecuted because of their 'action in the name of liberty'. Even though it subscribed to the Geneva Convention in 1951, it is only in 1954 that France was forced to broaden its definition of a political refugee to encompass all persons forced into exile because 'their lives or their liberties are found to be under threat by reason of their race, religion, or political opinions. Considerably broadened, it is true, but very recent nevertheless. Even the Geneva Convention was itself very limited in the manner in which it could be applied, and even at that we are still a long way from the idea of cosmopolitanism as defined in Kant's famous text on the right to (*droit de*) universal hospitality, the limits and restrictions of which I shall recall in just a moment. The Geneva Convention of 1951, which obliged France to improve its asylum laws, could only direct itself to 'events in Europe prior to 1951'. Much later, at the end of the 1960s, precisely at the time when there were signs of the beginning of a process which has dramatically deteriorated today, the area, place, and dates specified by the Geneva Convention (that is, the events in Europe prior to 1951) were enhanced by a particular protocol added to this convention in New York in 1967, and eventually extended to cover events occurring beyond Europe after 1951. (These are the developments which Hannah Arendt could neither have known about nor evoked when she was writing her text sometime around 1950.)

There is still a considerable gap separating the great and generous principles of the right to asylum inherited from the Enlightenment thinkers and from the French Revolution and, on the other hand, the historical reality or the effective implementation (*mise en œuvre*) of these principles. It is controlled, curbed, and monitored by implacable juridical restrictions; it is overseen by what the preface of a book on *The Crisis of the Right to Asylum in France* refers to as a 'mean-minded' juridical tradition (Legoux 1995: xvi). In truth, if the juridical tradition remains 'mean-minded' and restrictive, it is because it is under the control of the demographico-economic interest – that is, the interest of the nation state that regulates asylum. Refugee status ought not to be conflated with the status of an immigrant, not even of a political immigrant. It has happened that a recognition of refugee status, be it political or economic, has only come into effect long after entry into France. We shall have to maintain a close eye on these sometimes subtle distinctions between types of status, especially since the difference between the economic and the political now appears more problematic than ever.

Both to the right and to the left, French politicians speak of 'the control of immigration'. This forms part of the compulsory rhetoric of electoral programmes. Now, as Luc Legoux notes, the expression 'immigration control' means that asylum will be granted only to those who cannot expect the slightest economic benefit upon immigration. The absurdity of this condition is manifestly apparent: how can a purely political refugee claim to have been truly welcomed into a new settlement without that entailing some form of economic gain? He will of course have to work, for each individual seeking refuge cannot simply be placed in the care of the host country. This gives rise to an important consideration which our conventions will have to address: how can the hosts (*hôtes*) and guests of cities of refuge be helped to recreate, through work and creative activity, a living and durable network in new places and occasionally in a new language? This distinction between the economic and the political is not, therefore, merely abstract or gratuitous: it is truly hypocritical and perverse; it makes it virtually impossible ever to grant political asylum and even, in a sense, to apply the law, for in its implementation it would depend entirely on opportunistic considerations, occasionally electoral and political, which, in the last analysis, become a matter for the police, of real or imaginary security issues, of demography, and of the market. The discourse on the refugee, asylum or hospitality, thus risks becoming nothing but pure rhetorical alibis. As Legoux notes, 'what tends to render the asylum laws in France ineffectual for the people of poor countries is the result of a particular conception of asylum, one with a long and complex history, and one which is becoming ever more stringent' (Legoux 1995: xviii).

This tendency to obstruct is extremely common, not to Europe in general (supposing that one had ever been able to speak of 'Europe' in general), but to the countries of the European Union; it is a price that is oftentimes paid as a consequence of the Schengen Agreement – the accords of which, Jacques Chirac declared, have not been, up to now at least, implemented in full by France. At a time when we claim to be lifting internal borders, we proceed to bolt the external borders of the European Union tightly. Asylum-seekers knock successively on each of the doors of the European Union states and end up being repelled at each one of them. Under the pretext of combating economic immigrants purporting to be exiles from political persecution, the states reject applications for the right to asylum more often than ever. Even when they do not do so in the form of an explicit and reasoned (*motivée*) juridical response, they often leave it to their police to enforce the law; one could cite the case of a Kurd to whom a French tribunal had officially granted the right to asylum, but who was nevertheless deported to Turkey by the police without a single protest. As in the case of many other examples, notably those to do with 'violations of hospitality', whereby those who had allegedly harboured political suspects were increasingly charged or indicted, one has to be mindful of the profound problem of the role and status of the police, of, in the first instance, border police, but also of a police without borders, without determinable limit, who from then on become all-pervasive and elusive, as Benjamin noted in *Critique of Violence* just after the First World War.

The police become omnipresent and spectral in the so-called civilised states once they undertake to *make the law*, instead of simply contenting themselves with applying it and seeing that it is observed. This fact becomes clearer than ever in an age of new teletechnologies. As Benjamin has already reminded us, in such an age police violence is both 'faceless' and 'formless', and is thus beyond all accountability. Nowhere is this violence, as such, to be found; in the civilised states, the spectre of its ghostly apparition extends itself limitlessly. It must be understood, of course, that we are concerned here with developing neither an unjust nor a utopian discourse of suspicion of the function of the police, especially in their fight against those crimes which do fall within their jurisdiction (such as terrorism, drug-trafficking, and the activities of mafias of all kinds). We are simply questioning the limits of police jurisdiction and the conditions in which it operates, particularly as far as foreigners are concerned.

With respect to new police powers (national or international), one is touching here on one of the most serious questions of law that a future elaboration of our charter for the cities of refuge would have to develop and inscribe throughout the course of an interminable struggle: it will be necessary to restrict the legal powers and scope of the police by giving them a purely administrative role under the strict control and regulation of certain political authorities, who will see to it that human rights and a more broadly defined right to asylum are respected.

Hannah Arendt, in the spirit of Benjamin, had already highlighted the new and increased powers afforded to the modern police to handle refugees. She did so after making a remark about anonymity and fame which we should, particularly in an International Parliament of Writers, take seriously:

> Only fame will eventually answer the repeated complaint of refugees of all social strata that 'nobody here knows who I am'; and it is true that the chances of the famous refugee are improved just as a dog with a name has a better chance to survive than a stray dog who is just a dog in general.
>
> The nation-state, incapable of providing a law for those who had lost the protection of a national government, transferred the whole matter to the police. This was the first time the police in Western Europe had received authority to act on its own, to rule directly over people; in one sphere of public life it was no longer an instrument to carry out and enforce the law, but had become a ruling authority independent of government and ministries.
>
> (Arendt 1967: 287)

We know only too well that today this problem is more serious than ever, and we could provide much evidence to this effect. A movement protesting against the charge of what has been called for some time now 'violations of hospitality' has been growing in France; certain organisations have taken control of it, and, more widely, the press has become its mouthpiece. A proposal of 'Toubon-law', in the spirit and beyond of the laws known as 'Pasqua', has now come on to the agenda. Under examination in the parliamentary assemblies, in the National Assembly and in the Senate, is a proposal to treat as acts of terrorism, or as 'participation in a criminal conspiracy', all hospitality accorded to 'foreigners' whose 'papers are not in order', or those simply 'without papers'. This project, in effect, makes even more draconian article 21 of the famous edict of 2 November 1945, which had already cited as a 'criminal act' all help given to foreigners whose papers were not in order. Hence, what was a criminal act is now in danger of becoming an 'act of terrorism'. Moreover, it appears that this plan is in direct contravention of the Schengen accords (ratified by France) – which permit a conviction of someone for giving help to a foreigner 'without papers' only if it can be proved that this person derived financial profit from such assistance.

We have doubtless chosen the term 'city of refuge' because, for quite specific historical reasons, it commands our respect, and also out of respect for those who cultivate an 'ethic of hospitality'. 'To cultivate an ethic of hospitality' – is such an expression not tautologous? Despite all the tensions or contradictions which distinguish it, and despite all the perversions that can befall it, one cannot speak of cultivating an ethic of hospitality. Hospitality is culture itself and not simply one ethic amongst others. Insofar as it has to do with the *ethos*, that is, the residence, one's home, the familiar place of dwelling, inasmuch as it is a manner of being there, the manner in which we relate to ourselves and to others, to others as our own or as foreigners, *ethics is hospitality*; ethics is so thoroughly coextensive with the experience of hospitality. But for this very reason, and because being at home with oneself (*l'être-soi chez soi – l'ipséité même* – the other within oneself) supposes a reception or inclusion of the other which one seeks to appropriate, control, and master according to different modalities of violence, there is a history of hospitality, an always possible perversion of *the* law of hospitality (which can appear unconditional), and of the laws which come to limit and condition it in its inscription as a law. It is from within this history that I would like to select, in a very tentative and preliminary way, some reference points which are of great significance to us here.

First, what we have been calling the city of refuge, it seems to me, bridges several traditions or several moments in Western, European, or para-European traditions. We shall recognise in the Hebraic tradition, on the one hand, those cities which would welcome and protect those innocents who sought refuge from what the texts of that time call 'bloody vengeance'. This urban right to immunity and to hospitality was rigorously and juridically developed and the text in which it first emerged was, without doubt, the Book of Numbers:[3] God ordered Moses to institute cities which would be, according to the very letter of the Bible itself, 'cities of refuge' or 'asylum', and to begin with there would be 'six cities of refuge', in particular for the 'resident alien, or temporary settler'. Two beautiful texts in French have been devoted to this Hebraic tradition of the city of refuge, and I would like to recall here that, from one generation to the other, both authors of these essays are philosophers associated with Strasbourg, with this generous border city, this eminently European city, the capital city of Europe, and the first of our refuge cities. I am speaking here of the meditations by Emmanuel Levinas in 'The Cities of Refuge' ['Les Villes refuges', in *L'Au-delà du verset* (Minuit 1982), p. 51], and by Daniel Payot in *Refuge Cities* [*Des villes-refuges, Témoignage et espacement* (Ed. de l'Aube, 1992), especially pp. 65ff.].

In the medieval tradition, on the other hand, one can identify a certain sovereignty of the city: the city itself could determine the laws of hospitality, the articles of predetermined law, both plural and restrictive, with which they meant to condition *the* Great Law of Hospitality – an unconditional Law, both singular and universal, which ordered that the borders be open to each and every one, to every other, to all who might come, without question or without their even having to identify who they are or whence they came. (It would be necessary to study what was called *sanctuary*, which was provided by the churches so as to secure immunity or survival for refugees, and by virtue of which they risked becoming enclaves; and also *auctoritas*, which allowed kings or lords to shield their guests (*hôtes*) from all those in pursuit; or, what occurred between the warring Italian cities when one became a place of refuge for the exiled, the refugee, and those banished from another city; and we who are reminded of writers in this context can call to mind a certain story about Dante, banished from Florence and then welcomed, it would seem, at Ravenna.)

Finally, at this juncture, we could identify the cosmopolitan (*cosmopolitique*) tradition common to a certain Greek stoicism and a Pauline Christianity, of which the inheritors were the figures of the Enlightenment, and to which Kant will doubtlessly have given the most rigorous philosophical formulation in his famous *Definitive Article in View of Perpetual Peace*: 'The law of cosmopolitanism must be restricted to the conditions of universal hospitality.' This is not the place to analyse this remarkable *Article*, or its immense historical context, which has been excised from this text without trace. It was Cicero who was to bequeath a certain Stoic cosmopolitanism. Pauline Christianity revived, radicalised, and literally 'politicised' the primary injunctions of all the Abrahamic religions, since, for example, the 'Opening of the Gates of Israel' – which had, however, specified the restrictive conditions of hospitality so as to ensure the 'safety' or 'security' of the 'strong city'. Saint Paul gives to these appeals or to these dictats their modern names. These are also theologicopolitical names, since they explicitly designate citizenship or world co-citizenship: 'no longer foreigners nor metic in a foreign land, but fellow-citizens with God's people, members of God's household' (Ephesians II. 19–20). In this sentence, 'foreigners' (*xenoi*) is also translated by guests (*hospites*); and 'metic' – but see also 'immigrants', for '*paroikoi*' – designates as much the neighbour, from a point of view which is important to us here, as the foreigner without political rights in another city or country. I am modifying and mixing several translations, including that of Chouraqui, but it will be necessary to analyse closely the political stakes and the theological implications of these questions of semantics; Grosjean Leturmy's translation, in the Pléiade Library, for example, could literally announce the space of what we are interpreting as the 'city of refuge'. But that is precisely what I would like to begin putting into question here – i.e., the secularised version of such Pauline cosmopolitanism: 'And so therefore, you are no longer foreigners abroad (*xenoi*, *hospites*), you are fellow-citizens of the Saints, you belong to the House of God' (*sympolitai ton hagion kai oikeioi tōu theōu; cives sanctorum, et domestici Dei*).

When, in the spirit of the Enlightenment thinkers from whom we are drawing inspiration, Kant was formulating the law of cosmopolitanism, he does not restrict it 'to the conditions of universal hospitality' only. He places on it two limits which doubtless situate a place of reflection and perhaps of transformation or of progress. What are these two limits?

Kant seems at first to extend the cosmopolitan law to encompass universal hospitality *without limit*. Such is the condition of perpetual peace between all men. He expressly determines it as a *natural law* (*droit*). Being of natural or original derivation, this law would be, therefore, both imprescriptible and inalienable. In the case of natural law, one can recognise within it features of a secularised theological heritage. All human creatures, all finite beings endowed with reason, have received, in equal proportion, 'common possession of the surface of the earth'. No one can in principle, therefore, legitimately appropriate for himself the aforementioned surface (as such, as a *surface-area*) and withhold access to another man. If Kant takes great care to specify that this good or common place covers 'the surface of the earth', it is doubtless so as not to exclude any point of the world or of a spherical and finite globe (globalisation), from which an infinite dispersion remains impossible; but it is above all to expel from it what *is erected, constructed, or what sets itself up above* the soil: habitat, culture, institution, State, etc. All this, even the soil upon which it lies, is no longer soil pure and simple, and, even if founded on the earth, must not be unconditionally accessible to all comers. Thanks to this strictly delimited condition (which is nothing other than the institution of limit as a border, nation, State, public or political space), Kant can deduce *two* consequences and inscribe *two* other paradigms upon which it would be in our interest to reflect tomorrow.

1 First of all he excluded hospitality as a *right of residence* (*Gastrecht*); he limits it to the *right of visitation* (*Besuchsrecht*). The right of residence must be made the object of a particular treaty between states. Kant defines thus the conditions that we would have to interpret carefully in order to know how we should proceed:

> We are speaking here, as in the previous articles, not of philanthropy, but of right; and in this sphere hospitality signifies the claim of a stranger entering foreign territory to be treated by its owner without hostility. The latter may send him away again, if this can be done without causing his death; but, so long as he conducts himself peaceably, he must not be treated as an enemy. It is not a right to be treated as a guest to which the stranger can lay claim – a special friendly compact on his behalf would be required to make him for a given time an actual inmate – but he has a right of visitation. This right to present themselves to society belongs to all mankind in virtue of our common right of possession on the surface of the earth on which, as it is a globe, we cannot be infinitely scattered, and must in the end reconcile ourselves to existence side by side: at the same time, originally no one individual had more right than another to live in any one particular spot.
>
> (Kant 1972: 137–8)

It is this limitation on the right of residence, as that which is to be made dependent on treaties between states, that perhaps, amongst other things, is what remains for us debatable.

2 By the same token, in defining hospitality in all its rigour as a law (which counts in this respect as progress), Kant assigns to it conditions which make it dependent on state sovereignty, especially when it is a question of the *right of residence*. Hospitality signifies here the *public nature* (*publicité*) of public space,

as is always the case for the juridical in the Kantian sense; hospitality, whether public or private, is dependent on and controlled by the law and the state police. This is of great consequence, particularly for the 'violations of hospitality' about which we have spoken considerably, but just as much for the sovereignty of cities on which we have been reflecting, whose concept is at least as problematic today as in the time of Kant.

All these questions remain obscure and difficult and we must neither conceal them from ourselves nor, for a moment, imagine ourselves to have mastered them. It is a question of knowing how to transform and improve the law, and of knowing if this improvement is possible within an historical space which takes place *between* the Law of an unconditional hospitality, offered *a priori* to every other, to all newcomers, *whoever they may be*, and *the* conditional laws of a right to hospitality, without which *The* unconditional Law of hospitality would be in danger of remaining a pious and irresponsible desire, without form and without potency, and of even being perverted at any moment.

Experience and experimentation thus. Our experience of cities of refuge then will not only be that which cannot wait, but something which calls for an urgent response, a just response, more just in any case than the existing law. An immediate response to crime, to violence, and to persecution. I also imagine the experience of cities of refuge as giving rise to a place (*lieu*) for reflection – for reflection on the questions of asylum and hospitality – and for a new order of law and a democracy to come to be put to the test (*expérimentation*). Being on the threshold of these cities, of these new cities that would be something other than '*new* cities', a certain idea of cosmopolitanism, *an other*, has not yet arrived, *perhaps*.

– If it has (*indeed*) arrived . . .

– . . . then, one has perhaps not yet recognised it.

NOTES

1 [This chapter was first presented to a meeting of the International Parliament of Writers in Strasbourg 1996. One of the first goals of this organisation included the formation of an international network of Cities of Asylum, cities dedicated to offering haven to persecuted writers and intellectuals] (ed.).

2 See *Le Monde*, 27 February 1996. See also Legoux (1995).

3 Numbers XXXV. 9–32. Cf. I Chronicles 6. 42, 52, where the expression 'Cities of refuge' reappears, and also Joshua 20. 1–9: 'if they admit him into the city, they will grant him a place where he may live as one of themselves' (*Revised English Bible with Apocrypha*. Oxford and Cambridge: Cambridge University Press (Bibles), 1989: 199).

REFERENCES

Arendt, H. (1967) 'The decline of the nation-state and the end of the rights of man', in H. Arendt, *The Origins of Totalitarianism*, London: George and Unwin.

Legoux, L. (1995) *La crise d'asile politique en France*, Paris: Centre Français sur la Population et le Développement (CEPED).

Kant, I. (1972) *Perpetual Peace: a philosophical essay*, trans. M.C. Smith, New York and London: Garland Publishing.

Chapter 3: Architecture as evidence

Catherine Ingraham

The Melbourne conference, *Building Dwelling Drifting*, that originally gave rise to this essay substituted the word 'drifting' for 'thinking' – a wily substitution, I think, since the word 'drifting' updates (arrogant word) the *Dasein* to take account of a world in which Heidegger's philosophical concept of identity as Being[1] has fully yielded to the drift that, as Heidegger taught us, was drifting inside it all along; a world where plural beings find their identities-through-difference inside incessant streams of cultural displacement and migrancy by means of 'interstitial perspectives' as Homi Bhabha calls it (1994: 1–2),[2] and 'middle passages' (1994: 4–5). The word 'drifting' also flows back and forth into the words 'building' and 'dwelling' in a way that underwrites the temporality of those acts, the continuous emergent quality of their organization in cultures, and the impossibility of stopping them in one place in spite of long-standing beliefs that buildings are the firm, inflexible, ground for flexible acts of dwelling.

Language, of course, is the consummate cultural drift artist. Its drift, in a migrant world, has been both thematized and banalized by global computer networks; the literal mass movements of contemporary culture have found an interesting fit with the global spread of information culture. But, of course, we need to be careful of thinking in heroic terms about the success of the linguistic model or the information model. Within these successes are, among other things, the near successes of one or two languages over the others, Microsoft and Apple, English and Chinese; the increased modelling of computer space as secured corporate space; and the development of eco-touristic conservation and media forces that avidly consume global exotica. Were one looking for the edge in front of these movements, in the usual spirit of the avant-garde, one would find only cul-de-sacs. The only twenty-first-century avant-garde gesture that now seems possible is the paradoxical and regressive one of refusing the scientific desire, and its media offshoots, that have been with us since the Enlightenment; to let something happen in the jungle involving animals or plants, for example, without needing to record or represent the event in any form; to refrain from knowing. Such refusals of representation, desire and knowledge often go by another name, fundamentalism. We are only too familiar with the desire of fundamentalism not only to keep everyone at home, but to design the home as a place in which the movement implied by difference is a breach of security.

Architecture – building and dwelling – is a practice that has always belonged to the desirous and incessantly constructive forces of knowing and classifying, although the practice of architecture sometimes comes perilously close to a kind of fundamentalism. What I want to explore a little more here is how architecture – in the West and since the Enlightenment – seems to position itself, not primarily as a form of positivism, nor as a constructed object of knowledge (although both of these positions are true on occasion and in some respects), but as a very specific kind of evidence for the existence of a very specific kind of knowledge, or, perhaps, a specific kind of 'not-knowing'. And I want to examine this question with respect to some of the themes of the migrancy conference, in particular with respect to colonial and postcolonial conditions that open certain paths for migration (Castles 2000: 82). The role of 'place', in the analysis of global migrations and in what Homi Bhabha calls the 'jargon of the times', 'postmodernity, postcoloniality, postfeminism' (1994: 4), is often scrutinized. 'Place' is not equivalent to architecture but place and architecture, in cultural terms, are intimately connected. Architecture – buildings built not simply as constructions but as constructions with a symbolic import – simultaneously secures and activates ideas of place in several ways: through the various operations of property systems, symbolic transfers of meaning, economies of material productions, and through the maintenance of the discipline of 'architecture' itself.

ARCHITECTURE AND COLONIAL OCCUPATIONS

Migrancy is, by most contemporary definitions, the condition of not living in 'your country of origin'. Colonialism is a dislocating force that acts on and inside a culture and which, under certain circumstances, forces native occupants (non-migrants) to become migratory in order to maintain identity and to survive. Buildings, civic and religious buildings in particular, house and give identity to cultures and it is this, not surprising, fact that accounts for why colonialism necessarily involves the cumbersome and highly inefficient process of occupying territories, cities and buildings in order to occupy the institutional and infrastructural life of a culture. Equally, as one of many counter-moves to colonial history, colonial and postcolonial cultures often attempt to de-occupy space, migrating from one place to the next, restarting institutional and domestic life in different place, or even in the same place but as a reoccupation rather than a continuation of what came before. In general, during periods of both colonial occupation and postcolonial migration, the architecture of the background, and the background of architecture, is brought to the foreground. To a lesser degree, labour and political transmigrations also make us acutely aware of the normally almost invisible alliance between identity, in the large sense, and place, in the more specific architectural sense.

The felt degree and extent to which a space, any space, can be said to be occupied has always been, for me, primarily an architectural question. We acquire our most basic ideas and mythologies about bounding and occupying space from architecture. Architecture – the discipline and practice of thinking, designing and building buildings – and the subsequent occupation of these structures, is where culture produces, projects and processes its main ideas about space and occupation. The production of space is not, of course, linear in the sense that the phrase 'culture produces' suggests. The production of architectural space is never simply the production of abstract symbolic space. It is space produced out of an entangled network of cultural negotiations surrounding ideas of home, identity, community, propriety, property ownership, gender, aesthetics, and a multitude of other issues.[3] Living or working in a building is not a simple act. Buildings are also living in, and working on, their occupants. Among other things, architecture is a spatio-symbolic organization 'extruded' from our bodies (Leroi-Gourhan 1993: 242),[4] although multiple conflicting theories have been advanced about why and how we, as a species, have come to design and live in specific architectures. Once out in the world, so to speak, architecture makes a point of establishing its scale and material difference from the body that inhabits it because the idea of inhabitation is enlarged in a particular way by the architectural act. But, simultaneously, architecture extracts organizational energy from the action of life residing within it and vice versa. This can partly be understood by observing the relentless and diverse labour needed to maintain buildings in small and large ways. Buildings are almost live forces and operate, in some sense, according to similar principles of organic life that the quantum physicist Schrödinger characterized as a force that extracts order from the world around it (1962: 9–10).[5] It is no surprise, then, that architecture necessarily always entangles us in the complex space of identity, particularly when a space/identity affiliation is threatened by aggressive occupations from outside, but also by less aggressive, but no less powerful, de-occupations of space of migrant cultures. There are, for example, large populations of guest workers from South America living in New York City, many of whose immediate families live elsewhere. The buildings these workers live in are, for the most part, anonymous housing blocks on the periphery of the city. The anonymity of these buildings, often government housing projects, is not, paradoxically, entirely undesirable from the occupant's standpoint since it sometimes helps shield the occupant from civic and legal forces that are intolerant of civic anonymity. Insofar as migrancy means living away from your country of origin it also means the maintenance of an idea of origin that choreographs a path – even if it is a fantastical or virtual path – back to the country of origin. The architecture of these housing blocks, which we would typically deplore for their grotesque lack of environmental and psychological consciousness, conspires in some way with the migrant spirit of people who are making their money in one country and spending it in another country. The labour expended to make the money is exhausted in the marketplace and does not spill over into living space; what money is left after the work is done is reserved for expenditure elsewhere. Money and labour, in these cases, have split loyalties with respect to place, and the place of life after this kind of work is also provisional and split.

There are interesting literal dimensions to the question of architecture and identity, although we also have to hold the idea of the 'literal' accountable for views on architecture that are invested in keeping architecture inert, out of play. But the literal is always invoked in architecture, even if it proves elusive. The degree to which the literalness of architecture is suspended is the degree to which a particular kind of evidentiary scene is elided. By means of the literal, architecture seems to refute the 'split mirror' of identity and the disjunctive narratives of the present postmodern condition (Bhabha 1994: 4–18).[6] But it too plays a double game. Because architecture does not move in the same way as the face, body, or language moves, initially architectural 'agency' in matters of identity seems to come from the far periphery of the play of signs (Bhabha 1994: 189–90).[7] This is a longer discussion than will be pursued here, but the literalness of architecture guarantees that it will appear to lie outside of the movement of central matters of identity, even as those matters can be spatially and metaphorically located in architecture. In a sense, architecture is primary cultural evidence of the possibility of an external realm. When we are inside a building, we forget the outline of the outside; when outside, we forget the volume of the inside. Architecture is, for example, the thing that is fully left behind by migrant culture, left behind as a possession too large to carry away, as the thing/place clearly lost, and as the literal evidence of having passed from one place to another. In addition, architecture marks a particular kind of time that is connected to the passage of biological time, but also exceeds it. Temporality – which Homi Bhabha, with Lacan, styles as the gap of signification itself – in the case of architecture is akin to the temporality of death; death may be an ongoing process of decay that forms a continuum with life's ongoing processes, but death also is a relinquishment of the active agency that is life's mark. The literal externality of architecture, particularly when it has been left as the home of identity, signifies a loss of the agency of life – that is, life as the subject of one's own story. All of this makes architecture's exact 'double game', and its evidentiary game, hard to discern.

I want to trace some aspect of this double game inside one particular, mostly colonial, history, mainly the British occupation of India. I have not necessarily picked the best example, from the standpoint of migrancy, since the occupation of India by the British does not, initially, speak specifically to questions of migration. But the example does something else. It attempts to shift our view of culture, momentarily, from the animate life forces that contribute their vitality to any idea of culture to the inanimate material forces that are routinely thought to passively hold and represent that culture. I want to do this in order to explore how buildings – architectural buildings – participate as evidence in scenes of culture that, as in colonial and migratory periods, are in crisis.

When one culture moves into another culture its first move is frequently along economic vectors. As is well known, the British occupation of India started as an opportunistic mercantilism that gradually insinuated itself into the institutional and governing life of that country, an insinuation that was then supported by the overt military aggressions we are familiar with. This is both the parasitic nature of colonialism – it cannot survive without sharing some kind of institutional life with the host culture, even a wholly exploitative one – and, simultaneously, its point of vulnerability. As long as institutional life is shared there is the possibility of the slippage of control. Built into colonialism, in other words, are the seeds of its own undoing. This neat poststructural formulation, however, while reassuring in some way, is useless in identity politics because identity is where the full force of colonialism exerts itself and identity itself must always be invested in immediate survival. Identity – which is never a unified idea, but splintered in very particular ways in a colonial world – cannot afford to wait for colonialism to unravel itself at the institutional level. But I want to use this idea in a provisional, non-heroic way, to suggest that at least some of the internal 'undoing' of colonialism can be attributed to the relentlessly evidentiary character of architecture. We already know that the reverse is true: that architecture can advance and concretize colonial claims, and that architecture is often inimical to the establishment of ethnic identity.

Colonial powers are, by definition, faced with the inconvenience of housing themselves in a foreign place; this is considerably more than an inconvenience since a large part of colonial occupation is enacted through the logistical. One of the most complex, and instructive, instances of colonial occupation is the much debated Viceroy's House complex designed by the British architect Edwin L. Lutyens in New Delhi, India in 1918–31. As is well known, the British Raj was understood, by its European chroniclers in particular, to be more fully rooted, more fully represented, by means of the imported British architecture of the Viceroy's House. But Lutyens, in designing this complex of buildings, was influenced not so much by British architecture as by the interest of British architects in Palladio, the Italian Renaissance architect. The 'idea of order' (Irving 1981: 226) that the British felt themselves to be bringing to India by means of the entire processional architecture[8] of the governmental complex is inscribed in the classical symmetries and repetitions of Palladian architecture, but, also, in the imperial styles of Roman empire architectures such as Hadrian's Pantheon. It was in the style of Roman imperialism that Britain pursued its own imperialist adventures (Irving 1981: 195).[9] Palladio was not from Rome but from the Veneto region in Italy and, of course, lived long after the imperial reign of the Romans (AD 117–138). Palladio's work is also profoundly civic, not imperial; it is an architecture that attempts to domesticate questions of economy and function, and is typically characterized as a 'humanist architecture'. So Lutyens' use of Palladio in his design for an imperial capital, the specifics of which I will refer to here only generally, is confusing. On the one hand, the Viceroy's House is meant to install an imperial government, to anchor it deeply within a country and to command a space with a structure; on the other, it is a 'House', the Viceroy's house.

The Viceroy's House, like all buildings to some degree, was built largely by hand, using traditional Indian construction techniques. The Indian workers, about whom we know very little aside from a few photographs in the most well known, and most ecstatic, account of this project, *Indian Summer*, typify the colonial dilemma of how to act as both other and same to an occupied culture (Bhabha 1994: 66). Controlling the otherness of the Viceroy's House inside India is, in part, what has maintained its stature as an historical example of colonial architecture. But it would have been the antithesis of the British colonial style to import not only the architect and the building style, but also the materials and workers. The workers and materials are local; they are 'natives' who come from the occupied culture. The otherness of India and the sameness of India exist in both tension and repression in the Viceroy's House project (Bhabha 1994: 204).

It is hard to control the meaning of these types of structures, in truth, of all structures. Is this building, either during or after its construction, during or after its occupation by the British, a diorama of a reconstructed British-Indian 'family group', harmoniously arranged in front of our eyes? Or is this an evil predatory animal poised to swallow New Delhi? Generally, at least in architectural discussions, we resort to relatively benign discussions of culturally complex issues by giving accounts of the architect's intentions or describing a building's features. Lutyens' intentions were to exaggerate the 'British side' of the Viceroy House to such a degree that so-called 'Indian motifs' could find no purchase, although it was important that India be represented as a subordinate culture in the buildings by means of what Lutyens called 'emblematic ornament'. There were many arguments about how the building would be viewed from all parts of New Delhi; how the long avenues would enforce a particular reading of the building in relation to the city and the occupied culture. In spite of these elaborate cautions designed to regulate the significance (particularly its provenance) of the architecture, Indian motifs, animal motifs in particular, find their way onto, and into, the building – elephant reliefs ornament the entry gates, a bronze cobra sits on top of a commemorative fountain, ornate screens and bird cages enclose interior spaces, and so forth. The architectural narratives that look back on the history of this building rarely take up the debate of how, in spite of a colonialist insistence on the Britishness of the building, elephants and cobras came to be included, although the general assumption is that Lutyens, like all architects, gathers information from local and site-specific, as well as academic, sources. In general, the Indian motifs were understood to be primarily ornamental (that is, coming from outside the architecture) although they contributed to the overall British scheme of 'a better ordering of the world through the civilizing genius of the English-speaking races' (Irving 1981: 170, 277) by lending a 'touch of strangeness' to the overall design, the 'essential qualities of Indian architecture in "pure English idiom"' (Irving 1981: 273). Most of these historical narratives seem wholly disjunctive with the visual evidence. In the interest of gathering these incongruities together as 'architectural features' that can be summarized as a form of description, the enunciated intentions of the project are completely repressed: *Here is the tea garden, here is the entry court, here is the rose garden, here is the cobra, here is the south portico with the Indian guard, here are the lions of Britannica, here is the elephant.*[10] Description, in architecture, tries to pass a building off as the neutral sum of its parts, but is, in its deeper structures, really a form of lament for something that has been lost; in this case it might refer to the dawning futility of the British colonial project itself. And then, of course, there is the picture of Gandhi, the last picture in the account of the building, on the terrace of the Viceroy's House, comfortably seated in a rattan chair taking tea with the English Governor, the governor clothed in 'English idiom', Gandhi nearly unclothed.

The Viceroy's House is troubling because it presents, at a massive and hyper-symbolic scale, the drift of both the colonizer and the colonized from the isomorphism of culture and its artefacts; the drift from the home and the symbol of the home (that, of course, never fully holds the ground in the first place) that so much of colonial/postcolonial and migrancy discourse is about. The unavoidable hybridity of architecture (*all* architecture, finally) underwrites the *unheimlich* forces that Bhabha aligns with the disjunctive contemporary identities of displaced peoples. Architecture is also, in this sense, a split screen – hybrid infrastructures (Italian/British/Indian, Indian contractors/British architects) work against architecture's literal and expressionistic powers. India is an interesting example, because it was precisely by means of infrastructure that the British wanted to rule the country. Not incidentally, the modern movement in architecture was, in some respects, a direct response to this tendency of architecture toward hybridity (its dependence on ornament, for example) coupled with the increasing waves of displacement of people in the early twentieth century. Modernism makes its universalist claims and rejects the stylistic combinatory games of earlier periods, in the interest of liberating architecture from its enmeshed cultural systems of signification. It attempts to make architecture stand for itself, architecture alone.

The hybridity, irony, disjunctiveness that are some of the felt effects in buildings occupied by colonial aggressors – not thinking, now, of structures such as the Viceroy's House that were built to install colonial architecture but of pre-existing institutional building – is short-lived because buildings, even extravagant acts of architecture, quickly become isomorphic with the cultural context in which they are placed; most buildings gradually become almost invisible. This disappearance of buildings is, partly, the function of the concrete enactment of the never fulfilled desire for home itself – the re-establishment of familiarity between our bodies and our spaces and skins that we usually would identify as 'comfort', not a full or complete comfort (as mentioned above, the *unheimlich* is ever present), but a restless adjudication of ourselves and our spaces into brief moments of homeostasis that we both recognize and cultivate. Any disruption in the fabric of culture threatens this isomorphism and this homeostasis. During colonial periods one's own skin, one's national body and identity, and one's second skin, the architectures of state and home, are rendered strange. This is where the deepest threat of colonial aggression and violence resides. The post-colonial struggle is to regain an isomorphic relationship with cultural artefacts; to bring external symbolic life and internal everyday life back into alignment, although this is precisely what some postcolonial critics ideologically argue against, since it re-inaugurates the colonial cycle. It is understood as a politically complacent position with respect to the idea of home. But, what else is there to do? It would be better, some would maintain, to keep our institutional structures in a state of alertness to their own security and symbolic role in order to fore-stall new occupations, new violence (Bhabha 1994: 6).[11] The museum is, typically, at its outset an attempt to secure a certain institutional cultural alertness. But maintaining cultural occupancy of architectures and an operational daily life without isomorphism is a kind of tourism – although there are a multitude of different attitudes and postures between the touristic and the isomorphic. Chinatown in New York City, for example, is constructed for tourists, both Asian and otherwise, as well as for an immigrant Chinese population and long-term Chinese-American residents.

Colonialism, in its early stages, shares with tourism (not to mention architectural tourism) a short-term occupation of other cultures that draws buildings out of their places of hiding. Postcolonialism, which is the culture of movement between cultures, shares with tourism an initial indifference to which site, which architecture, is its place of settlement. Both the tourist and the immigrant/emigrant have given up, for a time, issues of settlement. But gradually, post-colonial and migratory cultures' main work is to sink back into the historical or nostalgic places of its culturally diverse beginnings. This is rarely achieved. The many Chinatowns and Little Italys of the world that signify the apparently neutral political ground occupied, as I mention above, by immigrants, long-term residents and tourists, always stand out from the urban fabric, from the *idea* of urban fabric. We can see that architecture, the apparently immovable evidence for the presence of culture, is always moving around in this process; put on stage, pushed into the background, 'displayed' as tourist destination, rendered invisible, and so forth.

ARCHITECTURE AND SCENES OF EVIDENCE: MUSEUMS AND ISLANDS

But I want to go back a little and consider the problem of evidence as a theoretical and historical problem. And, in addition, I want to link the problem of evidence with what I understand to be a few of the issues of migrancy – mainly, the maintenance of structures that support ethnic identity without the infrastructure to do so. Unlike an infrastructural colonialism (such as the British in India), migratory cultures abandon both their architectures and their infrastructural anchors. The question of evidence is an exceptionally interesting one and I think it goes beyond specific tactics of argument-making familiar to critical theorists, historians and scholars, because we are speaking not simply of types of evidence, but of the mechanisms that give evidence whatever force it possesses at any given moment. Evidence, particularly material evidence, is radically ambivalent, as we know from criminology where the very material item or testimony that was meant to corroborate one side of the argument ends up corroborating the opposing argument. Testimony, linguistic or written evidence, is, of course, multivalent by definition. In legal arguments, this multivalence is held in check by very specific instructions about how to say things.

At a symposium in New York in the 1990s on 'The architecture of display', sponsored by the New York Architectural League, the question of display in the projects presented there initiated for me this question of evidence. Many of the architectural interventions, which were the occasion for the symposium, tried to link displays – advertising displays in particular – with more urbanistic, four-dimensional experiences of space. This had the effect of disrupting the smooth commercial use of display, with the result that 'display' often became the 'display of evidence'. The examples I used in my presentation at that symposium were the natural history dioramas at the New York Museum of Natural History, where the display of stuffed animals in vitrines is viewed by the average museum-goer as a display of a natural nature re-enacted.[12] While the diorama-as-display of stuffed animals in a vitrine is picturesque, both naturalistic and scenographic (calculated), the diorama-as-evidence is about a murder, that is, the murder of the animal for the purposes of displaying its stuffed body. Once we connect with the scene of evidence, a certain distance necessary to the coherence of the spectacle collapses.

In some of the urban interventions commissioned by the Architectural League, architecture, or proto-architectures, reset the distance between the viewer and the scene by adding dimensionality, and a different sense of time, to the scene of display. Most of the sites chosen were unequivocally commercial (the Comme des Garçons clothing store, a movie theatre, a café). The re-dimensionalizing of the scene, in some cases and only for a short time, was meant to change the relation of the commercial to space, art and politics. In the same way we might be compelled, by certain framing devices, to come much closer to the window of a natural history diorama in order to see its artifice; be brought to look too deeply into the glass eyes of the animals. How long these architectures can hold the evidentiary scene in place, and how effective these scenes are in political or critical terms, is another question. Museums of immigration, for example, attempt to present the evidence of the vast transmigrations of people across the world. Here, too, problems of display and evidence present themselves.

At the Ellis Island Museum of Immigration in New York, for example, current displays alternate between dimensionalizing statistical information (to show what a million people looks like in volumetric and spatial terms); presenting individualized accounts of different 'passages' from other cultures into the US; accounts of types of transport; photographs of crowds of people looking up from the steerage decks of ships; photos of individual men and women surrounded by baskets and trunks and, often, children, staring into the camera with looks of fatigue on their faces. Artefacts of passage, such as baggage, family photographs, passports, lace shawls, shoes, little figurines from different cultures, steamer ship tickets, are gathered into different places of the museum. But there are also large, surprising, parts of the museum dedicated to displays about the operation and restoration of the Ellis Island facility itself. The dominant sense of Ellis Island, in terms of questions of evidence, is that the evidence of the massive migrations of people from different cultures into the US at certain points in history is not simply a matter of presenting numerical compilations and small biographies, but also a matter of grasping something about the buildings themselves; the oddly modest size of the buildings in relation to the number of people processed through them; the oddly ornate and festive style of the buildings in relation to their bureaucratic and ideological functions; the fact that the buildings were also detention centres where people were being medically scrutinized; and the fact that this switching point for millions of people is a small island of buildings that form some kind of 'gateway' to the enormous towers and densities of Manhattan, fifteen minutes away. The 'island', or the 'islanding' of buildings might be a way of typifying the evidentiary role of architecture in the face of cultural migrations – the building is extracted from its normal isomorphism and put on display. The more architectures such as museums and government structures, for example, are understood to represent the plurality of the passage through them, the more island-like they must become. Louis Marin and Frederic Jameson have written of necessary 'neutralization' that the island, as a utopia, must enact with respect to its referent – in Thomas More's utopia, for example, England had to be neutralized point by point (Jameson 1988: 85).

The passage to islands requires a temporary amnesia; the narrative of passage is always missing in the captain's 'log'. Ellis Island is meant to be precisely about moments of arrival, which lie between origins and ends. But it is a politically ambiguous space; the ferry transport to and from Manhattan by way of the Statue of Liberty mimics, at a small scale, the steamer ship transport of the immigrants but it turns out to be just a sightseeing tour; every attempt to 'write' the arrival, after it has happened, is waylaid into documentation of a prior life or a prior passage (a narrative of the origin of the journey) or documentation of the future (usually successful) life of the immigrant. The moment of the arrival itself – the evidence of which we visit Ellis Island to see – slips away. It is the moment for which there is no evidence. Buildings, particularly buildings connected with these kinds of passages, are evidentiary forces that orient the past and the future and, paradoxically, hold the place of the present but make it invisible. There is a place of the present and 'arrival', but the time of the present is absent; thus the passage into the place, which is temporally bound, is obscured.

New legal theorists and literary critics like Stanley Fish have been writing about evidence for years as something that is not found, but argued (Fish 1980), often from the standpoint of what is missing from the scene. In the discipline of palaeontology, Steven Jay Gould suggests that missing parts of the fossil record are not, in fact, missing but, instead, evidence of how evolution operates in leaps, arriving at various forms of 'punctuated equilibrium'. We immediately could supply a few of the nineteenth-, and twentieth-century scenes from which we have learned our contemporary lessons about evidence: Sherlock Holmes, Sigmund Freud, Edgar Allan Poe, Clarence Darrow, the 'missing link' controversies in palaeontology, courtroom sitcoms, hermeneutics, O.J. Simpson's glove and, now, genetic research. What we have learned is that evidence is not that which is right there on the ground and self-evident, but an argument, hermeneutical in character, that arrives from someplace else, plucks something out of a crowded visual (or textual) field and imports it into another realm, into the courtroom or onto the court of play. In Gould's case, the actual fossil provides proof not of its own immutability or participation in a long geological history, but of discontinuity, contingency and mutability (Oyama 1997: 509).[13] Fossils, in any case, were lying around on the ground for thousands of years before they became evidence. As Fish puts it, 'nothing can be evidence without being evidence *for* something'.

Historical and cultural evidence is, as I mention above, gathered in museums, although the museum, perhaps even more than most designated 'palaces of culture' is subject to the same isomorphism that erases the scene of evidence; erases the critical dimensionality that architecture supplied in the constructions associated with the 'Architecture of Display'. The Museum of Arts and Popular Culture (Metiers) in Paris is interesting to look at in this regard. This museum is about to succumb to the current French idea of museum-craft, best demonstrated by the new Gallery of Evolution in the Jardins des Plantes, which has the, by now, obligatory interactive information technology, freshened up taxidermic animals set in life-like settings, glass cabinets with butterfly species pinned and backlit, a pretty good café, and so forth. The more immediate antithesis to the Gallery of Evolution, however, is not the Museum of Arts and Popular Culture, which I will discuss in a minute, but the old Palaeontology Museum, also in the Jardins des Plantes. These rooms and herds of bones – the archive of skeletons collected by Cuvier in the nineteenth century for comparative anatomy studies – have been given back their skins and a semblance of aliveness in the new museum. As with the computer technology that is fleshing out our most powerful fantasies of real and mythical beasts – dinosaurs and dragons among them – while keeping them safe, the new museum specializes in the whole problem of 'bringing things to life' that have been, and still are, dead. This is a reversal of the role architecture played in the Display Symposium. Although I will not give details of the architectural renovation here, the design theories associated with that renovation included the idea that the space of the museum would act as a neo-biological milieu for renovated animal life.[14] Evidence of the dead, the bones of the Palaeontology Museum, have been converted into display. Taxidermic animals in mobile attitudes now 'walk' or 'swim' through the Gallery of Evolution.

Like the Palaeontology Museum, The Museum of Arts and Popular Culture, which is housed in a modest modernist building designed by Jean Dubuisson, celebrates the artefact (and not the visitor), but, like the Gallery of Evolution, these artefacts are displayed in 'life-related' ways. From the inside, the windows of the building have been darkened to create a deep interior space within which French rural history is archived by means of eerie displays of tools and objects from everyday life. These tools are not displayed in the familiar way, as a series of inert objects on shelves; instead, they are suspended from ceilings and set on tables in diorama-like, 'islanded', vitrines that are so darkly lit they seem cast in amber. There are no mannequins or dummies, so the ploughs, anvils, tables, forks, religious wands are all suspended in space, precisely located with respect to the missing bodies that seem to have just left the scene. Claude Levi-Strauss, the structural anthropologist, helped curate the exhibitions in this museum and it was, perhaps, his idea that these displays attempt to show the structure of culture through inanimate objects from both quotidian and spiritual parts of life. As Fredric Jameson writes in his essay about utopian discourse, Levi-Strauss' well-known interest in the 'structural study of myth' is inverted by Louis Marin's approach to the problem of More's Utopia. 'For Levi-Strauss, myth is a narrative process whereby tribal society seeks an imaginary solution, a resolution by way of figural thinking, to a real social contradiction between infrastructure [such as a kinship system] and superstructure [religious or cosmological system]', whereas for Louis Marin 'utopian narrative is constituted by the union' of the opposition between infrastructure and superstructure. Utopian narratives, such as those that refer to the history of passage through Ellis Island, neutralize the contradiction between, say, the place of origin and the destiny of the traveller (Jameson 1988: 77–9). Part of the Museum's attempt here also has been to try to exhibit aspects of 'utilitarian beauty': keeping the idea of labour (its history and economies) active in these material objects while subjecting them to the always desirous attention of the museum-goer. But, for the next part of this discussion, the interesting aspect of this museum is its complete commitment to the display of objects as evidence of the deep structures of culture, and its reinforcement of how tools are invariably marks of local, not universal, culture. The museum was designed during a period, the 1960s, when the gathering of cultural artefacts was under intensive scrutiny as an ethno-centric practice, and it comes very close to representing the way architecture has sought to represent itself, in the post-colonial age and the age of migrancy, as a resonant unmarked assemblage of buildings and sites that one gazes at from the outside, systematically editing out the hidden suspension wires, the absence of bodies (or the fact that the bodies are dead, which natural history dioramas are also always at pains to conceal), the erasure or darkening of the outer walls – which is the suspension of the various 'arrivals' of identity itself – the future of the scene, or the faltering of the idea of 'beauty' in the face of 'labour' (or perhaps 'life' is a better word), and vice versa. These architectures, like Ellis Island and like the Brewery building that I mention below, do not take an ethnic or culturally specific stand, but an ethnic and cultural argument (based on evidence and artefact) persists beneath in the fact of the buildings themselves.

As the information age increasingly interacts with tourism and revisionist histories, however, the Gallery of Evolution will become the preferred method of exhibiting architecture. Thus, the colonial history of buildings becomes more animated, more 'interactive', and, simultaneously, more deeply confused. The recovery of sacredness in the Brewery building in Perth, as Jane Jacobs (1996) has so astutely argued, necessitates an interactive Aboriginal park so that 'sacredness' can be staged in a secular way and all the histories of all the people can be preserved in some form. The introduction of noise (voice-overs, personal histories, information) to the dark silent scene of the artefact still falsifies the way in which the Brewery building itself, its style, its symbolic force, its continuance as object, maintains an ongoing, evidentiary, hegemony over the scene. While the Brewery/Aboriginal Park avoids exhibiting (as Jacobs also notes) the absolute and violent incompatibility between the specific kinds of secularity and sacredness at stake in this example – the secular property-based forces celebrated by the Brewery building and the non-property based forces of the Aboriginal relation to land and sacredness – the building continues to serve as evidence of property relations that include privatization, exclusive rights of ownership, one-site-one-owner, i.e. non-Aboriginal relations to property. Property evidence, which I talk more about in the next section, is thus added to the issues of the spatial-but-not-temporal present, hybridization, isomorphism (camouflage) and islanding (plinths and vitrines) that I have been exploring as parts of architecture's evidentiary role.

So architecture plays many sides of the equation – standing out and making an evidentiary argument, and then sinking back into isomorphism, a cultural camouflage that serves the various mythologies we summarize under the complex category of home. In this, it is always colonial in some sense. 'If the effect of colonial power is seen to be the *production* of hybridization rather than the noisy command of colonialist authority or the silent repression of native traditions, then an important change of perspective occurs' (Bhabha 1994: 119). Architecture produces hybridization, for one thing, because its usage is implicitly unfixed.

ARCHITECTURE AND SCENES OF EVIDENCE: EQUITY AND EXTERNALITY

Architecture has played an exceptionally interesting role in the securing of evidence. At the very least, there is rarely an historical argument about culture that does not use the passage through buildings or spaces as key pieces of evidence, and not just in architectural history but also in geo-political, military and economic histories. This evidentiary role of architecture is not activated solely in historical narratives that use buildings/spaces as a kind of reality check, or, say, in criminology, where buildings are used as harbours for illegality, nor even in architectural criminology as in Bernard Tschumi's *The Manhattan Transcripts*. It is at work constantly, for example, in the transferability of buildings/spaces as equity in Western cultures which, as I suggested above, is linked to the hybridization that is part of architecture's character. Bankers use the term 'equity' to refer to the residual value of mortgaged property that is in the long process of being transferred to its owner. Transferability of property is related to an implicit transferability of use and function that is part of what makes up architectural meaning. The Viceroy's House was built as a symbol of the British Raj but became, almost overnight, a symbol of Indian sovereignty. I don't mean to underestimate the scale and importance of the 'Home Rule' movement in India by pointing to the ease with which buildings meant to solidify foreign occupation became the sites of home governance. But it is an effect of space in general that it can be emptied and filled over and over again by radically different constituencies. Architectural space tries to direct this emptying and filling in highly specific ways, but it, too, is subject to the effects and indifference of space. The two occupations of the Viceroy's House may seem related (both were governmental) but the same building potentially could become, at some point in its future, a shopping mall, or housing for elderly people. Walls may attempt 'to signal the basic premise of legal discourse, which is to maintain governance over its own internal linguistic system', by defending against 'a foreign system of signs', (Douzinas and Nead 1999: 132) but the question of what is internal (home) and external (foreign) in architecture is not easily settled, not to mention the old difficulty of isolating a system of architectural signs.

I mentioned earlier in this essay that architecture is the primary cultural evidence of the possibility of an external realm. It is this 'external realm' that is left behind in migratory periods. I want to elaborate here a little more on the idea of the external as not only an object idea, but also as an existential and ontological idea. The term 'equity' also means tacit principles of fairness that correct or supplement law. These principles are not part of the proper domain of law, but have a correcting effect on law. How architecture, which usually seems indifferent to the specific politics of its use, might, nevertheless act in a correctional manner is related to the generally beneficent posture of architecture that we are used to attributing to the history of humanism. But actually, we should, instead, focus on the question of architecture's relative 'indifference' to its own use, an indifference that is more of a disinterest because of its pre-occupation with the production of aesthetic work.

In apparent contradiction to the hybridity of architectural use mentioned above – but, in effect, entangled with this hybridity – one of the most powerful forces that architecture exerts on culture is the maintenance of certain proprieties: how space is lived in and named; what type of building is most appropriate to what use; what materials belong to the exterior, what to the interior, and so on. These proprieties and typologies change gradually, and in important ways, over time – what used to be the parlour is now the living room, what used to be wood is now steel – but some typological paradigm is always in force. The familiarity of the terms of discussion, as in, say, the 'master bedroom', is a familiarity that is not pre-given or natural, but specific to particular moments in architectural history and culture. At the same time, it is precisely the compatibility, the isomorphism mentioned above, of these terms, and the spaces they refer to, with a particular cultural context and time that makes them effective and operational. The other powerful force that architecture exerts on culture – the force that, in its turn, contradicts and advances the specific proprieties of a building type or style – is the maintenance of the categories of property, property ownership and real estate; categories that have the power, mentioned above, to simultaneously anchor and transfer culture. Buildings are always owned, even if it is a communal ownership, even if the ownership is understood as the simple quantity of labour infused into the materials. Ownership implies that buildings are simultaneously rooted in the particulars of their proprietorial role and, as I mentioned above, transferable. I would not want to apply some universal principle of architectural ownership/transferability uniformly to all cultures, since the status of property is a sensitive indicator of cultural difference. And yet every culture might be said to have examples of the passage of a building from one set of hands to another, from parents to children, from individual to government, from government to government, from communal to private, and so on. Some of these transfers take place as a matter of routine and others are cataclysmic.

I am interested here not simply in the, always provocative, coexistence of two opposing tendencies of architecture – the tendency to anchor proprieties versus the tendency to transfer property or the holding of place but rendering the present invisible – but also in how this seeming paradox affects the political life of architecture's occupants. For example, during much of the history of colonial occupations, one of the roles of architecture has been to harden and close in indigenous structure. Tents become sheds, shanty towns become brick projects, quonset huts become government office buildings, and so on. Hardening is invariably meant to locate, by means of buildings, something that is seen to be either temporally precarious, such as provisional governments, or spatially difficult to locate, such as the poor or dispossessed who need to be propertied in some sense in order to be located and contained. In all these cases, architecture, as a paradox of stasis/motion, spatial present/temporal absence, and as a force or practice that calcifies and reifies in order to locate and appropriate culture, arrives on the scene from another place.

The evidence discussion above, and the short digression into the relation of property and identity, now coalesce into the following proposal: architecture arrives at the scene of property from another place, but, once at the scene, architecture proceeds to act as a guarantor or underwriter of that property in order to set up specific, local, temporally present, proprieties. Part of this is the straightforward act of building on a site in a culture where private/public property ownership is the necessary prerequisite to any kind of occupation. To build on the site is to actualize and enhance its property value. But because architecture comes from 'another place' – I am deliberately leaving the intricacies of this other place out of the picture in this account – it acts as if it were part of what, in law, would be called 'common law', the tacit law that supplements and underwrites property law, and which, as we also know, is where fundamental definitions of the self, dwelling, organizations of personal identity, and the already mentioned principles of equity are also formulated. William Blackstone, whose legal commentaries were influential, although controversial, in the formation of law in the US, defines 'title' as follows:

> Title is the legal ground of possessing that which is our own [. . .]. It is an ancient maxim of the law, that no title is completely good, unless the right of possession be joined with the right of property; which right is then denominated a double right. When to this double right the actual possession is also united, then, and only then, is the title completely legal.
>
> (Cheyfitz 1997: 47)

The transfer of a piece of property, which is brought about by the joining of the right of possession with the right of property is only made good when the 'actual possession' – which comes from a different place than the law itself – joins the group. Architecture, which always exceeds mere building and part of which is always off the site proper (we could name the off-site part generally as the 'aesthetic' realm although this will cause problems later), comes from the place of the 'actual possession' and goes on to guarantee the place of the double right of possession and property. For the moment, even outside the sphere of influence of English law, I think there is something like this double right operating. In Aboriginal cultures, for example, the stress is placed more on propriety than property – transferability of buildings is infrequent in these cultures because they do not subscribe to ideas of private property and yet use can still be relatively fluid. The excess of architecture over building – a theoretical formulation that is fascinating for its subtopics of the relation of ornament to structure, art to technology, and so forth – suggests that when architecture arrives at the scene of property, it makes a very specific kind of contribution to that scene: first, it brings itself as a hard material object to serve the legal collection of rights surrounding ownership and/or use, and, second, it brings the idea of 'surplus' into the idea of property. Even as property rights and laws hold the ground, and a building holds the ground, the architectural dimension of building exceeds the ground. In this excess or surplus, a different branch of knowledge is announced.

The Lacanian critic Joan Copjec writes: 'Human freedom makes radical evil [Kant's term] a structural inescapability. But radical evil contributes to the historical phenomenon, modern evil, only on one condition: the elimination of the perspective of the final judgement' (1996: vi–xxvi). Copjec's discussion concerns the character of this final judgement in Kant and Lacan. It is not a theological final judgement that Copjec wants to emphasize (and which she takes great pains to differentiate from fundamentalist currents in American culture), but a principle of externality that guides reason through its various paths and purposes – an understanding that the 'subject exceeds itself'. 'From the final judge, the subject learns not what it is, but that it is external to itself.' As Copjec asks: 'What is teleological judgement, what makes it possible, if not the fact that the subject exceeds itself?' Architecture, among other things, quite precisely underwrites, and acts as evidence for, a material externalization, a material excess, of the self over itself. The self, inside architecture, cannot be fully present to itself because it is doubled by the skin and symbolic envelope of the structure. It is not merely an extension of the self – a tool or technology – but the 'second skin', the 'envelope', around the self, inside of which the self 'dwells' and which constitutes the address, the identity, of the self. This is a very sketchy first part of the surplus question. The second part is the vast realm of architectural aesthetics. The intersection of the aesthetic with cultural proprieties and law is one of the ways we differentiate architecture from mere building. In Western cultures, the aesthetic dimension is understood, in legal terms, to be that which remains outside of the system. The law aspires to blindness with respect to *aesthetic* difference – the difference between faces for example – in order to act according to an abstract institutional logic. Thus, the identifying characteristic of architecture as an aesthetic performance legally secured is paradoxical at its heart – the usual paradox of an enlightened blindness.

Finally, to complete the picture, the architectural securing of identity by means of enclosure – and its supplemental, although external, role in reinforcing the structure of common law – incorporates in its assumptions another notion that emanates from the proprietorial role played by architecture, the notion of 'courtesy', a strange word, a courtly word. Courtesy, for the most part, has nothing to do with individual states of being. It is fully civic and communally formed as a linguistic or currency exchange that facilitates the movement of people through space, even if that means, on occasion, allowing them to stop and rest. Security, which is often civic in its need to protect a population is, nevertheless, fundamentally a constraint of movement. Security and courtesy are linked. The myriad courtesies (even if false) that enable movement both within and between populations, particularly in cities, and which constitute the economic potential of culture itself, are reduced and threatened by security systems when the balance between passage and obstruction is upset. One could study the relation of courtesy to security at Ellis Island, for example, at both the level of arriving immigrant – who is simultaneously welcomed and searched – and at the level of the contemporary tourist – who is simultaneously welcomed and scanned. The Statue of Liberty, since the terrorist attacks of 11 September, has been closed because it was felt to be a potential symbolic site for terrorist attack and yet its very existence signifies the exercise of courtesy over security.

I am using the word 'courtesy' to mean a ritualized set of manners that enable the passage of people through the world. It is important that the effect of courtesy is a surface affect. It has little to do with the genuine feelings or sincere emotions that also belong to civic life. Courtesy is an affect that emanates from the belief in culture itself. Specific courtesies belong to specific cultures and one of the current results of globalization is that many local courtesies are now rendered as touristic, with very little legal or property stake.[15] A frequently mentioned example is the ATM machine that can broker money globally by means of the flat electronic courtesies of saying 'hello' in different languages. The ATM machine is the customs official dressed up in machinic form. Although the machine is manipulated through language, it minimalizes and directs language as much as possible into the networked economy of money. Elaborate ritualistic language, local official language, or everyday language, would complicate matters immeasurably. It would make the machine less secure by suggesting that it had pretensions to be an interactive machine, perhaps pretensions to be the all-too-imperfect human; it would not be able to trade on the illusion of the impenetrability of the metallic machine. Even the Berlin Wall, with its barbed wire and no man's land, faced the erosive effects of courtesies that accompany human movement through space. It was courtesy, in some sense, that was responsible for the fall of the Berlin Wall – some fundamental triumph of speech and life over silence and death, although the intricate marriage between courtesy and security would suggest that this triumph is never wholly out of the reach of silence and death. Migration, as well as specific forms of identity disruption that happen during colonialism, are tied to the many manifestations of courtesy and security in quite precise ways. All the various mechanisms by which human beings are able to move themselves, or be moved, now involve the passage through frontiers and borders. There is no movement without the presentation of documents of birth, gender, place. This chapter has attempted to show that there is also no human movement across or within frontiers and borders – with documents of identity in hand – that is not consequential for architectural movement and no architectural movement that is not consequential for human movement.

NOTES

1 '[I]n *Being and Time* Heidegger began with an analysis of the meaning of man (*Dasein*), proceeding from there toward an understanding of Being, *Identity and Difference* asks about that very "relation" itself *as* the relation of man and Being. [. . .] What is new about [Heidegger's] understanding of identity as a relation is that the relation first determines the manner of being of what is to be related and the how of this relation' (Stambaugh 1969: 8, 11–12).
2 'What is theoretically innovative and politically crucial, is the need to think beyond narratives of originary and initial subjectivities and to focus on those moments or processes that are produced in the articulation of cultural differences. These "in-between" spaces provide the terrain for elaborating strategies of selfhood that initiate new signs of identity. [. . .] It is in the emergence of the interstices – the overlap and displacement of domains of difference – that the intersubjective and collective experience of *nationnness*, community interest, or cultural value are negotiated.'
3 I discuss some of these entanglements more specifically around the three points of property, propriety and the proper name in *Architecture and the Burdens of Linearity* (1998).
4 The hand is not only a tool but a 'driving force'.
5 'First, a physical organization, to be in close correspondence with thought (as my brain is with my thought) must be a very well-ordered organization, and that means that the events that happen within it must obey strict physical laws, at least to a very high degree of accuracy [. . .] the

physical interaction between our system and others must, as a rule, themselves possess a certain degree of physical orderliness [. . .] they too must obey strict physical laws to a certain degree of accuracy' (Schrödinger 1962: 9–10).

6 Bhabha discusses in these pages the *unheimlich* that informs the 'traumatic ambivalences of a personal, psychic history to the wider disjunctions of political existence' (1994: 11). The 'split-screen' refers to the 'private and public, past and present, the psyche and the social' relations that develop 'an interstitial intimacy. It is an intimacy that questions binary divisions through which such spheres of social experience are often spatially opposed' (1994: 13).

7 Bhabha discussed 'agency' as the 'return of the subject'. He refers to Hannah Arendt's theory of political matters in which the '*who* of agency bears no mimetic immediacy or adequacy of representation' in the '*what* of the intersubjective realm' (Bhabha 1994: 189). In any series of events in history we might point to an agent, the '"hero" of the story' as its subject, but we can never point to him as the author of the outcome.

8 'Because Lutyens planned Viceroy's House essentially as processional architecture, its forms a catalyst for movement, he expended much care and space on transition areas, especially the vertical linkages. The pivotal Durbar Hall is everywhere surrounded by stairs, eminently practical for large-scale entertaining and for evoking a useful impression of awesome imperial might' (Irving 1981: 202).

9 'Surely the Durbar Hall is no less than the image of a man-centred cosmos: to use Palladio's description of the Pantheon, it bears in its plan and dome "the figure of the world".' 'British imperialists routinely compared themselves with their most illustrious predecessors. The Romans had achieved dominion not simply by the sword, but by codified laws, a universal language, and the enticements of citizenship in a civilized community. Under the Pax Romana new highways and canals and safe shipping lanes linked disparate, distant lands to their general benefit. Order and imperium had been synonymous' (Irving 1981: 195).

10 This is an imaginary summary of the itinerary through Lutyens' 'British' building. Also see Catherine Ingraham (1998), Chapter 5, for a longer discussion of architecture, descriptive narratives and 'lament'.

11 Colonialism induces a radical redefinition of what cultural 'community' means.

12 See Donna Haraway's (1989) seminal discussion of the natural history museum in 'Teddy bear patriarchy'.

13 'Like other scientists, Gould frequently argues against the widespread idea that the course of evolution is somehow *necessary*: progressive, goal-directed, always moving from the less to the more complex, culminating in those marvels of reflective intelligence, ourselves' (Oyama 1997: 509).

14 See Ingraham, *The Discipline of the Milieu: architecture and post-animal life*, book manuscript in progress.

15 The Berlitz language guide, with its isolation of courtesy phrases that are necessary to survival from the larger context of the language, is a good example.

REFERENCES

Bhabha, H. (1994) *The Location of Culture*, London: Routledge.

Castles, S. (2000) *Ethnicity and Globalization*, London: Sage.

Cheyfitz, E. (1997) *The Poetics of Imperialism: translation and colonization from The Tempest to Tarzan*, Philadelphia: University of Pennsylvania Press.

Copjec, J. (ed.) (1996) *Radical Evil*, London: Verso Books.

Douzinas, C. and Nead, L. (eds) (1999) *Law and Image: the authority of art and the aesthetics of law*, University of Chicago Press: Chicago.

Fish, S. (1980) *Is There a Text in This Class?*, Cambridge, Massachusetts: Harvard University Press.

Haraway, D. (1989) 'Teddy bear patriarchy', in D. Haraway, *Primate Visions: gender, race and nature in the world of modern science*, New York: Routledge.

Heidegger, M. (1969) *Identity and Difference*, trans. J. Stambaugh, New York: Harper and Row.

Ingraham, C. (1998) *Architecture and the Burdens of Linearity*, New Haven: Yale University Press.

Irving, R.G. (1981) *Indian Summer, Lutyens, Baker and Imperial Delhi*, New Haven: Yale University Press.

Jacobs, J.M. (1996) *Edge of Empire: postcolonialism and the city*, New York: Routledge.

Jameson, F. (1988) *The Ideologies of Theory: essays 1971–1986. Volume 2, Syntax of History*, Minneapolis: University of Minnesota.

Leroi-Gourhan, A. (1993) *Gesture and Speech*, trans. A. Bostock Berger, Cambridge: MIT Press.

Oyama, S. (1997) 'The accidental chordate: contingency in developmental systems', in B. Herrenstein Smith (ed.) *Mathematics, Science and Postclassical Theory*, Durham, North Carolina: Duke University Press.

Schrödinger, E. (1962) *What is Life?*, Cambridge: Cambridge University Press.

Stambaugh, J. (1969) 'Introduction', in M. Heidegger, *Identity and Difference*, trans. J. Stambaugh, New York: Routledge.

Chapter 4: Mythforms

Techniques of migrant place-making

Paul Carter

> If you can't find the right surroundings it doesn't matter where you are . . .
>
> Franco Forte, Melbourne, Australia, 24 June 1985[1]

SPEAKING PLACES

Who has read Vincenzo Volentieri's 1951 migrant manifesto, *The Unspeakability of Places*? The answer is: no one. And for good reason. Volentieri was a Bicentennial hoax. On the eve of national celebrations, a journalist had asked one of Australia's leading pundits, about Australian identity. To secure it, our pundit had replied, 'a great creative genius' was needed. So I obliged, inventing the aforenamed migrant architect, and describing his manifesto as an attack on the 'cult of *placism*, which held that every place had its own individual spirit, which it was the artist's task to paint, describe or, in the jargon of the time, "capture" ' (Carter 1992a: 151). Volentieri introduces my topic, then, in two ways: he champions a non-placist, characteristically migrant, technique of place-making, and he also hints at its character. A non- or anti-placist place-making begins in a critical and creative reflection on the myth of prescribed origins.

A further preliminary word of explanation: the essentialism implied by the phrase 'characteristically migrant' is not mine. It alludes to the way the politics, poetics and economics of historically, geographically and culturally diverse experiences of migration become homogenised – lumped together as the more-or-less tolerable 'stranger within' – in white settler ideology and its territorially-exclusive discourse of self-producing nationhood. As this discourse dominates the terms in which national, regional and local governments conceptualise the making and re-making of places, any reflection on *techniques* of place-making needs to take it into full account.

Its assumptions find a litmus test in the terms used to define public art programmes associated with large-scale publicly funded place-making initiatives. There, a thematic sociologese obtains. The experience of migration takes its place alongside a nod in the direction of indigenous heritage, a carefully-neutral acknowledgement of the legacy of the colonial founders and a born-again environmentalism, in which a pre-development *genius loci* is rediscovered only to be recycled for post-industrial leisure consumption. As it is axiomatic in white settler ideology that the ground is given, these themes reinscribe the amnesia constitutional in colonial foundations. Located within a taken-for-granted prior clearing, whose architectural settlement is assumed, public artworks are theatrical. They make no difference. They do have, though, an immense ideological value: defining the future as a repetition of the past, they serve to suppress the wilful destructiveness involved in its production. In this way they reinscribe the settler myth of prescribed or immaculate origins.

Within placist discourse one myth has to be countered with another, better one. A stereotype – the migrant as the tamed but exotic stranger within – needs to be replaced by an archetype. This, at least, is what happens if, following the hint Elias Canetti gives us when he pictures migration as a group of people walking in single-file (Canetti 1978), the migrant is characterised plurally as *the ones who always come from elsewhere*. In exploring the place-making implications of yoking architecture and migrancy, this redefinition has three obvious advantages. One of these is historical. The other two bear more directly on imagining the conditions of a place-making in which migrants *qua migrants* enjoyed agency.

As one coming from elsewhere, the migrant's coming is no longer depoliticised. 'Migration is like an event in a dream dreamt by another,' John Berger writes. The migrant appears to 'act autonomously, at times unexpectedly', but everything he does 'is permeated by historical necessities of which neither he nor anybody he meets is aware' (cited in Papastergiadis 2000: 21). In this existential sense, we are all migrants. The critical point, though, is that the dreamer is colonialism and its twentieth-century heir global capitalism. The history of movement it dreams is based on a master–slave economy. And the slave, as Emile Benveniste notes, was always 'introduced from the outside'. This is the first yield of our archetypal redefinition. It relocates migrants historically. But it also suggests something else: that by an act of lucid dreaming, they might learn to control the dream that appears to direct them down preset routes.

Our redefinition suggests two further points. A migrant place-making is likely to incorporate movement. It will do this because it recognises the formal properties of movement. In placist myth, citizens are actors in someone else's set. They are the exercise of commanding prospects. The kinetic formation represented by Canetti's people in single-file has no place there. As a mobile collective viewpoint, it possesses no fixed position or perspective. The movement vector doesn't necessarily dissipate when it issues into the monumental spaces of the modern city. It may linger there as a catalyst to grouping. And grouping, as I have indicated elsewhere, is the activity that resists placism's rhetoric of instant meeting places. Grouping preserves the experience of arrival, 'the place of potential approaches' (Carter 2002: 192).

Finally, although Canetti's group advances in single-file, it advances walking, that is, bipedally. What's more, we are to surmise that it follows the leader because there is no prescribed road. Our archetypal migrants are track-makers and track-followers. The metaphysical linearism of placist design, and its ideological equivalent, the myth of linear progress, is of no use to them. The imprint of movement is a broken line, and the true progress achieved is no longer defined teleologically, but in the rhythm of repeatedly assumed poses, repeatedly abandoned – in 'the instant between two strides taken by a traveller' (Kafka 1954: 73). These poses are not beads strung out along a pre-destined line. They are to be thought of as a mode of spatial production, as a placing tradition in the making.

These opening remarks wouldn't be out of place in *The Unspeakability of Places*. An anti-placist poetics may in general terms promote the epistemological value of an attention to the lie of the land. It can assert the value of ephemeral architectures in which, in the medium of non-theatrical performances, poses fuse with historical traces to redefine places and their memories. But the question Volentieri stimulates is a practical one, a matter of *design technique*. And here, even if his essay hasn't survived, its title is helpful, as it puts us on the track of the *mythform*.

Placism derives its authority from an original mouthing into being, a *mythic* act of naming. Naming brings place into being, and the singularity of the name enables it to circulate like any other word discursively. The first step in an anti-placist design is to insist on the 'unspeakability' of places. This doesn't mean rendering them mute, but attending to the multiplicity of other speaking positions potentially meeting there. It is by tracking this silenced noise that a better myth may emerge. The better myth isn't another singular name, it is perhaps the design of those tracks, constitutionally a labyrinth. When Roland Barthes asks, 'What is characteristic of myth?' and answers himself, 'To transform a meaning into form', he not only describes story-making but place-making (Barthes 1972: 131). The coinage 'mythform' attempts to name this conjunction, one in which (to borrow Geoffrey Bardon's felicitous phrase) the place is made after the story, in which histories, instead of being represented monumentally and statically, are inscribed as tracks.

PLACING PLACISM

Migrant mobility may be constitutional but it is not trackless. Neither defined by twinned destinations, nor deterritorialised, it involves processes of localisation that also mobilise traces of that mobility. In migrant experience, Kierkegaard's contrast between becoming as a movement from a place and self-becoming as a movement at that place is a both/and formula (Kierkegaard 1989: 66).[2] Mobilisation of the first kind is evident when migrant subjectivity is built around 'nostalgia and actual circular journeys between homeland and host-land'. Mobilisation of the second kind is manifest in what Pulvirenti calls the 'active process of anchoring', by means of which stepping-off places are provisionally constructed which allow for further movement and change. Together these mobilities enable the migrant, first, to create a new speaking position and, second, to identify it (and himself) with a place. By these and other means migrants may become 'grounded' (Pulvirenti 2002: 221).

The limitation of this formulation is that it fails to give adequate weight to the prior act of territorialisation within which migrant 'identities are territorialised' (Pulvirenti 2002: 221). Only against the background of the pervasive placism which white settler ideology takes over from its colonial origins, can the distinctiveness of migrant place-making be measured. Otherwise, there would be nothing to distinguish the migrant's arrival from any act of colonisation. Yet, the difference of his arrival is well-established, residing precisely in his refusal to repress the traces of his mobility – by contrast, in white settler foundationalist myths, it is axiomatic that the people were always there, and that without them the land was nothing.

Placism, as Volentieri indicated, is the application of the picturesque landscape aesthetic to the design of new places. But the capturing of the genius loci depends on throwing a net over the scene, a conceptual grid. And this device rests on another assumption: that the view might slip away. The figure of place presupposes a boundless space. The desire to fix the scene is haunted by a fear that nowhere is fixed. The immobility ascribed to the place is a projection of the colonist's sense that the ground is not given – a typical agoraphobic symptom. Placism not only presupposes placelessness, but identifies it with the nightmare of anchorless movement. Both terms thus involve an act of environmental erasure, repressing the observer's subject position, or orientation, and the movement history informing it. Thus, the phrase used earlier, 'prescribed and immaculate', was deliberately chosen, for the authority of placism, whether in its picturesque modality or in the Platonic form of the surveyor's grid, resides in an appeal to a writing – a foundational text – *which has left no trace*.

In the 1870s zoologist Alfred Russel Wallace toured Canada and the US. On both aesthetic and utilitarian grounds, he deplored the way in which 'the whole country [had] been marked out into sections and quarter-sections (of a mile, and a quarter mile square)'. There had been 'no natural development of lanes and tracks as they were needed for communication between villages and towns that had grown up in places best adapted for early settlement'. Instead, 'the only lines of communication [. . .] are along these rectangular section-lines, often going up and down hill, over bog or stream, and almost always compelling the traveller to go a much greater distance than the form of the surface rendered necessary'. Wallace compared the colonial landscape unfavourably with the 'picturesque' English countryside – 'the narrow winding lanes, following the contours of the ground [. . .] the numerous footpaths which enable us to escape the dust of high-roads', and so on. He thought the former landscape 'raw and bare and ugly'; the latter he prized because it was richly clad, its buildings 'worn and coloured by age' (Wallace 1905: 191–2).

To understand how this passage illustrates the tenets of placism, two biographical data. Wallace's first employment was as a trainee land-surveyor working on the Trigonometrical Survey of England – the cartographic enterprise on which the implementation of the Enclosure Acts depended. Later in life Wallace became a prominent advocate of land nationalisation, the proposal to reverse the enclosure of the land and return it in standardised packages to labourers prepared to work it productively. Wallace saw the picturesque countryside through the window of the survey. The frame of enclosure focused it. And, in a move that oddly parallels his indifference to the conservation of those tropical habitats that inspired his evolutionary theory, he advocated a land-based programme of *social* evolution that would finally erase all trace of the old 'organic' system of winding tracks.

Wallace's description of the American landscape might suggest claustrophobia, rather than an agoraphobic fear of ground slipping away. But the conditions are twinned – 'agoraphobia, a sense of complete isolation, and claustrophobia, a complete merging of identity, are [. . .] two poles of a single existential dilemma' – and have their roots in an ideologically induced trauma (Carter 2002: 33). In the post-Cartesian mode, the observer is reduced to an all-seeing eye, and vision de-corporealised. The scientific traveller or rational colonist lacks the *gravitas* to settle. To come to rest is to risk an inertia that cannot be overcome. To go on is to risk the fate of the Flying Dutchman. Wallace does not object to the conceptual grid: it is its *physical* inscription that fills him with alarm. As a mapping device the linear net the survey throws over the land creates a set of ideal locations. Anxiety only occurs when it is found that these ideal representations do not correspond to the environment we inhabit. Then the fantasy of access to endlessly multiplying squares of land turns into its opposite: an experience of being hemmed-in and isolated. Nor is there any rational way out: to follow an infinitely-extendable section-line is to go nowhere, to be engulfed in a distance without proximities.

Wallace's landscape assessments reveal placism's basis in a dialectical relationship between the linear grid and the curvilinear picturesque. Migrant approaches to place-making need to be located within this ideological horizon. Indeed, to imply that 'anchoring' occurs within a featureless urban scene would be to internalise the host-culture's placism, and to recapitulate the terra nullius trauma. No doubt migrants *can* internalise this historical perspective. Italo-Australian poet Lino Concas defines his migration in existential terms. The migrant is 'an isolated human being, isolated in his movements and in his speech'. The migrant is one who says, 'We are what we are not', or 'We are, and we are not' (cited in Gunew 1982). Or, as another migrant writer, Jeltje, puts it: 'You walk around in circles, trying not to walk around in circles' (cited in Gunew 1982). These existentialist poses locate the migrant's movements in a tabula rasa environment. But this is an illusion, recapitulating the colonial myth of a blank, immaculate space ready to receive the white settler's inscription. As Wallace's remarks disclose, the migrant's isolationism depends upon a prior placing within his host-culture's placist dream.

The dream is not mere historical background radiation. It actively intervenes in shaping migrant techniques of self-becoming at that place. Grids and picturesque in-fill were designs on the land. To insert oneself into this design history is inevitably to engage with these inscriptive practices. Pulvirenti's finding that, among Italian Australian migrants, 'home ownership confers a sense of anchorage to Australia, a right to be in a land that is not inherently theirs', cannot be explained solely in cultural terms (Pulvirenti 2002: 228). Most first generation migrant 'homes' were and are located in late nineteenth-century houses laid out on a grid. The process of 'transforming the house into home', through which 'mobile subjectivities become anchored in place', occurs within a framework of planned undifferentiation. It is this which explains the fetishisation of the house, the baroque surplus of ornaments, memorabilia and other associatively valued objects which characterise the migrant interior.

This infill recapitulates *in parvo* the colonial painter's picturesque differentiation of his patron's property, but it shouldn't be mistaken for home in any Bachelardian sense:

> For here, where no two backyards or front lawns are really different because they are all different, where the emphasis is, tirelessly, on the novel, the quaint, the personal, such objects can never be representative; they can never conjure up a childhood place that existed inside the orchard of one's parents. [. . .] They remain depressively in the land of conscious intention, unnamed or but once named and nailed permanently to one, all too visible spot. They refuse to connect, to stretch out towards the enigma of a living space, to shadow paths and walls, streams and views.
>
> (Carter 1992b: 5)

Remobilisation, in this context, means unrepressing the placist dream, acknowledging its material legacy. In particular, if it is to furnish a migrant place-making technique, it involves tracking the design history of the line.

TRACKING THE LINE, OUTLINING THE TRACK

The modern line is a design. It is a line of thought. It does not copy or produce an image. It draws out a thought. In this sense an architectural design is not a symbolic representation, but a method of thinking. It is, indeed, the 'writing' which discourse draws out. This, at least, is the argument that Claudia Brodsky Lacour draws from her study of architectural imagery in Descartes' philosophical writings:

> Descartes' architectonic line [. . .] is a specifically one-dimensional construct without plastic reality. It does not illustrate the forms of nature, but [. . .] translates thought onto an empty surface. It reiterates nothing and represents no preexisting process, but commits an unprecedented form to being. Rather than develop inevitably from a given material core, *it is drawn*.
>
> (Brodsky Lacour 1996: 7)

Discourse is the act of drawing out the line. In order to give the line meaning, a system of notation must be invented, a form of writing that will spell out or make manifest the ideal writing of the architectonic line. This is the function of the algebraic symbolism that Descartes develops: his easily memorised symbols signify the physical content of geometrical proportions and relations in a way that can 'be forgotten in the rapid act of the drawing of a deduction' (Brodsky Lacour 1996: 7).

That act of forgetting is analogous to the 'transparency' said to occur when, through the act of design a 'mental intention' and a 'spatial plan' fuse and appear as one (Lefebvre 1991). The fusion is illusory, or at least ideologically sustained. Just as Descartes' 'well-ordered [modern] towns and public squares that an engineer traces on a vacant plan according to his free imaginings [or, fancy]' depend on erasing the traces of earlier, 'poorly proportioned' cities, (Brodsky Lacour 1996: 33) so with the line of thought: drawn out, its discourse is designed to cancel out every trace of former occupation, every memory of movement at that place. As Donald Verene observes, 'the deficiency of the critical philosophy which Descartes inaugurated, is apparent. What the moderns lack, what Descartes did not give us, is memory' (Verene 1997: 35). In place of memory, modern architects (as well as critical philosophers) substituted drawing. Brodsky Lacour shows, for instance, how Charles Perrault envisaged 'the "practice" of "executing plans" (*desseins*) and the "theory" of "appropriate proportions" [as] a single activity in which drawing manifests thought and nothing else' (Brodsky Lacour 1996: 132).

It is easy to draw our own line, showing the technical, as well as intellectual descent, of the trigonometrical survey, not to mention Modernist architecture from Descartes' 'design'. When, for example, Le Corbusier, contrasted the modern man who 'walks in a straight line because he has a goal and knows where he is going', with the 'pack-donkey' (qua pre-modern man) which meanders, 'zigzags in order to avoid the larger stones', in short, 'takes the line of least resistance' (Le Corbusier 1971: 11), he precisely recapitulates Descartes' double discovery – that the drawing out of the line of thought is cognate with the creation of a new historical subject, the cogito, or thinking 'I'. As Brodsky Lacour puts it, the new discourse 'dispels every regressive and recurrent myth of cognition as the effect of resemblance' (Brodsky Lacour 1996: 8). The point is that the modern line is not simply another figure of thought, but 'pragmatic and functional' (Brodsky Lacour 1996: 3). As a method of thinking space and spatial relations, embodied in the discourse of the survey and the rationally planned town, it drove out anthropomorphism. It is the violence of this imposition that Wallace registers in the US, the sense that there is nowhere to 'anchor'.

Anchoring is not only a matter of physical localisation. It occurs when the mobile subject begins to find a way of telling his story. It is through a new discourse that his subject position and his sense of finding a place at that place simultaneously come into being. Places are discursive constructions. But they need not necessarily conform to Cartesian projections. Etymologically, discourse signifies to run hither and thither, and implies the zigzag gymnastic of dialogue (Barthes 1979: 5). The Cartesian subject is nowhere and everywhere, like the line; he is detached, static and historyless. On this criterion, the migrant subject's constitutional mobility makes him pre-Modernist. The same confusion of 'stasis with order' and motion with 'rebellion and chaos' (Carter 1996) explains the incarceration of refugees – a phenomenon starkly illustrating the design of design, its pragmatic role in erasing from the white settler imaginary any memory of arrival from another place. This doesn't prove that the ones who come from elsewhere lack a discourse of place-making. It clarifies, though, the ideological character of the hardness and smoothness they encounter: the former erases every sign of former place-writing, while the latter is designed to resist new inscriptions.

Approached through a (short) history of the line, the migrant discourse of place-making recalls critiques of contemporary architectural linearism and over-rationalised urban design. But it is interesting how often these critiques reinscribe Cartesian aspirations. Writing about the application of Georges Bataille's idea of the *informe* or formless to architecture, Greg Lynn reflects, 'Geometry resists the play of writing more than any other language' (Lynn 1998: 42). The only satisfactorily formless writing, he thinks, will 'be written within architecture by architects' (Lynn 1998: 42). This is an attack on linearism in architectural design, but, in the light of Brodsky Lacour's analysis, its residual Cartesianism is apparent. Similarly, landscape historian, Catherin Bull argues against urban design and planning practices that make 'places more predictable and homogeneous' by saturating them with 'exotic imagery'. 'The city has value,' Bull maintains, 'because its story, in contrast to those told in the theatre, in soap dramas, in the virtual domain or at grand staged events that are now so much a part [. . .] of big city life, remains eternally unresolved, surprising, in the end unknowable' (Bull 1997).

Lynn and Bull identify 'non-design' with the recovery of different life-stories. Both recognise the discursive construction of place. Yet, in preserving the myth of the uninscribed, both display a Modernist, even Cartesian, nostalgia. Lynn may object to linearism, but he embraces the notion that architectural discourse does not develop inevitably from a given material core, but is drawn. What he objects to is a linearist orthodoxy that controls the free and formless play of the drawing hand. A post-geometrical architectural design remains a design, one that disguises the violence and material impact of its 'writing' by pretending it has 'no worldly analogue' (Brodsky Lacour 1996: 7). A similar paradox informs Bull's desire to inscribe the uninscribed. Her rejection of exotic imagery recalls the Viennese Modernist attack on neo-Baroque design, and its surplus of classically derived motifs and statuary. Modernism wasn't an architectural and urban *tabula rasa*. Scraping back International Style figuration and post-Modernist imagery won't prepare a page for future inscriptions. Modern streets, parks, downtown office-blocks and suburban grids are already fully written, even if the identity of the mental intention and the spatial plan renders the writing almost invisible.

The difference of a migrant place-making *technique*, then, is not stylistic. It is not another writing style that mimics immateriality. It begins elsewhere (in a double sense), in the material line or track. The trope of tracks or tracking has become prominent in recent critiques of Cartesian epistemology. Materiality has been a key term in blunting the reductionism inherent in semiotic accounts of meaning and meaning production. If, as a technique of place-making, migrant 'anchoring' can easily be assimilated to the discourse of non-design, then its focus on the track and tracking suggests another dialectical affiliation – to the wide-ranging critique of models of knowing predicated on a presence/absence opposition (whether the model is phenomenological or semiotic). The track, it is urged, is neither an absence nor a presence. It attests to an historical environment of knowing in which the cogito is immersed. It foregrounds the corporeality of the knower, and his existence amid a plurality of bodies. As regards reading, it reinstates the letter, the typographical medium, which is more than the passive bearer of thought 'and nothing else', and less than the symbol or representation of anything.

This revival of interest in the material trace suggests a new ichnology is possible, a science of tracks that, intersecting with the traditional Vitruvian term for site design, ichnography, substitutes for the 'language' of lines a hither-and-thither discourse of marks – blots, grooves, folds and scatters. In relation, though, to the elucidation of migrant place-making, the salient property of the trace is that it indicates a movement that can never be explained in terms of former presence. The trace has no origin because its materiality differentiates it from whatever made it. In this sense it is a writing free of nostalgia but imbued with the past. It communicates mobility in a stable form. The relevance of this to the migrant experience is evident in Emmanuel Levinas' famous, if obscure, characterisation of 'the face', whose 'wonder is due to the elsewhere from which it comes and into which it already withdraws' (Levinas 1996: 60). In Levinas' explanation, the face is not a mask, signifying what is hidden or absent. It is constitutionally other. As such, it signifies as a trace. That is, it is not a sign of something missing. The trace, Levinas explains, 'is the presence of that which properly speaking has never been there, of what is always past' (Levinas 1996: 63).

To invoke Levinas' post-Holocaust reflection on the Other and my responsibility for him is another way of reinserting the ones who come from elsewhere within history. In Levinas, elsewhere is not a geographical address but the state beyond being against whose background Being makes its epiphanic presence felt. Further paraphrase of his argument would be out of place here, but even this summary brings us to the critical (and creative) premiss of a migrant place-making practice. As a technique of tracing, it deals in marks that do not stand in for something else. To take Levinas' example – trying to wipe out any trace of his presence at the scene of the crime, a criminal leaves his fingerprints behind. The trace is what he could not avoid leaving behind – '*leaving a trace* is to pass, depart' (Levinas 1996: 62). Always left behind, the trace refers to a past always past. Because of its difference from what makes it, its materiality and its placedness, it 'does not simply lead to the past but is the very passing toward a past more remote than any past and future which still are set in my time' (Levinas 1996: 63).

As an act of tracing (as opposed to drawing out the line) migrant place-making disturbs the order of history. In the nation-making narrative the migrant is often represented as one without a history. This turns out to be a valid intuition. The migrant doesn't have a history, if that is measured in terms of a heritage of local signifiers. The migrant cannot point to the ruins of former migrant presences. Yet, as the maker of the trace, he has a *past*. 'The trace is the insertion of space in time, the point at which the world inclines towards a past and a time' (Levinas 1996: 62). Here, the white settler host-nation's authority based on 'being here first' collapses. For that past is not his – 'it does not signify his labour or his enjoyment in the world' – but is the condition of always coming from elsewhere. The trace is the sign of that unending approach.

MYTHOPOETIC DESIGN: 'SOLUTION'

The point has repeatedly been made that place-making is a *discursive* act. Names are not applied to prexisting 'places'. Speaking positions are not simply inserted into already-formed theatres. The placist myth, that stories are made after the place, has to be reversed: places are made after the story. But which story? Architectural Cartesianism has the effect of expunging from sites their past, but, as Bull's saturation of exotic imagery reminds us, this does not prevent new stories rushing in to fill the vacuum. In the ideologically levelled terrain of the nationalist narrative space, though, the difference of such stories is neutralised. In a way, public art programmes recapitulate the techniques of the nineteenth-century colonial surveyor, throwing a grid of equivalence over unlike historical topographies. The result is a picturesque multiculturalism, in which every story has a place, and where no history is allowed to leave a mark.

Cartesianism aimed to supercede mythic thinking. Instead, it engineered a new myth of its own – the line. The line, univocal, dimensionless, ideal, purposeful, manifesting thought and nothing else, inscribed the myth of scientific knowledge, a conception of truth in which memory played no part. In this context, a conclusion of Roland Barthes is relevant: noting that mythologies are immune to reason, Barthes asks himself how they may be displaced – and answers, by replacing them with better, 'artificial myths' (Barthes 1972: 135). This is not to lapse into new-age primitivism, but to advocate an invigorated historical discourse, one from which the 'past' is not expunged. Thus, extrapolating from the fact that, in the ordinary usage of the Cretan peasant, '"histories" are "differences"', anthropologist Michael Herzfeld observes that the negative assessment of myth's truth value has often been ideologically motivated, myth being opposed to an implicitly nationalist, progressivist idea of history (Herzfeld 1987: 42).

Mythic or symbolic thinking is not the exclusive preserve of pre-Modern or non-Western societies. It happens wherever the material ambiguity of appearances is acknowledged. As Paul Ricoeur explains:

> all symbols have a sign element within them while signs are not symbols. Signs find their primary identification in their one dimensional conceptually clear identity. [. . .] In contrast to the sign, the symbol is composed of polar dimensions to be identified not by univocity but by double intentionality.
>
> (Rasmussen 1971: 43)

It may be that, in this sense, migrant discourse is constitutionally symbolic, for in it every name always has a double referent, being metaphorical even in its literal application (see Carter 1992c: 186 *passim*). In any case, the practical challenge is clear. To bring mythic discourse within the fold of history, in such a way that it writes difference indelibly, a 'technical problem' must be overcome. A 'heuristic structure' has to be created 'to interpret this distinctive kind of language *without destroying it*' (Rasmussen 1971: 43). In the context of place-making, this is the intention of 'mythopoetic design'.

In a study of modern literary and artistic revival of Western myths, Harry Slochower argues that the recreative transposition of ancient stories into symbolic form has usually occurred '*in periods of crisis, of cultural transition*, when faith in the authoritative structure was waning' (Slochower 1970: 15). He also suggests that the mythopoetic process turns to myth precisely because it embodies 'the tradition of re-creation' (Slochower 1970: 15). That is, mythopoesis is a mode of invention that reinscribes what has gone before, rather than erasing it. Mythopoesis is invention with memory. Michel Serres makes the point that invention involves a movement from the local to the global. Unlike the scientist's global breakthroughs, inventive thought 'establishes a ground that will found local inventions to come' (Serres 1997: 99). The 'local' is not defined territorially. It does not lie 'inside' the global, but is wherever 'work' is done. The local is what comes into being through invention. The implications for a design practice are clear. As mythico-symbolic discourse is, by definition, the history of what happened *at that place*, invention in design practice means *local* invention. Further, the emergence of a reinscriptive design practice is likely to indicate a crisis, or at least loss of confidence and direction, within the host urban design and development community.

'Solution', a public spaces strategy for Victoria Harbor, Melbourne, which the property developer Lend Lease commissioned early in 2002, seems to bear out these conclusions.[3] The commission grew from a lively debate within the company's own design and management team. Existing developments at Melbourne's Docklands were dominated by high-rise apartment blocks. These isolated towers were erected on the simplest of landscape templates, and the early indications were that public art commissions of a 'plonk down' variety would be used to infuse the sites with a degree of picturesqueness. A group within Lend Lease wished to resist a design solution authorised solely by the prospect of maximising the short-term commercial return. Announcing their wish to find alternative design models, they convened (in October 2001) an interdisciplinary design workshop, drawing on a range of local, interstate and international expertise. One of the workshop's recommendations, that an integrated, 'global' public spaces strategy be developed, subsequently translated into the already-mentioned commission. As this background indicates, the 'recreative transposition' represented by 'Solution' emerged in an environment of corporate cultural transition.

'Solution' is an exercise in mythopoetic design. The ground pattern, or 'global template', is a mythform (Figure 4.1). It expresses, or reinvents a history of change. It is well described as the stable trace of many movement histories.

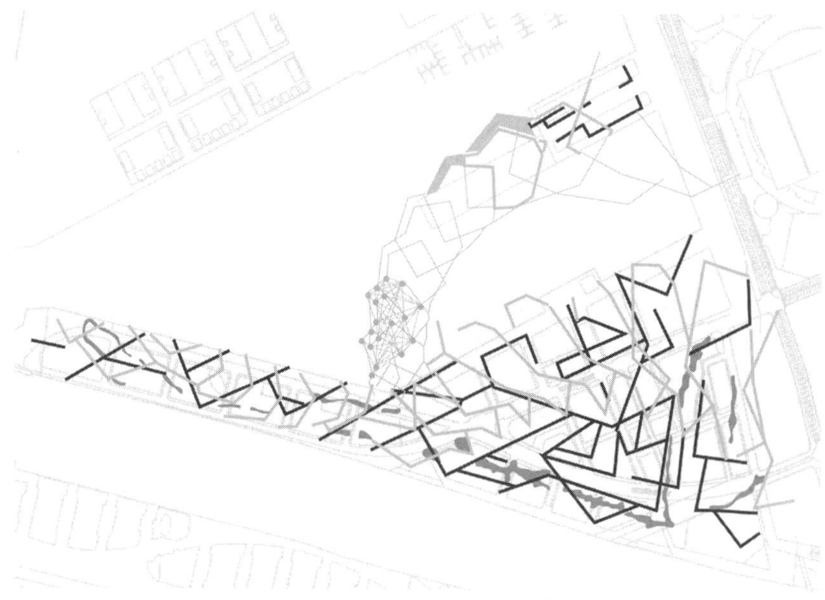

Figure 4.1
'SOLUTION' GROUND PATTERN.
(Drawing P. Carter)

But, as the trace of traces, it does not correspond to any particular history. What it inscribes is the past, always coming from somewhere else. In this sense, it's not only a mythopoetic design, but embodies a migrant technique of place-making. One effect of this is to redefine the meeting place. The migrant 'anchorage' that preserves the movement history is not a fixed, pre-existing destination. Localisation occurs wherever migrants arrive, and begin to reinvent their stories (and themselves) at that place. (In the context of re-inventing a formerly active port, the analogy between these discursive, as well as physical, arrivals and departures and the local to global translations of maritime trade is irresistible.) Instead of conceiving the meeting place theatrically as a central place – as a *chora* already opened up, passively ready to receive human action – it is considered a realm of multiple, unpredictable and endless approach.

A great sculptor of modern urban spaces, Alberto Giacometti, explained:

> Every moment of the day people come together and drift apart, and approach each other again to try to make contact anew. They unceasingly form and reform living compositions of incredible complexity. What I want to express in everything I do, is *the totality of this life*.
>
> (Hohl 1972: 31)

In a similar spirit, the dispersed, deliberately complex and redundant ground pattern of 'Solution' preserves the trace of possible meetings. The emphasis on tracing technique (as opposed to redrawing the line) emerges here. To meet Bull's requirement that design avoid curtailing the future invention of stories, something other than 'non-design' is needed. Non-design remains tied to the ideology of the line: having no memories, it can elicit none. By contrast, the trace remembers. But what it remembers is not this or that story, but the meandering, always duplex character of discourse itself. As it derives from no former presence, it does not lead to a presencing (or decisive meeting) in the future. The sum of possible anchorings, it signifies the always past and always future. After all, this describes our experience of the materiality of places: what we value in richly textured built spaces is not the architect's idea or mental intention, but the sense of the place's *resistance* to our passage. The 'face' of good built spaces conforms to Levinas' definition. It does not offer us an exotic, anthropomorphic mask, but a sense of 'the insertion of space in time'.

Obviously, the illustrated mythform remains linear, captured by placism. The satisfactory notation of a system of tracks needs further research. Until the *techne* adequate to a migrant place-making exists, it is a matter of interpreting the drawing in a different way. Here, two aspects of the reception of 'Solution' may point the way. The first was a tendency to 'read' the pattern as a figure graphically representing the *genius loci*. In its linear representation, the mythform looks like a pure drawing-out of the line. Its excess of connectivity may lack a Cartesian economy, but, as an elaborate drawing-out of the ideal line, it appears to discourse architecturally. However, this is in linear appearance only. The pattern is, in fact, a *local* invention, the reinvention and transposition of two movement forms meeting at that place. One is a composite of unbuilt harbour plans and developments, a palimpsest of unrealised ground figures. The other comprises a series of rotation figures derived from the apparent annual motion of certain locally symbolic stars. Neither movement form, even less the interference pattern resulting from their intersection, figures forth a 'history'. They materialise certain lines and ideal proportions *as traces*. They inscribe a tradition of passage.

The second reaction related to the materialisation of the pattern. The ideology of 'transparency', in which designers treat sites as blank sheets on which they draw their free imaginings, encourages a graphic literalism. Lines may be ideal projections but, in the context of a plan, they are read as outlines of *a future something*. Tracks cannot be interpreted in this way. The character of their materialisation remains undecided. Within placist ideology, they may be marked as a negative impression. If marked positively, the inscription may be dispersed, plural and unpredictable. Tracking, Rodolphe Gasché points out, draws differently, sometimes over and across itself. Its discourse is composed of potential crossroads, '*always already* and *always not yet*' (Gasché 1999: 267). The interrupted double line of the track is both a way of drawing places, and a way of thinking about them. 'The chiasm is one of the earliest forms of thought: it allows the drawing apart and bringing together of opposite functions or terms and entwines them within an identity of movements' (Gasché 1999: 273). Its rhetorical counterpart is the riddle. In Greek, the riddle takes its name from a kind of fish net – 'the riddle is braided in the same way as a fishnet, [. . .] through intertwinement of opposite terms' (Gasché 1999: 369, n.34). In the riddle of 'Solution', unceasingly forming and reforming living compositions of incredible complexity, people might remember an approach to 'the totality of this life'.

The technical 'Solution' to the materialisation may be insoluble on the screen or the drawing board. It may always remain a matter of interpretation, depending for its realisation on participatory, or analogue, movement and making acts. Rather than prescribe the outlines of buildings, 'Solution' indicates a multiplicity of possible meeting places. As regards negotiations between rival functions, programming priorities and design intents, it may be said to set the exchange rates, marking points of cross-over, gathering and leaving. The physical expression of this movement form may be fixed – in the hard form of differentiated material treatments and the localisation of various functional objects (including street furniture), but these placements will be seen under the aegis of migration, as traces of time. In this sense their inscriptive practice will be embodied in the unpredictable acts of grouping they choreograph. Without origin, the reinventions of a past that by definition remains futural, these groupings would faithfully capture the migrant's constitutional experience of coming from elsewhere:

> A successful grouping is chiasmatic, like the agora. It is poised between growing more dense or diffusing. In this moment of accidentally achieved balance, a maximum ambiguity obtains. The space between figures is flirtatiously charged. A surplus of possible paths of propinquity opens up.
>
> (Carter 2002: 199)

Although, until now, no trace of Volentieri's manifesto, *The Unspeakability of Places*, has been found, extracts from his *Sayings* have been published. In these I find the following advice to a newly arrived immigrant:

> Certainly the interference pattern is unsettling: it is nothing like the view from the hostel window. Do not yield to self-pity though: it is not nostalgia that blurs the picture but the clouds passing overhead. This dappled composite country is the place you will come to inhabit: your dreams are reverse genealogies, tracks leading into it. Until we get in and learn its name, 'Talk, talk' must do, I'm afraid.
>
> (Carter 1992d: 191)

This chapter is intended to indicate the kind of 'Talk, talk' useful in this process.

NOTES

1 Oral History Archive, Italian Historical Society of Carlton, Carlton, Victoria, Australia, tape copy 65 transcript.

2 'Becoming is a movement *from* that place, but becoming oneself is a movement *at* that place.'

3 Paul Carter, 'Solution' (presented July 2002) is a 28-page A3 landscape report with 42 figures. The body of the report is a 'site myth analysis' divided into three sections – micro-macro-cosmic analogies, colloidal forms and humid edges. The document also contains a number of 'worked examples' showing different design applications of the mythform and a public art strategy. The document is exclusively licensed to Lend Lease, whose permission (together with the author's) must be sought in order to reproduce any part of it.

REFERENCES

Barthes, R. (1972) *Mythologies*, trans. A. Lavers, London: J. Cape.

Barthes, R. (1979) *Frammenti di un discorso amoroso*, Torino: Einaudi.

Brodsky Lacour, C. (1996) *Lines of Thought: discourse, architectonics, and the origin of modern philosophy*, Durham, North Carolina: Duke University Press.

Bull, C. (1997) 'City: repository of dreams – realm of illusion experience of reality', *Urban Design International* 2 (3): 145–53.

Canetti, E. (1978) *The Human Province*, trans. J. Neugroschel, New York: Seabury Press.

Carter, P. (1992a) 'Grass houses: Vincenzo Volentieri, a bicentennial memoir', in P. Carter, *Living in a New Country: history, travelling and language*, London: Faber.

Carter, P. (1992b) 'Migrant Carnival', *Agenda* (Melbourne) 22, March.

Carter, P. (1992c) 'Post-colonial collage: aspects of a migrant aesthetic', in P. Carter, *Living in a New Country: history, travelling and language*, London: Faber.

Carter, P. (1992d) 'Getting in, from the sayings of Vincenzo Volentieri', in P. Carter, *The Sound In-between: voice, space, performance*, Sydney: NSW University Press/New Endeavor Press.

Carter, P. (1996) *The Lie of the Land*, London: Faber and Faber.

Carter, P. (2002) *Repressed Spaces: the poetics of agoraphobia*, London: Reaktion Books.

Gasché, R. (1999) *Of Minimal Things: studies on the notion of relation*, Stanford, California: Stanford University Press.

Gunew, S. (ed.) (1982) *Displacements: migrant story-tellers*, Waurn Ponds, Victoria: Deakin University.

Herzfeld, M. (1987) *Anthropology Through the Looking-glass: critical ethnography in the margins of Europe*, Cambridge: Cambridge University Press.

Hohl, R. (1972) *Alberto Giacometti: sculpture, painting, drawing*, London: Thames and Hudson.

Kafka, F. (1954) 'Third Octavo Notebook', in *Wedding Preparations in the Country, and Other Posthumous Prose Writings*, trans. E. Kaiser and E. Wilkins, London: Secker and Warburg.

Kierkegaard, S. (1989) *The Sickness unto Death: a Christian psychological exposition for edification and awakening*, trans. A. Hannay, London: Penguin Books.

Le Corbusier (1971) *The City of To-morrow and its Planning*, trans. F. Etchells, Cambridge, Massachusetts: MIT Press.

Lefebvre, H. (1991) *The Production of Space*, trans. D. Nicholson-Smith, Oxford: Blackwell.

Levinas, E. (1996) *Emmanuel Levinas: basic philosophical writings*, A.T. Peperzak, S. Critchley and R. Bernasconi (eds), Bloomington: Indiana University Press.

Lynn, G. (1998) *Folds, Bodies and Blobs: collected essays*, Brussels: La lettre volee.

Papastergiadis, N. (2000) *The Turbulence of Migration: globalization, deterritorialization, and hybridity*, Malden, Massachusetts: Polity Press.

Pulvirenti, M. (2002) 'Anchoring mobile subjectivities: home, identity, and belonging among Italian Australian migrants', in B. David and M. Wilson (eds), *Inscribed Landscapes: marking and making place*, Honolulu: University of Hawaii Press.

Rasmussen, D.M. (1971) *Mythic-Symbolic Language and Philosophical Anthropology: a constructive interpretation of the thought of Paul Ricoeur*, The Hague: Martinus Nijhoff.

Serres, M. (1997) *The Troubadour of Knowledge*, trans. S.F. Glaser and W. Paulson, Ann Arbor, Michigan: University of Michigan Press.

Slochower, H. (1970) *Mythopoesis: mythic patterns in the literary classics*, Detroit: Wayne State University Press.

Verene, D.P. (1997) *Philosophy and the Return to Self-knowledge*, New Haven, Connecticut: Yale University Press.

Wallace, A.R. (1905) *My Life: a record of events and opinions, vol. 2*, London: Chapman and Hall (2 vols).

Chapter 5: Why architecture is neither here nor there

Mark Rakatansky

When I say architecture is neither here nor there, what I mean is this: architecture is neither purely specific nor purely abstract, neither purely social nor purely formal, neither purely local nor purely global. Architecture, all architecture, is here *and* there, specific *and* abstract, social *and* formal, local *and* global. It is only a question of how and to what degree it attempts to enact this here and thereness, this specificity and abstraction, this socialness and formalness, this localness and globalness, in the work itself, in form and in content.

There is so much to say on these matters in such a short time that I will only be able to make a few small points, these points being points from some earlier themes of my work that resonate, in canny and uncanny ways, with the topic under discussion here.

I will begin from the beginning: from my first substantial essay: 'Spatial narratives' (Rakatansky 1992), to speak to the title: *Building Dwelling Drifting*: the conference's and the collection's play on Martin Heidegger's title for his 1951 essay 'Building dwelling thinking', an essay in which Heidegger celebrates all the homey, the *heimlich*, the canny aspects of dwelling, while repressing the unhomely, the *unheimlich*, the uncanny aspects. Take, for example, Heidegger's etymological derivations, his sleight of hand as he moves from word to word ('building', 'neighbour', 'peace'), from Old English to High German to Old Saxon to Gothic, until he gathers up what he was already looking for, a *heimlich* definition as follows: 'To dwell, to be set at peace, means to remain at peace within the free, the preserve, the free sphere that safeguards each thing in its nature. *The fundamental character of dwelling is this sparing and preserving*' (Heidegger 1971, original emphasis).

Well, as the title *Building Dwelling Drifting* suggested, there is already some drift here, some drift not only in his method, not only in his conclusion, but in the etymological derivations themselves, or perhaps it would be better to say: there is the attempt to repress any drift. Now, if you go to the dictionaries *Oxford* and *Webster*, you will find that the English verb 'to dwell' is derived from the Middle English *dwellen* (from the Old English *dwellan*) which means 'to lead astray, hinder', and is akin to the Middle Dutch *dwellen* which means 'to stun', and the Old High German *twellan* and the Old Norse *dvelja* which mean 'to delay, to deceive' – which in turn are all derived from the Indo-European base *dh(e)wel* – which means 'to mislead, to deceive, to obscure, to make dull'.[1]

And lest you imagine that it is only in cultures derived from North European bases that words related to the concept of home reveal an uncanny meaning: for the Sakalava, a tribe in Madagascar, among whom (I am quoting the anthropologist Gillian Feeley-Harnik) 'no one would refuse another entrance into his house *unless he were hoarding or hiding something*', the word *mody*, which means 'at home' or 'heading home' also means 'to pretend what one is not' (cited in Wilson 1988: 98).

Now, Heidegger's etymological repressions are just one manifestation of his later repressions of his earlier work, in this case, his earlier examinations of the concept of *Unheimlichkeit* in his *Prolegomena to the History of the Concept of Time*, his Marburg University lectures from 1925, which led to *Being and Time* of 1927, as David Krell has well noted:

> In *Being and Time* and in his Marburg lecture courses that led up to it, Heidegger defined human existence itself in terms of being *not-at-home* [. . .]. Section 30 of his 1925 *Prolegomena to the History of the Concept of Time* declares that human existence (*Dasein*) has essentially nothing to do with homey homes, that its very being is *Unheimlichkeit*, 'uncanniness', 'unhomelikeness'. Our being in the world, the world that serves as our only home, is marked by the uncanny discovery that we are *not* at home in it. *Dasein*, or being-there, when it is truly there, is an absentee; it is stamped and typed by *Unzuhause*, the not-at-home, the nobody-home.
>
> (Krell 1997: 93)

All this returns us to Freud, to his 1919 essay 'The uncanny', where he puzzles over that strange confluence of meaning between those two words that should have entirely opposite meanings: *heimlich* (the homey, the canny) and *unheimlich* (the unhomely, the uncanny). Freud, in the beginning of the essay, says that the 'The German word *unheimlich* is obviously the opposite of *heimlich*, *heimisch*, meaning "familiar", "native", "belonging to the home"; and we are tempted to conclude that what is "uncanny" is frightening precisely because it is *not* known and familiar'. In the course of the essay, undertaking his own etymological derivations from Daniel Sanders' *Wörterbuch der deutschen sprache* (1860) and the Brothers Grimm's *Deutsches wörterbuch* (1877), Freud reveals another meaning of *heimlich*: ' "concealed, kept from sight, so that others do not get to know about it [. . .] to behave *heimlich*, as though there were something to conceal [. . .] *heimlich* places (which good manners oblige us to conceal)".' Thus, Freud says, the 'uncanny is in reality nothing new or foreign, but something familiar and old-established in the mind which has been estranged only by the process of repression'. The *unheimlich*, far from being the opposite and outside of the *heimlich*, then, *is* the *heimlich* – it is what is already inside, the homey that returns as the unhomely (Freud 1958).

So let us say, then, between my staged sleight-of-hand here (emphasizing what is *unheimlich*) and Heidegger's sleight-of-hand there (emphasizing what is *heimlich*), the oscillation that Freud suggests, this migration between, this hybrid condition of, these two so-called poles provides the more relevant and productive model for the relations of dwelling.

This now brings us to Homi Bhabha, whose own scholarly hybridity on the subject of hybridity seems to me of seminal importance in thinking about these issues in relation to dwelling and migrancy.

Let us start first with the issue of dwelling, a passage say, from his essay 'Halfway house':

> Home may be a place of estrangement that becomes *the* necessary space of engagement; it may represent a desire for accommodation marked by an attitude of deep ambivalence towards one's location [. . .] home is territory of both disorientation and relocation.
>
> (Bhabha 1997: 11)

Bhabha succinctly marks and connects for dwelling what we inevitably speak of as two poles (estrangement and engagement, accommodation and ambivalence, disorientation and relocation), but, as he indicates, these are no more opposite poles than the *heimlich* and the *unheimlich*, the here and the there. There remains only a question of, let us say, proportion, or rather of the concept of proportion in the title, but not in the text of the essay 'Halfway house'. Halfway, no. Not half, not one-third, not two-thirds, but as he reaffirms in many penetrating ways through this essay, a constantly adjusting and readjusting measure, a hybridizing, a forever intermixing, the one in and of the other.

Bhabha carries this analysis forward to address these forms of relations of the local to the global, native culture and migrant culture:

> What it does suggest is that we have overemphasized, even fetishized, the relation between culture and national identity, or traditional, customary community. There is, of course a link between territory, tradition, and 'peoples' that serves certain functions of state and governance and bestows an important sense of belonging. But the strong, *nationalist* version of this relationship can lead to a limiting collusion that returns us to the dominant sociological paradigms of the nineteenth century. To be overly focused on the authenticity of national identity leads to an 'authoritarian' or 'paternalist' gaze – however well-meant – towards those who are part of the great history of migration. Authenticity unleashes a restrictive sense of indigenous or native 'belonging' [. . .] these questions of home, identity, belonging are always open to negotiations, to be

> posed again from elsewhere, to become iterative, interrogative processes rather than imperative, identitarian designations.
>
> (Bhabha 1997: 125)

This great history of migration (which includes but is not restricted to the current situations of migrancy),[2] as Bhabha says, has already changed our sense of what it is to be native and national, and thus how those architectural categories of vernacular, regionalist, nationalist and internationalist might need to be totally rethought, given the great history of migration of individuals and ideas in architecture (Palladianism in English architecture, Miesianism in American architecture, internationalism in the neo-vernaculars of Murcutt and Mockbee).

But if all aesthetic objects are already inherently hybrid, then how might an aesthetic object enact this condition of hybridity rather than just merely represent it, within the object, as an object, not just as an inadvertent representative of a cultural and historical condition? Here is what Bhabha suggests:

> Might this hybrid, culturally diverse landscape then make visible the rough edges, the complex negotiations of aesthetic values that find themselves not only 'outside' the artwork or in the social problematic of its production but 'inside' the work itself, both formally and effectively? Cultural contradictions, disjunctive historical spaces, identifications created on the crossroads – these are the issues that the arts of cultural hybridization seek to embody and enact rather than 'transcend'. It is an art that is no less valuable because it takes what is unresolved, ambivalent, even antagonistic, and performs it in the work, underlining the struggle for translation.
>
> (Bhabha 1997: 125)

In a number of his other essays, Bhabha has already suggested one set of tactics that an aesthetic hybridity might utilize (drawn from certain historical resistances to certain colonial authorities): that of mimicry, that of sly civility:

> a discursive process by which the excess or slippage produced by the *ambivalence* of mimicry (almost the same, *but not quite*) does not merely 'rupture' the discourse, but becomes transformed into an uncertainty which fixes the colonial subject as a 'partial' presence. By partial I mean both 'incomplete' and 'virtual'.
>
> (Bhabha 1994: 86)

The subject is incomplete and virtual because it is put into a set of 'conflictual, fantastic, and discriminatory "identity-effects" ', so that its location (its position) within its locale (its place) is revealed to be problematic, simultaneously located and dislocated, simultaneously localized and delocalized, simultaneously here and there. It is this question (and questioning) of identity through mimicry that

Bhabha draws from Lacan, and thus Bhabha's essay 'On mimicry and man' opens with the following quote:

> Mimicry reveals something in so far as it is distinct from what might be called an *itself* that is behind. The effect of mimicry is camouflage [. . .]. It is not a question of harmonizing with the background but, against a mottled background, of becoming mottled – exactly like the technique of camouflage practised in human warfare.
>
> (Lacan 1977a: 99)

Returning to the dictionary once again to look up 'mimicry' will not result in as dramatic a surprise as with 'dwelling', but will be useful nonetheless. Now, in the Oxford Dictionary, 'mimicry' is defined in a somewhat broad manner, as: 'ridicule by imitation (person, manner, etc.); copy minutely or servilely; (of thing); resemble closely'. The later definition indicates the close relation between mimicry and mimesis, but for now, before we return to the potentially transgressive aspect of what it could mean to 'resemble closely', let us concentrate on the second half of the second definition: to copy servilely.

Architecture is always a mimic to itself, all architecture is already mimetic, is already mimicking what has been previously stated, constructed, even the most 'extreme' avant-garde projects maintain the mimicry of social and cultural programming. When a client comes to you and asks you to design a house, you don't say: 'what's a house?' You say: 'how many bedrooms would you like?' You say: 'do you need a separate dining room?' You say: 'what sort of appliances do you want in your kitchen?' And so forth. Ditto a conference centre. Ditto a library. Ditto an art museum. Ditto an office building. This is architecture's and society's compulsion to repeat, which is its defence against actively questioning the constitutive attributes and motivations of its forms. This is the whole cultural and ideological force of architectural practice, from the most conventional practices (with their Professional Pattern books and Professional Standards books and Building Type books and Manufacturer Catalogues) to the most avant-garde practices (which use the exact same books and references but bend the walls and roofs around a bit). I am, in case you are wondering, as an architect not exempting myself here: this is the cultural transmission that one inevitably has to engage with.

We should not forget that Roger Caillois, whose essay on biological mimicry so influenced Jacques Lacan's ideas of identification, spoke primarily of mimicry as a 'renunciation', 'a depersonalization by assimilation to space', a 'temptation of space', in other words, as a potential trap (Caillois 1984).

How might one escape this trap, this spatial assimilation, this compulsion to repeat the environment as already given, whether one's homeland or away-land or new homeland? Precisely by enacting it as a temptation, as a trap, as a compulsion to repeat, as Freud suggested, by using the compulsion to repeat against itself:

> We render it harmless, and even make use of it, by according it the right to assert itself within certain limits [. . .] to display before us all the pathogenic impulses [. . .] only by living through them in this way will the patient be convinced of their power and existence.
>
> (Freud 1963: 164–5)

Not serviley but with sly civility: Bhabha's concept of mimicry and sly civility is close in concept to the Greek idea of *mêtis* (or cunning intelligence), which is less about ridicule than about how the 'only way to triumph over an adversary endowed with *mêtis* is to turn its own weapons against it' like 'the feint employed in wrestling (*palaisma*) of eluding the grasp of the adversary and then, by reversing one's body, turning against him the force of his own thrust' (Detienne and Vernant 1991: 36):

> Why does *mêtis* appear thus, as multiple (*pantoie*), many-coloured (*poikile*) shifting (*aiole*)? Because its field of application is the world of movement, of multiplicity and of ambiguity. It bears on fluid situations which are constantly changing and which at every moment combine contrary forces that are opposed to each other [. . .]. In order to dominate a changing situation, full of contrasts it must become even more supple, even more shifting, more polymorphic [. . .]. It is this way of conniving with reality which ensures its efficacity.
>
> (Detienne and Vernant 1991: 20–1)

To be 'almost the same, but not quite', to be 'both against the rules and within them' (Bhabha 1994: 89), as Bhabha suggests, is to reveal the rules of the game, the rules of social construction, which once revealed might be seen no more as absolute, essential, matters of fact, and might then be possible to change. According to Brecht:

> 'A representation that alienates is one which allows us to recognize its subject, but at the same time makes it seem unfamiliar', in order to 'free socially-conditioned phenomena from that stamp of familiarity which protects them against our grasp today'
>
> (Brecht 1964: 192)

Thus, just as one does not have to introduce drift into dwelling (it is already there), one does not have to introduce mimicry into conventional modes of discourse or representation, (servile) mimicry is precisely what conventional forms already are. One just has to operate on these conditions to reveal these conditions at work – at the scale of the site, the programme, the individual spaces, the tectonic elements – to find the unfamiliar within familiarity, to find mannerisms in the manner, the mannerisms of form and content, mannerism being the irresolvable enfolding of the here and the there, the convention and its swerve, straight up with a twist, 'almost the same, but not quite'.

Thus, the architectural question is not answered merely by choosing whether forms have either the appearance of mobility *or* stasis, nor whether they have the appearance of being either specifically localized *or* generalized. To localize an architectural event is not to root it in some essential and proper place, some irreducible form of dwelling, but to find it enmeshed, enfolded, in a field of non-localized relations. In design or discourse, the specific, the here, is only interesting to the extent it draws forth the general, the there, and the general is only interesting to the extent it can be conveyed in and through specific occasions.

This perpetually alternating here and there is already evident in Lacan's concept of the mirror stage, where (and when) you, the subject, in front of a mirror, around the age of eighteen months, become aware of yourself as a self as *here*, as a whole image rather than just the disjunctive fragmentary bodily sensations that was your self up to that moment. But this image, your image, is not located in you, it is located elsewhere, in front of you, *there* in the mirror, in advance of you, and henceforth your identity will always circulate between internal and external, specific and general, attempts at and acts of identification (Lacan 1977b: 1–7).

In Lacan's essay on the mirror stage (the essay where Caillois' concept of mimicry makes its first appearance), he refers to 'the spatial captation manifested in the mirror-stage' ('*la captation spatiale que manifeste le stade du miroir*'), but to find the word 'captation' you would have to reach for the bigger *Oxford* with the smaller print (at the same time reaching for the accompanying magnifying glass out of its drawer in the double-volume slipcase). This *Oxford* says the word is 'obsolete', which is probably why the otherwise welcome new translation of *Écrits* renders this phrase as 'the spatial capture' (Lacan 2002: 6), but the often passive and finished sense of capture misses the more active and desirous sense of captation: 'a catching at, an endeavour to get', a seeking after identity, or as the newer double-volume version of *Oxford* (which no longer designates the word as obsolete) has it, 'an attempt to acquire something', as in the sense of *ad captandum*, something '(designed) to appeal to the emotions',[3] or as my French dictionary translates it, an 'inveigling'. You don't capture your identity in the space of the mirror, it is in this seeking after your identity that you are forever in the act of being captured, captured in the space between yourself and the mirror, in these spatial temptations of identity circulating between your inner and outer world, your 'self' and your 'environs'. We are always tempted to endeavour after these identities, spatialized as they always give the appearance of being, as insides and outsides, homelands and awaylands (even if for the migrant, homeland is now the one that is away), here-lands and there-lands.

This seeking to acquire something that will never be acquirable as a fixed entity (but will always be alternating), this appealing to (alternating) emotions, is further played out, within and between selves, in the *fort-da* 'game' of Freud's grandson: that repeated enunciation of the alternating absence (*fort*) and presence (*da*) of some small *object* (the little bobbin) that the child – in response to the presence then departure of his mother (Freud's daughter) – enacts for and in himself, by making his object become absent, throwing it to where he cannot see it, uttering '*fort*' (gone) and then pulling it back into view with a '*da*' (here). Freud: 'I eventually realized that it was a game and that the only use he made of any of his toys was to play "gone" with them.' As in Lacan's mirror-stage, Freud's grandson is in fact eighteen months old at the time of these observations: as in the mirror-stage, the subject makes of himself the object of his own operation *and* observation: a piece of himself (*his* toy) is repeatedly tossed away or hidden and then retrieved – peek-a-*boo* – in order that the 'here' (what is 'present') is not separate from, is not opposed to, but already enfolded in, the 'there' (what is 'absent'), and it is this perpetually enfolded relationship that the child enacts (Freud 1959: 8–11).

This enactment of absence and presence may take place on a psychological and a social level, in relation say, to the mother *or* the motherland – playing gone with them – enacting the desire *and* the fear, the appeal, the endeavour, for both separation and belonging, independence and association – personally, culturally. So if various migrant populations still, as Stephen Cairns says, 'manage to throw-up new tactics of attachment [. . .] through the projection of a hyper-stable architecture, an architecture that announces fixity, permanence', then this very hyperness already anticipates his 'yet' that follows, anticipates an equally hyper enactment of separation: 'Yet, in turn, this fixity and permanence is itself constituted through memory and the experience of a profound mobility.' Experienced, that is, through an alternating of separation and the need to draw what is now there, here.

But why should we be surprised at that, any more than we should be surprised that even the most avant-garde of houses maintain whole areas and categories of homeyness? Why not just weave this hybridity into the story of our architecture, rather than repress it, why not work off of and through it?

If dwelling had no drift, then this alternation of absence and presence might be understood as an attempt of resolution and mastery of this splitting, as some have suggested about the *fort-da* scene. But as Lacan observed, already noting in 1964 the Heideggarian (why not put a name on it) *post-war* tendency (or need or desire) to contain the alienating effects of absence and drift:

> There can be no *fort* without *da* and, one might say, without *Dasein*. But, contrary to the whole tendency of the phenomenology of *Daseinanalyse*, there is no *Dasein* with the *fort*. That is to say, there is no choice [. . .]. The function of the exercise with this

> object refers to an alienation, and not to some supposed mastery, which is difficult to imagine being increased in an endless repetition, whereas the endless repetition that is in question reveals the radical vacillation of the subject.
>
> (Lacan 1977a: 239)

It is these various radical vacillations that as Bhabha says, 'the arts of cultural hybridization seek to embody and enact rather than "transcend"'. They do so by performing their own hybridity within the aesthetic object, their own mimicry of close (but not too close) resemblance, to return to that last dictionary definition at last.

This dialogue of resemblance is a form of comparative double-description. As Gregory Bateson said, it doesn't take one to know one, it takes *two* to know one. As in binocular vision, which is a lie that tells a deeper truth. Each eye sees the same thing, more or less, but between that more and that less, between that shift and overlap, is the deeper depth of perception. Binoculars, the mechanical ones, are like having another set of eyes, allowing you both close attention and distance from the object of your attention. The way the group of children I met on my first day in Nakuru, looking through my binoculars, shaking their heads and clicking their tongues in disbelief and belief, would point first far and then draw that pointing finger back near to themselves. Bringing the there and the here into relation. And binoculars, even when they are drawing what's near even nearer, give you some distance on it, so you can see it anew, in its familiarity and unfamiliarity.

So, unlike human binocular vision, which achieves depth at the cost of resolving difference, aesthetic bi-nocular operations most productively achieve depth by putting into play sameness and difference, not by resolving but by exaggerating samenesses and differences, both collapsing *and* keeping some distance, keeping two almost similar conditions apart in order to draw them deeper into relation and depth. Exposing the desire for resolution even as it reveals the impossibility of resolution.

This is why Bhabha insists on the necessity to avoid the easy resolution of (cultural) difference: 'Hybridity [. . .] is not a third term that resolves the tension between two cultures' (Bhabha 1994: 113). To see how they are both separated from and tied up each with the other, or as he says, 'less than one *and* double' (Bhabha 1994: 100). Less than one because the dominant identity has lost its unified status through the difference revealed by multiple description: not unified because multiplied. But perhaps it would be more precise to say not doubled, at least not, as the dictionary definition goes, copied servilely. Not copied exactly, but playing at resemblances, thus copied slyly. Almost doubled, but not quite. Less than one and not exactly double. Less than one and slyly doubled.

The hybrid play of resemblances is a 'process of classificatory confusion' that Bhabha has described as 'the metonymy of the substitutive chain of ethical and cultural discourse' (Bhabha 1994: 91). This play is metonymic because ethical and cultural discourse is already *within* the social circumstance, and as for architecture it is already within the architectural circumstance: the building. Architecture of course is articulating its ethical and cultural discourse all the time, but it mainly does so as rote repetition (of fixed classifications of building types, programme spaces, elements), as a compulsion to repeat, as servile mimicry. The possibility and ability to draw this ethical and cultural discourse forth in order to rearticulate it – so we can see it in the act of its act – is precisely what architecture may yet find a way to do, in its own becoming hybrid in and through itself, in and through its own aesthetic operations: by being less than one and slyly doubled.

'Less Aesthetics, More Ethics': this was the theme, the provocation, of the 2000 Venice Biennale, and my response to this provocation (in the Biennale competition *Città: Terzo Millennio/The City: Third Millennium*), as in my earlier response to the title of Bhabha's 'Halfway House', was this: let's not play the percentages, let's not play at totalizing proportions if it becomes a matter of re-apportioning, if more of one aspect always results in less of another (that was always the problem of colonialism and of migrancy). Proportion is more productively understood as an enfolding, as an entanglement, as relations, not as definitive allotments. So if more ethics is what you're after in architecture, then you'll need *more* not less aesthetics. Ethics, by definition, is not that which is morally proper, but the *discussion* of what might be considered to be – at any given historical moment – society's moral relations. Ethics means a field of discussion, not of prescription, and for a good discussion, an articulate discussion, you need more (not less) articulation and re-articulation. All architecture is ethical, just as all architecture is social – in that all architecture is entangled in the ethical and social conditions of its time and culture. So if architecture is to be more ethical then that can only mean it needs to be more articulate of its ethics, and so it needs more aesthetics to be more articulate – but an aesthetics that recognizes and articulates, enacts, its own and our own entanglements.

Michel Foucault has already suggested this entanglement of ethics and aesthetics in his tracing of the genealogy of ethics from its development in Antiquity as an 'aesthetics of existence'. 'This art of the self involves the ways individuals constitute themselves and are constituted as ethical subjects in relation to the rules and values that are operative in a given society or group, the agencies or mechanisms of constraint that enforce them, the forms they take in their multifariousness, their divergences and their contradictions' (Foucault 1985: 29; see also Foucault 1997). Earlier in his work Foucault had examined another aesthetics: the development of politics as an aesthetics of the state in Europe during the seventeenth and eighteenth centuries. This marked the beginning of the political rationality of those systems of 'rules and values that are operative in [. . .] society', as the state involved itself 'as agency and mechanism' in the demarcation and numeric regulation of time as schedule and location as address, as well as in the development and administration of infrastructural networks of transportation and communication for the distribution and regulation of individuals and goods (in public interventions such as urban development and welfare management) (Foucault 1980).

That the personal and the political are entangled, that ethics is a form of aesthetics, that aesthetics is a form of ethics, the spatial circumstances of migrancy makes abundantly clear, from the level of the city to the level of an individual domestic shrine. The ways in which migrants occupy space, from local housing to urban contexts, have often put into question some of the most fundamental architectural categories of the host architectural culture: ideas of proper one-to-one correspondences of rooms to familial domestic use are reconceived in relation to the multiplicity of extended families, the proper delimitation of the public and private edge of commercial use (the strict demarcation of the storefront) is put into question by the opening and extension of the store into the sidewalk and street.

These uncanny doublings of spatialized cultures, almost the same, *but not quite*, bear the marks and connections that Bhabha charted in 'Halfway house': estrangement and engagement, accommodation and ambivalence, disorientation and relocation. These occur in and through architectural and sub-architectural elements: sidewalks, storefronts, doorways, windows, walls, storage and display areas, enacting as these do the constitution of self and community through the engaged and conflictual interactions of identities, public and private, domestic and urban. Therein lie a great many bi-nocular lessons for those of us, architects, trying to learn from the issues of migrancy, even if, or especially because, we may never have the occasion to design specifically for those circumstances.

In this process of identifications and cross-identifications, as Ernesto Laclau suggests, cultural and political identities (and I would say architectural identities)[4] are never fixed and unified: these identities will always fail, but there will also always be the failure of those failures, as further attempts to shore up identity are effectuated in order to fill the lack generated by this failure:

> Failure will trigger new acts of identification [. . .] which attempt (vainly) to master those destructuring effects [. . .]. This is why there is a permanent and alternating movement whereby the lack is rejected and invoked, articulated and annulled, included and excluded.
>
> (Laclau and Zac 1994)

In these matters, architects still have much to consider from Krzysztof Wodiczko's multimedia 'industrial designs' for immigrants that mimic the walking staff and backpack of the wanderer, his *Alien Staff* and *Ægis: equipment for a city of strangers*, which stage and frame the collection and commentary of memories and memorabilia, with visual and audio recordings of the user's migrancy stories as well as places to display artefacts related to those stories, allowing both closeness and distance for the user from their own travails, a bi-nocular ability of the object and the user to both inhabit and stand outside of these stories of location and dislocation (Wodiczko 1994, 1999; see also Rakatansky 1994, Deutsche 2002).

This sly doubling 'results in the *splitting* of colonial discourse so that two attitudes towards external reality persist; one takes reality into consideration while the other disavows it and replaces it by a product of desire that repeats, rearticulates "reality" as mimicry' (Bhabha 1994: 91).

This close attention to repeat yet rearticulate reality, to draw forth new relations from and through conditions of authority, is a metonymic rather than a metaphoric operation,[5] in that it finds from within the object and what is contingent to the object the material to export, to rearticulate, rather than completely replacing it with some totally foreign imported material – it works the relations between the native *and* the foreign, between the exported *and* the imported. Which is why, looking from the other way around, if we architects do import lessons from migrant cultures into non-migrant projects, we still have to find within our own architectural and critical culture the basic material to export, to rearticulate, from within our own objects.

Importing and exporting, from here to there: some years back, in the late 1980s, I read an interview with the Japanese Butoh dancer, Kazuo Ohno, conducted with the assistance of the performance team of Eiko and Koma. Ohno's most famous performance is entitled 'Admiring La Argentina' which he created at the age of 71, an homage to 'La Argentina', Antonia Merce, the Spanish dancer, famous for adopting and developing the dances of the Gypsies (certainly one personification of migrancy), whom he saw perform at the Imperial Theatre in Tokyo in 1929, when he was 23. Ohno credits this experience as the one that instigated his desire to become a dancer, and his performance is a remembrance of that moment and that dancer. Like all homages this one involves a certain form of mimicry, a certain bittersweetness of time and place and circumstance now past, and thus Ohno performs this work dressed in 'a long yellowed dress and a withered flower hat'. As the final question in the interview, Ohno was asked what it was like to go from everyday life as a (then, in the late 1980s) 80-year-old Japanese man to a stage performance enacting the dance of a (then, in 1929) 43-year-old Spanish woman. His response, as conveyed by Eiko and Koma: 'He says he doesn't commute.'

If there is a widespread interest today in the work of Shigeru Ban – I'll just restrict my comments here to one architect who is involved in some form of practice immediately related to certain forms of migration – it is due to the fact that his work on refugee shelters following the Kobe earthquake and the Rwanda crisis (both from 1995) are not unrelated to his work for his most affluent clients.

In other words, the degree of interest in his work, in the long run, will match the degree to which he doesn't commute but circulates between equally significant inhabitations of his practice. From the fixity of his temporary material (cardboard tube) shelters in Kobe, say, to the temporariness of position of his mobile rooms in his house in Kawagoe. From here to there:

> Even in disaster areas, as an architect, I want to create beautiful buildings, to move people and to improve people's lives. If I did not feel that way, it would not be possible to create works of architecture and to make a contribution to society at the same time.
>
> (Ban 1999)

And from there to here:

> Architects are generally very egoistic, including me, I'd like to build my monument, too; there's no doubt about that. But it's not the only thing I want to do. I wanted to use my skills and knowledge for a society. The reason I worked for Kobe and Rwanda, is, obviously, the humanitarian feeling, but also to develop my ideas further and apply them at the same time, as long as I'm satisfying the humanitarian need. The two things are mixed together.
>
> (Obrist 1999)

This mixing is never simple, never without consequences, never always successful, but nevertheless it happens, here and there, and it is from this alternating positioning that questions about the architectural articulation of this migration may be asked.

Ban's work is rightfully well known for its purity, its exquisite elegance, but this purity, this exquisiteness threatens to conceal some of his more intriguing projects, no less elegant, but with greater conceptual depth and play, mannerist play, subtle mimicries of his deepest inspiration, Ludwig Mies van der Rohe.[6] For example, in Ban's aforementioned Kawagoe House (2001) with its 'universal space', but with rooms and not just (curtained) partitions now mobile. Or in the Curtain Wall House (1995) with its mobile two storey external tent sheet that plays off of the idea of the curtain wall Mies was so known for, as well as the domestic curtains Mies was so increasingly resistant to, as well as the super-scaled curtains Mies did use in his and Lilly Reich's Silk Exhibit of the *Exposition de la Mode* (1927) and his IIT Chapel (1952), as well as Ban's own Shelter 1 tents for African refugees (1995). Or in the Sagaponac Furniture House (2001), which is a direct play on Mies' unbuilt Brick Country House (1924), only what was, there, linear 'structural' brick walls is now, here, a series of lines and cells 'comprised of modular, full height furniture units which become elements of structural support, spatial division and storage' (Ban 2001), closets upon closets, this again in relation to Mies whose love of closets was only matched by his love of domestic curtains and whose clients were known to incredulously ask others 'You mean your architect *lets* you have closets?'

But then Ban's purity reasserts itself again, more minimalist than Mies, more monocular than bi-nocular, for once again the storage units, judging from all the interior photographs of his projects, are there to keep everything '"concealed, kept from sight, so that others do not get to know about it [. . .] to behave *heimlich*, as though there were something to conceal [. . .] *heimlich* places (which good manners oblige us to conceal)"'. Whereas all the storage units and curtains, rather than being so mono-, suggest the bi-nocular possibilities of concealing and revealing, *fort* and *da*, given that there are many social stories – canny and uncanny, *heimlich* and *unheimlich*, homeland and awayland – to tell, in the entire range of his work, not just in the affluent houses but especially in the refugee shelters and housing for where the cardboard tubes suggest all manners of possible storage and display, and where the display of some of what was there (in one's home before the disaster) may be all the more poignant and needed here (in the refugee shelter).

Now it may seem that we have come a far way from the concerns of social migrancy, if the most significant migration the owners of the Sagaponac Furniture House will have will be between their city home and this their country house in the Hamptons, but if Ban's furniture house series (four have been built to date in Japan and China) began as designs for affluent clients, then this series has also included his design for mass housing for the Kobe earthquake survivors (1996), and the lessons learned from any one of these explorations in pre-fabricated construction may well be useful towards the other, say, for some yet future migrant housing. Because if we say one type of use is social architecture and one isn't, then aren't we just ghettoizing all over again, with yet another badly thought-out binary opposition. What might make architecture social is that it enacts what is social in its condition, within its architecture, not just in its circumstance, so a Hamptons vacation house may be considered to be a form of social architecture as well, if, that is, the architect her- or himself were to consider it and design it as such. So then, even though the client commutes, the (intentions and attentions of the) architect doesn't (have to). Isn't that what social architecture is: the exploration of what is social in whatever design one is designing? Which of Ban's projects would fall under that classification – or by being hybrid might put into play a productive 'process of classificatory confusion' – are some questions that his work engagingly suggests.

I have to tell you, before I finish, the origin of the title for this chapter. It begins in 1989, long before I wrote these words, at another conference in which I was speaking (in fact making my first public presentation of 'Spatial narratives'), but at this particular moment I was listening to another speaker. His talk consisted primarily of what he considered to be fundamental propositions on space, all of which I considered to be overly obvious, binarily oppositional and therefore underthought as propositions. Propositions such as: 'A maze is complex space and an urban retail street is simple space' (you could of course argue quite the opposite:

a maze is homogeneous space, and even the simplest street is filled with all kinds of social and architectural complexity) or 'A plaza is public space and a bedroom is private space' (Joan Copjec has brilliantly analysed how in the film *Double Indemnity* the very publicness of a space might allow for private transaction (Copjec 1993), and as for the guarantee of the privateness of the bedroom, well, not in over a quarter of the so-called US where it's still illegal as I am writing these words, if you are gay, to do what's done in a bedroom, and where still in the state of Louisiana any homo or hetero oral or anal is punishable by law). This speaker I am referring to had a long litany of such oppositional propositions, choreographed with both hands flung to the right for one side of the binary and then to the left for the other side of the binary. It ended at last with what he considered the most obvious opposition of all: 'Either you are here [. . .]' (hands to the right) 'or you are there [. . .]' (hands to the left), and then as if in a fit of pique at how fundamentally fundamental this final fundamental principle was, he burst out: 'you-can-not-be-here-and-there-at-the-same-time-this-is-clear-no?' (hands right, hands left, hands front with palms raised towards the heavens).

What I hope is clear is this: I didn't believe that then and there and I still don't believe that now and here. Architecture, and you, and I, are neither here nor there, but always here and there at the same time.

After all, there it is, now, years hence, and somehow these words have managed to migrate (to strain this word one last time) here, into your hands and your eyes, wherever and whenever in the world your hands and your eyes may be.

NOTES

1 *The Compact Edition of the Oxford English Dictionary* (New York: Oxford University Press, 1971) and the *Webster's New World Dictionary* (New York: William Collins and World Publishing, 1978). I would like to thank James F. Gramata for pointing out this etymology to me.

2 All nations and peoples have at their heart origin-myths that involve their own great history of migration (Virgil's epic of Aeneas bringing the Trojans to found Rome, all the Biblical migrations from Eden to the Flood to the flight from Egypt, the Navajo's sojourn through the Four Worlds), which is why nations are always worried about the next set of immigrants to arrive, who may arrive as they once did, to settle and overtake their new home as their new homeland – one displacement leading to the displacement and replacement of another – that *heimlich* story is all too familiar and thus all too *unheimlich*.

3 When Oxford adds the word *vulgus* in parenthesis after the phrase *ad captandum*, then this appeal becomes an appeal to the emotions of, as it says, 'the rabble', the crowd, just as for all our inner sense of the specialness of ourselves, what appears before us here in the mirror (or in a

photograph or in the holiday video) is a common human being, just another face, there, in the crowd.

4 See Rakatansky 1995.

5 'The metonymic strategy produces the signifier of colonial *mimicry* as the affect of hybridity – at once a mode of appropriation and of resistance, from the disciplined to the desiring' (Bhabha 1994: 120).

6 'One of my favourite buildings is the Farnsworth House by Mies van der Rohe. This was a revolutionary work that achieved complete continuity between inside and outside by means of a totally glazed exterior. However there is no physical continuity as in traditional Japanese residential spaces, where various openable screens exist between inside and outside. The "Curtain Wall House" was formed with an authentic exterior curtain wall. Other works are a response to the "Universal Space" proposed by Mies, that is, the idea of a fluid space generated under a large continuous roof by means of furniture-like cores and partitions' (Ban 1999).

REFERENCES

Ban, S. (1999) http://www.archilab.org/public/1999/artistes/shig01en.htm.

Ban, S. (2001) http://www.housesatsagaponac.com.

Bhabha, H. (1994) *The Location of Culture*, London: Routledge.

Bhabha, H. (1997) 'Halfway house', *Artforum* 35 (9) May: 11–12, 125.

Brecht, B. (1964) 'A short organum for the theatre', in J. Willet (ed.) *Brecht on Theatre*, New York: Hill and Wang.

Caillois, R. (1984) 'Mimicry and legendary psychasthenia', *October* 31: 16–32.

Copjec, J. (1993) 'The phenomenal nonphenomenal: private space in *film noir*', in Joan Copjec (ed.) *Shades of Noir*, London: Verso.

Detienne, M. and Vernant, J.-P. (1991) *Cunning Intelligence in Greek Culture and Society*, Chicago: University of Chicago Press.

Deutsche, R. (2002) 'Sharing strangeness: Krzysztof Wodiczko's *Ægis* and the question of hospitality', *Grey Room* 6: 26–43.

Feeley-Harnik, G. (1980) 'The Sakalava House (Madagascar)', *Anthropos* 75: 580.

Foucault, M. (1980) 'The politics of health in the eighteenth century', in M. Foucault *Power/Knowledge*, New York: Pantheon: 166–82.

Foucault, M. (1985) *The Use of Pleasure*, New York: Random House.

Foucault, M. (1988) 'The political technology of individuals', in Luther H. Martin, H. Gutman and P.H. Hutto (eds) *Technologies of the Self*, Amherst: The University of Massachusetts Press.

Foucault, M. (1991) 'Governmentality', in G. Burchell, C. Godon and P. Miller (eds) *The Foucault Effect: studies in governmentality*, Chicago: The University of Chicago Press.

Foucault, M. (1997) *Ethics: subjectivity and truth*, New York: The New Press.

Freud, S. (1958) 'The "uncanny" ', in S. Freud, *On Creativity and the Unconscious*, New York: Harpers.

Freud, S. (1959) *Beyond the Pleasure Principle*, New York: Norton.

Freud, S. (1963) 'Further recommendations in the technique of psychoanalysis: recollection, repetition and working through', in S. Freud, *Therapy and Technique*, New York: Collier.

Heidegger, M. (1971) 'Building dwelling thinking', in M. Heidegger, *Poetry, Language, Thought*, New York: Harper.

Krell, D.F. (1997) *Architecture: ecstasies of space, time, and the human body*, Albany: State University of New York Press.

Lacan, J. (1977a) *The Four Fundamental Concepts of Psycho-Analysis*, New York: Norton.

Lacan, J. (1977b) *Écrits: a selection*, trans. A. Sheridan, New York: Norton.

Lacan, J. (2002) *Écrits: a selection*, trans. B. Fink, New York: Norton.

Laclau, E. and Zac, L. (1994) 'Mining the gap: the subject of politics', in E. Laclau (ed.) *The Making of Political Identities*, New York: Verso.

Obrist, H.-U. (1999) 'Hans-Ulrich Obrist interviews Shigeru Ban, Paris May 1999', http://amsterdam.nettime.org/Lists-Archives/nettime-l-9908/msg00079.html.

Rakatansky, M. (1992) 'Spatial narratives', in J. Whiteman, J. Kipnis and R. Burdett (eds) *Strategies in Architectural Thinking*, Cambridge, Massachusetts: MIT Press.

Rakatansky, M. (1994) 'Krzysztof Wodiczko: disfiguring – refiguring', *Assemblage* 23: 18–27.

Rakatansky, M. (1995) 'Identity and the discourse of politics in contemporary architecture', *Assemblage* 27: 9–18.

Wilson, P.J. (1988) *The Domestication of the Human Species*, New Haven: Yale University Press.

Wodiczko, K. (1994) 'Alien staff', *Assemblage* 23: 6–17.

Wodiczko, K. (1999) *Critical Vehicles: writings, projects, interviews*, Cambridge, Massachusetts: MIT Press.

Chapter 6: Migration, exile and landscapes of the imagination

Andrew Dawson and Mark Johnson

This chapter concerns situations in which migration and exile informs constructions of place and locality. However, the focus of the chapter is not on the migrant or exiled per se: those who see themselves or are seen by others to be living in a state of variously enforced separation from 'home'. Rather, we are interested in situations in which the imagining of migration and exile become constitutive parts of the construction and experience of place and landscape. Migration and exile, we suggest, may be as much about cognitive movement as they are about the actual physical movement of groups and individuals from one locality to another.

Writing on migration and exile has thus far primarily focused on the experiences of those living in exile, i.e. individuals or groups who have either left (or have been forced to leave) their 'home' and/or those who see themselves as living in a state of separation from their 'home'. Thus, for instance the structure of a recent edited volume on migration and exile (King, Connell and White 1995) is laid out largely in terms of what might be called the social biography of exile – that is, of leaving, arrival and return. The focus of analysis is the sense of 'betwixt and between', of being between 'here and there' which characterizes the experience of the exiled, and which is seen to incite responses which centre around the idea of return.

Recent writing has, of course, critically problematized the notion of 'return', demonstrating that while the experience of exile may at times lead to the search for 'roots', it also may act to destabilize fixed notions of shared history and ancestry. As White (1995: 1–19) suggests, the experience of return never effects a simple recovery of origins. Rather, the experience of exile not only calls into question cultural authenticity, but also disrupts linear narratives of time and place, since each and every place, time and event is reconstituted in a relation in which none is given ontological priority. Leaving, and the place one has left, are constituted through the process of relocation and return and vice versa. In this way of narrating and experiencing exile, the betwixt and between, is not something which can in any simple way be resolved. Indeed, for some, it is particularly the transient – one might say liminal – quality of exile, of routes over roots which provides important sites of resistance to hegemonic discourses of place-based identity (Clifford 1997; Gilroy 1993).

Important though these critical interventions have been, the notion of movement and passage celebrated in writing on migration, diaspora and exile still works within a framework in which there are individuals and groups who inhabit movement and passage and those who do not. In this way, writing on exile continues to authorize a particular group of individuals – the exiled, the migrant, etc. – as bearers of a particular kind of existential truth, whether it be the truth of a traumatic nationalism or the truth of the traveller. Indeed, as Malkki (1995: 513) notes, while 'refugees' continue to be viewed as individuals out of place and in crisis, exiles, as well as migrants, nomads, travellers and diasporas (see, for example, Clifford 1992; Eades 1987) have recently become the romantic figures for anthropologists and others who seek to move anthropology away from what are regarded as static views of people and culture confined to and conditioned principally by particular places, towards a view of people and culture as mobile, creolized and hybrid, increasingly inhabiting non-places (Auge 1995).

Studies of this variety constitute an invaluable contribution to the inventory of contemporary issues we must tackle. However, as a recipe for the transformation of anthropology's substantive foci it is absurd (maybe even ethnocentric), a call for nomadology rather than anthropology. As Hammann *et al.* (1997) have recently pointed out, for example, 98 per cent of the world's population never physically moves to another place on anything like a permanent basis, and the greater proportion of this 98 per cent hardly move at all. Paradoxically, moreover, rather than challenging the static, place-based view of people and culture, the study of movers and variously displaced persons reaffirms a static view of the relationship between people, place and culture, re-creating the division between those who are 'emplaced' and those who are 'out-of-place', the sedentary and the non-sedentary, fixed vs. fluid, roots vs. routes, isled vs. ex-isled.

What we seek to emphasize, above and beyond the actual physical movement of individual subjects, are two things. The first is the physical movement individuals confront in their conditions of physical fixity – the intercultural import-export of goods and ideas (Clifford 1992), the translocal networks Olwig (1993, 1997), and appropriation of cultural otherness (Massey 1991, 1992) through which the specificity of local places and identities are made. The second, however, are individuals' vicarious movements [. . .] the sense in which people move imaginatively or cognitively in time and space in constructing their identities and experiencing particular places (Rapport and Dawson 1998). Moreover, as the case studies on which we draw demonstrate, while emplacement suggests fixity and roots, it is often achieved through language which metaphorically invokes spatial and temporal movements and relocations. Similarly, the discourse of migration, displacement and exile is as much the property of the seemingly most fixed or rooted individuals as it is of those who live physically transient lives. In sum, we argue that place and identity are rarely made or inhabited in a singular or straightforward manner, but are most often constructed and experienced as a variety of both literal and metaphorical roots and routes (Tilley 1999: 177–84).

MIGRANT MINDS AND PLACES OF THE IMAGINATION

The former coal-mining town of Ashington, in north-east England, would seem to be a particularly apt context to test out the thesis that emplacement should be treated as an active search involving cognitive movement in time and space, for here is a place whose residents have been characterized in the sociological literature as facing a triple-faceted fixity. Many are socially fixed, working-class with little opportunity for social mobility. Most are spatially fixed (isolated and geographically immobile). Finally, there is a sense in which this increasingly elderly population of residents are temporally fixed. With death nearby, time is running out.

The particular event we wish to focus on is the conflict that emerged in one particular old people's club surrounding the issue of the representation of community. The case is interesting because it demonstrates how competing discourses of fixity and movement, and particularly residency and migration, play out in struggles over the depiction of place and collective identity. At the time of research several clubs were approached by local government who sought the involvement of elderly people in the running and construction of a local museum of mining. Participants from each club were asked to choose one from among them who with others would act as voluntary curator, record local poems, songs and passages of dialect for broadcast in the museum and serve on an advisory body concerned with the design of the museum's displays.

In the event two fairly resolute candidates and groups of backers emerged. A ballot was called by club leaders, and in the days leading up to it a fairly conflictual debate took place. The conflictual nature of the debate was hardly surprising. First, in the eyes of participants the advisory body on which the successful candidate would serve was responsible for nothing less than playing a leading role in the construction of a visual and oral representation of the community. This kind of activity is the very *raison d'être* of the clubs. Second, the debate focused on the issue of the ownership of rights to community definition. Third, the divergent biographies of the respective candidates lent the debate a particularly polarizing set of substantive issues around which claims to ownership of definitional rights were contested. One of the candidates was a former school head teacher, an activist in the local historical movement and a lifelong resident of the town.[1] The other was a former miner who in the economic depression of the 1930s had temporarily moved for work to the coalfields of Kent, Canada and America. In terms of class at least, the social profiles of the two groups of supporters reflected broadly those of the two candidates.

The first set of issues were, then, those of class and occupation. The right of community definition accorded to the former miner was represented as stemming from his direct erstwhile involvement in mining. The second key issue was residency. The right of community definition accorded to the former headmaster was represented as stemming both from his unbroken residency in the town and the fact that, as a long-term resident and activist within local historical circles, he had become an expert in the histories, songs, poetry and dialect of the local mining, working class.

With change, wrought largely by the demise of mining, the seemingly 'objective' referents of community are steadily disappearing. As such, a sense of community is increasingly obtained at a second remove, through learning rather than direct experience. Moreover, the central images of community are part of a cultural fiction that becomes ever more elaborate as they are celebrated in the burgeoning local history societies, writing groups and the local museum. It is clear that community is being refined as a discourse by a middle class that manipulates images and symbols that have only a condensed historical meaning for them, rather than a more personal historic link. What is important to note is that through his mastery of apparently mining- and working-class-specific cultural forms, the middle-class former head teacher was able to represent himself as more working-class than the working class. Here, then, personal identity is dislocated from the objective referent of class and relocated via the mastery of working-class memorabilia into a privileged relation to a historical place.

The teacher's claims to represent community, in other words, were based not simply on long-term residency but on his rootedness in the particular lifeway and landscape of an imagined historical place. By contrast, the miner's claim to represent community was based not simply on his working-class credentials, but more importantly on his experiences of the larger landscape inhabited by the international working class and of which Ashington was seen to be a part. This was achieved by a critical reappraisal of the idea of the 'local', a critique and argument that resonate with a series of strands of socialist thinking in which the idea of 'local' community was seen as intimately connected with the paternalistically oppressive objectives of pre-nationalization mining companies, whose strategies of control involved the discursive construction of 'local' places and communities (Dawson 1990: 30–8). In other similar thinking, such as that of the internationalism of the Communist Party of Great Britain in the 1930s (a politically formative era for many of the club participants), local community identity is represented as a form of class consciousness.

The point here is that through deployment of the discourse of the international community of the working class the former itinerant miner who had spent much of his life exiled from the local community could represent himself as more of the community than others with histories of permanent residency. Here, then, community identity is effectively dislocated from the objective referent of place. In real terms this consisted of a re-presentation of migration and, to an extent, temporary economic exile as a rite of passage to emplacement and community membership. Three, often explicitly stated, reasons were given for why this should be so.

First, migration was claimed as an origin(al) experience of belonging. Much was made of the newness of Ashington, a town that simply did not exist before the onset of the mining industry in the eighteenth century. The argument was embellished with subtlety. For example, in commenting on the complexity and cleverness of local language, one supporter of the former miner was able to add the descriptive term 'polyglottal buzz' to that of the 'pitmatic'. The term pitmatic refers to a process whereby mining terminology is developed for metaphorical usage in the description of everyday reality. The term polygottal buzz refers to the multifarious inputs to the language, from the migrant settlers who were the area's first significant population.

Second, mirroring an emphasis on spatial segmentation in the way that community is constructed, migration was represented as heightening, through lived contrast, consciousness of a community whose distinctiveness derives from juxtaposition with the world beyond its boundaries. Third, mirroring socialist internationalism, migration and temporary exile was represented as enabling consciousness of a community of the working class which, because locally suppressed, is realized principally in its international aspect (see also Olwig 1993). Conversely, and somewhat paradoxically given the use of socialist internationalist ideas, through localizing these three discourses, of origins, hybridity and internationalism, migration was represented as a quintessential characteristic of local community and culture. In essence, apart from the fact that it is a working-class coal-mining town, what distinguishes Ashington from the isolated agricultural communities that surround it is that it is a migrant town per se, it has a kind of 'been-to' culture, and, in at least some cases, its people are conscious of its international locatedness.

It is no doubt true that the people depicted in this case study face extreme conditions of social, spatial and temporal fixity. However, it is clear that their competing definitions of community that are constructed through a process of identity location and dislocation, are also engineered through engagement in a kind of movement. At one level people move socially, to working class from the objectively perceived social status of middle class, for example. At another level they move temporally to defining moments of community: to Ashington's moment of inception, to its depression-years era of intermittent wage migration and to the era of the rise of socialist internationalism. Finally, they move spatially, to the southern locus of their exploitation and depreciation, and from local community to international community to internationally located local community. As part of this process, migration and exile are represented often as defining features of community and place.

In essence, while these people face conditions of fixity, they seem like many others to engage cognitively in movement. Furthermore, we may be able to describe fixity and movement as interdependent modalities. There may be a situation where the imagination of other places and times informs images of community constructed in the here and now that people seek to instil in perpetuity, in this case in the bricks, mortar, display cabinets and cassette tapes of a heritage museum, perhaps so as to overcome the crises of discontinuity that impending death threatens: movement gives on to fixity gives on to movement. Here, then, are home bodies and migrant minds, for whom place is fashioned and remade as a route for, as much as it is the root of, identity.

ROMANCING HUE: LOVING AND LEAVING PLACE

While the lives of rural miners in Britain are mistakenly imagined to be both thoroughly fixed and firmly emplaced, precisely the opposite might be said of popular imaginings of the Vietnamese. Indeed, refugees and exiles are a recurrent theme both in Vietnamese history and in imaginings of Vietnam. Exile figures as an important part of the story of anti-colonialist struggle in Vietnam, a badge of honour bestowed by the French on errant emperors and early nationalist thinkers alike. In the more recent past, in terms of Western (particularly Anglo-American) media, after the war itself it was the image of 'boat people' and refugees – individuals who whether through their own or other's choosing set off on perilous journeys – that dominated news stories on Vietnam and the Vietnamese. What the rest of the world initially saw simply as another story of third world refugees, however, has more recently been variously rewritten in terms of 'exile': of leaving, arrival and return, part of the stories through which immigrant Vietnamese communities living outside of Vietnam narrate their lives (Dorais, Chan and Indra 1988; Nam 1993; and see also Young 1998 for a Western journalist's recent reflections on one Vietnamese family's story of flight into exile).

Within Vietnam itself, there continues to be much discussion about both the original movement of Vietnamese during the war and more recent migrants who together make up the diasporic Viet Kieu (Vietnamese living outside of Vietnam). These discussions raise complex issues linking economics, politics, kinship, gender and personal identities. Our interest here, in particular, is in the way in which exile, or the possibility and imagination of migration and exile and of exiled imaginings – that is to say, discourses of and about the exiled – informs everyday constructions and relationships to place and landscape in the emerging tourist centre and 'world heritage site' of Hue, the former imperial capital and current seat of the people's committee of Thua Thien Hue province in Central Vietnam.

'Hue is more lovely as a reminiscence than as a place to live.' This expression is found in the introduction to the chapter of a book on the traditional arts and crafts of Hue (Thong 1994). Immediately striking is the way in which the book situates Hue as a place in relationship to a sense of nostalgic longing and loss. The author, a history professor at the local university, suggests that this saying encapsulates how many people feel about Hue. People who go away from Hue, he suggested, remembered with fondness the aesthetic beauty of the City and the romance of the perfume river, but most people who live in Hue are actually tormented by the weather, particularly the long rainy season which usually causes extensive flooding. Other individuals, however, interpreted this saying in different ways. On the one hand, some individuals felt that there was a special quality about Hue and people from Hue, which always made people wish to return. On the other hand, many individuals, young people especially, bemoaned the lack of economic opportunities and job possibilities, as well as the all-too-quiet life of a sleepy provincial town where most shops and restaurants closed at 11 o'clock. For these individuals, it was not the weather, but the sense of cultural and economic stagnation which at times made living in Hue difficult to bear.

Hue, both people and place, are, perhaps increasingly, constructed and to a certain extent 'policed' as the living embodiment of a traditional Kinh or Viet cultural aesthetic. Strict zoning regulations have been adopted in order to protect, so far as possible, the 'unique' interplay of natural and man-made features which characterize the Hue landscape. A tightly imposed curfew has been placed on women working in the evening, with most activity in hotels, restaurants, karaokes ending by 11 pm, in order to protect, so far as possible, 'the modest beauty and charm of the social landscape'. Significantly, this reconstruction of Hue – marked among other things by the renovation and conservation of monuments and the reopening of fine arts training departments, as well as by the growth of private entrepreneurial activity such as hosting 'traditional'-style meals – is being produced as much by discourses originating outside of Hue (among others by Viet Kieu or overseas Vietnamese) as it is by the discourses of State and people living there.

One internet site, 'Hue Net' (www.geocities.com/Tokyo/2579/), compares Hue with other 'ancient capitals in SE Asia' and points to its representativeness as an 'Oriental city'. The authors note how all the monuments are 'in sublime harmony with nature', a harmony which is seen to be mirrored in the 'courteous, mild and quiet' people of Hue. 'Both life and landscape here are poetical, bringing self-confidence and worrilessness to everybody.' The site is apparently maintained by a Viet Kieu. It is not possible to document here the direct material effects or consequences of such apparently naive and nostalgic images or imaginings on Hue. More importantly, however, for the purposes of this chapter, is the perception among local people of the impact of overseas Vietnamese on the locality.

Young tour guides (both women and men) with whom one talks, for instance, continually commented on overseas Vietnamese men coming back to Hue to find 'real' Vietnamese women – 'Hue women' – as wives. One tour guide mentioned that there had been 10,000 overseas Vietnamese visitors in Hue the previous year, and that he and his friends reckoned Hue was now short 1,000 women as a result. Whether or not their characterization of the Viet Kieu is accurate, what is of interest here is the way in which both for the tour guides and other individuals living in Hue, the Viet Kieu (men especially) are commonly viewed as being motivated by a longing for return, a rediscovery of their Vietnamese roots and the desire for an authentic, if regal, Vietnamese woman: a longing which was set against the presumed loss of Vietnamese identity in the countries within which they were newly settled.

In fact, tour guides and other individuals have a complex relation with exile and the exiled. On the one hand, the longing and desire of the exiled is read and constructed by these individuals as proof of place and evidence of an essential truth of the self; e.g. why would the exiled return unless there were not, in fact, something quintessentially Vietnamese about the place and people? At the same time, this essential truth was always called into question by the fact that many of these same individuals expressed a desire to be and/or to live elsewhere and otherwise, places and lives which were more often than not constructed as being in complete opposition to the dominant visions and viewings of 'Hue'. For example, the same tour guide who said that the Viet Kieu had taken away 1,000 local women, lamented the fact that his family had narrowly missed out on emigrating to the US. More than about the relative desirability of one place over another, however, it was fundamentally about the possibility of different subject positions which enable different versions and relations to place, including home place. The paradox is that it is the imagined longing of the exiled which in part creates the burden of an authentic self which they see themselves as carrying.

In order to further illustrate the complex and often contradictory ways in which both the imagining of exiles and the possibility of migration (in this case to Saigon) inform constructions of place in this particular locality, here is a love story of sorts between two individuals encountered there, Tuan and Hein. Tuan had at that time recently returned to Hue from Saigon where he had spent two years living with his uncle and working as a waiter in a restaurant there. While he was in Saigon, he said, he longed to get back to Hue, though the longing was tempered by the pleasure of living in an urban cosmopolitan centre and of earning a decent wage. He originally came back to Hue, he suggested, only because he had decided to go to University and pursue a degree studying English. On completion of his degree course, his original intention was to return to Saigon to find a job with a multinational firm whom he had heard paid very good wages for University graduates who were able to speak English. Tuan was being forced to rethink his plans, however, because he had met and fallen in love with Hein.

Hein had completed a degree course in French and worked in the Hue post office. She also worked in her family's business, a relatively expensive restaurant which prepared and served food in the 'manner of the former royal court'. The restaurant was in fact part of the family home, with guests served on the verandah surrounded by landscaped bonsai gardens. The picture of Hein which Tuan painted was a kind of quintessential Hue individual: he mentioned several times how she loved and served her parents, how she not only was well educated, but also was specially talented in preparing traditional Hue dishes. Indeed, Tuan and Hein recounted how on two separate occasions, foreign visitors – one a French Caucasian, the other French Vietnamese (Viet Kieu) – had unsuccessfully sounded out the possibilities of marrying Hein because of her 'beauty, talent and charm'. The only cloud in this otherwise fairy-tale picture of romance was that unlike Tuan, Hein was apparently fixed on staying in Hue, despite the fact that, as she herself said, Vietnamese gender and kinship protocols specify that women should follow their partners, rather than vice versa.

For Tuan, the question as to whether or not to leave Hue was complicated in a number of ways by Hein's apparent refusal to leave Hue. Leaving Hue for Saigon provided economic opportunities which Tuan clearly thought would enable him to embark on a successful and prosperous career and increase his social standing and prestige. If he stayed in Hue, the potential for increasing his economic and social status would be greatly diminished and he would be continually reminded of his inferior status vis-à-vis his wife and his wife's parents, both of whom were influential and affluent individuals. Tuan's desire to leave Hue, however, was not only about his desire to transcend his present social and economic status, but was also about the possibility of exploring both other places and alternative selves: possibility spaces which Tuan, like many other young people in Hue, does not see as being readily available in the local landscape.

What of Hein, who unlike Tuan, did not give any overt indication of ambivalence with Hue, and certainly no sense of being oppressed by the place which she appears to have chosen for herself. First of all, having chosen to live in Hue, not desiring to move, not having physically moved, does not mean to say that she experiences no movement. Apart from anything else, Hein is in frequent contact with tourists and travellers who pass through her family's restaurant. Hero's mother has also previously worked abroad in Iraq as a doctor. Both her mother's stories of living and working abroad and her day-to-day contact with travellers, from places either physically or conceptually distant, present possibilities for cognitive movement, through whom she might, as with the tour guides, imaginatively explore other possible selves and view home place from a different perspective.

But why in particular does Hein not want to leave Hue with Tuan? One possible answer lies in the fact that the longing and love of Tuan for Hein is akin to, and mirrored in the desiring gaze of Viet Kieu men, for both of whom Hein is the objectification of an essential sense of place and location. Recall for instance that Tuan has experienced the kind of longing for Hue similar to that which he and others attribute to the exiled. His return to Hue is then complicated by the fact that he falls in love with Hein, as do other Viet Kieu men, on their return from exile. Hein thus becomes the site for Tuan's identification of an essential Hue self, a part of his self, of his place and identity which he wishes to take with him, while at the same time he is actively engaged in the process of leaving and reinventing identity, place and self. For Tuan, that Hein seemingly refuses to leave becomes another instance of the burdensomeness of this part of himself which, as it were, refuses to let him leave. What he cannot, or does not, wish to see is that the object of his desire is a subject who, like himself, does not wish to be confined or contained, but also has and experiences alternative selves. The crucial difference is that whereas Tuan sees the exploration of alternative selves as necessitating physical relocation, for Hein, the exploration of alternative selves lies in a kind of exiled imagining, an act of self-imposed exile from the categories through which she is continually being constructed as a passive and docile body. By choosing to live in Hue, Hein simultaneously confirms her status as a Hue woman, one located 'at home', and destabilizes the social fictions that keep her 'in place'. Moreover, while constructed as passive and docile, she incorporates, through the contacts she makes, her own exiled imaginings. In this way a conceptually rooted place of past-presents – the idea of an essential and original Hue – is transvalued in such a way that the actual physical locality can become a route to alternative future-presents. In this case it seems a moot point as to whether or not the would-be physical migrant and exile – Tuan – or the migrant mind and exiled imagination – Hein – is the more rooted or routed.

CONCLUSION: ON MIGRANT MINDS AND EX/ISLED IMAGININGS

In this chapter we have essayed the argument that the making of place, like the making of identity, involves both literal and metaphorical movement. While drawing on recent theorists who have emphasized routes over roots, what we have sought to demonstrate is that the exiles search for roots, no less than the unfolding of migrant routes takes place within landscapes of the imagination. As we suggested in the introduction, however, imaginings of exile, no less than the cognitive movement of migrant minds, are never singular and straightforward but often involve contradictory expressions and desires, both literal and cognitive dissonances which are never completely reconciled.

Migration and exile are often written about as a movement away from that which is familiar and self-same, which either leads to nostalgic attempts at recovery or to a liberatory experience from the self. We wish to disrupt this oppositional logic of either roots or routes to posit a more complex relation of both/and, which we suggest might be written as the ex/isled. In particular we think ex/isled is a useful metaphor for rethinking identity processes in general, because it not only evokes the sense of leaving, which is a longing and a carrying with, but also is evocative of destination not yet achieved, and of return never fully realized. Exile points to the possibility of experiencing self and place as 'other', or, more precisely, of the experience of self and place as located in the movement between and in acts of identification with other possible selves and places. Indeed, it is important to reiterate the point often lost in discussions of self and others that in experiencing self as other, we experience the other as self.

Finally, in trying to think through the making of place and identity, we wish to reconceptualize liminality as the awareness or realization of the betwixt and between, in order to get away from its being seen as a temporary stage in the process of movement from one fixed state or place to another. We want to see it as proximal and immanent in all acts of identification, including the construction of and acts of identifications with particular places. That is to say we do not conceptualize liminality in Van Gennep's (1960) or Turner's (1974) sense of discreet phases, states or places, between which lie a temporary and transitional period which is resolved. To do so would simply be to affirm fixed states of being. Indeed, even if one takes a dynamic version of Van Gennep and Turner which sees social life as a continual series of changing states, of lots of little series of beginnings, middles and ends, this still does not capture what we are after. It is true that we are born, we live and we die, for most, though by no means all, in one physical and seemingly familiar location – but living, the place we are at in the present, is a condition of in-betweenness, a crossroads of various real and imagined comings and goings.

ACKNOWLEDGEMENTS

We would like to thank the following for their comments and contributions to the formulation of the chapter: Barbara Bender, Judith Okely and Nigel Rapport. Research in Vietnam was sponsored by a grant from the British Academy South East Asia section.

NOTE

1 This section develops a case study presented elsewhere (Dawson 1998).

REFERENCES

Auge, M. (1995) *Non-places: introduction to an anthropology of supermodernity*, London: Verso.

Clifford, J. (1992) 'Travelling cultures', in L. Grossberg, C. Nelson and P. Treichler (eds) *Cultural Studies*, London: Routledge, pp. 99–116.

Clifford, J. (1997) *Routes: travel and translation in the late twentieth century*, Cambridge, Massachusetts: Harvard University Press.

Dawson, A. (1990) *Ageing and Change in Pit Villages of North East England*, unpublished thesis, University of Essex.

Dawson, A. (1998) 'The Dislocation of Identity: contestations of home community in Northern England', in N. Rapport and A. Dawson (eds) *Migrants of Identity: perceptions of home in a world of movement*, Oxford: Berg.

Dorais, L.J., Chan, K.B. and Indra, D. (eds) (1988) *Ten Years Later: Indochinese communities in Canada*, Montreal: Canadian Asian Studies Association.

Eades, J. (1987) *Migrants, Workers and the Social Order*, London: Tavistock.

Gilroy, P. (1993) *The Black Atlantic: modernity and double consciousness*, London: Verso.

Hammann, T., Brochmann, G., Tamas, K. and Faist, T. (eds) (1997) *International Migration, Immobility and Development: multidisciplinary perspectives*, Oxford: Berg.

King, R., Connell, J. and White, P. (eds) (1995) *Writing Across Worlds: literature and migration*, London: Routledge.

Malkki, L. (1995) 'Refugees and exile: from refugee studies to the national order of things', *Annual Review of Anthropology* 24: 495–523.

Massey, D. (1991) 'A global sense of place', *Marxism Today*, June: 24–9.

Massey, D. (1992) 'A place called home?', *New Formations: Journal of Culture, Theory and Practice* (The question of home) 17 (Summer): 133–45.

Nam, W.P. (1993) *Ways of Exile: poems from the first decade*, London: Skoob Books.

Olwig, K.F. (1993) *Global Culture, Island Identity: continuity and change in the Afro-Caribbean community of Nevis*, Reading: Harwood Academic Press.

Olwig, K.F. (1997) 'Cultural sites: sustaining home in a deterritorialized world', in K. Hastrup and K.F. Olwig (eds) *Siting Culture: the shifting anthropological object*, London and New York: Routledge.

Rapport, N. and Dawson, A. (eds) (1998) *Migrants of Identity: perceptions of home in a world of movement*, Oxford: Berg.

Thong, N.H. (1994) *Hue, Its Traditional Handicrafts and trade guilds*, Hue: Thuan Hoa Publishing House.

Tilley, C. (1999) *Metaphor and Material Culture*, Oxford: Blackwell.

Turner, V. (1974) *The Ritual Process: structure and anti-structure*, Harmondsworth: Penguin.

White, P. (1995) 'Geography, literature and migration', in R. King, J. Connell and P. White (eds) *Writing Across Worlds: literature and migration*, London: Routledge, pp. 1–19.

Van Gennep, A. (1960) *The Rites of Passage*, London: Routledge & Kegan Paul.

Young, G. (1998) *A Wavering Grace: a Vietnamese family in war and peace*, Harmondsworth: Penguin.

Chapter 7: Building Hong Kong

From migrancy to disappearance

Ackbar Abbas

In the years immediately after the Sino-British Joint Declaration returning Hong Kong to China, it used to be said: those who can afford it, get a foreign passport and leave; those who can't, get the Basic Law and stay. What needs to be added is that, in either case, the experience of migrancy is unavoidable and sometimes also paradoxical. Take the case of passports and emigration. Many of those who made major sacrifices to get one did so not in order to leave, but in order to stay. In other words, the signification of getting a passport has changed. It is now essentially an insurance on the possibility of future movement, in case of disaster, not an indication of the imminence of departure; a point that Britain does not, or pretends not, to understand in refusing to grant right of abode to the majority of citizens of its former colony. Migrancy means, therefore, not only changing places; it also means the changing nature of places. Like colonialism, migrancy too can take an extensive or intensive form. In the latter case, we can be migrants without going anywhere.

Hong Kong has experienced both forms of migrancy. For example, it is said that it was an act of emigration, the flight of 21 Shanghai industrialist families to Hong Kong after the communist revolution, that formed the basis of the city's industrial development. They brought with them their capital and business expertise. But since then, the nature of Hong Kong as a place has gone through a series of mutations and reinventions, as it moved from local manufacture to global finance. On the one hand, we find its increasing inscription in a global economy; on the other, the residues of a colonial history and a special relation to China; the overlapping and *non-synchronised* histories producing an always unfamiliar sense of place. The latest episode of course is when Hong Kong as a British colony becomes Xiang Gang, one of China's Special Administrative Regions. The late Deng Xiao-ping's promise of '50 years without change' is belied by the fact that the city is changing daily right in front of our eyes, though not necessarily in ways that we can see. Whether one goes or stays, the experience of migrancy is inescapable.

It is not surprising, therefore, that cultural theory, particularly what is known as cultural studies, has adopted migrancy both as a subject of study and as a methodological trope. We can think about contemporary cultural theory as bequeathing to us, first of all, a more inclusive and anti-elitist notion of culture, placing now at the centre what was once on the margins. Culture now would include the study of mass culture, subcultures, working-class youth cultures, the cultures of 'ethnic minorities', the critiques of race, gender, colonial discourse and so on. But besides a widened notion of culture, cultural theory gives us, even more importantly, a *changed notion of culture,* where culture itself is now not just an expanded field, but a field of instabilities and destabilisations, indeed of migrancy. Hence, the prevalence in recent cultural theory of tropes such as nomadism, travel, the space-in-between, the interstitial rather than the institutional, 'third spaces' and so on, all of which work to combat a too domesticated view of culture based on established models.

Important as this second line of argument in cultural theory may be, there is, nevertheless, a danger, namely a tendency to associate migrancy too easily with intellectual mobility, or with 'free play' and 'sliding signifiers', and to downplay disparities between the intellectual project and socio-political exigencies. In this connection, the work of Edward Said is both exemplary in alerting us to the dangers I am alluding to, and at the same time, an inadvertent exemplification of such dangers. I am thinking of the final section of *Culture and Imperialism* (1993), significantly entitled 'Movements and migrations'. There, Said rightly insists on the crucial difference between theoretical liveliness and 'the massive dislocations, waste, misery, and horrors endured in our century's migrations and mutilated lives', and rightly emphasises the fact that 'the bravura performances of the intellectual exile and the miseries of the displaced person or refugee are [not] the same' (Said 1993: 332). Yet in the very same paragraph, both migrant and intellectual are somehow transmuted and brought together as twin sources of the energies of liberation, 'energies whose incarnation today is the migrant, and whose consciousness is that of the intellectual and artist in exile, the political figure between domains, between forms, between homes, and between languages'. And it is this association of migrant and intellectual that makes it possible for Said 'to regard the intellectual as first distilling then articulating the predicaments that disfigure modernity – mass deportation, imprisonment, population transfer, collective dispossession, and forced immigration'. Note the terms 'distilling' and 'articulating' – at this point, Said's language comes perilously close to saying that it is the intellectual who speaks for the migrant.

When we consider the politics of migrancy in a place like Hong Kong today, it is necessary both to hold on to Said's reminders, as well as to change the terms and foci of analysis. To begin with, it cannot be a matter of addressing exclusively the plight of intellectual exiles and political refugees, even if these are the cases that for different reasons attract the most attention. There are also other more mundane migrancies, a whole grey area accompanied not by violent displacements but by a series of small dislocations; associated with little shifts in experience that are not only not traumatic, but often not even noticeable. This is the migrancy of everyday life, a widespread and generalised form of migrancy which, I have already suggested, is the result of changes in urban space and the nature of place. What I want to suggest now is that this everyday migrancy, too, needs to be addressed, all the more so because it is defined by no images of outrage and gross injustice, and also because, in spite of this, it has the quiet capacity to falsify everyday experience.

Let me illustrate with an architectural example of housing estates introduced by British colonialism. This is Wah Fu Estate in Pokfulam, one of the first government-subsidised low-rental housing estates built in Hong Kong. Any visitor who ventures beyond the main tourist areas will find many of these housing estates – on Hong Kong island, in Kowloon and the New Towns. For those who have heard about the notoriously high cost of Hong Kong property, it may be surprising to learn that, in fact, over 50 per cent of the population live in low-cost government estates. Next to Singapore, Hong Kong has the world's largest housing programme relative to the size of the population, making it more like a welfare state in this respect than a colony and the quintessential capitalist enclave. What the paradox points to is that important mutations have taken place in colonialism and capitalism, which take one form in the era of imperialism and another form in the era of globalism. For a long time now, colonial space in Hong Kong has stopped being simply a space of greed and exploitation, taking on more elusive qualities. For example, we will have to try very hard if we want to show that there is indeed a correlation between, on the one hand, the government-subsidised housing estates, and on the other hand, the high cost of property elsewhere in the private sector (among the highest in the world) and the low cost of labour. In other words, in spite of appearances, and whether by accident or design, building housing estates, too, serves in the long run the interests of the capitalist state, but – and this is the point I want to emphasise – at a level that is not immediately perceptible. The example is a lesson in visual culture. It shows that something has happened to images. Colonial space as migrant space means that images of the city now tell us little directly about the city. What we see is not what we get. Capitalist history *disappears in the benevolent images of the housing estates.*

In this context, to disappear does not mean to become non-existent. It means rather that appearances (images) are far from self-evidential, although they conspire to be so. I will have more to say about this problematic of disappearance which architecture in Hong Kong shares with cinema. For the time being, what I am proposing is a redirection of attention from the politicised figure of the migrant who forces on us the awful truths of contemporary history, to the ordinary spaces of migrancy, with its capacity to falsify experience, including the experience of history; a redirection of attention from the 'true' to the 'false', from the truth of migrancy to the falsity of disappearance. As history disappears, in the structures, images, and events of everyday life, our methodological starting point will have to be what Walter Benjamin called 'the object riddled with error'. What I am suggesting is that, besides a politics of events, which of course is still necessary, we also need another complementary politics, a politics of disappearance where epistemological disorientation counts as a political fact.

Let me briefly consider in the shadow of such a politics a more complex example: the Hong Kong Handover. Representation of this event, which is without question of great historical importance, is polarised around two images, which are really mirror images of each other. In both, Hong Kong history disappears.

One image is of the Handover as liberation from colonialism and the reintegration of Hong Kong to China, even though 'colonialism' in this old sense has long been over. To celebrate the occasion, there were firework displays, performances and parades, some of which were incredibly but amusingly ridiculous, like the dance of the credit cards to represent Hong Kong as a global city, and the parade of world currencies to show Hong Kong as a world financial centre – with the placard for the British pound displayed inadvertently upside down! Perhaps worse were the serious performances, notably the symphony commissioned from the New York-based Chinese composer Tan Dun, featuring the cellist Yo-yo Ma. *Symphony '97* is a programmatic piece, but it is a programme of clichés with quotes from Richard Strauss and Beethoven to symbolise the West, the use of the much publicised 2,500-year-old Chinese bells to symbolise the East, and movie music and a children's choir to symbolise the present and future of Hong Kong, all performed in great earnestness. Architecture, too, played a part. The Handover ceremony itself, attended by Chinese dignitaries like Jiang Zemin and other state representatives from all over the world, took place in a new building, an extension to the Convention and Exhibition Center, a visually striking building on the waterfront of Causeway Bay that vaguely resembles the Sydney Opera House. We are told that the wing-like roofs are supposed to symbolise the new Hong Kong as a bird about to take flight. But what, we might ask, prevents us from seeing it as a predatory bird that has just landed? These competing interpretations, though, are really beside the point, because what is essential is only that the building looks spectacular and photogenic. The result, as we see, is something designed like a film set. It is literally an Exhibition Hall where history is an exhibit, a history that will be telecast live all over the world. But this history, of mediatised facts and events, is beginning to look by the day more and more staged, turning those who believe it into 'victims of the set' (Virilio); that is to say, the set as set-up.

The other image of the Handover is apprehension over the death of democracy, even though Hong Kong under British rule never had any democracy to speak of, or indeed until recently, made any demands for it. Who speaks for democracy now? First and ironically, the British ex-governor Chris Patten who, in a final policy speech, outlined what he called '16 benchmarks' for a democratic society, at the moment when the bench was being pulled away from under him. The other voice, the Democratic Party, presents a different case. It is the political party with the most popular support but now marginalised from the new SAR government; led by figures like Martin Lee, widely respected for his elegant intransigence and sincerity; a party that forged its unity in the wake of the Tiananmen Massacre. Yet what is a little disturbing is that even they resort to spectacle and crude melodrama in their representations of history. For example, in its last 4 June rally before the Handover, in Victoria Park, they commissioned a Danish sculptor to produce a work called the 'Pillar of shame'. Its message is all too obvious. The sculpture is made up of contorted faces. Placed in the middle of Victoria Park, it alludes in an overtly ironic way to the 'Monument to the people's heroes' in Tiananmen Square itself, thus turning Victoria Park into almost a replica of the Square; while everyone holding up a lighted candle that night was turned into a 'Goddess of Democracy'. It seems to me that the images of the Handover from either side are a kind of simplification, just as Tan Dun's *Symphony '97* is as much a piece of kitsch as the 'Pillar of shame'. And it is in these simplifications that history appears and disappears.

Let me try now to draw some working principles from the discussion so far. The rule seems to be that the more complex the space, the more simplistic the images used to represent it will tend to be. In other words, in case of confusion, reach for the cliché. In Hong Kong today, history is both a matter of great urgency and strangely absent. A large part of it seems to have slipped away into some other dimension, migrated elsewhere, but – and this is the important point – not without leaving its mark on the cultural space of the city, particularly on architecture and cinema. Like the invisible man in James Whale's cinematic masterpiece of special effects, this history is perceptible not directly but only through the *effects* it has on things around it. Tracing this other history, of migrancy and disappearance, requires a shift in attention away from the immediacy of events to the space in which they take place. Such a spatial history will have to count architecture and cinema among its primary sources of historical evidence.

What I propose to do now is to give not a history or a survey of Hong Kong architecture, but to look at some ways in which migrancy and disappearance are part of its form and substance; in other words, to examine the relation between migrancy and architecture at a crucial moment in Hong Kong history. It is construction, as Walter Benjamin noted, that occupies the role of the subconscious. I will do so by outlining four themes: (a) anamorphosis and Hong Kong architecture; (b) architecture as the allegorical representation of global networks; (c) infrastructure and the 'city as airport'; and, after a discussion of the Hong Kong cinema, (d) the question of 'straight' and 'perverse' architecture.

ANAMORPHOSIS

Perhaps one way of catching the elusiveness of disappearance is to compare it to anamorphosis and the visual surprises it produces. Anamorphosis is the use of a distorted grid, and painters concerned with the problematics of perception have long been fascinated by it. A very recent example is a work by the American, Mark Tansey, called '*Judging*'. Looked at directly, the painting shows a panel of judges, as in sports or beauty contests, awarding wildly different marks to what looks like cloud formations. However, viewed from the side, viewed distractedly, the cloud formations begin to resemble Michelangelo's *Last Judgement*. In Hong Kong architecture there is no obvious use of distorted grids and few surprises. Nevertheless, the combination of stable building forms in the midst of an unstable problematic history creates its own distortions. Let me give two examples, and it is not by accident that they are both examples of preserved public buildings, where the question of 'history' is itself foregrounded.

The first example is the auditoria complex of the Hong Kong Cultural Center designed by the government Architectural Services Department in the mid-1970s, but only completed in 1989; that is to say, at a moment when the question of a separate Hong Kong 'identity' was very much on the public mind. (Today, this has already changed, and all the talk is of the Handover as a 'return home'.) The Cultural Center is built on the site of the demolished Victorian-style Hong Kong-Canton railway station. Consider the design. The main structure which houses the auditoria is one of those modernist placeless structures which could be from anywhere, looking like nothing so much as a giant ski slope. As if to compensate for the neglect of the local, one significant design detail was introduced. The clock tower in red brick from the demolished railway station was saved and incorporated into the overall design.

At one level, this 'quotation' from Hong Kong's architectural history is the expression of a sense of historical moment, giving to the Cultural Center a sense of local history, the preservation of cultural and urban forms as the preservation of cultural identity. But at another level this 'history' is no more than decorative, like an instant patina added to the new, as in the many examples of 'antiques' that we can buy on Hong Kong's Hollywood Road. As such, this 'history' has no power to stir memory.

I might try to suggest something about the function of the clock tower by comparing it to that strange-looking, hard to construe, anamorphic object floating on the bottom of Holbein's famous painting *The Ambassadors*, a painting that Lacan analysed in his discussion of the gaze. In both cases, something in the visual field does not seem to 'fit'. It is, however, the difference between the two cases that I will emphasise, and that tells us something about a space of disappearance. Lacan's analysis is by now well known (Lacan 1978: 79–90). Faced with *The Ambassadors*, the viewing subject caught in the gaze, i.e. in the perspectival space that dominates most of the painting, cannot construe the distorted anamorphic object as the representation of a skull. The gaze, therefore, is a channelling and socialising of desire by exclusion: it makes one space, the perspectival one, recognisable and turns the space of the anamorphic image into an hallucination, and so excludes it from easy recognition. But when we do recognise it, there is a sense of shock. The skull is both a *memento mori*, and a destabilisation of the power of perspective. Anamorphosis in Holbein opens up the visual field to critical attention. Consider now the case of the Hong Kong clock tower, which dates from the heyday of Hong Kong's colonial history and which might raise difficult questions about how such a history can now be perceived. However, unlike Holbein's skull, this anachronistic structure seems to present no difficulties for perception at all. In fact, the clock tower is seen *too easily*, and is too quickly assimilated into the overall spatial ensemble (as a general instance of 'Hong Kong history'). Space is homogenised, as 'old' and 'new', 'modern' and 'traditional', are placed together in contiguity and continuity. Note that there is, here, also a spatial programming and socialising of desire, but it operates through *inclusion*, in that it consists of making us accept, without shock or protest, the most blatant discontinuities as continuities. This is disappearance as a kind of second-level or reverse anamorphosis, because in this instance, the historical contradictions are covered over by the *seamlessness* of the implied historical narrative. Thus, it is preservation-as-history, as instant history or as substitute for history, that brings about the disappearance of history. Unlike Holbein's skull, which provokes, the function of the clock tower is to make us forget.

My second example is Flagstaff House, and I can deal with it more quickly. Flagstaff House is a fine colonial-style building constructed in the 1840s. First used as the headquarters of Jardine, Matheson and Company, the first and most important *hong* in Hong Kong, and then as headquarters of the British military, it was later converted into a residence for the commander of the British forces. More recently, with the withdrawal of the British military presence in Hong Kong, there was some debate on what to do with the building. Eventually, the government's Architectural Services Department decided to preserve it by turning it into a museum to house a magnificent collection of Chinese teaware. This was done in 1984, and in 1989 the building was declared a monument. In this way, a historically significant building is saved from the bulldozers and the general public gets an education in Chinese culture. All sides, it would seem, stand to benefit from such an arrangement, and there is some truth in this. However, there is a certain, presumably unintended, irony here, not only in the dates 1984 (the year of the Joint Declaration) and 1989 (the year of Tiananmen) but also in the historical associations that tea has with the Opium Wars and the British gunboat diplomacy that secured Hong Kong for Britain in the first place. This reincarnation of a British military establishment in the form of a museum of Chinese teaware skims over the monumental barbarisms of the nineteenth century by aestheticising them out of existence. Flagstaff House could be read, therefore, as an example of the disappearance of history: not in the sense of history's having come to an end, but in the sense of its blind, uncritical preservation. The metamorphosis of Flagstaff House is also an anamorphosis.

MIGRANCY AND THE ALLEGORICAL REPRESENTATION OF GLOBAL NETWORKS

As a kind of rebuttal to the sentimental and fictitious myths of identity seen in the two public buildings is the daily experience, not always comfortable, of Hong Kong's inscription in the global economy. Here, I will be referring not so much to obvious architectural symbols of global capital like I.M. Pei's China Bank building or Norman Foster's Hong Kong Bank building, but to cases where globalism is more indirectly or allegorically represented. Before we come to that, let me say something about the global city.

According to Manual Castells, not only is Hong Kong a global city; his very educated guess is that the Hong Kong-Shenzen-Canton-Pearl River Delta-Macau-Zhuhai metropolitan system is, in fact, a megacity in the making, which though 'only vaguely perceived in most of the world at this time, is likely to become the most representative urban face of the twenty-first century (Castells 1996: 409). What concerns me, however, is what Castells has to say about the spatial characteristics of megacities: '[W]hat is most significant about megacities is that they are connected externally to global networks and to segments of their own countries, while internally disconnecting local populations that are either functionally unnecessary or socially disruptive' (Castells 1996: 404). This is interesting because, though Hong Kong is not yet a megacity in the physical sense, the pattern of global connections and local disconnections that Castells outlines is, nevertheless, already there in some of Hong Kong's urban spaces, allegorically represented in an anticipatory and sometimes brutally frank way. These spaces are fixated on a speculative future, just as the spaces we have just discussed are fixated on a fictitious past. We can distinguish between two kinds of allegorical representations: by means of gentrification, and by means of indifference.

The most obvious example of gentrification in Hong Kong is the entertainment area around Lan Kwei Fong. The area has now spilled over into Staunton Street, which some PR people are already calling the new SoHo, because it happens to lie south of Hollywood Road. Not too long ago, Lan Kwei Fong was just an unremarkable and unfashionable bit of space on the commercial periphery of Central, with its narrow streets, little shops and low-grade offices, local restaurants, flower stalls and street cobblers. Lan Kwei Fong was just part of Hong Kong's anonymous urban vernacular. Then a string of smart restaurants began to appear in the area, followed by European-style beer halls serving special brews, coffee bars, Hong Kong's only jazz club, art galleries and just generally stylish meeting places. The flower stalls and street cobblers are still there, next to hi-tech chrome and Plexiglass shop fronts. We find here more than just a mixed space, a juxtaposition of the Western and the local. The local is preserved, but in the process becomes dislocated. Gentrification here means not just a general upgrading, a rise in class; it means essentially a specific appropriation and infiltration by an elsewhere of the local. The elsewhere gets a local habitation and a name. So it is that in Lan Kwei Fong we get a factitious sense of being in Hong Kong, Europe and America all at once, of being here, there and everywhere – just like in the Beatles' song! It is true of course that locals, too, go to Lan Kwei Fong, but only those who can afford it: an 'economic' way of selective exclusion.

My second example of the allegorical representation of global networks is the recently built mall-and-entertainment complex called Times Square. The name itself, like the Staunton Street SoHo, is an allusion to elsewhere, specifically, to New York; the difference is that it is not, as in Lan Kwei Fong, an elsewhere that infiltrates the local, but an elsewhere that is quite aggressively indifferent to, and disconnected from, the local. One surprising thing about Times Square is its choice of location, on Russell Street which at the time was a local market street. The mall, however, is not so much sited in a local area as it is a para-site of the local, and not integrated with it. It was designed as an autonomous inner-looking space, indifferent to its surroundings, strangely dislocated. Visitors to the mall can ride up and down on its glass-cased elevators, and thus protected by the mall itself, look out with a certain pleasure straight into the interiors and rooftops of the run-down apartment houses just a few metres away on the other side of Russell Street. Since the mall's construction, some distinctive places have opened up across the street. Besides the usual multinational retailers like DKNY, Guess and so on, we also find a kind of simulacrum of the old street food stalls known as *Dai Pai Dongs*, but now made relatively comfortable and hygienic. In the simulacral version, the food is local but the prices are international.

INFRASTRUCTURE AND THE 'CITY AS AIRPORT'

Spaces like Lan Kwei Fong and Times Square would not have been possible in Hong Kong before the process of Hong Kong's increasing inscription in the global economy began in earnest. These spaces are indirectly and allegorically the representations of this process. They give us at the level of everyday social life the spatial experience of the global, which can be defined as essentially the breaking down of boundaries of all kinds: spatial, temporal and experiential. From this point of view, they are doing at the level of social life what the new airport is doing at the level of infrastructure. Let me say a quick word about this.

Unlike the old Kai Tak Airport, which is situated right in the middle of the urban area, the new airport at Chek Lap Kok is 21 miles from the city, but only about 25 minutes away by rail. Therefore, it is not so much the airport being distanced from the city, as the city being integrated to the airport with a number of major infrastructural projects, including new highways, railways and bridges. The result, according to Nanoori Matsuda, a professor of architecture at the University of Hong Kong, will not be the 'airport as city', something large and self-contained, but separate and distinguishable from the city, like London's Heathrow for example; rather, it will be 'the city as airport', something very different, where the *boundaries* between airport and city are erased. Infrastructure now becomes the *interface*, that is to say, more than and different from a mere system of connections, and more and more of the city will begin to be absorbed by this interface. The airport is designed to handle 38 million passengers a year, a number that will rise to 45 million by the end of the century. Compare this with a present population of around six million, and we see how the transit passenger will replace in importance the citizen who inhabits the city. In the not too distant future, the question of the nature of citizenship in the megacity will have to be asked.

'STRAIGHT' AND 'PERVERSE' ARCHITECTURE

According to Paul Virilio, airports are 'a foreshadowing of future society: no longer a society of sedentarization, but one of passage [. . .] one concentrated in the vector of transportation' (Virilio and Lotringer 1983: 64). However, Virilio's statement needs some qualification, for even though migrancy may well be an everyday reality, this does not necessarily mean it has to be recognised as such or built upon. For example, one way of forgetting the question of migrancy is to make architecture narrowly practical and predictable, to make it predominantly a question of economics and construction techniques. This, in fact, is the present state of Hong Kong architecture. In Hong Kong there is more building and rebuilding taking place than in practically any other place in the world, but very little reflection on building. These are architecture's self-imposed limits; it limits itself to the praxis of building and ignores the parapraxis. But in keeping to the straight and narrow, Hong Kong architecture shows its historical myopia: it does not see that techniques of construction are part of a larger cultural field.

The question that still needs to be asked, of course, is how 'static' architectural forms can address the issues of migrancy and disappearance. It is at this point that a discussion of the cinematic and the relation of cinema to architecture may prove quite illuminating. In the cinematic, it is through the movement of images that the appearance of stable shapes and forms is produced, what Godard ironically calls truth at 24 frames per second. Cinema resolves the opposition between 'stability' and 'movement'. The cinematic gives us this visual paradox: the static is not the opposite of movement, the static is a *function* of movement. It is possible to imagine, therefore, a relation between architecture and the cinematic that has nothing to do with shots of buildings in films, but has to do with the way in which both share a common problematic: how time enters to complicate the grid of stable forms and images. This is how we can understand what Paul Virilio calls 'the aesthetics of disappearance':

> The question today therefore is no longer to know if cinema can do without place but if places can do without cinema [. . .] literally as well as figuratively, from now on *architecture is only a movie*; an un-habitual motility is successor to the habitudes of the city.
>
> (Virilio 1991a: 64–5)

And this is why Virilio says elsewhere that the study of urban space today will have to learn not so much from Las Vegas, as Robert Venturi and company asserted, as from Hollywood (Virilio 1991b: 26).

What, then, can Hong Kong architecture learn from Hong Kong cinema? My own sense is that if the Hong Kong cinema became so riveting from the 1980s onward, it is precisely because it took the risk of addressing the problematics of migrancy and disappearance and found ways of doing so (see Abbas 1997a, 1997b). It did this not through 'realism', but by presenting to us a space that slips away if we try to grasp it too directly; a space that cinema coaxes into existence by whatever means at its disposal, including the fantastic. To take a classic example, in a film like *Rouge*, director Stanley Kwan reinvents the popular genre of the ghost story. The film is about a woman who committed suicide in the 1930s returning to the Hong Kong of the 1980s in search of her lover. Kwan uses the ghost figure as a device for temporal juxtaposition, to evoke something about the nature of time, space and affectivity in the contemporary city. He uses a ghost to catch a ghost. In this and other examples, it is by abandoning a narrow idea of relevance that Hong Kong cinema registers something that might otherwise be missed.

The film I want to say something about now is Wong Kar Wai's *Happy Together*, partly because it is a film that seems to be quite carefully constructed around the complexities of migrancy. The story centres around three men, a homosexual couple from Hong Kong and a Taiwanese, who somehow drifted to Buenos Aires. To begin with, there is a spatial symmetry of opposites. At one level, Buenos Aires is the antipode of Hong Kong, the other side of the world. Day in one place is night in the other, summer is winter and so on. There is even a Georg Baselitz-like shot late in the film of Hong Kong upside down. But at another level, the spatial experiences are not that different. Buenos Aires is shot the way Hong Kong is shot in Wong's other film *Chungking Express*: in fragments and in medium shots. These are no long shots of the city or clichéd shots of the architectural skyline as *the* city. Both cities take on the quality of what Gilles Deleuze has called *any-space-whatever*: ordinary spaces which have somehow lost their particularity and system of interconnectedness. In this sense then, 'here' and 'elsewhere' are exchangeable, 'home' itself loses its specificity and 'homelessness' its pathos. Yet, in spite of this 'drifting', the characters themselves hold on to some notion of someday returning home, just as even after repeated disappointments they still look for happiness. 'Space' and 'affectivity' are not congruent with each other – but it is around these incongruities and *oscillations* that the film is built up. In one sense then, the title *Happy Together* is ironic. It suggests that, in a migrant space, happiness goes together with disappointment, and this is as true of homosexual love as of any other kind. The characters always miss the right moment; they cannot be happy *and* together at the same time. Yet, in another sense, the title is not ironic at all, because the characters remain eudaemonists, believers in happiness, always ready to come together and, in the key phrase of the film, 'start over again'. We find here what I will call *serial eudaemonism*, which might just be the migrant form of happiness.

What question, then, does cinema pose for Hong Kong architecture? It shows that in the main, architecture has not come out of the closet. What we see is basically 'straight' architecture, 'interesting' architecture, i.e. architecture very much concerned with doing the right thing; whether it is acquiring the services of renowned architects that can provide a 'brand name' building, or following trends like 'postmodernism', or more generally studying the building code to get the most square footage out of expensive land. This is because it is either insensitive or indifferent to the larger social space of architecture, and represses the experience of migrancy and disappearance, which appear in buildings only as parapraxis. As a result, space is in danger of being deprived of what does not fit conventional ideas of affectivity and pleasure. It is deprived of perversity and fascination. It is deprived of choice. But like Wong's eudaemonists, I would like to ask how Hong Kong architecture can 'start over again'.

What, then, should Hong Kong architecture be like? The only, admittedly tentative, way to answer this question, it seems to me, is not by being prescriptive (we know where that leads), or by amateurishly designing a building. It would be more useful and practical to open up a critical dialogue that involves architect and non-architect, to come together with the architect to create a critical community which shows that architecture is not constructed by the architect alone. In the Hong Kong case, this may be a matter of learning from disappearance.

REFERENCES

Abbas, A. (1997a) 'The erotics of disappointment', in J.-M. Lalanne, D. Martinez, A. Abbas and J. Ngai (eds) *Wong Kar-wai*, Paris: Editions Dis Voir.

Abbas, A. (1997b) *Hong Kong: culture and the politics of disappearance*, Minneapolis: University of Minnesota Press.

Castells, M. (1996) *The Rise of the Network Society*, Oxford: Blackwell.

Lacan, J. (1978) *The Four Fundamental Concepts of Psychoanalysis*, trans. A. Sheridan, New York: N.W. Norton.

Said, E. (1993) *Culture and Imperialism*, New York: Alfred A. Knopf.

Virilio, P. (1991a) *The Aesthetics of Disappearance*, trans. P. Beitchman, New York: Semiotext(e).

Virilio, P. (1991b) *The Lost Dimension*, New York: Semiotext(e).

Virilio, P. and Lotringer, S. (1983) *Pure War*, trans. M. Polizotti, New York: Semiotext(e).

Chapter 8: Conflicting landscapes of dwelling and democracy in Canada[1]

Katharyne Mitchell

> I grew up in Shaughnessy, on Balfour Street, and have watched closely the changes happening within it. I am saddened and disgusted when I walk through it today to see so many of the trees and houses gone, only to be replaced by hideous monster houses!! I talked to a construction worker who was working on one of these new atrocities they call a house [. . .] he said, and I quote, 'the house is a piece of shit, and will probably be falling to pieces in ten years.' So, is this what Shaughnessy is to become? We need assurances that the character of the neighbourhood will be maintained!
>
> (Letter to Vancouver City Council, 10 April, 1990)

Imagine Walter Benjamin's angel of history looking back from the twenty-first century. This Shaughnessy neighbourhood, a landscape of creative destruction in fin de siècle Vancouver, BC, draws his particular interest. Is it because the houses truly are 'pieces of shit' that are 'falling to pieces', the piles of debris growing skyward at an especially alarming rate? Or does the angel take a philosophical turn and, like Benjamin himself, seek to understand how a particular urban landscape entered the public consciousness and held sway over its imagination, how it was a 'precise material replica of the internal consciousness, or rather, the *un*conscious of the dreaming collective?' (Buck-Morss 1991: 39).

The nineteenth-century shopping arcades of Berlin and Paris were, for Benjamin, potent historical artefacts, public spaces that could illuminate not just the physical experience of a particular time and place, but the actual consciousness of an entire metropolitan generation. Benjamin was drawn to these buildings because of their central role in a narrative of capitalism and modernity, a narrative that he wished to both elucidate and debunk. The arcades, as public paeans to progress and the commodity, served as the perfect conduit for this comprehensive critical project: their advanced technological construction, saturated years of consumer glut, and early demise provided, for Benjamin, the material evidence of 'all of the errors of bourgeois consciousness [. . .] as well as all of its utopian dreams' (Buck-Morss 1991: 39).

The Parisian arcades are seen and used as evidence of rupture in the seeming seamlessness of capitalist progress. But what of these new 'atrocities they call a house' constructed in the somewhat less famous locale of Shaughnessy Heights? What intervention in the narrative of capital and the commodity is witnessed here? How has this contemporary landscape provided the material evidence of a moment of rupture sufficient to attract the special attention of the *Angelus Novus*?

The ruptures here are now familiar moments in the landscapes of dwelling and migrancy in the global era. The architecture of a suburban landscape entered the public consciousness of a population and formed a psychical as well as material condensation point for residents because it refracted, in inescapable detail, the profound changes jolting the society. The so-called *monster* houses named in the letter above, were purchased largely by a wealthy group of migrants from Hong Kong, who entered Vancouver in a special business immigration programme designed to attract economic migrants to Canada. Many of these migrants transferred capital with them, and their interest in investing this capital in Vancouver housing and commercial buildings helped to trigger a wider, speculative real estate frenzy in the city. With the purchase of monster houses, along with other substantial chunks of real estate throughout the city, the Hong Kong economic migrants quite literally brought contemporary, often paradoxical forces of dispersion, dwelling and diaspora 'home' to the heretofore protected spaces of suburban Shaughnessy Heights. In addition to looking at the conflict-laden struggles over the reconstitution of dwelling – its meanings and associated desires – which this caused, I also want to focus, in particular, on the specific conflicts that arose around the zoning related to these extra-large houses, and on the ways in which the land use decisions and controversies within the neighbourhood spurred a rethinking of democracy and the public sphere in the city and the country at large.

Shaughnessy Heights is a wealthy, upper-class neighbourhood located in the west-side of Vancouver (Figure 8.1). One of the features of rapid change evident in Shaughnessy and many of the city's other west-side neighbourhoods in the 1980s was the demolition of older homes dating from the nineteenth and early twentieth centuries, and the construction of new and extremely large houses in their place. These larger homes came to be known as monster houses. Such houses generally extended to the edges of the lot, were built to the maximum allowable height, and often occupied the maximum lot surface coverage and square footage. They were commonly large, rectangular and relatively boxy in form, and were typified by such features as a grand entranceway with double doors, a two-storey entrance hall and large, symmetrical, unshuttered windows (Figure 8.2). Many of these windows incorporated glass brick detailing. The external finishes of these houses generally consisted of brick or stone veneer on the ground floor, with stucco, vinyl or cedar siding on the first.

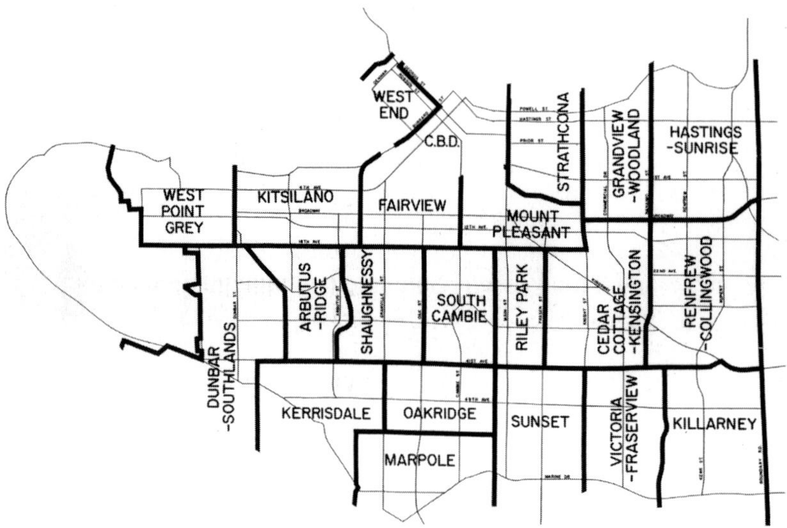

Figure 8.1
VANCOUVER NEIGHBOURHOODS.
(All figures in this chapter are by the author)

Figure 8.2
A 'MONSTER HOUSE' IN KERRISDALE.

Figure 8.3
A TYPICAL ENGLISH COTTAGE-STYLE HOUSE IN KERRISDALE, LOCATED OPPOSITE THE HOUSE IN FIGURE 8.2.

Often, the area around the house was paved and fenced, while the landscaping was usually quite sparse. The newly constructed houses contrasted vividly – in form, structure, scale, aesthetic and urban sensibility – with the historicist styles of the existing residential architecture in its picturesque suburban streetscapes (Figure 8.3).

The vivid contrast in architectural styles and urban attitudes that the new housing generated provided a highly visible manifestation of the economic and cultural changes then under way in Vancouver. Most of these changes were associated with the transnational flows of capital, culture and people from Hong Kong and Taiwan – flows which increased sharply in the 1980s and early 1990s. These expanded transnational movements across the Pacific were facilitated by federal regulatory shifts in the areas of immigration, finance and land control. New Canadian immigration procedures initiated in the 1980s, for example, allowed those with money to jump the processing queue and enter Canada ahead of others awaiting visas.[2] Following Thatcher's signing of the 1984 treaty which ceded control of Hong Kong to China in 1997, tens of thousands of wealthy Hong Kong Chinese took advantage of this newly permeable border and moved to Canada to establish citizenship.[3]

In addition to the easing of immigration restrictions, financial borders were also deregulated, allowing easier and quicker foreign investment in numerous sectors of the economy, including real estate (Tickell 2000). With respect to the regulation and control of land, provinces such as British Columbia began a vast campaign to sell off Crown land, much of which had been acquired during the previous provincial administration. This privatization of large swathes of land provided a great stimulus for global real estate players such as Li Ka-shing to invest in the region. His acquisition of the former Expo '86 lands (comprising one-sixth of the Vancouver downtown) was but one of numerous ventures by Hong Kong business interests into Vancouver real estate during the latter part of the decade (see Gutstein 1990).

The long-standing connections between Canada's major west coast city and the cities of the Asian Pacific Rim were thus strengthened and accelerated by the processes of global restructuring affecting each region. The physical transformation of Vancouver's built environment associated with these heightened connections was immense and was met with great dismay from a large section of the local population. Cultural and economic changes visibly demonstrated in the proliferation of monster houses in the west-side, threatened various kinds of identity for established Vancouver residents. As a result of the perceived threat to established values, aesthetics and atmosphere in neighbourhoods such as Shaughnessy Heights, efforts were made to arrest these changes through what were perceived as openly public avenues of land use opinion and decision-making. As I will show later, however, this understanding of 'the public' and who constituted it, quickly became a major source of contestation.

Changes in the urban landscape of Shaughnessy Heights focused public consciousness on the processes and repercussions of the transnational flows characteristic of late capitalism. The primary condensation point for these processes of change was the monster house, a residential form in stark contrast with the architecture of the pre-existing streetscape. Conflict associated with the construction of monster houses occurred in putative public and democratic spaces such as local meeting halls and City Council chambers, and through neighbourhood property rights associations, urban planning sessions of the local Council, and the media. I argue that in these institutional spaces (both actual and discursive), through the struggles and resolutions connected with the monster house affair, a formative Canadian understanding of the liberal public sphere was contested and reworked. In the Vancouver context, the vigorous, highly racialized contestation over the urban landscape in spaces widely perceived to be democratic and public served to open up and call into question the meaning of the public; at the same time this contestation helped to expose past exclusions in the formation of public space and the public sphere, to engender a crisis in the accepted meanings of democracy and citizenship, and to trigger a rethinking of their relationship to contemporary Canadian society.

In my discussions of the liberal public sphere, I draw on the Habermasian notions of an ideal public sphere as a setting in which rational, equally empowered actors are able to deliberate concepts of justice and the future of society (Habermas 1989). In contemporary Canada, the ideology of the public sphere as a site of rational discourse is an important foundation and a key rhetoric. For a society founded on liberal democratic ideals, such as Canada, the public is the space where 'intuitive ideas' pave the way for a consensus on justice; it can also be understood as an arena of 'neutral principles' which allows the state to justify its policies on neutral, purely procedural grounds.[4] In the following section I examine the actual workings of institutions associated with the public sphere in the arena of land use decision-making. I show some of the historic exclusions from the so-called spaces of rational debate and individual choice in architecture and urban planning institutes, real estate agencies, and property owners' associations. Despite the ideal of rational decisions made for the public good by elected officials or volunteer leaders of society (e.g. those participating in property owners' associations), in effect most land use decisions have never encompassed all of the public. This is clearly manifested in both historic and contemporary class and ethnic exclusions from access to the information necessary for informed choice and from the discussions and decisions involving land and property in the neighbourhood of Shaughnessy Heights.

HISTORICAL EXCLUSIONS: OR THE POVERTY OF THE 'PUBLIC' SPHERE

Shaughnessy Heights was fashioned as an exclusive suburb of Vancouver since the Canadian Pacific Railroad subdivided the land in 1909. Through various exclusionary tactics of zoning, pricing, marketing and the imposition of informal covenants, the area was established for, and remained controlled by, wealthy Anglo-Canadians throughout its early history. This interest in Shaughnessy Heights as an exclusive suburban development continued through the Second World War, and the carefully defined borders between east-side and west-side communities in Vancouver became further entrenched during these years. While east-side and downtown neighbourhoods were seen as ethnically mixed, west-side neighbourhoods, such as Shaughnessy, remained coded as 'white' through the Second World War, and in some areas well into the 1970s. Family incomes in the neighbourhood were consistently the highest in the city (see Vancouver Local Areas 1985, 1988; Barman 1986: 114–15).

Although Shaughnessy Heights had been protected by strict zoning covenants since the original Canadian Pacific Railroad (CPR) subdivision of the land, these regulations became even stricter in the 1980s in response to the increasing threat of streetscape change. In May of 1982, after a background report was prepared by the Vancouver City Planning Department (at the instigation of the SHPOA and at municipal expense), the City Council rezoned the Shaughnessy local area from RS-4 (One Family Dwelling District) to a special zoning category called FSD (First Shaughnessy District).[5] The Director of Planning wrote of the role of the SHPOA in this change:

> Early initiatives undertaken by the Shaughnessy Heights Property Owners' Association were instrumental in drawing City Council's attention to the need for a new plan in

> Shaughnessy. SHPOA played a key role in responding to those pressures threatening to destroy the historic and aesthetic character of First Shaughnessy by developing a set of goals and recommendations for the area.
>
> (Vancouver 1982: ii)

On the same day as this shift in zoning status, the City Council further approved a series of 'design guidelines' for the area, amended the subdivision by-law, and established the First Shaughnessy Advisory Design Panel (Vancouver 1989). The design panel was established to serve as an additional level of protection against unwanted development by reviewing proposed developments with respect to both the original Shaughnessy by-law and the First Shaughnessy Design Guidelines. These extremely detailed guidelines specified the preservation of such architectural design features as roof, entrance and fire escape treatment, as well as broader principles of massing and siting. The correct roof treatment, for example, was delineated in three main points: roof slope, which stipulated the levels of roof pitch in the order of a 1:1 ratio; roofscape, which called for the use of gables and dormers to accentuate volume; and roof silhouette, which drew attention to the 'appropriate' sequence of volumes and roof lines along the streetscape (Vancouver 1987: 21). The language for the preferred entrance treatment was a similarly complex tri-partite set of recommendations, such as:

> Space leading up to the main entrance of the principal building should be treated as an 'antechamber' that emphasizes the transition from the street to the house. This antechamber effect is created by: defining the front yard as a semi-enclosed 'vestibule' through the arrangement of trees, hedges, walls or other landscaping devices.
>
> (Vancouver 1987: 22)

All of these verbal guidelines were accompanied by illustrations of the preferred designs and of existing houses in Shaughnessy Heights.

The SHPOA attempted to extend these strict guidelines to Second and Third Shaughnessy (the southern end of the district) with a preliminary design report in 1984. In this report, the growing desire to keep out the new, extra-large houses and to retain the old houses was explicit. The old houses were described as 'interesting without being overpoweringly busy in appearance', while the new houses were seen as ostentatiously decorated, 'thin and flat' (cited in Ley 1995: 194). One of the primary characteristics of the older landscape that was heralded in many of the reports was its quality of 'neighbourliness'. In the Design Guidelines adopted by City Council in May, 1982, for example, it was claimed that:

> the combination of sensitive siting, design and use of materials creates a sense of harmony or neighbourliness in Shaughnessy. In part, the brief period in which most

> homes were built accounts for the development of a particularly attractive and enduring streetscape. The original homes do not compete with each other in composition, massing, siting, colour, quality and use of materials and architectural style. It is in effect a balanced form of architectural expression.
>
> (Vancouver 1987: 13)

In this statement, as in many others, neighbourliness is heralded as involving an attractive and *enduring* streetscape, as well as a non-competitive, balanced and harmonious atmosphere. It is precisely this celebration and reification of neighbourliness and community that will be taken up in the latter sections of the chapter. Further efforts to establish stricter zoning amendments to both massing and house style in South Shaughnessy and the adjacent southern neighbourhoods of Kerrisdale and Oakridge were undertaken jointly by the City Council and the SHPOA in 1988 and 1990.

NEIGHBOURHOOD CHARACTER AND SOCIAL REPRODUCTION

Why was there a threat of streetscape change at this particular moment in time? Why were there even stricter massing and architectural design stipulations added to the earlier, already rigid regulations? Why the closing of ranks around seemingly insignificant details such as the preservation of roof, entrance and fire escape treatment in the 1980s? Much of the fuss over changes in streetscape design in Shaughnessy arose in the early 1980s in response to the rapid transformation of many east-side communities in the prior decade. A number of extremely large houses, known locally as 'Vancouver Specials', appeared in east-side neighbourhoods in the 1970s. These new houses provoked fear that the carefully regulated borders demarcating communities would be lost in the advent of rapid urban transformation. With the disappearance of an exclusive architectural and landscape design, residents worried that the ability to preserve the 'character' of neighbourhoods would also be lost. In a public hearing of 1985, a spokesperson for the SHPOA expressed anxiety about the burgeoning Vancouver Specials and urged rapid action on a first set of proposed regulations for the neighbourhood. His comments were reported in a local west-side newspaper: 'You get three or four of these in a couple of blocks,' he explained, 'and all of a sudden you have completely changed the character of a neighbourhood.' Executive Secretary of the organization, Evelyn Mackay, said the 'threat' of Vancouver Specials had shaken the confidence of Shaughnessy residents in their ability to preserve the character of their area. 'This is a real threat to a neighbourhood–to have these oversized houses suddenly spring up on a street which we thought was safe and secure forever,' she remarked (Spence 1985: 7).

By the late 1980s, the incipient 'threat' to west-side neighbourhoods seemed confirmed, as the number of demolitions in the area skyrocketed

(Vancouver 1992). Numerous houses and five-storey walk-up apartments in west-side areas were torn down, some to be replaced with luxury condominiums, but most falling to what soon became widely referred to as the monster houses (*Vancouver Monitoring Program* 1992; *Vancouver Trends* 1992). The new houses varied in form and style in different neighbourhoods but were uniformly large in comparison with the other houses which remained on the street.

Before the arrival of the monster houses in the late 1980s, the restrictive planning measures enforced on lot divisions and lot and house prices in the northern third of Shaughnessy had ensured that any variation occurred only within a spectrum of extremely high-end designs and materials. The most common style for the area was the English Tudor manor, and the general ambience of the neighbourhood was that of the English landscape tradition (Kalman and Roaf 1974: 145–64; Holdsworth 1981, 1986: 29–30). The gently contoured lawns, scattered clumps of bushes and trees, irregular, curved shapes and natural-looking borders were patterned on the landscape tradition of Capability Brown and Humphry Repton, English garden and park designers of the eighteenth century.

The use of English architectural and landscape symbols in Vancouver's west-side neighbourhoods was deliberate. The CPR, which owned most of Point Grey, intentionally modelled the elite subdivision of Shaughnessy Heights on the pastoral myths of the English countryside (Duncan and Duncan 1984: 270; Duncan 1994). By claiming an ongoing, albeit transformed English tradition in the new spaces of Vancouver, an easy, unhurried grandeur and an idyllic, pre-industrial way of life gradually became recognized and incorporated as the symbols and codes of the new suburban elite of 'British' Columbia. The appropriation and reworking of these aesthetic symbols over time enabled residents of these neighbourhoods to feel pride of place, security and well-being, and to assume a universal notion of the 'appropriateness' of this landscape. Much of the anxiety of loss expressed in the late 1980s related not to the demolition of actual buildings or trees, but to a more general fear concerning the possible diminution, deprivation and dispossession of this Anglo-Canadian way of life.

For the Shaughnessy residents, this general atmosphere of fear, and the direct threat they felt to their way of life stemmed from the entry into the neighbourhood of wealthy Hong Kong Chinese 'business' immigrants, many of whom purchased the so-called monster houses in the late 1980s and early 1990s.[6] Owing to family ties, a good climate, and relative proximity to Hong Kong, a large percentage of this economic class chose to settle and purchase residential property in Vancouver in the late 1980s. Much of the residential investment was made in elite, relatively underpriced and highly desirable west-side neighbourhoods such as Shaughnessy Heights. This residential investment was just one component of major capital flows between Hong Kong and British Columbia in the late 1980s and early 1990s in the amounts of 1–2 billion dollars annually (Canada 1989; Macdonald 1990; Nash 1992: 3).

Despite government attempts to channel capital into productive sectors, the majority of Hong Kong money went into property investment. Larence Lim, a real estate broker at Goddard and Smith Realty Ltd, said of the real estate market in Vancouver in late 1989: 'The saturation point for Hong Kong investment in Vancouver real estate hasn't been reached yet because people now look at this city in a global context, whereas ten years ago only western Canadians were considered potential purchasers' (cited in Farrow 1989). The *Financial Post* estimated that in 1990, foreign investment in privately held real estate in Canada nearly tripled from the 1985 figure of US$1.2 billion. If the debt portion (bank financing) of the real estate transactions were included, the total investments of 1990 would exceed 13 billion (Fung 1991: 18).

The arrival of an outside group, perceived not only as a different class fragment, but also as a different race, signified the loss of exclusiveness in what had previously been an extremely homogeneous neighbourhood. Changes in the streetscape, including the demolitions of older houses, the removal of mature trees and the construction of extremely large houses, reflected many of the wider changes that were occurring in the socio-economic profile of the community at large. The inability of existing planning regulatory frameworks to protect the streetscape, which was felt to be a public good rightfully owned by community residents, was mirrored by its inability to protect the desirable character of the neighbourhood from change. This situation was understood in terms of 'loss' because it represented the rupture of a naturalized landscape of exclusion by the entry of groups which had historically been rendered as inappropriate to that landscape.[7]

Shaughnessy's streetscape operated historically as a repository of symbolic capital – a symbolic capital predicated on a double movement that generates and sustains both a sense of exclusivity and distinction from the excluded. The generation of this category of the excluded, the outsiders who live in different places and have different cultural tastes, allows the consolidation of an internal social identity within a limited and bounded locale. As Bourdieu (1984: 56) wrote:

> it is no accident that, when they (tastes) have to be justified, they are asserted purely negatively by the refusal of other tastes. Not only does taste identify a particular way of life with a particular class fragment through daily practices of consumption and lifestyle, it also legitimates that taste and casts others into doubt.

The ability to distinguish between tastes – good and bad, beautiful and 'atrocious', highbrow and lowbrow – aids the confirmation and marking of social identity. The anguish of the reaction against the streetscape changes in Shaughnessy betrayed the profound fear that the symbols of the established and dominant Anglo-Canadian group were being eroded, and with them, the chance of sustaining the rare rights and assets dependent upon a privileged position in social and geographical space.

Prior to the 1980s, the Shaughnessy streetscape was, aesthetically speaking, a space that remained separate from the other spaces within Vancouver. From its inception, the neighbourhood of Shaughnessy Heights had been deliberately produced for an elite group. This deliberate inaugurating move, however, was abstracted through time, so that by the late twentieth century, the relations between this particular neighbourhood and the Anglo-Canadian elite of the city appeared natural and appropriate. Following the norms of everyday life and given the 'proper' moral order, it came to seem 'natural' that this historic relationship between certain kinds of spaces and certain kinds of people would be quietly but inexorably reproduced. The particular transnational movement of capital and people arriving in tandem, that I have sketched, however, altered this stasis in ways that, to local residents, were new and shocking.

RECONSTRUCTING BORDERS AND RENORMALIZING THE LANDSCAPE

In the following section I examine the participation of the Vancouver City Council and several local newspapers in the effort to manage the transformation of the city occasioned by these massive flows of people and capital from Hong Kong. I argue that the reputedly neutral spaces of rational debate in such civic contexts came to be strongly coloured by categories of normality and abnormality, such that the new Hong Kong Chinese residents, and the house forms that were associated with them, came to be cast as inappropriate additions to the existing landscape. Despite a rhetoric of open discussion, these public arenas came to serve primarily as a vehicle for a dominant (Anglo-Canadian) discourse concerning the past and future of Shaughnessy Heights and other west-side neighbourhoods throughout the 1980s.[8]

This reconfiguration of public space and public discourse around the wrestling for control of neighbourhood aesthetics can be exemplified through a particular instance of grass roots action in which the residents of one small area of Third Shaughnessy (the southern end of Shaughnessy Heights) attempted to maintain the norms of space and design through legal action. John Pitts, a Shaughnessy resident, spent C$15,000 to draft a by-law to rezone nearly 200 houses between 37th and 41st and Granville and Maple streets. By-law 6694, labelled Preservation District No. 1 by the residents and sarcastically titled the 'Pitts-Stop' by city planners, was approved and passed by City Council on 24 July, 1990. The intent of the new zoning was 'to preserve the single family usage and character of the district outlined [. . .] with special regard to encouraging retention of existing dwellings and regulating demolition and replacement of them as a Conditional Use'.[9] The by-law reduced floor-space ratio to just below the FSR set by a City Council zoning amendment of 1990, and demarcated stringent property set-backs specifically designed to end the construction of monster houses in the neighbourhood.

Numerous west-side social movements followed with similar agendas, some aimed at preventing the removal of trees, while others focused more sharply on the demolition of houses and low-rise apartment buildings. At the same time as the physical changes were contested, a fierce ideological battle was waged in the media. Countless articles, editorials and letters to the editor on what came to be known as the 'Asian Invasion', emphasized the strangeness of the new houses and, implicitly, the new house buyers (e.g. Cox 1988; Wiseman 1988; Shaw 1989; Taylor 1989). In the late 1980s, there was a concerted effort to 'renormalize' the landscape, to bring back the appropriate taste for west-side neighbourhoods. These efforts involved making the outsiders themselves appear 'monstrous'. In one letter to the editor in 1990, a Vancouver resident wrote:

> I agree wholeheartedly with the sentiments of Shaughnessy homeowner Donald Tuck (Monster Mishmash, March 28 issue): 'we're concerned with the nature of the neighbourhood'. If I am not being too naive on the subject of 'monster houses', I ask: Who, in this day and age of family planning, vigilant birth control methods, and the 'norm' of 2.5 children per household, could possibly make use of houses containing seven–nine bedrooms and seven sets of plumbing plus two kitchens [. . .]. That is, if they are being used as 'single family dwellings'?
>
> (Courier 1990)

The concept of the 'normal' Canadian family is crucial here, as those occupying the new monster houses were cast as either odd, by virtue of having large, extended or fecund families, or operating illegally, by building basement suites. The definition of the norm, of what is appropriate behaviour for the neighbourhood is clearly an important site of contestation. Outlining the normal and the abnormal *in spatial terms* establishes both physical and cultural borders; defence of these bordered spaces can thus be made on both natural and moral grounds.[10]

Dismay over the inefficacy of old borders and landscape meanings was accompanied by a growing fear of the economic and cultural power of the new Hong Kong residents. Anxiety over the construction of extra-large houses and the extended families that inhabited them, sparked fears of a takeover; the newcomers were quite literally 'taking up too much space'.[11] The fear of competition for limited resources, particularly for space in the desirable Shaughnessy enclave, was refracted through other concerns, such as schooling. Many white residents who spoke with me in interviews felt that the Chinese students were 'too competitive', or 'too one-track minded'. They worried that their own children, who were more 'well balanced', would lose out to this new group scholastically. Several also expressed dismay at the high cost of expensive English as a Second Language (ESL) courses, which they felt siphoned off resources from after-school activities and art programmes.

The City Council responded to these fears by working closely with property rights associations and urban activist organizations such as the SHPOA, the Kerrisdale Concerned Citizens for Affordable Housing and the Kerrisdale/Granville Homeowners' Association in an effort to ameliorate the urban transformations. Public hearings were frequent throughout the late 1980s and early 1990s on the general topics of appropriate land use and on specific downzoning amendments. After years of debate and following the passage of three zoning amendments for west-side neighbourhoods in 1988, 1990 and 1992, a series of public hearings in September, 1992 addressed two more proposed options for downzoning in South Shaughnessy. These hearings soon became a lightning rod for the disparate communities interested in Shaughnessy's future landscape.

THE PUBLIC HEARINGS OF 1992: REWORKING DEMOCRACY AND THE IDEA OF THE PUBLIC

The most openly confrontational events between the older, Anglo-Canadian residents of Shaughnessy Heights and the more recent Hong Kong Chinese residents in the neighbourhood occurred in the autumn of 1992. In a series of six long and agonizing public hearings on the topic of downzoning in South Shaughnessy, the polarization of these two groups became immediately apparent. In the public hearings a majority of Shaughnessy Heights Property Owners' Association (SHPOA) members advocated restrictions on future redevelopment in the area. The general propositions of regulation and preservation were similar to the restrictions enumerated in earlier amendments. A group composed almost entirely of recent Chinese immigrants from Hong Kong, quickly formed an ad hoc committee in opposition to these proposed development restrictions. This committee, which later convened as the South Shaughnessy Property Owners' Rights Committee (SSPORC), campaigned strenuously against the downzoning. Aided by a number of developers, most prominently Barry Hersh, a housebuilder and president of the West Side Builder's Association, the campaign used allegations of racism to discredit the SHPOA and its followers.

After the first meeting in September, leaflets were sent to Chinese homeowners in the area, urging them to ask Chinese friends from the lower mainland parts of the city to attend the rest of the hearings in a show of public alliance. The question of linguistic transparency soon became an important issue. At the public hearings, Hong Kong Cantonese speakers complained that the survey distributed by the Vancouver Planning Department had not been translated into Mandarin,[12] thus reducing their accessibility to the information necessary to make informed decisions about the proposed downzoning change.[13] Some of these speakers spoke Cantonese at the hearing and engaged in the debate by using an English interpreter. At several points, they were heckled by Anglo-Canadian members of the audience for not speaking English.

The widespread publicity of this racial polarization (the hearings were televised and reported globally), and the manipulation of the definitions of racism by both the Chinese residents and developers indicated new stakes in the battle over urban design and control of the Shaughnessy streetscape. Public hearings are generally presented as models of democratic debate and spaces of rational decision-making, but most land use decision-making, as noted in the discussion of Shaughnessy's landscape history, has rarely functioned this way. Prior debates over appropriate land use in Shaughnessy generally led to restrictions which excluded certain members of the public by class and ethnicity (see also Anderson 1991). The six hearings in 1992 represented the first time that a radically different interpretation of the community good for a west-side area was promulgated and instituted by a group not composed primarily of Anglo-Canadian residents.

For the first time in the city's history, large numbers of wealthy capitalists who were perceived as 'non-white', moved to west-side neighbourhoods that were formerly protected from this type of influx by virtue of their high prices and exclusive zoning covenants. This outside group was able to form alliances with local capitalists for a pro-growth agenda that threatened the carefully established symbolic value of west-side neighbourhoods. By raising the spectre of racism, which could be easily buttressed by the historical evidence of racism implicit in prior zoning measures, the Hong Kong Chinese and west-side builders effectively controlled the public hearings and defeated the SHPOA-led effort to restrict further development in the neighbourhood. As a further warning to their Anglo-Canadian opponents, some members of the SSPORC publicly threatened to write to Chinese friends and contacts in Hong Kong and worldwide, to warn that Vancouver was a racist society, and to advise against further investment in the city (Interview, November 1992).

In defence of their position against downzoning, many Chinese speakers extolled the virtues of what they considered to be the Chinese way of life. Rather than contesting cultural difference, Chinese homeowners in Shaughnessy used it to their advantage, lecturing enthusiastically about family, respect for the elderly, communal closeness, education and hard work – and contrasting these values with what they saw as the lazy, unfamilial and undemocratic values of Anglo-Canadians. Similarly, they appropriated the meanings of racism and nationalism to their advantage, decrying English-only language survey forms as inherently un-Canadian and neighbourhood rezoning proposals as manifestly racist.

The understanding of what constituted the community good became a major source of contestation. Definitions of what it meant to 'be Canadian' or to 'live in Shaughnessy' were opened up for interrogation and negotiation. Rather than simply contesting the Anglo-Canadian definition of 'Chinese-ness' and, relatedly, the places it was deemed Chinese were to live, however, financial power and cultural savvy gave this new immigrant group the means to completely invert this process of racial and spatial definition, and allowed them to publicly set in play dominant Chinese definitions of 'Anglo-ness'.[14] The new Chinese home-owners in Shaughnessy were able to ally themselves with developers, realtors and politicians eager to join capitals in new, increasingly international business ventures. This slight shifting of the economic and political power ballast in the neighbourhood allowed the public voicing and material representation of Anglo-Canadian values and norms as they were perceived from the outsider's perspective. The spaces of rational discourse, an integral component of the liberal public sphere, were thus employed to contest implicit notions of justice and the 'common good', which had operated in the neighbourhood since its inception. Through this process of contestation and inversion, some of the actual spaces of the public sphere (public meetings on land use) were exposed as traditional spaces of hegemonic production for a dominant group.

To give final weight to this inversion, many of the Chinese residents voiced their concerns in Cantonese, and deliberately employed the conceptual vocabulary of popular democracy in defence of their individual and economic rights. They further spoke of these rights as integral to the Canadian liberal and secular welfare state. In the hearings, much to the dismay of their Anglo-Canadian listeners, Chinese-Canadian speakers invoked notions of freedom, family, individual rights, property rights and democracy itself in defence of their position. One Chinese-Canadian speaker (using an interpreter) said:

> I live in Shaughnessy and we built a house very much to my liking. The new zoning would not allow enough space for me [. . .]. I strongly oppose this new proposal. Why do I have to be inconvenienced by so many regulations? This infringes my freedom. Canada is a democratic country and democracy should be returned to the people.[15]

The threat to established norms that this position heralded became clear in an interview with a SHPOA member. She said to me:

> I can't describe to you how it feels to be lectured to about Canadian democracy by people who have to use an interpreter [. . .]. Lectured about laziness, how we don't need big houses because we don't take care of our parents like the Chinese do [. . .], I cannot understand how *anybody* could go to another country and insist they can build against the wishes of an old established neighbourhood. The effrontery and the insolence takes my breath away.[16]

Historic zoning patterns and landscape struggles in Shaughnessy Heights give some indication of how public spaces have been implicated in the reproduction of a dominant Anglo-Canadian elite in Vancouver. The contemporary conflict over downzoning also demonstrates how, by using alternative concepts of appropriate behaviour and justice, and by employing the vocabulary of individual rights and popular democracy, the recent Chinese residents in the community were able to contest and even dominate this public space in the early 1990s.

TRANSNATIONAL MOVEMENTS AND LOCAL LANDSCAPES

Why is the struggle over the public landscape of Shaughnessy Heights occurring now? What is significant about this particular historical and geographical period? Why is *this* the moment that has caught the special attention of the *Angelus Novus*? Many scholars have shown how the restructuring of the global economy in the past fifteen years has greatly affected the organization of capital, labour and finance worldwide (Harvey 1987, 1989; Smith 1989; Thrift 1990, 1992; Sassen 1991). With this general restructuring process, an increasing globalization of production, finance, trade and information has initiated a widespread renegotiation of local borders and of local-global articulations (Pred and Watts 1992; Pred 1995). As old borders and cultural understandings are reworked, new kinds of spaces are often opened up in the interstices. In the case of Shaughnessy in the late 1980s and early 1990s, I suggest that the transnational flows of capital and culture characteristic of global restructuring have opened new spaces of negotiation around the shaping of the Shaughnessy landscape.

In a time when new kinds of citizens and publics are being formed, old borders are more easily eroded. In the past, the position of people as legal subjects in the public sphere generally occurred through the ownership of commodities in the market. But in Vancouver until relatively recently, it was safely assumed that legal subjects would be limited to those of Anglo heritage. First Nations people and non-Anglo immigrants did not generally own commodities in the market. The entry of a significant influx of people with both money and claims to citizenship within the public sphere is a contemporary phenomenon and, I believe, reflective of the transnational movements of late capitalism.

With alternative interpretations of the common good aired publicly in the battle over downzoning in Shaughnessy, the heretofore normalized conceptions of the suburban landscape were shown to operate historically in the interests of a dominant, racially exclusive class.[17] More importantly, the struggles emerging with new forms of transnational articulations were not merely over particular landscapes and spaces, but over the ideology of the public sphere itself.[18] The Chinese immigrants into Shaughnessy used the language of popular democracy in order to contest the status quo of representative democracy.[19] The normalized understanding of democratic principles in representative democracy as the 'freedom to choose' (what has become more and more the freedom to choose a commodity rather than the freedom to think and organize politically), was highlighted by this action.[20] As the deep flaws in any actual realization of the ideals of equal participation and rational choice were thus brought to light, the legitimacy of state policy and of democracy itself became suspect.

Clearly, the power of architecture to serve as place-holder for the materialist and psychological desires of the past is disrupted by contemporary migrancy. Reflecting the tumultuous dislocations of late capitalism, the migrant and the architect are thrown together in reformulating the landscapes of dwelling and moving, of being and becoming. In earlier moments of rupture, this instability was perceived with considerable anguish. Benjamin (1978: 163) wrote of the Parisian arcades:

> each epoch not only dreams the next, but also, in dreaming, strives toward the moment of waking. It bears its end in itself and unfolds it – as Hegel already saw – with ruse. In the convulsions of the commodity economy we begin to recognize the monuments of the bourgeoisie as ruins even before they have crumbled.

This is a melancholy image, borne out in many respects by the fascist years to follow. But this is a new era, and perhaps the cracks in the monuments can also represent moments of possibility in our time. Does a shifting landscape, even a placid, suburban landscape such as Shaughnessy Heights, indicate the potential for both literal and metaphorical spaces of difference? *Can* 'the public' become an intellectually bloody and agonistic space, relieved of its entrapment by anaemic and never-to-be-realized categories of neutrality and egality? *Can* migrancy force a reworking of hegemonic narratives, sedimented over the course of generations in the spaces of the neighbourhood and the nation?

I believe our ability to grasp these possibilities rests on our deep understanding of the interconnections between the economic and the socio-cultural; the ways that building, dwelling and mobility are always implicated in the circulation of capital; the ways that architecture and migrancy always bear the stigmata of capitalism. If we are to expand the possibilities for positive disruption it will come through our inexorable quest for social justice. Perhaps this notion will help us to revalence Benjamin's image of ruins, and turn the *Angelus Novus* back to the future.

NOTES

1 This paper is adapted from the publication, 'Conflicting geographies of democracy and the public sphere in Vancouver BC', *Transactions of the Institute of British Geographers*, NS 22, 1997: 162–79. Republished with permission of the Royal Geographical Society. Special thanks to Stephen Cairns for his expertise and advice in editing the original manuscript.

2 The business immigration programme was clearly targeted at wealthy Hong Kong residents seeking citizenship outside Hong Kong in advance of 1997. In order to qualify for the 'investor' category, the applicant needed a proven track record in business and a personal net worth of at least C$500,000 by the time of application. He or she was further obligated to commit a certain amount of this money to a Canadian venture over a three-year period. During the 1980s, British Columbia required a minimum investment of C$250,000.

3 From 1984 through 1991, Hong Kong led as the primary source country under the business immigration programme, jumping from 338 landed immigrants in 1984, to 6,787 by 1990. The total number of landings from Hong Kong in 1990 was 29,266, up nearly 10,000 from the year before. Statistics show that approximately 35–40 per cent of business immigrants to Canada settle in Vancouver. See Lary (1992); Canada (1989) and BC Stats (1991).

4 The theory of the public as a space of 'intuitive ideas' is forwarded by John Rawls; that of 'neutral principles' is advanced by Charles Larmore. See Allejandro (1993).

5 First Shaughnessy occupies the northern edge of the district. It is the oldest third of Shaughnessy Heights and has adopted the strictest zoning guidelines. As Duncan (1994) has noted, the founding principle of these guidelines has been the preservation of an English architectural style and landscape tradition.

6 The exact numbers of Hong Kong Chinese buyers in the neighbourhood are difficult to ascertain and are widely debated. Several real estate-based estimates indicate approximately 80 per cent of the monster houses were purchased by families from Hong Kong or Taiwan. My own observation is taken from surveys, telephone interviews and participant observation in neighbourhood meetings in Vancouver between 1990 and 1992. See Pettit (1992) and Ley (1995) for similar findings.

7 Feelings of anger and a deep sense of loss were strongly articulated in many of the in-depth interviews that I conducted between 1990 and 1992; these feelings were also expressed in scores of letters to the editor and to City Council during the late 1980s and early 1990s.

8 This was the case through most of the decade, although by 1989 the ways in which the monster house debates were represented in the media and discussed in municipal meetings were highly contested. For example, the widespread contestation of the *Vancouver Sun*'s coverage of Hong Kong led to an in-house discussion of the newspaper's methods and to the general airing of the issue of racism in the city at large. In the weekend issue of 1 April, 1989, the paper devoted an entire page to letters to the editor concerning the Hong Kong coverage. The role of big business in these types of interventions is discussed in Mitchell (1993).

9 From a draft of the proposal to create a new zoning by-law schedule submitted to Vancouver City Council on 15 February, 1990. This draft was given to me by John Pitts.

10 Foucault (1979, 1980) and Bourdieu (1990) discuss the power of definition over the 'normal' and the 'natural' and how these concepts are institutionalized and reproduced spatially and culturally. Anderson (1991: 29) links these concepts to the production of racial categories in Vancouver and their establishment in particular places such as Chinatown.

11 See Gilroy (1991) for a discussion of a similar employment of racial ideology in Britain. He notes that the fear of competition over limited resources is exacerbated by the representation of black people as abnormally fecund; i.e. by 'out-producing' white people they will attain greater access to desirable resources.

12 Cantonese is considered a dialect and is never used for formal documents, so the written language – even for Cantonese speakers – is Mandarin.

13 Benny Hsieh Chung-pang, the founder of the ad hoc committee, noted ironically that the refuse collection circular had been translated into six languages, whereas the SHPOA-designed questionnaire was written in English only.

14 For a discussion of this kind of representational reversal and its power dynamics in black culture, see hooks (1992).

15 This testimony at the public hearing of 5 October, 1992 is cited in Ley (1995). For a further discussion of the arguments presented at these hearings see, in particular, pp. 196–9.

16 Interview, November, 1992.

17 See Hall (1988) for a discussion of hegemony as tendency rather than fact. The understanding of hegemony as a shifting and highly contested process gives weight to the argument that certain moments in the production of hegemony allow for greater negotiation and resistance than others.

18 The ideological importance of the public sphere – particularly in relation to urban spaces – is detailed in Mitchell's study of People's Park in Berkeley, California (Mitchell 1995: 116–17).

19 In Williams' (1976: 85) examination of the social etymology of the term 'democracy', he notes the different usages of the word in the modern era. In the more radical tradition, democracy meant popular power; in the liberal tradition, 'democracy meant open election of representatives under certain conditions (democratic rights, such as free speech) which maintained the openness of election and political argument'. In the contemporary period, these two usages often 'confront each other as enemies' – as was evident in the struggle over the meaning of democracy in the public sphere in Shaughnessy Heights in 1992.

20 Appadurai writes: 'These images of agency are increasingly distortions of a world of merchandising so subtle that the consumer is consistently helped to believe that he or she is an actor, where in fact he or she is at best a chooser' (Appadurai 1990: 307).

REFERENCES

Allejandro, R. (1993) *Hermeneutics, Citizenship and the Public Sphere*, Albany, New York: State University of New York Press.

Anderson, K. (1991) *Vancouver's Chinatown: racial discourse in Canada, 1875–1980*, Montreal: McGill-Queen's University Press.

Appadurai, A. (1990) 'Disjuncture and difference in the global cultural economy', *Theory, Culture and Society* 7 (2–3): 295–310.

Barman, J. (1986) 'Neighbourhood and community in interwar Vancouver: residential differentiation and civic voting behavior', in R. McDonald and J. Barman (eds) *Vancouver Past*, Vancouver: University of British Columbia Press.

BC Stats (1991) 'British Columbia immigration highlights', May, 90: 4.

Benjamin, W. (1978) 'Paris, capital of the nineteenth century', in W. Benjamin, *Reflections*, trans. E. Jephcott, New York: Shocken Books.

Bourdieu, P. (1984) *Distinction: a social critique of the judgement of taste*, Cambridge, Massachusetts: Harvard University Press.

Bourdieu, P. (1990) *In Other Words: essays towards a reflexive sociology*, Palo Alto, California: Stanford University Press.

Buck-Morss, S. (1991) *The Dialectics of Seeing: Walter Benjamin and the arcades project*, Cambridge, Massachusetts: MIT Press.

Canada (1989) 'Immigration to Canada: a statistical overview', *Employment and Immigration Canada*, November.

Courier (1990) 'Letter to Editor', 4 April.

Cox, S. (1988) 'Buying up their new world', *Vancouver Sun*, 27 February.

Duncan, J. (1994) 'Shaughnessy Heights: the protection of privilege', in S. Hasson and D. Ley (eds) *Neighbourhood Organizations and the Welfare State*, Toronto: University of Toronto Press.

Duncan, J. and Duncan, N. (1984) 'A cultural analysis of urban residential landscapes in North America: the case of the anglophile elite', in J. Agnew, J. Mercer and D. Sopher (eds) *The City in Cultural Context*, Boston: Allen and Unwin.

Farrow, M. (1989) 'Hong Kong capital flows here ever faster', *Vancouver Sun*, 21 March.

Foucault, M. (1979) *Discipline and Punish: the birth of the prison*, trans. A. Sheridan, New York: Vintage Books.

Foucault, M. (1980) *Power/Knowledge: selected interviews and other writings 1972–1977*, C. Gordon (ed.), New York: Pantheon Books.

Fung, V. (1991) 'Hong Kong investment funds pour into Canada', *Financial Post*, 17 June.

Gilroy, P. (1991) *'There Ain't No Black in the Union Jack': the cultural politics of race and nation*, Chicago: University of Chicago Press.

Gutstein, D. (1990) *The New Landlords: Asian investment in Canadian real estate*, Victoria, British Columbia: Porcepic Books.

Habermas, J. (1989) *The Structural Transformation of the Public Sphere*, trans. T. Burger with F. Lawrence, Cambridge, Massachusetts: MIT Press.

Hall, S. (1988) 'The toad in the garden: Thatcherism among the theorists', in C. Nelson and L. Grossberg (eds) *Marxism and the Interpretation of Culture*, Chicago: University of Illinois Press.

Harvey, D. (1987) 'Flexible accumulation through urbanization: reflections on "post-modernism" in the American city', *Antipode* 19 (3): 260–86.

Harvey, D. (1989) *The Condition of Postmodernity*, Oxford: Basil Blackwell.

Holdsworth, D. (1981) 'House and home in Vancouver: the emergence of a west coast urban landscape 1886–1929', unpublished thesis, University of British Columbia.

Holdsworth, D. (1986) 'Cottages and castles for Vancouver home-seekers', *B.C. Studies*: 69–70.

hooks, b. (1992) 'Representing whiteness in the black imagination', in L. Grossberg, C. Nelson and P. Treichler (eds) *Cultural Studies*, New York: Routledge.

Kalman, H.D. and Roaf, J.H. (1974) *Exploring Vancouver*, Vancouver: University of British Columbia Press.

Lary, D. (1992) 'Trends in immigration from Hong Kong', *Canada-Hong Kong Update*, Summer: 6.

Ley, D. (1995) 'Between Europe and Asia: the case of the missing Sequoias', *Ecumene*, 2 (2): 185–210.

MacDonald, P. (1990) 'Canada to trim numbers of independent class visas', *Hong Kong Standard*, 26 January.

Mitchell, D. (1995) 'The end of public space? People's Park, definitions of the public and democracy', *The Annals of the Association of American Geographers*, 85 (1): 108–33.

Mitchell, K. (1993) 'Multiculturalism, or the united colors of capitalism?', *Antipode* 25 (4): 263–94.

Nash, A. (1992) 'The emigration of business people and professionals from Hong Kong', *Canada and Hong Kong Update* (Winter).

Pettit, B. (1992) 'Zoning, the market, and the single family landscape: neighbourhood change in Vancouver, Canada', unpublished thesis, University of British Columbia.

Pred, A. (1995) *Recognizing European Modernities: a montage of the present*, New York: Routledge.

Pred, A. and Watts, M. (1992) *Reworking Modernity: capitalisms and symbolic discontent*, New Brunswick, New Jersey: Rutgers University Press.

Sassen, S. (1991) *The Global City: New York, London, Tokyo*, Princeton, New Jersey: Princeton University Press.

Shaw, G. (1989) 'The Hong Kong connection: how Asian money fuels housing market', *Vancouver Sun*, 18 February.

Smith, M. (1989) *Pacific Rim Cities in the World Economy*, New Brunswick: Transaction Publishers.

Spence, C. (1985) 'Being neighbourly – by law', *Courier*, 18 December.

Taylor, P. (1989) 'Hong Kong yacht people buy up Vancouver', *Sunday Telegraph*, 4 June.

Thrift, N. (1990) 'The perils of the international financial system', *Environment and Planning A* 22: 135–40.

Thrift, N. (1992) 'Muddling through: world orders and globalization', *Professional Geographer* 44: 3–7.

Tickell, A. (2000) 'Global rhetorics, national politics: pursuing bank mergers in Canada', *Antipode* 32 (2): 152–75.

Vancouver (1982) *First Shaughnessy Plan Background Report*, City of Vancouver Planning Department, May.

Vancouver (1987) *First Shaughnessy Design Guidelines*, City of Vancouver Planning Department, October.

Vancouver (1989) *First Shaughnessy District*, City of Vancouver Zoning and Development By-law, City of Vancouver Planning Department, December.

Vancouver (1992) 'Permits and Licenses Department', City of Vancouver Planning Department.

Vancouver Local Areas 1971–81 (1985) City of Vancouver Planning Department, August.

Vancouver Local Areas 1986 (1988) City of Vancouver Planning Department, October.

Vancouver Monitoring Program (1992) City of Vancouver Planning Department.

Vancouver Trends (1990) City of Vancouver Planning Department.

Williams, R. (1976) *Keywords*, New York: Oxford University Press.

Wiseman, L. (1988) 'On guard for thee', *Vancouver Magazine*, December.

Chapter 9: Too many houses for a home

Narrating the house in the Chinese diaspora

Jane M. Jacobs

The scale and extent of human mobility in contemporary times has added a new inflection to a question that has long pre-occupied scholars: this being the matter of 'what is home?' or, more precisely and following Agnes Heller (1995), 'where are we at home?'. These questions are both minor and major. They implicate something as ordinary as 'the house' and as extraordinary as our sense of belonging. Martin Heidegger's well-known essay from 1951, 'Building dwelling thinking', provides one starting point for thinking about how a building like a house is attached to an experience like dwelling (Heidegger 1975). He investigates how dwelling requires building (as a process and as a thing) and how, in turn, building helps constitute our sense of dwelling. Heidegger draws at one point on the example of a farmhouse in the Black Forest, which he uses to illustrate how building both cultivates and expresses dwelling. His conception of 'proper' dwelling relies, then, on the example of a house that is embedded in its place of origin – where building and dwelling and location come to be co-constitutive. Through an architectural diagnostic, a dwelling such as Heidegger's farmhouse might occupy the category of 'the vernacular'. Through a sociological diagnostic, we might think of it as a type of 'ancestral home'. Such models of 'proper dwelling' are being radically transformed in contemporary times. Not least, current levels of mobility act as a force of compromise. Mobility compels our lives to be full of radical open-ness, proliferating differences and multiplying loyalties. It produces flows of information, people and things that do away with, or render residual, what might be thought of as monogamous modes of dwelling. Within this restructured world, both vernacular architectures and ancestral homes come to assume new positions and are sutured into our modes of dwelling in quite different ways.

Although ending with the example of the deeply embedded Black Forest hut, Heidegger's essay is, in spirit, not especially prescriptive about the geographies and architectures of 'proper' dwelling. Indeed, part of his concern is with the matter not simply of how we dwell but '*how far* the nature of dwelling reaches' (Heidegger 1975: 147). Current levels of mobility suggest that the idea of reach touched upon by Heidegger needs to become fully activated in our explanations of dwelling and home. Reach was certainly something that geographer Anne Buttimer felt necessary to consider in her 1980 account of home and sense of place. Buttimer (1980: 170) proposed that places should be thought about by way of two 'reciprocal movements': on the one hand, an inward-facing concept of 'home' and, on the other, what she called the 'horizons of reach' that extended outward from that home. Buttimer proposed this binarized model as a way of diagnosing the extent to which a place was 'centred' (a good thing, from her perspective) or decentred (an undesirable thing). But perhaps the potential of the idea of reach is not as an opposite force to the idea of home, but as a constitutive force in contemporary home making. For example, we might think about applying a concept of reach to the ways in which mobility often stretches the idea of home well beyond any pre-given notion of origins. In a complementary manoeuvre, we might draw our attention to the processes by which we reach, through a range of everyday practices, not only for certain houses but also for certain ideals of home. Elspeth Probyn (1996: 19) calls this the 'movement of desiring belonging'. Her phrase points, in the first instance, to the way in which dwelling is built out of spatial, affective and sociological efforts. Furthermore, it confirms that one's sense of being 'at home' is not something simply bequeathed by long association with one place, but an active matter of becoming that can reach across far more complex spatialities and reflect more expansive relational ranges. In a mobile world, one's sense of home is not a geographical given, but emerges out of various building activities: how we respond to the strangers with whom we come to be proximate; the ways we orient ourselves in unfamiliar places; the things we assemble to make the houses we live in feel homely; the multiple scales that we negotiate to gather to us that which is familiar.

This chapter seeks to explore not simply the matter of how we come to feel at home in a mobile world, but how *the architecture of home* is implicated in that process. My concern is specifically with the interface between the emotional experience of feeling at home and the architectural materiality of the house as formed through the drama of mobility. I do not explore this interface sociologically, but by way of the feature film *Floating Life*,[1] which charts the sometimes comical, sometimes tragic experiences of one diasporic Chinese family. Pina Werbner (2000: 8) has argued that diasporas 'produce and reproduce themselves socially, culturally, and politically' and that they do so through strategies that are 'embedded in cultural technologies and underpinned aesthetically'. In short, being diasporic entails cultural work. Such work, and specifically the ways in which it implicates media practices (including film), has been well documented (see as examples Chow 1993; Nacify 1993, 1999; Sun 2002). I offer the film *Floating Life* as one example of such cultural work, as undertaken by the recent Hong Kong diaspora. It provides an illustrative narrative of the experiences of the Hong Kong diaspora, and tells us specifically of the way the architecture of the house is drawn into contemporary narratives about, and representations of, home and transnational sociality for this group.

THE HOUSE IS (NOT) A HOME

It has long been accepted that the concept of home is far more than a synonym for the architectural thing called a 'house'. The matter of being at home can always transcend the matter of 'house' to incorporate the wider question of dwelling. For Mary Douglas (1991) the house is merely a physical space that is animated into the state called 'home' by the regular doings of its residents. Home emerges, she suggests, out of social processes (*processes in time*) that are always more than the architectural container of the house itself (*something in space*). So having a house is not sufficient in and of itself to provide one with a sense of being at home. In the context of this observation, we might speculate about the ways in which the contemporary phenomenon of widespread human mobility might be transforming this socially produced relationship between house and home. Does mobility increase the distance between the architectural entity called 'house' and the social and affective state of being at home? Or does mobility simply transform the logic of the processes by which homely dwellings are built out of the raw material of the house?

In her article 'Where are we at home?', Agnes Heller (1995) specifically contemplates the implications of extreme human mobility for the modern sense of being at home. She identifies (1995: 7) two 'representative kinds of home-experience': 'the spatial home-experience' and the 'temporal home-experience'. The spatial home-experience is 'geographically monogamous' (Heller 1995: 2), there is no movement. In this example of home-experience it is *place* that furnishes one with the sense of the 'familiar' (Heller 1995: 5) and ensures life proceeds in such a way that there is a maximum level of transparency. Heller usefully provides us with a caricature of someone who might just live such a life: the old man who has stayed in the same rural village all his days. Heller depicts a *mode* of dwelling as opposed to an actual dwelling type, but it is not too difficult to see that we are being called back to the idea of Heidegger's Black Forest hut and, if not actual vernacular architecture, then certainly the idea of it.[2] In contrast, Heller (1995: 7) posits the 'temporal home-experience' as something that is decidedly modern (or as she suggests, postmodern). This is the experience had by the person who travels incessantly: staying in hotels, speaking many languages and being 'geographically promiscuous' (Heller 1995: 1). Such folk live in the 'abstracted place of nowhere and everywhere' (Heller 1995: 6). This example of home-experience is brought to life by Heller through the figure of a female professional whose concept of home is defined not by walls or localities but simply by where her pet cat lives. This figure and her way of life suggest a world in which house and home are radically uncoupled.

If one were to take this literally then it might be imagined that a mobile world eschews the architecture of the house entirely. But is this really the case? People on the move are not all the same and it is important to register here that much contemporary human mobility is not associated with the stratospheric lifestyle represented by Heller's transnational professional. For the refugee and the migrant, being housed is often an imperative, and coming to feel as if one belongs a yearned for future state. For many migrant groups home ownership is an obsession. In Australia, for example, high rates of home ownership have for some time been recognized as a defining feature of a range of post-war migrant groups, including recent arrivals from Hong Kong (Bourassa 1994; Pulvirenti 2000). Migration, in particular, involves a complex system of inhabitations that incorporate architectures as various as the ancestral home, the departure lounge, the vehicle of passage, the temporary shelter and the new house. As such, architecture is always being called upon to structure the spatiality of a mobile world. And when the migrant comes to that point when journeying stops and settling begins – be it reluctantly, precariously, temporarily or even dispersedly – the architecture of the house is specifically implicated (for better or worse) in one's efforts to reinstate a sense of being at home.

Migrancy places into question monogamous modes of dwelling, but it does not do away with the matter of the house or locality. Recent accounts of home within the specific context of the changes generated by an intensification of human mobility tend to emphasize the ways in which the migrant's sense of home is split between here and there (see, for an overview, Rapport and Dawson 1998: 6–9). Once one's concept of home comes to be understood as 'plurilocal' (Rouse 1991) then the role the house has to play in one's ability to be at home needs rethinking. Under such conditions does the house matter more, or less? John Berger (1984: 64) acknowledges that the idea of home has been so irrevocably transformed by modern intensities of mobility that it can no longer function as the stable physical centre of one's universe and, as such, is 'no longer a dwelling'. Rather, it transforms itself into a far more mobile and adjustable concept, as Rapport and Dawson (1998: 27) put it: 'a home that can be taken along whenever one decamps [. . .] a mobile habitat and not [. . .] a singular or fixed structure.'

The house so conceived becomes one point in a more dispersed and disjunctive geography of dwelling, one that is no longer bound to a single place but sutured into a relationally linked range of localities. For the migrant it is this dispersed relational geography that must be negotiated in the building of dwelling. It shapes the affective scope of home, it constitutes the materialities of taste that come to be displayed in the house, it determines the extent of various economies of exchange, and it stretches the home's rituals of living. As such, the initial journey made by a migrant is but one of the many shifts that come to characterize life after migration. Settling is not simply about coming to terms with one new place, but about many places. Once re-settled, the house becomes a point in a widely orchestrated set of what Elspeth Probyn (1996: 19) calls 'surface shifts'. These might entail overseas communications, far away memories, long-distance travellings, re-inventions of traditions, and much more. It is from the base provided by the house that the newly arrived migrant negotiates their new circumstance. This is the pivotal point from which one re-orientates oneself, not simply to one's new neighbours, new nation and new society, but also to one's old home, one's memories, one's responsibilities to family left behind or moved on elsewhere. This is a concept of home which replicates a version of Doreen Massey's (1994) 'progressive sense of place', a spot that is articulated with multiple sites and scales. This is not the vernacular house, although it is a house that may well contain any number of 'shifted' vernacularisms. This is not the ancestral home, although it may be a home that comes to embody that idea in any number of ways and localities. This is the mobile home and regardless of what kind of house it is, it calls into being flexible architectures of inhabitation.

HOMES THAT ARE (NOT) HOMELY

How are the houses drawn into experiences of modern mobility animated by this new geography of shifting surfaces? And what diagnostic concepts are available for us to understand the architecture of home brought into being by such mobility? Freud's concept of the uncanny has provided many contemporary commentators with a useful conceptual frame for thinking through the unsettled (and often anxious) experience of home in an age of migrancy. The uncanny, as outlined by Freud in his famous essay of 1919, bears directly upon the question of one's sense of home in a modern changing world. Freud elaborates the uncanny by way of two words whose meaning, which at first seem diametrically opposed, in fact circulate through each other: these being, *heimlich* ('home') and *unheimlich* ('unhomely', meaning unfamiliar or strange). An uncanny experience occurs when something familiar (like one's home) is rendered somehow and in some sense unfamiliar; one has the experience, in other words, of being in place and out of place *simultaneously*.

A number of scholars have associated the uncanny with the ambivalent sense of home or place associated with migration (e.g. Kristeva 1991; Bammer 1992). For architectural critic, Anthony Vidler, the uncanny is a pertinent trope for thinking about contemporary architectural and urban practice in a mobile world. It captures, he argues, the 'peculiarly unstable nature of "house and home"' in a world characterized by 'social and individual estrangement, alienation, exile and homelessness'. It brings into view the experience of 'the de-domesticated [modern] subject' (1992: x), who is engaged in the struggle for 'domestic security' (1992: 12). Vidler assembles an expansive collection of architectural, artistic and urban projects that speak to the unhomely in modern times. Inspired as these works might be by the conditions that invoke the uncanny as a trope of our time, few directly touch the experience of migrancy or, indeed, the matter of the architectures of migrant living.

I wish to capture a more everyday sense of the architectural uncanny as it relates to and reflects the migrant experience of housing and home making. Freud's essay on the uncanny is particularly relevant to the migrant experience because it has at its heart a concern with the consequences of disorientation. That is, the anxieties that arise when one is exposed 'to a world one does not fully know one's way about in'. As Freud (1987: 341) noted, '[t]he better orientated in his environment a person is, the less readily he will get the impression of something uncanny in regard to objects and events in it'. As shown in the film *Floating Life*, it is often a very ordinary domestic architecture that becomes central to the worlds (new and old) migrant families negotiate. Often enough this architecture is foreign, but in many ways it is also a familiar architecture, taking up increasingly standardized domestic architectural features and reflecting suburban architectural types that travel the globe through various virtual circuits. Yet, under the disorienting effects of migration, this entirely ordinary architecture can often come to feel extraordinary and can give rise to an uncanny experience. The house is both familiar (it is a house onto which one's movable idea of home might be traced) and unfamiliar (not the home one remembers or feels one might need).[3] Furthermore, when one migrates one does not simply leave one place and start up another place afresh. In moving, one's former homeland is not simply abandoned, nor is one's former dwelling simply forgotten, nor even many of its appurtenances left behind. Some things, some family, some memories and some routines go with the migrant into the new context where they must be reassembled within the opportunities and constraints of new types of housing. Other people and things stay behind or move on to other places and so one engages in an on-going process of re-orientation. Notions like the uncanny – the unhomely home – provide a useful tool for diagnosing the logics of migrant dwelling for it registers the surface shifts that vibrate through stable homes that migrants strive to build in their new worlds.

THE SURFACE SHIFTS OF *FLOATING LIFE*

The film *Floating Life* depicts such processes of transnational disorientation and reorientation as they occur in relation to a family – the Chans – cast to the four winds by the 1997 return of the British Crown Colony of Hong Kong to the Chinese. The Chans are typical of what some commentators have described as 'reluctant exiles' (Skeldon 1994). Like many recent Hong Kong exiles, they follow in a much longer tradition of Chinese migration. Not surprisingly this tradition of migration has come to define and extend two of the key analytical categories associated with human mobility: 'diaspora' and 'sojourner'. A number of the features assumed to define a diaspora fit the experiences of the overseas Chinese. Most notably, their dispersal has been understood to have been from a specific original centre (China). Furthermore, those dispersed retain a collective memory (often mythologized) of that original homeland and see it as the place to which they or their descendants would (or should) eventually return. As Safran (1991: 83–4) suggests, diasporic groups have a specific 'ethnocommunal consciousness' which ensures that a (real and imaginative) relationship to the ancestral home is sustained despite their mobility (see also Werbner 2000; Anthias 2001).

McKeown (1999) notes that nominal uses of the term diaspora not only name a social group (in this case the 'Chinese diaspora') but also activate an essentialized understanding of homogeneity within the diasporic group. This he calls 'diaspora-as-exile' (1999: 311). McKeown distinguishes the nominal use of the term 'diaspora' from more recent adjectival extensions that apply the term to a non-essentialized notion of diasporic identity (see also Schnapper 1999). McKeown (1999: 309) refers to this as 'diaspora-as-heterogeneity'. This second notion of diaspora not only brings into view distinctions in the quotidian character of the diasporic group, it also registers 'the rising self-consciousness and status of diaspora as a way of life' (McKeown 1999: 311). A film like *Floating Life*, made as it is by an Australian-Chinese who has herself fled Hong Kong, is a product of just such a self-conscious moment.[4] As a narrative of the recent Hong Kong exile it extends the idea of the 'Chinese diaspora' and actively constitutes how that category is understood and how its experiences are seen. The film is itself an artefact of an emerging self-conscious culture of diasporic Chineseness. As will be shown, such narratives of the Chinese diaspora do not activate simplistic stories of a people exiled from a Chinese homeland (diaspora-as-exile) but instead a more complex social geography 'circulating in all directions around the world' (diaspora-as-heterogeneity) (McKeown 1999: 330; see also Werbner 2000).

Another term, and one that is more traditionally associated with the overseas Chinese is that of 'sojourner'. 'Sojourner' describes that category of migrant who is only away from their homeland *temporarily*, and who always assumes that one day they will return (Siu 1952; see Yang 2000). Sojourners are not interested in assimilation and, as such, they have often been portrayed negatively. This concept now has a new vitality because of the way in which recent Hong Kong 'exiles' have behaved. These 'modern sojourners' (Skeldon 1994: 11) have households that are split across two or more countries, with the (primarily) male household heads staying in Hong Kong while the rest of the family establishes a residence elsewhere in Australia or Canada. These men then commute long distances in order to maintain contact between their work life and home life, and because of this are often described as 'astronauts' (Pe-Pua *et al.* 1996: 1). The term 'astronaut' was taken from the Cantonese term '*taikon-gren*', which has a supplementary meaning of 'empty wife' and, as such, implicates the home specifically. It evokes the fact that such transnational households are made up of houses that at any one time may be somehow incomplete, without a husband or without a wife.

OF MONSTER HOUSES

I would now like to turn to the houses of *Floating Life*. The idea of the house is centrally important in the film, structuring how we come to know this diasporic Chinese family, spread as it is across three countries: Hong Kong, Germany and Australia. The house, and specifically the presence of many houses, is the device that is used to confirm that this family is geographically dispersed. The houses they inhabit are also varied in style: a suburban 'monster house' (Australia), an apartment (Germany), another apartment (Hong Kong); a Federation-style house (Australia), an ancestral home (China) and a vernacular farm house (Germany). I will, in this chapter, speak at length only of the houses in Australia and Germany where the two eldest daughters of the Chan family are carving out new homes. The many houses of *Floating Life* are not simply the privileged *context* of action in this film. Interactions within and with the houses constitute a key part of the film's action. In this sense the houses are positioned as animated components in the daily lives of their inhabitants: setting off thoughts, dictating action, mediating well-being, expressing identity. In structuring her film so, Law instates the house as central to the lives she depicts. And although the lives of this family 'float' they are also pinned to specific localities and negotiate the demands of those localities, including the locality closest in – the house itself.

A House in Australia. As Mitchell (this volume) observes, the Hong Kong diaspora in Canada engages in a form of conspicuous housing consumption. Cities like Vancouver have neighbourhoods dotted with what non-Chinese locals dub 'monster houses'. These houses are large and often have an aesthetic that, Mitchell's research shows, is at odds with specific Anglo-Canadian notions of suburban beauty. It is into one such 'monster house' that Ma and Pa Chan, with their two youngest sons, move when they arrive in Sydney (Figure 9.1). The house is not theirs. It is owned by their second daughter, Bing, and her husband. Bing has been in Australia for some time; she migrated first with the express purpose of forging a new life so that her wider family could join her. This is her second house, one she has bought to accommodate the extended family. As Bing puts it: 'This is my second house. This is a 100 per cent clean tidy and secure house.' When the rest of the family first see the house they are duly impressed: 'It is like a movie,' says one of the sons; 'It's so beautiful,' says Pa; 'I'm glad I came, I like the kitchen best,' says Ma. But this new house is not as it seems. It carries with it the after-effects of the traumas Bing experienced when alone in her first

Figure 9.1
THE CHAN FAMILY ARRIVE AT THEIR NEW 'MONSTROUS' AUSTRALIAN HOME.
(All figures in this chapter are reproduced with permission from Hibiscus Films)

months in Australia. The house is infected by Bing's paranoias and fears about Australia. It quite literally takes on monstrous ways, interfering with the Chans' ability to settle.

A house in Germany. The first-born daughter of the Chan family, Yen, lives with her German husband and their daughter, Mui-Mui, in an apartment in Germany. They have just moved in and we are introduced to this home at a point where settling in is very apparent: boxes are being unpacked, walls painted, new beds bought. Yen's household is generally happier than the other households represented in the film. But this house also has its share of unwanted disturbances that must be dealt with in order for Yen and her family to feel properly settled. Not least, Yen is tortured by the thought of her increasingly unhappy mother in Australia, and racked by her sense of guilt for not properly fulfilling her filial duty. At one point she despairs: 'The happier I am in Germany, the more it hurts.'

A house without a tree. This is the first house that Bing, as the lone first migrant of the family, occupies in Australia, and it is introduced by way of a flashback. This is the house that stands at the frontier of this family's movement to Australia and, appropriately, it is located right at the edge of the city – beyond its fence is a treeless expanse and even the odd kangaroo. Locating this first house at the geographical margins of the city reminds us that for most migrants – even relatively well-equipped Hong Kong migrants – the first experience of a migrant destination is through peripheral spaces. Bing initially came with her husband, but he has returned to his job in Hong Kong leaving Bing alone to establish a base for those to follow. Hers then is the quintessential 'astronaut' home, a household without a husband and she the

Figure 9.2
BING, TERRIFIED BY THE NOISES SHE HEARS AT NIGHT IN HER FIRST AUSTRALIAN HOME, HUDDLES ATOP A TABLE, PHONING HONG KONG.

'empty wife'. Bing feels out of control in this house, frightened by its isolation, scared of the unfamiliar creatures that she hears crawling through it at night (Figure 9.2).

DETAILING A FLOATING LIFE

Brick veneer. Architecturally speaking the walls of a house offer protection, managing the interface between inside and outside, the domesticated and the wild, the private and the public. The walls that structure the houses of *Floating Life* do not always function in this way. The part they play in an architecture of security is unreliable: some walls are not what they seem, others create discomfort, some entrap instead of protect, others open the way to sheer horror. One of the key architectural features of contemporary suburban architecture in Australia is the use of relatively cheap and light construction materials. Exterior walls are commonly brick veneer and interior walls constructed from plasterboard, each covering a timber frame. No sooner had the newly arrived Chans decided their new home was 'beautiful' than their daughter Bing abruptly delivers the 'truth' about this suburban house and its failings in terms of providing a safe and secure haven from the hostile world out there: 'I'm telling you, houses here aren't very solid [as she taps the plasterboard walls]. Thin as paper!' When Ma and Pa take out the altar that has been carefully brought all the way from Hong Kong and try to find a place for it within the new home, daughter Bing warns them that this house cannot accommodate their usual ways: 'It's a wooden house, you can't burn incense. A little fire would burn it down.' Ma and Pa are mystified. Ma asks curiously 'That flimsy?' Pa, who has noticed that the house

Figure 9.3
THE CHAN FAMILY TRAPPED BEHIND THE GLASS DOORS OF THEIR SUBURBAN HOME.

was brick, is even more sceptical: 'The outside wall is brick,' he says, and he goes to open the large sliding glass doors in order to check that his own eyes are not deceiving him.

Sliding doors. The large sliding glass doors of this house are typical of the generously proportioned apertures that work to seamlessly join the inside rooms to the outside in Australian suburban homes. But in Bing's house such openness is only a source of anxiety and this door, like all the others, is securely locked. Bing explains: 'There are lots of burglaries. We've got locks on the windows and doors. Plus an alarm and a smoke detector.' When Pa finally gets the door open and starts to step outside, Bing's anxiety intensifies: 'Got a hat, Pa? The sun's dangerous. That hole in the ozone layer . . . three out of ten Australians has skin cancer, a terminal disease.' Bing builds her case as to why the family should not go outdoors, including the dangers of killer wasps, redback spiders and vicious dogs. In Bing's '100 per cent clean, tidy and secure' second home the walls are so impenetrable that they come to entrap the newly arrived parents and their sons who rarely go out and, when they do, get lost, attacked by a dog and even frightened by a 'boxing kangaroo' (Figure 9.3).

Not quite an attic. Bing's own paranoia stems from her experiences when she was alone in the very first home she had in Australia. There, Bing experiences a building sense of terror, and the greater the anxiety the more she tries to 'secure' the home by adding locks and alarms, security doors and cleaning incessantly. One day Bing decides to enter the only unsecured and unclean space left in her home, the relatively small cavity between the ceiling and the roof. In suburban Australian homes this space is largely unoccupied. It is far too compressed to be thought of as an 'attic' and it certainly carries no trace of the

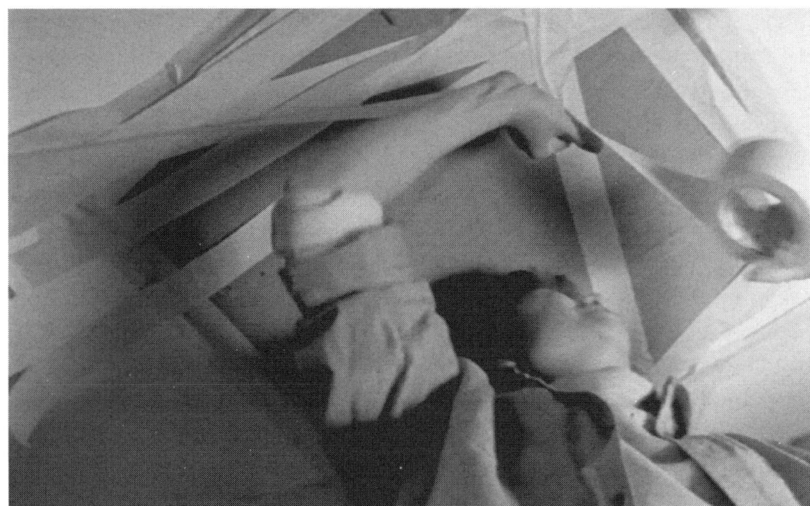

Figure 9.4
NOT QUITE BACHELARD'S ATTIC.

meaning that Bachelard (1969: 18–19) attaches to attics, those 'rational spaces' in which 'all our thoughts are clear' and 'fears are easily rationalized'. As Bing enters the roof cavity she is faced with darkness and through the torchlight she makes out what for her is an illogical assembly of roof supports, cobwebs, electrical wiring and other detritus. Utterly traumatized by this glimpse of irrational filth secreted away in this cavity, she exits and frantically seals off the manhole with tape (Figure 9.4).

Surface effects. The eldest daughter, Yen, has a happier home than that inhabited by her Australian-based family. Having just moved in to this apartment we first see the family together painting the walls. As Yen paints she talks to her husband about her concerns for her family newly arrived in Australia. In the midst of her painting and fretting Yen's skin begins to itch. She is increasingly 'irritated' in her new house. As Yen's itch worsens she decides that there is something wrong with the house and that it needs to be set right. She subjects it to the corrective powers of feng shui. Rearranging the furniture does not appease her growing sense of discomfort: she suggests to her husband they move to Australia, she frets that her daughter Mui-Mui is reluctant to speak Cantonese and to know Chinese ways. One night she breaks down and the inability of her newly painted and properly arranged house to provide a sense of home is made clear: 'I don't know where my home is,' she laments, 'where is my home?'

The stairs 1. The stairway is a transit passage within a house. It is not a space for permanent occupation. As an architectural feature designed for vertical movement it has risk built in to it. Certain added features, like the balustrade, are designed to reduce that risk. Other features, like the landing, provide rest points in order to make the up and down journeying more manageable

In this sense, the stairway offers an architectural metaphor for the dynamic of the migrant family, and perhaps for the migrant house as a whole. In *Floating Life* this space is featured in two dramatic moments in the Chans' migrant experience. It is on the stair that the pressures of 'settling' boil over and set the family asunder. It is on the stair that certain vernacularisms return to reinstate order and well-being.

When they first arrive, Ma and Pa have little option but to accept the hospitality and advice of their daughter, Bing. They are in the care of Bing, she being their official family-reunion sponsor, the main breadwinner (with her husband) and the owner of the house. This results in a strange inversion of the relations of authority in the family, with Bing assuming the role of the temporary 'elder'. Ma even loses authority over the one space and the one task that was always understood to be hers, the kitchen and cooking. The disruptive effects of the inverted structure of authority come into view around the 'problem' of the Chans' two teenage boys. Bing also assumes responsibility for how her younger brothers will settle. She urges them to assimilate by banning them from speaking Cantonese at home. But she admonishes them for assimilating in the wrong ways (such as buying certain magazines). One day Bing raids her teenage brothers' room removing 'contraband' and dirty clothes and dumping them on the stair landing. The family gathers there to witness Bing's rage: the boy's are sullen and silent; Ma tries to suggest everyone come to the table to eat. Bing spectacularly turns upon her mother and asserts her authority: 'You're here as migrants, not to enjoy life. You're leaving your country, OK? My rules or back to Hong Kong!'

The stairs 2. The fight on the stair landing ruptures the family and Ma and Pa take the boys and move into their own home. Bing is devastated and has a breakdown that sees her confined to her room, not eating and not bathing. It is at this point that certain vernacular artefacts and rituals come to be actively reinserted into the logic of homemaking in this Australian-based branch of the Chan family. Ma, resuming her proper place in the family structure, catches a bus to Bing's house and, once there, makes soup and, most importantly, sets up the altar that Bing had so adamantly discouraged. The altar is set up at the base of the stair in front of the (opened) front door to the house. It is in the midst of this architecture of apertures, thresholds and thoroughfares that Ma does her work of healing her daughter and making this house right again. Bing is drawn out of her bedroom and sits on the stairway listening to her mother pray to distant ancestors to help them to 'plant our roots in this soil'.

Let me linger here with this scene on the stairwell, with a mother praying to distant ancestors at a movable altar positioned between the stair and an open front door (Figure 9.5). At this point in the film the narrative tells us, much as it did with Yen's use of feng shui, about how Chinese traditions cannot just travel, but inhabit new houses and be used to bestow upon those new houses and

Figure 9.5
VERNACULARIZING THE THRESHOLD OF THE NEW HOUSE.

those that live in them a proper sense of belonging. This is of course a very inviting, empowering and, some might say, romantic migrant story. By depicting an adaptable tradition-on-the-move an idea of ancestral Chinese-ness is not simply sustained as some residual thing back there, but as an enlivened thing that can be set to work in what ever here and now it is required.

AS MANY ANCESTRAL HOMES AS NEEDED

The scenes on the stairway offer, then, a way for this film to narrate a mobile and adaptable 'tradition' into the core of movement itself. There is one other figure that is called upon to demonstrate a similar point, and in a way that is explicitly (as opposed to metaphorically) architectural. This is the figure of the ancestral home. I use the term 'figure' here because the narrative of *Floating Life* suggests that, contrary to what we might imagine, the ancestral home is more than a single, non-replicable thing. As noted earlier, the 'overseas Chinese' have long been seen as retaining attachments to the homeland. In terms of the house, this translates into the idea of the ancestral home. One might imagine that in a film that depicts the Chinese diaspora, there would be just one ancestral home. But in *Floating Life*, there are three houses that come to assume the role of 'ancestral home'. This film deals with the idea of the ancestral home under diasporic circumstances, not by doing away with it altogether, but by multiplying it. The idea that an 'ancestral home' can only ever be unilocal and bound to one place is dispensed with. The first ancestral home we see in *Floating Life* is the house we might imagine to be *the* ancestral home, the one that retains the aura of the authentic. This house is back in China and the family have not lived in it for over 50 years. We come to know of this house through the reminiscences of Pa and one of his old friends, and we see it only through a snapshot taken by Pa's friend (Figure 9.6a). It is, in this sense, more of an idea than part of the lived social geography of the family. It is an ancestral home that is not known through dwelling as such but by way of various mediated experiences. It is *the* ancestral home, but it is at the same time a virtual ancestral home.

When Pa and Ma leave Bing's house with the boys they move into a Federation-style house in the countryside. Made of stone, with a typical corrugated iron roof, surrounded by a wide veranda and located in a picturesque garden setting with established trees, the house is utterly different to the house Bing provided for her family. It is in this solid, older home that Ma and Pa reconstitute their family and the practices and rituals they feel appropriate to sustain it. It is here that Pa sets about planning and building a lotus pond just like the one he remembers near the ancestral home in China (Figure 9.6b). In this new 'old home', Ma and Pa create another ancestral home for their family. Of course, the ability of this house to play convincingly the part of the new ancestral home in *Floating Life* depends not simply upon us being told it is so, but upon the way its architectural features furnish it with a certain authenticity relative to the architecture of the suburban monster house. The older, Federation-style house assumes an air of authenticity that we imagine surpasses anything that might emerge from a suburban house with its brick veneer, its paper thin walls and its balustrades that stop short, in a space somewhere between function and ornament (see Figure 9.5).

There is yet one more ancestral home suggested in *Floating Life*, this being an aged, two-storey, stone farmhouse in Germany (Figure 9.6c). This is the house of Yen's German mother-in-law, Mui-Mui's grandmother, and it functions in the film in a way that is reminiscent of Heidegger's Black Forest hut with which I opened this chapter. In the film, this house is called 'Mui-Mui's house' and the final scene of the film shows this as the home that we presume will become the locus of Yen's Chinese-German daughter's rooting in her birthplace. The final scene of the film shows Mui-Mui running towards this house and metaphorically running towards a future that incorporates a house grounded in someone's local tradition and linked to someone's local ancestry. Again, it is an architecture constituted out of stone, solid walls and age that allow this home to take up the role as one of the many 'ancestral homes' now needed to service a family as dispersed as the Chans. But for all of the solidness that seems to be required of the architecture that comes to fill the category 'ancestral home', we see also in these examples the way in which the most foundational of dwelling figures – the ancestral house – undergoes routine surface shifts in the making of the migrant dwelling.

Figure 9.6
AS MANY ANCESTRAL HOMES AS YOU NEED: (a) VIRTUAL; (b) LOCAL; (c) ONERIC.

CONCLUSION

Floating Life is part of a representational field that does much more than depict a certain diasporic condition. It is a film that actively constructs a narrative about how such a diasporic experience might be seen and understood. In so doing it plays its part in constituting the Hong Kong diasporic identity. It is part of the cultural work that such migrant groups do in order to adjust their narratives of self so that they properly reflect the expanded field of associations and experiences that come with migration.

The materiality of the house matters in the stories told about how migrant senses of 'homeliness' are made and remade. The architecture of the house is actively called into the service of home making in a geographically promiscuous world that is defined by movement, networks of association and multi-local loyalties. The arrangement between the architectures of the house and senses of identity, homeliness and belonging may be complicated and made more self-conscious under migrant conditions, but it is certainly not done away with. Indeed, it might be argued that under the pressure of the disorientations and estrangements created by migration the house is called upon both more intensely and more flexibly to underscore identity. This then, is not Heller's transnational who has little apparent need for either a house or architecture of home. It is a migrant condition in which the materiality of the house remains fundamental to the building of more flexible and geographically promiscuous modes of dwelling. Home becomes an array of houses threaded like beads upon a string that links these floating lives. In this system of house and home, ideas of tradition as well as vernacular things and modes, are activated in novel ways. In *Floating Life*, for example, they are given an important role in the ways the Chan family come to settle properly in their new homes. Moveable altars, long-distance prayers to the ancestors and transnationally applied techniques of geomancy, all play a role as specifically 'Chinese' vernacularisms that are imported into these new settings in order to make the Chans' various new houses properly inhabitable.

Floating Life so fully implicates the architecture of the house in its depiction of how Chinese diasporic identities are formed and diasporic senses of belonging constituted that there seems to be no limit to the number of houses that might be threaded upon the transnational string that joins the Chan family. This capacity of the diasporic condition to thread into a meaningful relationship a seemingly limitless number of houses, is best illustrated by the case of the ancestral home. It might be imagined that a diasporic condition would make the idea of the ancestral house fade away (as hinted at by the depiction of the ancestral home in a snapshot). Or, alternatively, that nostalgia and longing might enhance the power of authenticity that can be claimed by the never-seen ancestral house. But *Floating Life* depicts yet another diasporic outcome for the ancestral home. In this film new ancestral homes are made by the appropriation of existing houses by the dispersed branches of the Chan family. So while the Chans are estranged from their 'real' ancestral home, they actually draw to their family two more, one in Australia and one in Europe.

This account of one narrative framing of the role of the house in the home-making of a diasporic family is intended to leave us with a restructured sense of how we dwell in a mobile world – one that is more suited to the geographical, sociological and affective peculiarities of the condition of migrancy. Migration transforms the way we think about Heidegger's original formula of the co-constitutive nature of building, dwelling and location. It forces us to activate his useful asides about 'how far' and 'reach', and place them actively and constructively into the formula of building, dwelling, location. By so doing we are not captured by the yearning for monogamous modes of dwelling, authentic vernacular architectures or ideas of lost ancestral homes. Rather, we can be captivated by the array of surface shifts that allow the complex and multi-local material and affective assemblies necessary to sustain meaningful modes of dwelling in the condition of migrancy.

NOTES

1 *Floating Life*, 1995 Australia, 95 mins. Production Company: Southern Star/AFFC/Hibiscus Films. Producer: Bridget Ikin. Director: Clara Law. Screenplay: Clara Law, Eddie Ling-Ching Fong.

2 This parallels what Marc Augé (1995: 47), writing around the same time, describes as 'anthropological place', which is something constituted not only by experiential fact but also by a compelling mixture of 'indigenous fantasy' (the desires of those who 'belong' to imagine themselves as always 'belonging') and 'ethnologist's illusions' (the desire of those outside to see those who 'belong' as always 'belonging').

3 Mandy Thomas's (1997) study of Vietnamese home-making in Australia has shown how the typical suburban house often does not comply with a varied array of Vietnamese criterion about what a 'proper' home should have.

4 Director Clara Law has explored themes about the disorientation and trauma of Chinese migration to New York in *Farewell China* (1990) (see Sun 2002).

REFERENCES

Anthias, F. (2001) 'New hybridities, old concepts: the limits of "culture"', *Ethnic and Racial Studies* 24 (4): 619–41.

Augé, M. (1995) *Non-places: introduction to an anthropology of supermodernity*, trans. J. Howe, London and New York: Verso.

Bachelard, G. (1969) *The Poetics of Space*, trans. M. Jolas, Boston: Beacon Press.

Bammer, A. (1992) 'Editorial', *New Formations*, 17: vii–xi.

Berger, J. (1984) *And Our Faces, My Heart, Brief as Photos*, London: Writers and Readers.

Bourassa, S.C. (1994) 'Immigration and housing tenure choice in Australia', *Journal of Housing Research* 5: 117–37.

Buttimer, A. (1980) 'Home, reach and the sense of place', in A. Buttimer and D. Seamon (eds) *The Human Experience of Space and Place*, London: Croom Helm.

Chow, R. (1993) *Writing Diaspora: tactics of intervention in contemporary cultural studies*, Bloomington, Indiana: Indiana University Press.

Douglas, M. (1991) 'The idea of "home" a kind of space', *Social Research*, 58 (1): 287–307.

Freud, S. (1987) 'The "uncanny"', in A. Dickson (ed.) *The Pelican Freud Library: art and literature*, vol. 14, Harmondsworth: Penguin Books.

Heidegger, M. (1975) 'Building dwelling thinking', in M. Heidegger *Poetry, language, thought*, trans. A. Hofstader, New York: Harper and Row.

Heller, A. (1995) 'Where are we at home?', *Thesis Eleven* 41: 1–18.

Kristeva, J. (1991) *Strangers to Ourselves*, New York: Columbia University Press.

Massey, D. (1994) *Space, Place and Gender*, Minneapolis: University of Minnesota Press.

McKeown, A. (1999) 'Conceptualizing Chinese diasporas, 1842 to 1949', *Journal of Asian Studies* 58 (2): 306–37.

Naficy, H. (1993) *The Making of Exile Culture: Iranian television in Los Angeles*, Minneapolis: University of Minnesota Press.

Nacify, H. (ed.) (1999) *Home, Exile, Homeland: film, media and the politics of place*, London: Routledge.

Pe-Pua, R., Mitchell, C., Iredale, R. and Castles, S. (1996) *Astronaut Families and Parachute Children: the cycle of migration between Hong Kong and Australia*, Centre for Multicultural Studies, University of Wollongong, Canberra: AGPS.

Probyn, E. (1996) *Outside Belongings*, New York and London: Routledge.

Pulvirenti, M. (2000) 'The morality of immigrant home ownership: gender, work and Italian-Australian sistemazione', *Australian Geographer*, 31 (2): 237–49.

Rapport, N. and Dawson, A. (eds) (1998) *Migrants of Identity: perceptions of home in a world of movement*, New York: Berg.

Rouse, R. (1991) 'Mexican migration and the social space of postmodernity', *Diaspora* 1 (1): 8–23.

Safran, W. (1991) 'Diasporas in modern societies: myths of homeland and return', *Diaspora*, Spring, 83–99.

Schnapper, D. (1999) 'From the nation-state to the transnational world: on the meaning and usefulness of diaspora as a concept', *Diaspora* 8 (3): 225–53.

Siu, P. (1952) 'The sojourner', *American Journal of Sociology* 58 (1): 34–44.

Skeldon, R. (1994) 'Reluctant exiles or bold pioneers: an introduction to migration from Hong Kong', in R. Skeldon (ed.) *Reluctant Exiles?: migration from Hong Kong and the new overseas Chinese*, Hong Kong: Hong Kong University Press.

Sun, W. (2002) *Leaving China: media, migration, and transnational imagination*, Lanham Maryland and Oxford: Rowman and Littlefield Publishers.

Thomas, M. (1997) 'Discordant dwellings: Australian houses and the Vietnamese diaspora', *Communal/Plural* 5: 95–114.

Vidler, A. (1992) *The Architectural Uncanny: essays in the modern unhomely*, Cambridge, Massachusetts: MIT Press.

Yang, P.Q. (2000) 'The "sojourner hypothesis" revisited', *Diaspora* 9 (2): 235–59.

Werbner, P. (2000) 'Introduction: the materiality of diaspora – between aesthetic and "real" politics', *Diaspora* 9 (1): 5–20.

Chapter 10: Emigration/immigration[1]

Maps, myths and origins

Mirjana Lozanovska

This chapter investigates the vernacular built forms of the village of Zavoj, in the Republic of Macedonia. It is concerned with the way these built forms are configured within a particular migratory dynamic, and with the ways they come to be understood within a particular range of architectural field research techniques, representational systems and knowledge regimes.

A PLACE OF ORIGIN AND A SITE OF DEPARTURE

The village of Zavoj is configured here as a site of emigration, a site of departure and a place of origin that is significantly mediated through a particular site of immigration, namely Melbourne, Australia. These terms 'emigration' and 'immigration' make explicit a troubling dynamic between places that often remains unrecognised within the more generalised term, 'migration' since they connote common movement. Together, these terms can reveal the ways that places appearing to be disparate – such as Zavoj and Melbourne – are, in fact, linked by the migrant's departure and arrival.

In the particular case of migration between Zavoj and Melbourne, these terms immediately activate a number of other distinctions. Zavoj can be perceived as Other to the settler-west of Melbourne, as a place of the non-western subject, a place seemingly off the map of the globalised economy, a place amenable to specific rather than generalised knowledges, a place not normally registered in the canons of architecture. But here, the 'em-' and the 'imm-' of migration seek to bind together these apparently diverging distinctions so that west and non-west, city and village, place and subject, case-study and theory, building and architecture are brought into more intimate and complex relationships. The migrant is centrally germane to this dynamic, his/her imaginative and existent mobility sets up, and then complicates, these oppositional relationships.

The migrant departs from a place of origin and embarks on a journey to a site of promise and growth. Any place of origin can be configured in terms of a temporal immobility, of stasis, in the memories of those who leave it behind.

As a site of emigration, however, Zavoj already absorbs the image of the new city of Melbourne, the migrant's destination. The promised city is imagined through stories, through fabrications by those who have already made that journey and have returned, through a strange mixture of the experience of a journey in space and its narration in language (Berger and Mohr 1975: 23). The process of emigration radically alters places of origin. Such places are not necessarily fixed or stable or passive or mute points of departure.

In this context, there are two questions to be approached. The first asks 'What becomes of Zavoj, the place of emigration, after the departure of the migrant?' The second question is methodological. It is concerned with the styles and manners for examining built and urban forms that are overcast by an ahistoricity of the vernacular, inherited in both migration and architectural discourse. Here we can ask, 'If disciplinary boundaries are produced through a mapping of canonical sites of significance how does migration (as a practice of mobility) impact upon this?'

It is clear that Zavoj needs to be examined, initially, as a problematic of geographic mapping, of locating (and siting) a non-canonical site. Furthermore, Zavoj poses a particular set of problems of architectural representation, of sighting, measuring and documenting. What does it mean to produce a plan of the village of Zavoj? The drawing practices required for the production of a plan are themselves heavily implicated in the norms of the architectural canon. How are these to be negotiated in the representation of Zavoj? Finally, the study of Zavoj is a problematic of citation. As academic producers of the canon, what do we address within the borders of writing, research and teaching? In other words, once we decide to turn our gaze somewhere else, what do we make of *and for* that place?

ABJECTION

Society depends on an established order and a stable human subject, and yet psychoanalytic theories of abjection analyse 'the ways in which "proper" subjectivity and sociality are founded on the (impossible) expulsion or exclusion of the improper, the unclean and the disorderly' (Grosz 1986: 108). The abject is a precondition to the human subject and to the symbolic order of society, but my emphasis here is that it accompanies that order, it 'hovers at the edges or borders of our existence, haunting and inhabiting regions supposedly clean and free of any influence or contamination' (Grosz 1986: 108). It can reappear when triggered by a traumatic event like migration. Migration invokes the abject in two ways: individually, in which the child is differentiated from the maternal space and constructed as a unified, independent subject; and socio-culturally, in which proper places (the city) is divided from improper places (the village). The not-yet-migrant often speaks of a compulsion to leave the village, pre-empting the journey of migration. As such, this kind of theory is useful for examining the figure of the migrant, as well as the site of emigration (the vernacular architecture of the village, Zavoj) and the site of immigration (the migrant house and the city of Melbourne, Australia) (Lozanovska 1997).

The village is redefined as a maternal space. The village haunts the migrant as a 'return of the repressed', the guilt associated with a disavowal of the debt owed to maternity (Grosz 1986: 107). Spatial boundaries between the migrant's body and the migrant house, and between the village and the city are put to question. Kristeva obliquely points to this, for example, when she refers to abjection as the 'degree zero of spatialisation', adding 'abjection is to geometry what intonation is to speech' (cited in Burgin 1991: 26). If the city is site of immigration, it is built on the pre-condition of the village. As a primordial spatiality, the village haunts the city's geopolitical structures. Migrant houses attest to an intense relationship between the migrant's body and the house. The migrant is, 'a tireless builder, the deject is in short a *stray*. He is on a journey, during the night, the end of which keeps receding' (Kristeva 1982: 8). The house is not an architecture that can sublimate the condition of the abject, rather it becomes a relentless process of rebuilding and maintenance.

At stake for the migrant is ongoing abjection, s/he might fall into the gap between the subject and the object (Kristeva 1982). The migrant's incapacity to sublimate this abject condition is exacerbated by the 'foreign' symbolic order s/he is inserted into. S/he is perceived as the site of the abject within the symbolic order of the proper city, because the proper city cannot fully expel its pre-condition of immigration. The migrant has an ambivalent role in relation to both the western subject and the (non-migrant) peasant, revealing a complexity within subject positions (Deleuze and Guattari 1987; Chow 1993).

Further, this spatial condition of the abject is also implicated in the ways the migrant attends to a map of the world. If for the migrant, the 'other place' already has a presence and hovers at the edge, the migrant's techniques of mapping offer a limit to the fantasy of the 'other place' as unknown, a limit to the exoticisation of the 'other'. Rather, the location of sites (as a practice of the migrant) is connected with the continual making and remaking of the self. This practice, then, is a process whereby the migrant constructs, and is constructed by, a location, a place, a space. It may be named an abject geometry, a fluid time-space representation. Layered upon this abject space-time of migration, almost as a superstructure, appears the formal measurement and documentation of maps and plans. Geographic space and geometric space given to us in this way, by maps and by orthographic projections, emerge as an overlay on something altogether more opaque.

Boundaries between disciplines, between language, the body and architecture are contested by an abject condition of migration and, becoming blurred, result in a complex spatial field, rather than a disciplinary platform. How might we characterise the disciplinary boundaries of architecture whose parameters enclose the living spaces of the migrant both before and after migration? In the next section two aspects of the architectural canon are identified as significant points of intersection between architecture and migration.

THE CANON(S)

The primitive hut and the vernacular-classicism conception significant to the canon of architecture are identified as sites of the abject. Each contains the ways in which the canon of architecture cannot completely exclude or expel that which it regards as improper and contaminating. The classical canon dominates architecture as a superior and universal tradition, and also as something that has been challenged, since the eighteenth century by the notion of historicism (Colquhoun 1989). Alan Colquhoun deals with this binary conception of architecture in his essay entitled 'Vernacular Classicism'. Here, he discusses the rise of the idea of the 'primitive hut' in eighteenth-century European architectural theory, principally through the writings of French cleric Marc-Antoine Laugier. Colquhoun suggests that Laugier's citing of the 'primitive hut' was not concerned with the 'real' Mediterranean vernacular, positioning Laugier precisely and centrally within the classical canon. Laugier's concern, Colquhoun argues, was with the dissemination of the classical doctrine – at a time when other architectural cultures had already started to influence (and undermine) the traditional certainties of the classical.

Laugier's interest in the Mediterranean was a search for the symbolic origin of classical architecture rather than the exploration of contemporary Mediterranean vernacular. Colquhoun argues that 'when we define *vernacular* in terms of the eighteenth-century notion of the primitive, we are involved in an argument that is characteristically classical', and that 'this process entailed, not the discovery of vernacular building, but the *revernacularization* of classicism with which to substantiate a myth of origins' (Colquhoun 1989: 30). The distinction made between the vernacular and classicism is problematic – it is neither clearly delineated nor overcome. It may be possible to argue, for example, that the origins of Zavoj (and the origins of architectural discourse) might also be related to the idea of the 'primitive hut'. Yet, at issue here is the negotiation of a space for vernacular architecture, attempting to resist its appropriation within the discourse of the classical canon and, simultaneously, addressing unresolved tensions within the classical discourse.

HISTORIES

It is to the improper within the proper that I now turn. The configuration of space as an associative field between geography, geometry and dwelling confronts the traditional definitions of place (the place of origin, the place of settlement, the place of the home). To locate architecture within this particular intellectual context raises the question of a history of architecture as a history of (social) space. As such, this is investigated in the writings of Michel de Certeau (1984) and Henri Lefebvre (1991), among others.

Lefebvre's notion of 'social space' and de Certeau's concepts of spatial practices and dwelling, suggest a much more complex and interactive relation between space and its physical order than that normally entertained by traditional architectural discourse. Furthermore, together they support a role for time in relation to space, in particular by giving space a specific temporality. It follows from this that one way of defining a field of the vernacular, an ontological field of dwelling and spatiality, is to see social space as a condition within architecture from which to speak to the classical canon.

MIGRANCY

The figure of the migrant is constrained by a specific historical time (1950–75), place (from a village in the Balkans/Southern Europe to a city in Australia/Canada/US), and a specific local/global economics (from one type of working class to another type of working class). For the path of migrancy explored here, there were a number of superstructural formations.

Perhaps the most crucial of these was the 'White Australia' policy. The intention of this policy was to control non-British immigration to Australia over the period between federation in 1901 (the moment that brought together the former colonies into the modern nation state of Australia) and the Whitlam government in 1972. While simultaneously advocating the superiority of British culture the 'White Australia' policy also, paradoxically, produced one of the world's most ethnically diverse countries. The purpose of the policy, however, was to select immigrants from specific socio-cultural – and even racial backgrounds – for their particular capacity to assimilate into Australian society. It was an exclusionist policy conceived along explicitly racial lines. In particular, it sought to eliminate Asian immigration, which had been fairly widespread in Australia for over a hundred years. In practice it also differentiated between northern and southern Europeans, with an institutional preference for Nordic, Aryan types (Kunek 1993). These policies constructed Australia as a nation with clearly established British origins, and with a monolithic frontier of Anglo-Celtic culture (Gunew 1988).

Clearly, such immigration policies are also obliquely designed to assure members of the dominant culture that the migrant is unthreatening. The desire for such reassurance stems from the host culture's memories of its own prior acts of colonisation and processes of settlement, of its own Anglo-Celtic histories of departure and arrival. Nostalgia for origins is common among all migrants, yet when origins such as Macedonia are invoked, and they do not coincide with the origins of the host culture (England and Ireland), there can be a sense of disjuncture and disquiet. The migrant who is associated with origins which differ from those which the host culture promulgates inevitably turns into the (transcendental) foreigner, the figure of the dislocated subject, the bitter/sweet sense of the stranger within each one of us. This figure of the migrant (Berger 1975) is pivotal to recent theories of identity construction and human subjectivity as explored, for instance, by Julia Kristeva (1991), Edward Said (1993) and Stuart Hall (1996). Tracing the complex and interlinked relationship between self and place (both imaginary and real) we can see that Macedonia and Australia are constantly renegotiated through histories of migration, through collective memory and through imaginary projections between the sites of emigration and immigration. The history of Zavoj is entangled with the history of Melbourne.

Like many other villages in Europe in the process of industrialisation, Zavoj came to be seen as 'underdeveloped'. Many of its residents simply had to leave in order to live (Berger 1975). In contemporary global economic contexts, villages like Zavoj have no reason to continue existing. And yet the vision of the global village is both contingent on, and constituted through, actual villages, such as Zavoj, as its unacknowledged place/space. The unembellished story of the migrant is one instance of this unacknowledged relationship. The host-citizen, perceiving and representing the metropolis as a village – a site with social and racial frontiers, turning cities into villages – is another. We see these boundaries shifting in Australia (and other sites of the Diasporic and Old Worlds), projecting the myth of place through strategies to remove the guest, the migrant and the refugee. The concept of the global village presents dire consequences – who will be cast outside of the global village – who will be rendered invisible in its representation?

THE PLAN(S) FOR ZAVOJ

It perhaps comes as no great surprise that Zavoj lacks architectural visibility and location on the great map of architectural cultures. But when thinking about maps as tools of travel, it is perhaps possible to introduce a 'non-place' onto the architectural map. Zavoj, then, is bought into visibility and focus, and thus becomes an object of desire – traced by a line between itself and Melbourne, Australia (Figure 10.1). Desire, in this context, is the line of myself as author located within the text and here oscillating between architect, academic and migrant: siting Zavoj, mapping Zavoj, representing the built environment of Zavoj, telling the story of Zavoj.

Zavoj was paced, measured, checked through orientations to the sun, and adjusted by the angles of walls. Fragments of Zavoj recorded on A3 sheets were overlaid into a single smooth orthographic plane, and these were taped together

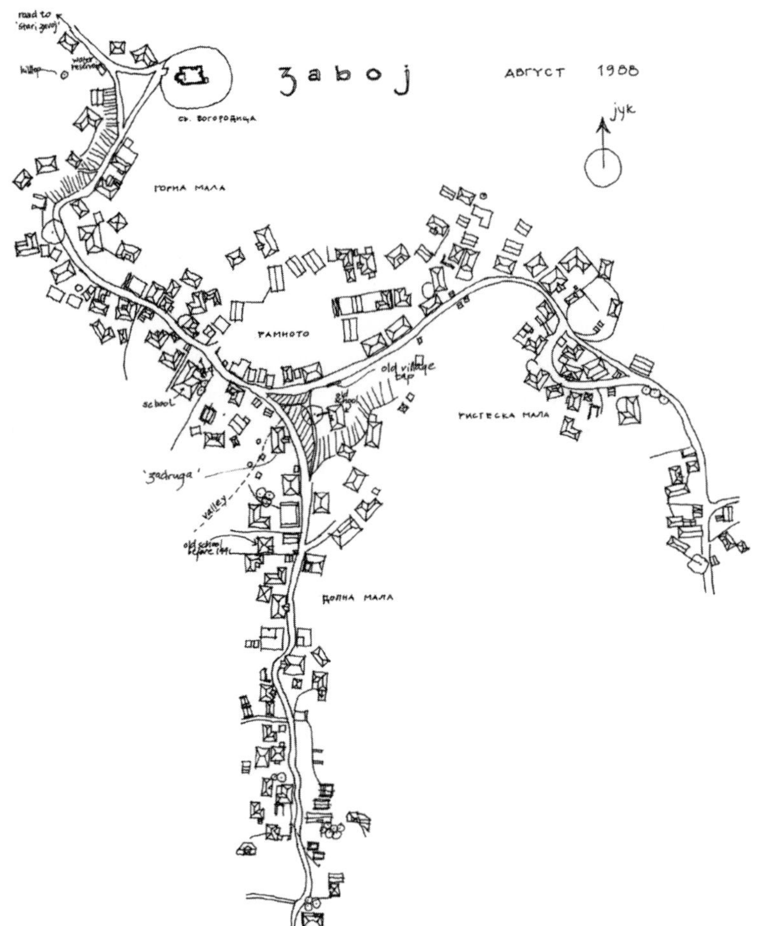

Figure 10.1
THE PLAN OF ZAVOJ, IN THE REPUBLIC OF MACEDONIA. THIS PLAN IS NOT THE REPRESENTATION OF REALITY, BUT ALLUDES TO AN IMAGINARY FIELD THAT IS EXTRACTED FROM THE DRAWING.
(All figures – drawings and photographs – in this chapter are by the author)

to give a comprehensive sense of the whole village. Additional adjustments were made with drafting tools – crosschecking according to observations and photographic documentation – before it was integrated into a single, smooth, orthographic plane. Discrepancies were present but were erased from the representation of the final drawing.

Luscombe and Peden, discussing architectural representation, argue that plans and sections make it possible to see a building's interior from a distance (Luscombe and Peden 1992: 9). Conversely, architectural drawings of buildings and cities after the fact of disintegration and change act as historical documents that inevitably participate in the circulation and citation of architecture. As a corollary of having a plan, Zavoj is subsequently able to participate in discursive practices. The plan makes the village representable, visible and legible.

Robin Evans, architectural historian and theorist, explores another type of pleasure in the plan (Evans 1995). He argues that there is an 'active imagination in the drawing' and that while drawings themselves do not think, imaginative intelligence lies dormant in the plan (and the section and elevation) because orthographic projection is, itself, the product of intense imagination (Evans 1986). He is referring here to orthographic projection specifically as a peculiar method of representation, where the imaginary lines from the object are perpendicular to the picture plane, and are always directional and parallel within themselves. Such a characterisation offers precision and measure of the object, but in order to avoid too much disfigurement, the buildings that are frontal, rectangular and flat are most accurately represented due to their affinity with the surface of the paper.

The plan of the village thus both reveals and conceals a truth about the relationship between reality and representation: it has no reference to the real and yet inherent within it is the ability to perceive the thing represented. The making of a plan of Zavoj – a village site that is, in reality, abandoned and disordered – produces the village as a unified and preserved whole, that the village both is and is not. The plan, in this sense, alludes to an imaginary field of the village, not the representation of a reality, but something that is envisioned through our imaginative extraction from the drawing: an image of the village as an ideal place, a place of (the author's) idealisation (Colquhoun 1989: 12, 28). The plan also becomes a site of encounter between Zavoj, author and (migrant) reader(s), weaving dialogues of personal and intellectual histories reinforcing the interrelated history of Zavoj and Melbourne. Such pleasures in the plan might again turn it back into an abject geometry between improper and proper places (Figure 10.2).

Desire, seen as the architectural academic's projection, has the uncanny effect of destabilising the (western) subject partly through (dis)placing the self onto a foreign site of fieldwork. A panoramic black and white photograph can complement the empirical representation and can offer a breadth of vision and an atmosphere of an impossible perspective. The village is on a mountain, a few buildings are dotted on its topography, a white cube-church reflects the light and is, itself, illuminated. To gaze at the image exemplifies the unleashing

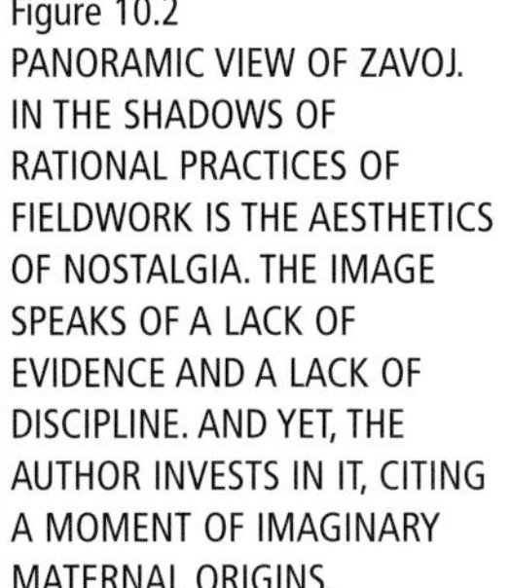

Figure 10.2
PANORAMIC VIEW OF ZAVOJ. IN THE SHADOWS OF RATIONAL PRACTICES OF FIELDWORK IS THE AESTHETICS OF NOSTALGIA. THE IMAGE SPEAKS OF A LACK OF EVIDENCE AND A LACK OF DISCIPLINE. AND YET, THE AUTHOR INVESTS IN IT, CITING A MOMENT OF IMAGINARY MATERNAL ORIGINS.

of nostalgia, a nostalgia that 'may paradoxically undo the concept of the unique and unitary self' (Gunew 1994: 115). In the shadows of rational practices of fieldwork is the aesthetics of nostalgia. Critiques of the politics of fieldwork, in particular the technique of participant-observation, are well known (Clifford 1997: 19–27). But this image conjures a snapshot from a travel diary. It speaks of a lack of evidence and a lack of discipline. And yet, the author invests in it, citing a moment of imaginary maternal origins. The everyday lives of the villagers engaging in their own travels also view this panorama. They are not always in the village centre. The object of study, the place, Zavoj, has another narrative and other histories that negotiate the discursive boundaries of the discipline.

A plan/map of the village of Zavoj also attests to the complex arguments of de Certeau. The map is ultimately a product of (architectural) discourse. As a master discourse of *proper places*, it thus 'collates on the same plane [plan] heterogeneous places, some *received* from a tradition and others *produced* by observation' (de Certeau 1984: 121). While tradition is included within the logic of the plan, its form of representation alters its constitution. The inhabitants always already know the village and its context. Spatial and geographic knowledge about the village for its inhabitants is generated through multifarious means *other* than plans and maps; daily itineraries are organised within and in relation to the layout of the village; everyday practices produce an associational sense of the relative location of things; people's movements are interlaced with mental, cultural and territorial charts accumulated over time. The purpose of the plan is to consolidate memory, to make history.

So it is that the field academic wishing and intending to fill the gaps of history and knowledge about Zavoj is compelled to produce a map, to make a plan, before everything is lost. Making history, in this context, is a crucial and imperative exercise. To not act is to disown the place.

But do the black solid lines on the white surface of the architectural plan cast into oblivion all the labours, the movements, the bodies, the histories on which their inscription is contingent? The plan, together with other drawings and representations, constitutes an architectural frontier, a system of representation in which temporal relations are reduced to (and reconstituted as) spatial relations and the strange realness of the everyday is gone: 'the map gradually wins out over these figures; it colonizes space; it eliminates little by little the pictorial figurations of the practices that produce it' (de Certeau 1984: 121). It is in this context that the consequence of visibility and invisibility of the plan as representation becomes relevant to a study of Zavoj (Lozanovska 1995, 1999).

Architectural discourse, embodied as it is in graphic representations, casts these spatial practices into pre-history, into a pre-architectural era. They are frequently scribbled as notes in the margins of the plan, the section, and in the footnotes, they are displaced from the central discursive site. The trace of architecture is not the site of memory, but something much more absolute. Is it 'actual repression (the forgetting of what one has forgotten)?' enquires Sneja Gunew in another context (1994: 115). Representations of vernacular architecture signal that the discipline repeatedly and repetitively avoids the site as a discursive history. Is this, then, the site of *indifference* to other co-existing architectural cultures? (Grosz 1989; Lefebvre 1991: 70).

Drawing the vernacular building of Zavoj does not guarantee the universality of the classical canon. More useful is Evans' argument that there is a blind spot between drawing and its object – how will things go, how will they travel in between, and what will happen to them on the way? 'To draw from' and 'to be drawn to' better describe the processes of translation, transportation, transfiguration, transition, transmigration, transfer, transmission, transmutation, transposition, that mediate drawings and buildings. The imaginary field of drawings affects knowledge and human subjects, as well as their object.

LOGS, CARTS, BENCHES, HOUSES

But where on the plan of the village are women's meeting places? Where are the sites for women's gatherings? Often the women amble somewhat distractedly within the village; they meet spontaneously and find somewhere where they can sit together. This might be on a pile of logs, an unused cart, or some benches by a house (Figure 10.3). There are no organised or even recognised places for women to meet. Each day, and in contradiction to their apparently pre-destined, pre-mapped lives, there are stories and contradictory movements, spatial trajectories, meanderings that traverse across paths and places, that weave places together.

Figure 10.3
WOMEN'S MEETING PLACE. IN CONTRADICTION TO THEIR SEEMINGLY PREDESTINED, PRE-MAPPED LIVES, THESE WOMEN TELL STORIES ABOUT TRAVELS TO MOUNTAINS, OTHER TOWNS AND COUNTRIES.

The effect is a proliferation, an abundance of meeting sites, a plenitude of spaces that are impossible for the plan to constitute. Such sites have no definition as a notable place per se – until the women meet there. It is through their meetings, their conversations, that spaces are transformed. So it is that women's meeting sites are at once non-existent, not on the plan, and yet exist everywhere in space. They cannot be marked on the plan and cannot be represented within the transparency of the rational white surface, but this does not mean that women do not meet in the village. 'They are at work everywhere', intertwining with the architectural frontier as its spatial Other. Conversations with the women moved from themes of work, poverty, family to the secret pleasures of walking, and walking alone in the mountains. They prefer to live in the village, even after their husbands have died, and their children have left. Why? They have not led such parochial lives. Many travel regularly to small nearby towns, and some have travelled to the shores of other continents, to the dream cities of Diaspora. One woman described her impressions of Melbourne during her visit to her daughter's house: *zatvor*, 'prison', she stated emphatically, always locked up inside, nowhere to walk. The women of the village are, themselves, travellers and their travels suggest a poetics of freedom, rather than the constraints of tradition and locality.

De Certeau proposes that *space* is in contradistinction to *place*. While strategic technologies of power and knowledge have already acted in the production of a place, space occurs as the effect of a number of intersecting forces which may be in conflict. Yet, for that time these forces produce a multivalent space, a space produced by a specific situation and a specific moment. A space cannot be simply identified as a stable place. While the strategic means (of the strong) invest in the 'mastery of place through sight', the tactical movements

Figure 10.4
WOMAN SITTING. WE LOOK AT THIS IMAGE OF THE WOMAN WITH A STICK IN ONE HAND, SITTING, SOLITARY, IN SILENCE. IT REMINDS US OF RODIN'S THE THINKER, EMBLEM OF WESTERN CIVILIZATION AND REASON. AND YET SHE IS A WIDOW IN BLACK, IN AN EMPTY VILLAGE, SOMEWHERE AT THE MARGINS OF THE MAP OF GLOBAL ECONOMIES. WE DO NOT KNOW WHAT SHE IS THINKING. THIS SUBJECT OF ARCHITECTURE EVADES OUR REPRESENTATION OF THE PLAN. YET, THE ARCHITECTURE OF THE VILLAGE IS SUSTAINED THROUGH HER SPATIAL STORY.

(of the weak) carry out a labour that constantly transforms places into spaces (de Certeau 1984: 118). We may call these 'spatial practices', and a narration of them, 'spatial stories'. This labour is persistent, subtle, tireless, ready for an opportunity, and scattered over the terrain of the dominant order (de Certeau 1984: xix, 34–8, 117). The architectural project is concerned with the documentation of the physical, presenting an order and division of space in its manifestation as a place. Spatial stories, argues de Certeau are 'treatments of space', a way of thinking about the built environment that complements the architectural tradition (de Certeau 1984: 122). The inhabitants' words and stories both distract from and compel the architectural documentation of place (Chow 1993: 52; Gunew 1994: 119). The writing of the 'inhabitations' (Irigaray 1993), 'uses' (Lefebvre 1991), 'practices' (de Certeau 1984), the 'making do' in and of space are gestures towards a representation which stages an archi-textual field between image, orthographic projection and narratives of daily life (Figure 10.4).

VILLAGE MYTHS

The tale about the origin of Zavoj speaks of the horror and sacrifice that preceded its founding and construction. Everyone in the village knows the story, which goes like this: one day, a few hundred years ago, the woman serving at the inn laid the table ninety-nine times for hungry travelling merchants. At the end of this she had run out of food and had nothing left to feed anyone. A group of Turks[2] broke their journey and went to the inn demanding food and drink. Angered by what they saw as her inhospitality they slaughtered her, put her in the *sac*[3] and had her for dinner. At this the villagers protested, fighting broke out and the village folk eventually disbanded towards Prilep, Bitola and Ohrid (three towns in the vicinity of the village). Three brothers stayed behind and settled at the site where they had overnight *koshari*[4]to shelter in. The brothers established the present village of Zavoj.

It is clear that two pre-eminent stories precede the founding of the village. The first is one of cannibalism: the foreign men devour the woman's body. In doing so they take more than they are offered; they are no longer the guests of the woman, they are her murderers. But they are also no longer strictly foreign. Through eating the woman they appropriate an identity that is part familial and part foreign, the bloodlines are mixed. The second foundational story is that of the battle between these foreign and familial men over territory. Once her body has been devoured, the men must battle each other. The battlefield itself is marked by the spilling of blood and flesh. In this battle, the men are also sacrificed and both familial and foreign blood soaks into the earth. It is up to the myth to resolve/correct such impure mixtures of the ground and foundation for reconstruction. Where is the woman? She disappears in the text.

Figure 10.5
KOSHARA. A FOUNDING SHELTER FOR THE MYTH OF THE ORIGIN OF THE VILLAGE OFFERS A PRIMORDIAL TEXTURE TO LAUGIER'S PRIMITIVE HUT.

The woman's evaporation and the battle between the men facilitates a third 'scene': the founding of a site and the construction of the village. The *koshari* are huts known only to men. Conversely, women have no access to the knowledge of how to claim *their* territory. The body of woman is also food for thought; she is the stuff (the original inspiration) of spatial origins. In this sense, space prior to the establishment of the village is defined as female in contrast to the 'hut', which is defined as male. The shepherds are travellers; they re/turn to their huts for a protected place to rest and sleep. In replacing the female space, the (m)other space, the hut is sometimes engendered as mother. The *koshara* mediates a man's relationship to space and territory (Figure 10.5).

The classical canon of architecture is entangled with the field and frontiers of this myth of the origin of the village. This occurs via the architectural edifice, which associates Laugier's Primitive Hut with the *koshari*/shepherd's huts. This tale speaks to us from the mythical unconscious and involves the dichotomies of male/female, body/territory, food/village, familiar/foreign, offering a kind of primordial texture to the primitive hut as the canonical object of Laugier's essay. Significantly, the hut as architectural edifice is a strategy for settlement. It transforms the environment from one type of space to another type of space, from an uninhabitable forest to a space defined through the logic of the architectural edifice. The construction of the architectural edifice renders space into place, renders a forest into a 'system of frontiers, which effects a division of spaces', a territory. The hut in the foreground of the image frames our view of the vast space above a mountainous landscape. While the gable form poetically mimics the mountain peaks and its woven roof makes associations with baskets, its central vertical post indicates that this structure is as much about surveillance of the land as it is about the poetics of journey. The hut acts as a fortress, a site with frontiers.

Laugier's Primitive Hut is a return to the primitive as a way to substantiate the myth of origins for the classical language. But, as this myth of origins of the village reveals, it is also a return to territorial claims and conquests, and these are historically evident in the processes of European colonisation. Cultural and blood lines are intermingled – as suggested in the myth. If the canonical texts of architecture and urbanism are intertwined with primordial myths and peasant tales, they also participate in scenes of cannibalism, the battlefield, and the original territorial gesture of architecture, a site where urban construction and borderlines are established on obscene yet uncertain grounds.

EMIGRATION/IMMIGRATION

Let us return to the 'em-' and 'imm-' of migrancy by examining the return journey migrants undertake to their place of origin, the village of Zavoj, for a celebration. Holidays associated with such celebrations are what de Certeau calls a turn: a migrational return to the site of emigration, departing from the city of immigration. In de Certeau's terms this return can be described as a *tactic*: a way of operating for people who are displaced, for people who are 'Othered' by the forces that establish dominant regimes of place. It is a mode of action determined by not having a place of one's own: 'The space of a tactic is the space of the other. Thus it must play on and with a terrain imposed on it and organized by the law of a foreign power.' The *tactic* though 'is neither a pathetic nor a romantic response to an analysis of power, it is always in an active relation to strategic forces' (de Certeau 1984: 34–8). The migrant must be reactive and organised to enable this return to the place of origin (Figure 10.6).

The house in the village that provides a proper place for the return of the migrant is a maternal space in relation to the other cities of immigration, but a patrimonial house in relation to the village and its myth of origins. Although there are limited documents of the ownership of the land, the land in the whole vicinity is mapped according to ownership and paternal lineage. Migration is a global force that interacts with existing property laws to produce an incongruous built environment. The village comprises more than 100 houses of which about 80 are old and in a state of disrepair. Scattered through these are new houses, small and minimalist, corners of an old house demolished and a new fragment rebuilt, new houses left eternally incomplete and sites of ongoing construction. These are uninhabited. In the image the old part of the house indicates inhabitation and dwelling by the strings of peppers hung on its sunny wall. The newly built part remains unfinished and uninhabited. The image presents an aesthetics that result when migration drives intersect with property and expedient construction. New veneers and empty houses make explicit an estrangement between the

Figure 10.6
ZAVOJ IS THE PLACE OF ANOTHER ARCHITECTURAL CULTURE. AN AHISTORICITY OF VERNACULAR ARCHITECTURE IS INHERITED IN BOTH MIGRATION AND ARCHITECTURAL DISCOURSE.

migrant and the village. Architecture's objective is absolutely complicit with property. Its apparent purpose is to claim the rights of territory and, literally, to put a stake in the land.

In an essay titled, 'Abjection and architecture: the migrant house in multicultural Australia' (Lozanovska 1997), I examined the migrant house in Melbourne. Zavoj and Melbourne are associated through the house(s) built by migrants in each site of emigration and immigration. In Melbourne, the immigrant house is divided between its formal exterior appearance and presentation, and an interior constituted through a mixture of cultural paraphernalia, customs and languages. It is also divided between its role in relation to the migrant inhabitants and its role in relation to the dominant culture of its host context. Distinctive territorial forces determine the architectures of both the Zavoj and Melbourne migrant house. The Melbourne migrant house articulates a symbolic architectural aesthetics. Its claim for territory might be perceived as architecturally excessive in various ways: in scale, in the duration of the materials (concrete, brick), in the security marked by the fence, gateways and doors, in ornament (lions and eagles), and in an extreme order marked by the control of nature (Lozanovska 1997: 113). It insists on ongoing maintenance and inhabitation. In contrast, the house in Zavoj is a project of incomplete construction, of expedience and fleeting visits. It is a site of the abject because the migrant does not dwell in the village.

In the village the migrant formalises space; converting it into property. This is no tactical movement; the migrant is much more strategic in relation to the space of the village. The women and men who have not emigrated move in and around the property of migrants, often using them tactically, turning them back into spaces. Animals, too, like the pig shown traversing the path, and nature, act onto these semi-abandoned buildings. To dwell indicates the treatment of architecture. Images of unfinished houses with steel rods protruding up into the sky and down into the concrete structure present a parody of Coop Himmelblau's project House Vektor II (Haus Meier-Hahn), Dusseldorf. Anthony Vidler states that this project:

> with its impaled roof, illustrates almost too directly, but uncomfortably enough, the will to destroy the house of classical architecture and the society it serves [. . .]; [it] encapsulates didactically, if not architecturally, the twin ambitions of Himmelblau to drive a stake at once through the house and through the specific humanist body it represents.
>
> (Vidler 1992: 80)

It presents a metaphoric rendition of the battle between familial and foreign men described in the myth of origin.

Could the discourse of migration and the poststructuralist discourse of the death of classicism converge over the loss of this other forgotten body, a body of another spatiality? The maternal body that makes food but that is, herself, consumed is entirely repressed by Coop Himmelblau and dominant architectural discourse. The migrant must build to believe in a fiction about ownership and territory, a scene that repeatedly suppresses the loss of this other spatiality and body (Lefebvre 1991: 355).

Building practices cover over memory and produce architecture as speculative and aspirational. A proper architectural edifice, like Laugier's primitive hut for example, transfers the processes of building into a metaphysical realm, a rational system of knowledge that overcomes both memory and amnesia. Coop Himmelblau's House Vektor II, reveals that a return to humanism 'is a movement backward within a closed episteme' (Colquhoun 1989: 31); a way to close the circuit of the architectural canon and again renew its origins. The Zavoj migrant house reveals an economics of construction in which the building of a new house to stand for the 'place of origin' remains an empty house, a house void of dwelling.

In migrant houses in both Zavoj and Melbourne, the loss is the space of dwelling, the space of inhabitation, the field of spatial practices and spatial stories. It constitutes an architectural loss presented as an unresolved tension within the dominant architectural canon: the place of dwelling and the ontological within architecture. What can we call this architecture? In architectural discourse it goes by the term 'vernacular'. In this chapter it is signalled by the vernacular architecture of the village, the other 'non-migrant' architectural context of Zavoj. It reflects back a history that is traditionally non-discursive, a history that is descriptive and that does not participate in a history of the present. Vernacular architecture is left out of critical discourse falling in the gap between the classical humanist house and its deconstruction and the migrant house and its construction. And yet it constitutes the spatiality on which they are built.

The migrant is unable to fully forget. Internally, the migrant house in Melbourne, the site of immigration, is in a dialectical relationship with the vernacular architecture of Zavoj, it struggles with its role in relation to the loss of this vernacular, this space of dwelling (Lozanovska 1997). It might be called 'little Macedonia' and offer the spatiality for the practice of the other language that is identified as a 'mother tongue' in relation to the hegemonic culture. But, these are gestures that signal the loss, rather than ways of reconstructing a vernacular. They have a temporal limit to their real practice, and they are a strange hybrid form of cultural and building practice. The migrant house has severed its relation to the myth of origins of the village and it has no other myth of origin to substitute it. The migrant must move on.

Zavoj, the site of emigration, is cited momentarily in the context of canonical discourse through the site of immigration, Melbourne. But this specific moment of citation signals that which cannot be included in a critical discourse on architecture: the co-existence of a village like Zavoj, a place of another origin, contemporaneous with Melbourne. This other place is constituted through a vernacular architecture *and* it is a site of ongoing dwelling and inhabitation. Zavoj is both a specific reality which represents the limit of the universalising canon, and an idealised village which represents the place of other architectural cultures.

NOTES

1 An earlier version of this essay was presented at the 3rd 'Other Connections' conference, *Building Dwelling Drifting: migrancy and the limits of architecture*, Melbourne, 1997. It introduced to the architectural forum the idea of 'migration' in its divided form between emigration and immigration.

2 This is a reference to the occupation/colonisation of Macedonia, by the Ottoman Empire, for 500 years, from the 1400s to the 1900s.

3 *Sac* is a traditional cooking pot set into the earth with hot coals placed on the lid and underneath.

4 The word '*koshari*' (plural) was used by the villagers for 'shepherd huts' scattered over the agricultural land. Its other meanings include basket '*koshara*' (singular) and fortress. The word '*koliba*' is also a term that means 'shepherd hut'.

REFERENCES

Berger, J. and Mohr, J. (1975) *A Seventh Man: migrant workers in Europe*, Cambridge: Granta Books.

Burgin, V. (1991) 'Geometry and abjection', in J. Donald (ed.) *Psychoanalysis and Cultural Theory: thresholds*, London: Macmillan.

Chow, R. (1993) *Writing Diaspora: tactics of intervention in contemporary cultural studies*, Bloomington: Indiana University Press.

Clifford, J. (1997) *Routes: travel and translation in the late twentieth century*, Cambridge, Massachusetts: Harvard University Press.

Colquhoun, A. (1989) *Modernity and the Classical Tradition: architecture essays 1980–1987*, Cambridge, Massachusetts: MIT Press.

de Certeau, M. (1984) *The Practice of Everyday Life*, trans. S. Rendall, Berkeley: University of California Press.

Deleuze, G. and Guattari, F. (1987) *A Thousand Plateaus: capitalism and schizophrenia*, trans. B. Massumi, Minneapolis: University of Minneapolis Press.

Evans, R. (1986) 'Translations from drawing to building', *AA Files* 12: 3–18.

Evans, R. (1995) *The Projective Cast: architecture and its three geometries*, Cambridge, Massachusetts: The MIT Press.

Grosz, E. (1986) 'Language and the limits of the body: Kristeva and abjection', in E. Grosz, T. Threadgold, D. Kelly, A. Cholodenko, E. Colless (eds) *Futur*Fall: excursions into post-modernity*, Sydney: Pathfinder Press and the Power Institute.

Grosz, E. (1989) *Sexual Subversions: three French feminists*, Sydney: Allen and Unwin.

Gunew, S. (1988) 'Home and away: nostalgia in Australian (migrant) writing', in P. Foss (ed.) *Island in the Stream*, Sydney: Pluto Press.

Gunew, S. (1994) *Framing Marginality: multicultural literary studies*, Melbourne: Melbourne University Press.

Hall, S. (1996) 'Who needs identity', in S. Hall and P. du Gay (eds) *Questions of Cultural Identity*, London: Sage Publications.

Irigaray, L. (1993) *An Ethics of Sexual Difference*, trans. C. Burke and G. Gill, Ithaca: Cornell University Press.

Kristeva, J. (1982) *Powers of Horror: an essay on abjection*, trans. L.S. Roudiez, New York: Columbia University Press.

Kristeva, J. (1991) *Strangers to Ourselves*, trans. L.S. Roudiez, New York: Harvester Wheatsheaf Press.

Kunek, S. (1993) 'Brides, wives and single women: gender and immigration', *Lilith: A Feminist History Journal* 8 (Summer): 82–113.

Lefebvre, H. (1991) *The Production of Space*, trans. D. Nicholson-Smith, Oxford: Blackwell.

Lozanovska, M. (1995) 'Excess: a thesis on [sexual] difference and architecture', unpublished thesis, Deakin University.

Lozanovska, M. (1997) 'Abjection and architecture: the migrant house in multicultural Australia', in G. Nalbantoglu and W.C. Thai (eds) *Postcolonial Space(s)*, New York: Princeton University Press.

Lozanovska, M. (1999) 'In and out of place: a study of the village Zavoj, Macedonia', *Self, Place and Imagination: cross-cultural thinking in architecture*, selected proceedings from the 2nd International CAMEA Symposium, The University of Adelaide, Australia: Centre for Asian and Middle Eastern Architecture.

Luscombe, D. and Peden, A. (1992) *Picturing Architecture: graphic presentation techniques in Australian architectural practice*, Sydney: Craftsman House.

Said, E.W. (1993) *Culture and Imperialism*, London: Vintage.

Spivak, G.C. (1990) *The Postcolonial Critic: interviews, strategies, dialogues*, New York: Routledge.

Vidler, A. (1992) *The Architectural Uncanny: essays in the modern unhomely*, Cambridge, Massachusetts: MIT Press.

Chapter 11: Earthquake weather

Sarah Treadwell

> And yet observe: that thin scraggy, filthy, mangy, miserable cloud, for all the depth of it, can't turn the sun red, as a good business-like fog does with a hundred feet or so of itself. By the plague-wind every breath of air you draw in is polluted, half round the world; in a London fog the air itself is pure, though you choose to mix dirt with it, and choke yourself with your own nastiness.
>
> (Ruskin 1905: 29)

John Ruskin, in his weather essay, 'The storm-cloud of the nineteenth century' (Ruskin 1905), having lovingly described the colour and configuration of clouds and winds, succumbs to an agitation that is palpable. The formal world that he traced was shaken at that moment by the science of vibrating particles; wave theory stirred the trees outside the window of his study in a troubling manner. The weather in the latter part of the nineteenth century had changed for Ruskin, becoming marked by the appearance of a 'plague-wind' characterized by tremulous and agitated qualities. This plague-wind, polluted by dead men's souls released by war and by smoke from factory furnaces, was also contaminated by 'dirt' that was airborne 'half round the world'.

Ruskin's distress is, in part, activated by his recognition of the wind's capacity to exceed boundaries, architectural, regional, national, and by his intuition that it also signalled change. Dirt thickened English air; new weather patterns seemingly carried traces of foreign wars and factories that could not be controlled or easily resisted. Ruskin saw the changing meteorological formations of the nineteenth century as omens with grim social consequences.

This chapter follows Ruskin's 'plague wind' 'half round the world' taking his agitation about nineteenth-century weather as a point of entry into an examination of a particular trajectory of settler migration between the British Isles and New Zealand. The immigrants in this case were settler colonials, departing the old country to establish new lives in New Zealand, a territory deemed in imperial eyes to be available for economic exploitation and constructions of a new (and always flawed) England.

'Weather', in this chapter, is invoked and practised as a metaphorical representation of a particular moment and variety of nineteenth-century immigration which still sends ripples into contemporary times. As weather is always about future conditions mapped with signs from the past, so too architecture is caught in a complex oscillation between forms of representation that carry with them both the past and technologies that imagine the future, in the present. Anxiety about weather is a consequence of its unpredictability and colonial architecture suffered a similar anxiety as it negotiated new forms arising from projected conditions and changing technologies.

Jonathan Hill points out that one of the traditional and defining roles of building is to provide shelter against inclemency and that the exclusion of weather is fundamental to this purpose (Hill 2001: 69). Hill critically engages with weather as an architectural material working it 'as a metaphor of the outside pouring into the discipline of architecture' (Hill 2001: 69). Weather, metaphorically, streams through the seeming tight fit of English architecture, finding gaps in its structure, weaknesses and intervals in its foundations, which are the sites of colonial ambivalence and the possibility of new constructions. Architectural approximations and ephemeral weather conditions are engaged as watery reflections of the both denied and enforced occupancy of colonial Aotearoa/New Zealand. As Andrew Ross suggests:

> weather has always been the most reliable witness that the world would soon change. If I had to come up with a metaphor for my kind of futurology then I imagine it would be something like *social meteorology*. A meteorology on the ground and of the ground, as well as from the air [. . .]. A meteorology that builds fronts from below in addition to one that sees the fronts coming in advance.
>
> (Ross 1991: 13)

Weather metaphors are activated in this chapter, along the lines that Ross suggests, as mechanisms for registering architectural anxieties and for acknowledging the capacity for change associated with migration. Metaphors of weather, in their capacity to overlap conditions of similarity and estrangement, allow a registration of effects across disjunctive spaces and times, from Europe to the Pacific, from the colonial to the present. The weather-borne agitation of the nineteenth century, exemplified in Ruskin's writing, travelled with the immigrants who left England for Aotearoa/New Zealand. Tracking waves of clouds that mark global motion, tumultuous waves of watery passage, they shipped to the other side of the world in contractual waves of increasing and dislocating populations.

> Then we soon got out into the open seas. We had a nice time till we got out of the Bay of Biscay, then we had a fearful gale. The sea ran mountains high. It commenced

> on New Year's night, it kept on for three days and three nights; we were all battened down below. It broke all the bulwark on one side of the ship [. . .]. The Captain's wife was washed out of her cabin three times – they thought she was dead. It was a terrible time; there was crying and screaming and praying.
>
> (Sarah Higgins, Nelson, 1842 (Drummond 1960: 84))

Mountains of water (momentarily earth flowed) cast out internal security. Sarah Higgins, no longer fixed in geologically secure space, became dependent on the force and flow of weather and time. Weather, however, was also subject to construction: English weather travelled with her into Southern skies to become strange. Weather, while framed as mutable, cast as fluid, was also a cultural product that came to be known relationally. For instance, as Homi Bhabha has pointed out, to invoke English weather is to acknowledge difference, a changeable relation between the soft grey 'quilted downs' of England and its 'daemonic double: the heat and dust of India' (Bhabha 1990: 319). In the context of the colonial passage the boundaries of such 'imaginative geographies' shift like the weather in both familiar and unpredictable patterns.

According to Vladimir Janković (2000), attitudes towards nineteenth century weather in England tended to be shaped by local and particular observation. A specificity of weather that was dependent on notions of other weathers and memories of different climates, and which only reluctantly attached to slow-building, global theories of meteorology. This concern for local English weather patterns, familiar, peculiar and changeable, coincided with and supported understandings of the nature of place. While nineteenth-century meteorology over time saw a shift from interest in the singularity of weather phenomena towards generalized patterns, from a lunar rainbow towards a concern for global atmospheric motions, the everyday, parochial attitudes to weather remained in place. It is this weather that fled with the immigrants to distant lands. Mechanisms of location and place made mobile.

Understandings of weather and weathering were to be complicated for the immigrant by the duration and spacing of the long sea voyage to New Zealand, and by the climatic reversals that resulted. Wrenching away from habitual configurations, English immigrants leaving for New Zealand imagined that they would see English weather in Southern skies, but as they drew closer to the coasts of Aotearoa/New Zealand[1] the seasons swapped and the winds reversed. Other traces of comfort, the sweet/sour smell of familiarity, travelled with them into exile, altering through the passage of time and space the already variable constructions of home. Coal dust dropped from the cold London air to settle in the travelling trunks (thick with fabrications of home) packed into the hold of the immigration ships.

HOLDING PATTERNS

Detached from locality, mobile on the outside surface of an ocean, the already faltering sense of continuity and continuation became intensified in voyaging childbirth. Birth, in these conditions, was no longer the guarantor of progress nor the means of embedding the domestic in a secure homeland through a fecund maternal body. Rather the maternal body, like the fast disappearing 'motherland', became a site for splitting, a disruption of the idea of place, (still-born, the small bodies were slipped into the water) followed by a new domestic condition to be characterized as external, dusted with foreignness.

> 17 January. 'Expect to have an addition to our passengers today. Poor Mrs Davie whose child died the day before we sailed is sick today. God grant her a good time. It is very hot and the staterooms are very close yet he who tempers the wind to the shorn lamb can take care of her even although circumstances look bad. Half past four a baby is born [. . .] and the mother is well, so is the child [. . .] she is to be named for the ship, Clara [. . .].'
>
> (From the journal of Margaret Peace 1864 (Porter *et al.* 1996: 65))

Waves of weather chased the immigrants across the surface of the globe. Confined in the ship and held in confinement by waves of contractions that exerted their own sort of barometric pressure, the immigrant woman in childbirth would have been barely able to catch the gleam of light reflecting on enclosing sheets of canvas. Sea noises echoed her own laboured breathing. 'Walled up in this elsewhere, the pregnant woman loses her sense of community, it suddenly seems empty to her, seems absurd or comic at best: the movement of a surface disconnected from its impossible depths' (Kristeva 1981: 160).

Within the hold of the ship there were no horizons, no limits, but in their stead an expansive pulsing black surface. Away from salt laden wind and the froth and foam of water, waves of contractions forced life through another passage; the silence of holding broken by the agitations of new arrival. Bodies separating, dividing, and leaking into an amorphous exteriority; slippery skin surfaces rubbing as child and mother slid apart. Interiority repeatedly and convulsively reversed as the immigrants sought new possibilities of occupation; home would persist only as a surface construction on the skin of the new land.

There would be, for the colonists, a much desired and impossible return to a maternal home; separations being remembered through mechanisms of loss. An inevitable rejection of natal security was enacted on the sliding sea and, later, would be re-enacted in the convulsions of the land (familiarly invoked as 'Mother earth') that the immigrants would attempt to settle. Was it possible, as Elizabeth Grosz has asked, that the 'effects of depth, of interiority, of domesticity and privacy [could] be generated by the billowing convolutions and contortions of an outside, a skin?' (Grosz 2001: 64).

Cast out, constructed in exile, the idea of domesticity would become in Aotearoa/New Zealand an external condition, removed from 'Home', no longer tied down by an atavistic attachment to local ground. Recast as temporary and mobile, pioneering domesticity became a momentary involution in a changeable cyclical pattern, rearranging the linear temporalities of history and passage.[2] Conditions of domesticity, fabricated in the hold of a ship's passage as enclosed yet excluded (cast off from home, cast out of self), were borne across the seas to Aotearoa/New Zealand to structure colonial enterprises as always outside. Waves of weather, of labour, of colonists were painful and persistent.

BORDER WEATHER

Following journeys of up to 170 days, settler ships drew near their destination off the coast of New Zealand. But impending arrival did not necessarily resolve immigrant anxieties. Landfall did not offer a stability against which to secure domesticity. Long low clouds on the horizon anticipated winds that would subsequently whip across the narrowness of land carrying smoke from local fires, whiffs of food and death, foreshadowing the turbulence of new associations. Wind that had filled the sails or, at times, prevented forward passage, on arrival formed eddies, producing a confusing convolution of movement. It swept the immigrants into the space and matter of an already occupied land. Victorian traveller, Thomas Arnold, sailing on the *John Wickcliffe* neared New Zealand in 1848 and wrote later:

> From Desolation Island we had a quick run to the longitude of New Zealand. It was stormy weather when we came upon the coast. The mountains of Stewart's Island [. . .] loomed dimly through the mist of rain. Coasting along the Middle Island, we came up on the night of the 20th of March with the latitude of Otago. In the morning we were becalmed off the land, near enough to see the surf breaking on the white beach, and almost to distinguish the individual trees of the virgin forests that clothed the hills. A wind sprang up in the afternoon, but it was from the wrong quarter. We were beating to windward all that afternoon, and all through the night. By sunrise we had weathered Cape Saunders, and were close in to the land. The captain was scanning anxiously every point that we ran past, trying to make out the heads of the harbour.
>
> (Arnold 1861: 247–8)

An anxious longing for the land emerges from this passage. The writing constructs a desired (clothed yet 'virgin') land as dimly visible, tantalisingly there and not there. Land which was to be the end of the journey, firm ground after months on a changeable, unstable sea, was, instead, strangely watery. At the moment of (deferred) arrival, sea and land, surf and the white beach, became one. Foaming water and particles of white sand tossed together, a literal merging of two opposed conditions. Even the movement through the sea was described in terms of the land, 'Coasting along', and the sea itself became static and fixed as they were 'becalmed'.

Land, inferred as the source of unseen interference patterns, (waves crossing the ship's progress doubled the troughs of doubt, the peaks of anticipation), was half sensed across sea space appearing in a misty thickening of the horizon. The arrival of the ship, puncturing the edge, revealed the imagined security of the land to be, instead, a porous boundary, a variable limit consisting only of sodden particles of earth dissolving into the enclosing horizon of the ocean.

LANDFALL

A land that flexed awaited the colonists. 'New Zealanders [. . .] are more likely than most to experience earthquakes on a fairly regular basis – about 100 a year, according to some estimates, although, on average, only one of these would exceed a reading of 6 on the Richter scale' (Rogers 1996: 8). The very motion and atmosphere of weather inhabited the land and, with a mobile earth, placement became radically unreliable. As the ground waved in fluid movements it reverberated with storm-sounds; weather noise of matter. Immigrants, encountering the rumbles and motion of earthquakes for the first time, carefully recorded the weather and wind directions, 'rather close and sultry [. . .] the wind came up from the Southward to Eastward, blowing half a gale of rain' (*Wellington Independent* 1848: 1), as they sought to understand the tumultuous rejection of new foundations.

Weather, a surface condition of matter, is, in Aotearoa/New Zealand, lodged in the volcanic and earthquake-prone land to produce 'earth-storms' that shake out foundational security undermining the domestic figuration of colonization.[3] Surface became everything, folding interiors into external constructions; tectonic plates slid apart and rifts opened. Meteorology 'on the ground', as Ross puts it, is possible in New Zealand in a particular and literal sense given the liquid quality of the land. If the sea voyage denied the possibility of permanence and underlined the uncertain fixity of anchors, these conditions would not be ameliorated on landfall. Foundational security, at the heart of architecture's enterprises, became doubtful on arrival. Mobility, lightness and a propensity to tremble marked the nature of the new constructions that settlers necessarily had to construct.

> In 1840 the first settlers landed at Petone beach. Having no tents, they built themselves whares composed of toi-toi and flax [. . .]. One night there was an earthquake '*happened*' around the agitated occupants, thinking the Maoris were shaking their building down, rushed out in the most *primitive* of costumes, but saw no one, and at last concluded that old mother earth had been seized with one of her tremors.
>
> (Turnbull 1889: 10)

In Aotearoa/New Zealand, swept by wind and named after a cloud, the turbulence of the weather was allied to the literal agitation of the earthquake-prone land. This material meteorological condition became, for the settlers at Petone near Wellington, also conflated with negotiations with indigenous occupants, the Maori. The desired colonial house, where language and social instruction took place, was designed and constructed in such a way as to exclude unwanted connections. If dry and self-contained the house might be felt as proof against the uncertainties of cloudy encounters, and proof against the possibilities of a two-way exchange with local indigenous inhabitants and local climatic/geological conditions. However, with earthquakes and wind came a consequent foundational mobility, and the possibilities of exchange, translation and alteration came within.

EARTHQUAKE, WELLINGTON 1848

Thomas Arnold, in Wellington 1848, later wrote:

> On the night of the 16th October, between one and two, A.M., the whole household was roused from sleep by the shock of an earthquake. It seemed to me in my dreams that a storm of wind was blowing – that it blew harder and harder – that it shook the very house – under which impression I awoke and found myself indeed being rocked violently from side to side in my bed, like an infant in the cradle, not however by the powers of the air, but by the mysterious forces pent up within the breast of the earth. [. . .] The sensation produced was singular and awful, its chief element being the feeling of utter insecurity, when that which we familiarly think of as the firm and solid earth was thus heaving and rolling beneath us.
>
> (Arnold 1861: 254)

Arnold, in his dreams, imagines a wind shaking the house but awakens to a subterranean nightmare of an earthquake which undermined his notions of stability and placement, of home and domesticity. Air wind became an earth wind, earth/mother's breast rocking a cradle, reducing the grown man to some sort of new beginning. Beginnings that were also attempts to ignore the resistances and upheavals of the land.

In a letter to his mother Thomas Arnold elaborated on the earthquake:

> For about a minute the bed was violently shaken from side to side; every plank in the house creaked and rattled, the bottles and glasses in the next room kept up a sort of infernal dance, and most of them fell. When the shock was past, there came a few spasmodic heavings, like long drawn breaths, and then all was still. But for the rest of the night and all yesterday there were slight shocks at intervals. In the morning we found that the kitchen chimney which is of stone, was cracked right through.
>
> (Arnold 1848: 91)

Waves of the earth sprayed out parts of the house, undoing the efforts of placement, vibrating the quiescent. Each component that constituted the house was divided from the other, separation and agitation preventing any maintenance of domestic wholeness. The loss of centre, the failure of the imaginary heart of home, embodied by the now disconnected and incapacitated chimney, completed the dissolution of domesticity. Henry Sewell, a colonial politician heavily involved in issues of land titles, also recorded, in his journal, a distressed response to ground tremors.

> In truth an Earthquake is an awful thing. The Earth is seized with a fit, and you do not know to what height the convulsion may grow. The effect of it is I think quite peculiar. The solid earth, the very embodiment of the principle of stability, becoming unstable, destroys your confidence in every thing. You cannot run away from it, and you cannot sit still under it, for it is every where.
>
> (Sewell: 1980: 120)

While fear prevented any chance of seeing the house as beneficently uncertain, there are nevertheless moments of exhilaration in Arnold's account of the earthquake; the house dances and breathes like an animal. It is as if 'in the fissure made by an earthquake' that Cixous identifies, 'when material upheaval causes radical changes in things, when all structures are momentarily disoriented and a fleeting savagery sweeps order away, that the poet lets women pass through for a brief interval' (Cixous 1997: 170). The household as a unit that both contained women and excluded the public realm, was undone by the loss of structures that maintain disciplinary boundaries. In particular, it was the agitation of the physical structure of the house that, subject to failure, gave a strange life to previously inconsequential inhabitants leaving gaps for emergent conditions. Fissures, already present within the social structure of domesticity, widened, such that the frailty of patriarchal order, as represented in colonial strategies of settlement and building, was manifest and other possibilities briefly surfaced.

EARTHQUAKE DRAWINGS

These themes to do with the social and material uncertainties and ambivalence of colonial constructions, appear in some 1848 drawings of earthquake damaged architecture. They are exemplified, in particular, in the effects that the earthquakes had on colonial architectural structures.

A series of earthquakes in Wellington in 1848 caused widespread damage to the colonial buildings of the settlement. Robert Park,[4] a surveyor and engineer, and John Marshman,[5] later to be an emigration agent for settlement in the South Island of the country, recorded the devastation. Their careful sketches depicted the brick and stone slump of the 'permanent' buildings of the colonists.

The upright propriety of the erections has faded, sloughing off surface rigidity, and revealing timber hatching beneath. Bracing 'guy ropes' stretched out, away from the distressed skin and uncertain foundations, to pin the building into the landscape.[6]

Edward Roberts from the Royal Engineers Office, in a letter from Wellington in 1848, described the damage that Park and Marshman drew:

> The Colonial Gaol on Mount Cook, a substantial Brick building of two stories containing 16 separate cells all arched over, was fractured at each corner, both ends were disjointed from the longitudinal walls forming the corridor and every arch was split longitudinally.
>
> (Roberts 1848)

Marshman's drawing of the Colonial Gaol (Figure 11.1) depicts a sudden catastrophic exposure of the interior revealing a caricature of domesticity. This interior consists of discrete cells, closed spaces of detached individuals. The image of community that might have been read in an intact architecture has now been revealed as a proliferation of isolated persons. The gaol has been rendered an exaggerated version of the English family home as advocated by missionaries and colonists as an antidote to the communal, and much disparaged, form of the local settlement. A familial structure of separated rooms that isolate individuals in the context of an hierarchically structured whole is now exposed; the room as cell, the house as prison.

Shaking apart the enforced communality of imprisonment, always premised on a societal privileging of individual accountability, the earthquakes moved the architecture from the defensive to the indefensible. The face of the building with minimal slits for light and air has crumpled. With the loss of the gable end, the failure of domestic sheltering becomes a possibility. Gathered under one seemingly collective roof, the isolation of individuals, prisoners or family, is laid bare. Unlike the walls which crumbled, the roof failed in a clinical sectioning leaving no ragged ends or torn sheeting. The roof is cleanly opened to show a lace work of timber, interconnecting members elastically working together despite the collapse of the monolithic form.

In Marshman's drawing the viewer is separated from the gaol by a picket fence that cuts across both ground and image. The image links the seemingly innocuous white painted pickets of twenty-first century suburbs to the pointed stakes that were used to construct stockades and the sharpened stakes with which the surveyors marked out new divisions in the land. Pickets, part of military and industrial terminology, watch, define and defend boundaries.

Edward Roberts described the damage done to the Ordnance Store, Manners Street by the earthquakes: 'The 3rd shock threw out the two ends of the Ordnance store, and fractured the front from the bottom to the top' (Roberts

Figure 11.1
JOHN MARSHMAN 'COLONIAL GAOL', OCT. 1848.
(An Enclosure to a Report from the Royal Engineer War Office, Ordnance Office, in-letters, (WO44) 183 Public Record Office)

1848). The Ordnance Store, that was recorded in ruins after the earthquakes, held the arms and military equipment that were inherently part of colonial occupation. Arms were accumulated and stored against the perceived threat of local Maori chiefs, Te Rangihaeata and Te Rauparaha, to ensure the acquisition and maintenance of land holdings, and to enforce new societal orders.

In the image of the Ordnance Store by Robert Park (Figure 11.2), a soldier stands rigidly upright; he guards, firearm in hand, the sudden exposure of the internal dimensions of colonial space. The smooth white face of the Ordnance Store is wrinkled and cracked, folded and slumped; the interior gapes open. Stability and rigidity, epitomized by apparently massive masonry walls underneath a plaster surface, were found to be illusory. Expectations of security are dissolved as the building that holds the fortifying power of the military is revealed to be dependent on a lightweight, timber frame.

Another building is depicted alongside the collapsed Ordnance Store: a smaller timber structure. This building has apparently remained intact, except for its only rigid component, the masonry hearth and chimney. Following the earthquake the rigidity of the chimney has seemingly fled leaving a small emissive pile on the ground. Such phallic loss of countenance was common after the quakes, indeed, a post-quake report stated that 'Every chimney in the settlement is down, or seriously injured, so much so as to require being rebuilt' (Miles 1848: 77).

John Marshman drew 'Messrs Hickson & Co's Store' (Figure 11.3) in its distressed state following the quakes. A figure stands surveying the debris. The

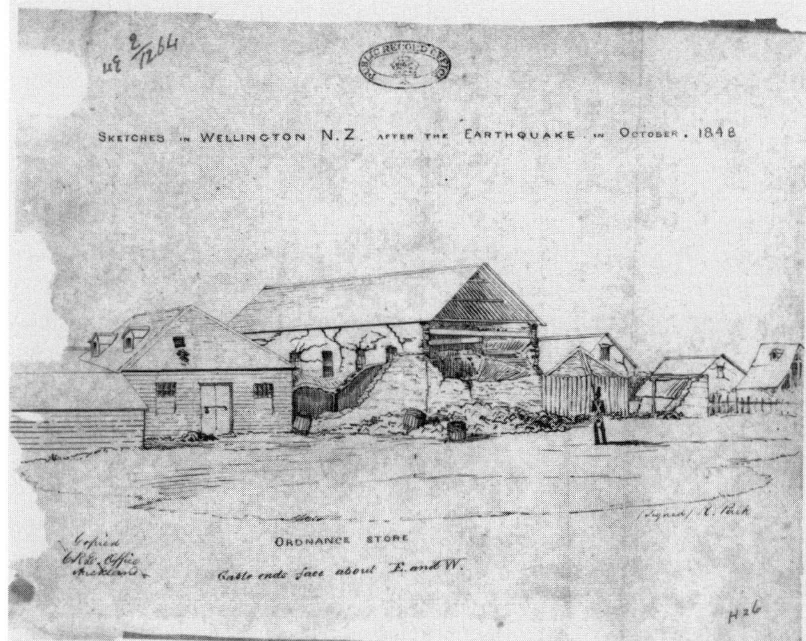

Figure 11.2
ROBERT PARK 'ORDNANCE STORE', OCT. 1848.
(An Enclosure to a Report from the Royal Engineer War Office, Ordnance Office, in-letters, (WO44) 183 Public Record Office)

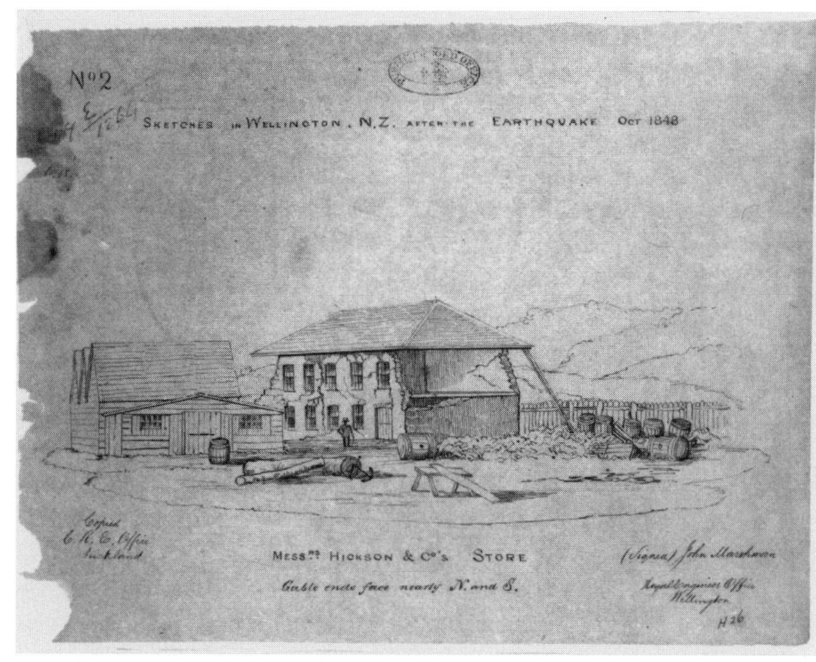

Figure 11.3
JOHN MARSHMAN 'MESSRS HICKSON & CO'S STORE', OCT. 1848.
(An Enclosure to a Report from the Royal Engineer War Office, Ordnance Office, in-letters, (WO44) 183 Public Record Office)

walking stick in his hand seems to prop his shaken ego against the unstable land. This image of support is repeated at a larger scale in the building itself with a temporary strut depicted that emerges from the rubble wall to bear the weight of the roof.

Architecture as a mechanism that facilitates the production of social form, collecting and distributing bodies in space has not in this form, at that moment, endured. The colonial enterprise is usually understood to be economically motivated (Williams and Chrisman 1994: 2). New territories beyond Europe became sites for amassing materials to enrich the colonial power and the circuits of exchange and consumption were supported by the ability of colonial authorities to collect and store such materials. Prosperity may have been redolent in the masonry face that looked down on the timber structure across the yard. Now pitiful, the architectural face shows lines of distress, the body of the building no longer collects, and the matter of commerce, bricks and barrels, have spilt back onto the land.

In the foreground, a tree trunk and a plank are symmetrically arranged so as to suggest a transformation from natural object to cultural artefact; beyond this scene is the redundant masonry structure juxtaposed against the new form of lightweight timber building. An image that could be taken to represent a nineteenth-century concern for progress and yet such concerns are also resisted by the attention given in the drawing to the masonry building. An anchor rests against the end of the tree trunk, a literal image of the possibility of positioning within a condition of fluidity, indifferent to linear notions of progress. Rather than foundations that weigh down upon the ground, the anchor and the prop suggest that a more responsive architectural relationship to land might be required in the colony.

In the depiction of the sorry state of Hickson's enterprise the adjacent timber buildings seem self-contained and secure. Horizontal and vertical boards mesh together in flexible structures that accept the liquidity of the land as did the woven *whare*, the huts made from flax and nikau (an indigenous species of palm), built for the settlers by local Maori.

In these drawings the attempts to fix and stabilize that which refused stability, in the recordings that try to stop time for a moment, it is obvious that it was the timber buildings that survived earthly upheavals. Serjeant of Police Wm. Miles wrote in his 1848 report surveying the earthquake damage in Wellington that 'The wooden buildings, even of the poorest description, have suffered no injury. The reason is obvious; for when one part yields from the shock, the part opposite must follow and they will return in the same manner, all being tied together' (Miles 1848).

A land that vibrated and trembled, like Ruskin's plague-wind, shook the sealed containers of English propriety; stone and brick could not prevail. Winds that blew the immigrants to New Zealand, eddying trade winds circulating labour and wealth, racing westerlies, tracking whales in Southern oceans, accelerated through the tight gap of Cook Strait[7] and into the pores in the woven *whare* inhabited by English immigrants and Maori alike. Strips of leaves, of timber, wet and green, swelling and shrinking, forming miasmas, small climates and atmospheres leaking in and out. Domestic conditions were formed from excluded external conditions; houses were literally enclosed in *weatherboards*, segments of climate sliced for protection. To be within the weather (boarded) house is still to be outside architecture and outside English domestic configurations, and to anticipate a new condition of occupancy.

DEBATE AT THE PHILOSOPHICAL SOCIETY, WELLINGTON, 1888

Despite the series of violent earthquakes in Wellington in 1848, colonial architect Thomas Turnbull confidently pronounced that, because of civilization, architecture in Aotearoa/New Zealand would not, in the future be subject to anything other than mild quakes. The shaking down of colonial forms of society and the production of what he saw as civilized life in the colony would, according to Turnbull, subdue the quaking of the earth.

In the discussion at a Wellington Philosophical Society, some years after the 1848 quakes, Turnbull stated that because New Zealand had reached a suitable state of civility 'Mother Earth' would therefore inflict no more severe tremors than had already been experienced and he would consequently be able to build in masonry. He concluded that 'we may feel in our souls that these islands are as safe and secure as the land which has sustained the Pyramids for thousands of years: more steady than the foundations on which the Greeks erected their matchless temples' (Turnbull 1889: 19).

The ability to build in masonry, to project effects of solidity in stone and brick, was to be the result of taming the land and the people through the agency of a 'civilization' that was dependent on force of arms. Englishness could still the earth. Turnbull acknowledged, however, that to achieve the appropriate stability for masonry construction it might be necessary to float the massive buildings on rafts of timber (Turnbull 1889: 18). In defence of a monumental and immobile architectural conception he had to obliquely acknowledge the viscosity of his new country through the principle of floating foundations; a principle that has subsequently become ubiquitous in New Zealand.

EDGECUMBE EARTHQUAKE

The legacy of fluid ground that the English settlers confronted remains palpable in contemporary Aotearoa/New Zealand. Grounds for occupancy are still contested: old patterns of English migration are washed over with new arrivals from

Polynesia and Southeast Asia, and the possible settlement of land claims made by indigenous Maori populations still invokes disturbance by challenging principles of property ownership. Domesticity continues to be made and remade in patterns that seemingly anxiously repeat the first migrants' confrontations with instability, and the initial longings for impossible security.

On 2 March, 1987, an earthquake measuring 6.3 on the Richter scale shook the eastern Bay of Plenty, in the North Island of New Zealand. It severely damaged the town of Edgecumbe, and to a lesser extent the surrounding towns of Whakatane and Kawerau. No deaths could be directly attributed to the quake but a number of the town's residents sustained injuries. The quake had been preceded by a swarm of smaller tremors.

Charmaine Baaker, married two days before the quake, was at home packing for her honeymoon. The description of her experience in the Edgecumbe earthquake was published in the *New Zealand Herald* newspaper on the 10th anniversary of the event:

> She [. . .] became aware that there were none of the usual bird noises not even a breeze. There was an eerie, uneasy stillness, but she told herself to stop imagining things and get to work. She had begun packing when the house shook sharply.
>
> (Hanning 1997: G1)

Before the quake an unsettling absence of noise is noted, like the silence recorded by the colonists who expected no sound from land desired as an emptiness. Uncanny stillness, 'earthquake weather', no wind that might stir the earth. A 'noisy silence' preceded upheaval.[8] Then:

> 'right from the coast, I saw the whole ground moving, it was rolling like the sea towards me.'
>
> (Hanning 1997: G1)

Land, rolling in waves, 'like the sea', recalling immigrants' passage from sea to beach and further inland, removing fixity, pointing to the provisional nature of occupation. The land itself was broken into particles, dust like spray, spume, obscuring familiar outlines.[9] Local knowledge was clouded.

> 'As it came closer there was a rumbling that grew and grew and I knew it was coming to get me.'
>
> (Hanning 1997: G1)

Land is a source of bitter contention in New Zealand. Bloody occupations, violent acquisition, dilatory settlements all make residency troubled and turbulent. The mobile earth is a literal upheaval of the grounds for dwelling.

> As the rumbling engulfed her, the house seemed to come alive with evil intent.
>
> (Hanning 1997: G1)

To domesticate is to tame, make safe, make productive and is achieved by bounding, binding and containing. Domestication as a colonial project is threatened by that which is to be tamed, and attempts were made to reinforce boundaries; external surfaces are obsessively maintained underlining the impropriety of rupture. Kept at bay is the potential flow of domesticity that, like a flow of words, objects, blood, seems messy and disruptive. Boundaries, however, were constructed as porous; the house as container, occupied by Charmaine Baaker, was a site of violence within a context of comfort.

> 'I tried to move to the doorway, but the fascia boards on the frame began to split off.'
>
> (Hanning 1997: G1)

Door and window frames bind up the raw edges of the walls and legitimize such openings as 'proper'. Openings are tolerable within a framework where all can be known and property can be apportioned and claimed. Frames that trim gaps in the surface control and emphasize any disruption of the containing structure. Window and doorframes provide authorization for penetration.[10]

> 'I couldn't stand up, I couldn't move. I thought I should shelter under the table, but I couldn't catch it. It was dancing around the room.'
>
> (Hanning 1997: G1)

The table was an item of furniture that the colonists insisted upon. Paul Carter asks, 'What history of violence does its pretence of smoothness, its equalisation of places conceal?' (Carter 1996: 23). As distinguishing implement,[11] the table lifted Europeans over an already owned and historied land, insisting on new relationships of body to ground. But the table on which the Treaty of Waitangi, the formal inaugurating document of the colony, was signed, on which Christian blood and flesh was eaten, is no longer a shelter or attachment but now gathers its own momentum.

> 'Then the microwave leapt off the top of the fridge as if some huge hand had thrown it, and the fridge started walking towards me. There was a big squelching sound and the sink came away from the wall and water was pouring out where the taps had been.'
>
> (Hanning 1997: G1)

The scene is a recurrent stereotypical nightmare, a micro-wave hiccup in a flow of technology. Such animation reveals an underlying belief that machines might be self-moving, self-designing, or autonomous.[12] Represented as actively partaking in cataclysmic destruction, the animating technology of domestic space seems to serve as a latter-day revival of the fear of an uncooperative indigenous work force.

> She said that when the fireplace was 'sucked backwards out onto the lawn' leaving a huge hole in the wall, she knew she had to get out.
>
> (Hanning 1997: G1)

The chimney falls and an opening occurs. This a moment in which paternal complicity between projects of domestication and colonization might be recognized. The chimney and fireplace are iconic forms, asserting hierarchical and heterosexual 'family values' that persistently inform many architectural representations of New Zealand.

> Worst of all, 'the walls were going up and down so that the skirting boards seemed like gums chomping up and down on the floor. I had bare feet and I was trying to keep them away from the skirting boards. I thought the house was going to eat me.'
>
> (Hanning 1997: G1)

The carefully constructed skin of domesticity had seemed to be impervious; its tight surfaces resisting intrusions. A skirting board covers the gap between floor and wall. Between the wall and ceiling a junction is rendered safe with a scotia. The scotia, however, as Hersey revealed in his discussion of the antecedents of classical architecture, is named for the realm of darkness (Hersey 1988: 21).

> 'I went into the toilet, but the floor moved away from the bowl, and I could see the ground underneath. I ran out of there, and got to the back door. When I opened it there was a gap between the frame and the concrete steps, and it was opening and closing. I thought if I jumped I might mistime it and it would cut my legs off.'
>
> (Hanning 1997: G1)

Movement of the floor presents a glimpse of the ground beneath, site of both uncertain darkness and anticipated architectural constructions. In the intermittent interval between house and ground, the clashing jaws of the earthquake, was a potential collision between domestic confinement and escape. A collision that carried with it, in this instance, a threat of immobility that is also the premise of the sealed enclosure of a family home.

> 'I decided to try the ranch slider in the lounge, and ran back in and through to it. Just as I got to it, it buckled and a big V-shaped piece of glass broke.'
>
> (Hanning 1997: G1)

The newspaper concluded:

> Charmaine [. . .] married two days before the quake, suffered trauma which may have caused the breakdown of the marriage, and which she says has brought her nine years of hell. The wreckage of the house in which she had experienced mind-numbing terror was bulldozed into a hole in the ground: the workmen doing the demolition were amazed that she hadn't been killed.
>
> (Hanning 1997: G3)

Charmaine Baaker was photographed (Figure 11.4) standing beside her husband of two days.[13] He holds a piece of earthquake damage, a broken vessel; 'A vessel [that was] both a container and a conduit, the sea and the ship' (Bloomer 1991: 49). Charmaine Baaker holds out her wedding dress covered with

Figure 11.4
CHARMAINE BAAKER AND HER HUSBAND BY THE RUINED HOUSE. BLACK AND WHITE PHOTOGRAPH, *NEW ZEALAND HERALD*, MARCH 1987. Reproduced with permission from the New Zealand Herald

flowers and promises of fertility. It is, like the broken petals of the bowl, offered up as a placation. The house, once sealed in with promises of perfect happiness and completion, has shrugged off its containing skin of Englishness, abandoning its attempts at stability; bricks litter the path. Charmaine Baaker perches on shaky ground and the woven nature of the house beside her is revealed.

Architect Thomas Turnbull's strange and dislocated reaction to the radically inhospitable earthquake weather of 1848 wells up and spills into the present as the past is cyclically 'restated as an object without conclusion' (Said 2000: 17): 'With regard to the earthquakes one foot high, described by Mr Fitzherbert in 1848, reliable old settlers allow there was nothing of the kind although there may have been atmospheric illusion[s] that produced something approaching [. . .] their appearance' (Turnbull 1889: 19).

NOTES

1 Aotearoa, the Maori name for New Zealand, can be translated as the land of the long white cloud.
2 The linear conception of time which passes is aligned with 'two types of temporality (cyclical and monumental) [which] are traditionally linked to female subjectivity in so far as the latter is thought of as necessarily maternal' (Kristeva 1986: 192).
3 See discussion by Anne McClintock (1995: 43).
4 Robert Park, 1812–1870; engineer, surveyor and artist, arrived in New Zealand in 1840 with the surveying staff of the New Zealand Company and was, in 1842, appointed Town Surveyor in Wellington (Platts 1980: 189).
5 See evidence of Marshman's views on weather in New Zealand in his panegyric on emigration to Canterbury, New Zealand (Marshman 1862).
6 'That with this faith [in the absence of severe earthquakes] [. . .] we may continue to cultivate the arts and sciences, and in civilisation march on abreast of the other great families of the Anglo-Saxon race that are to be found in every quarter of the globe' (Maskell and Turnbull 1889: 18).
7 Cook Strait is the narrow and dangerous stretch of water that separates the North Island from the South Island of New Zealand.
8 See discussion of this issue by Auckland art critic Francis Pound (Pound 1994: 88–90).
9 Elizabeth Diller commenting on the Blur Pavilion for the Swiss EXPO, 2002, wrote: 'Blur takes on the uncertainty of the future epitomized in the weather. When we speak about weather, it is assumed that we are talking about nothing, or that more meaningful forms of social interaction are being avoided. But is not the weather, in fact, a potent topic of cultural exchange, a bond that cuts through social distinction and economic class, superseding geopolitical borders?' (Diller 2001: 139).

10 '[T]he frame you bear with you, in front of you, is always empty. It marks, takes, marks as it takes: its fill. It rapes, steals. Could it be that what you have is just the frame, not the property? Not a bond with the earth but merely this fence that you set up, implant wherever you can? You mark out boundaries, draw lines, surround, enclose. Excising, cutting out. What is your fear? That you might lose your property. What remains is an empty frame. You cling to it, dead.' (Irigaray 1992: 24.)

11 'Perhaps a more striking contrast is not to be found than in Rauparaha and his son. The old man, with a great deal of natural sagacity, cunning to a proverb, and deeply implicated in every deed of blood which has darkened the history of this part of the island in his generation, has all the vices and qualities which belong to a savage; but his only son – the last of his race (the others having fallen in the different wars in which their parent has been engaged), destined to continue his father's name and succeed to his authority – has profited by the lessons and examples of civilisation. Both he and his wife are always dressed after the European fashion. His house is composed of wood, built on the native construction, but with wooden floors, doors, and glazed windows; and is furnished with chairs and tables and a bed. As he is about to remove with the rest of the tribe to the new village, he has not thought it worth while to incur further expense or trouble in altering his present dwelling. He always uses at his meals plates and knives and forks; the table is covered with a white tablecloth; and both he and his wife sit at the table in the European manner, on chairs.' (McKillop 1849: 261.)

12 See discussion on this issue by Donna Haraway (1991: 152).

13 The photograph is also reproduced in Anna Rogers' account of the earthquake (Rogers 1996: 151).

REFERENCES

Arnold, T. (1848) 'Letter to his mother Oct. 17th', in J. Bertram (ed.) *The New Zealand Letters of Thomas Arnold the Younger with Further Letters of Arthur Hugh Clough*, Auckland: University of Auckland.

Arnold, T. (1861) 'Reminiscences of New Zealand', *Frazer's Magazine* (August).

Bhabha, H. (1990) 'DessemiNation: time, narrative, and the margins of the modern nation', in H. Bhabha (ed.) *Nation and Narration*, London: Routledge.

Bloomer, J. (1991) 'Towards desiring architecture: Piranesi's *Collegio*', in A. Kahn (ed.) *Drawing/Building/Text*, New York: Princeton Architectural Press.

Carter, P. (1996) 'Turning the tables – or, grounding post-colonialism', in K. Darian-Smith, L. Gunner and S. Nuttall (eds) *Text, Theory, Space*, London: Routledge.

Cixous, H. (1997) 'Sorties: out and out: attacks/ways out/forays', in A.D. Schrift (ed.) *Logic of the Gift: toward an ethic of generosity*, New York: Routledge.

Diller, E. (2001) 'Blur/babble', in C. Davidson (ed.) *Anything*, Cambridge, Massachusetts: MIT Press.

Drummond, A. (ed.) (1960) *Married and Gone to New Zealand: being extracts from the writing of women pioneers*, Hamilton: Paul's Book Arcade; London: Oxford University Press.

Grosz, E. (2001) *Architecture from the Outside: essays on virtual and real space*, Cambridge, Massachusetts: MIT Press.

Hanning, P. (1997) 'The struggle to forget', in *The New Zealand Herald*, Saturday, 1 March.

Haraway, D. (1991) *Simians, Cyborgs, and Women: the reinvention of nature*, New York: Routledge.

Hersey, G. (1988) *The Lost Meaning of Classical Architecture*, Cambridge, Massachusetts: MIT Press.

Hill, J. (ed.) (2001) *Architecture: the subject is matter*, New York and London: Routledge.

Irigaray, L. (1992) *Elemental Passions*, New York: Routledge.

Janković, V. (2000) *Reading the Skies: a cultural history of English weather, 1650–1820*, Manchester: Manchester University Press.

Kristeva, J. (1981) 'The maternal body', in *m/f,* 5 and 6.

Kristeva, J. (1986) 'Women's time', in T. Moi (ed.) *The Kristeva Reader*, Oxford: Blackwell.

McClintock, A. (1995) *Imperial Leather: race, gender and sexuality in the colonial contest*, London: Routledge.

McKillop, Lieut. H.F. (1849) *Reminiscences of Twelve Months' Service in New Zealand*, London: Richard Bentley. Reprint (1973) Christchurch: Capper Press.

Marshman, J. (1862) *Canterbury, New Zealand, in 1862*, London: New Zealand Examiner Office.

Maskell, W.M. and Turnbull, T.A. (1889) *Discussion on Earthquakes and Architecture*, Wellington: Lyon and Blair Printers.

Miles, W. (1848) 'Return of the principal houses injured', in G.A. Eiby (ed.) (1980) *The Marlborough Earthquakes of 1848*, DSIR Bulletin 225.

Platts, U. (1980) *Nineteenth Century New Zealand Artists: a guide and handbook*, Christchurch: Avon Fine Prints.

Porter, F. and Macdonald, C. (eds) with MacDonald, T. (1996) *My Hand Will Write What My Heart Dictates: the unsettled lives of women in nineteenth-century New Zealand as revealed to sisters, family and friends*, Auckland: Auckland University Press with Bridget Williams Books.

Pound, F. (1994) *The Space Between: Pakeha use of Maori motifs in modernist New Zealand art*, Auckland: Workshop Press.

Roberts, E. (1848) 'Clerk of works, in a letter to Capt. Collinson, Commanding Rl. Engrs, Southern Division, New Zealand, 27th October', Public Record Office, London, WO44/183.

Rogers, A. (1996) *New Zealand Tragedies: earthquakes*, Wellington: Grantham House Publishing.

Ross, A. (1991) *Strange Weather: culture, science and technology in the age of limits*, London: Verso.

Ruskin, J. (1905) 'The storm-cloud of the nineteenth century', in *The Complete Works of John Ruskin*, New York: Thomas Crowell & Co.

Said, E.W. (2000) 'The art of displacement: Mona Hatoum's logic of irreconcilables', in Mona Hatoum, *The Entire World as a Foreign Land*, London: Tate Gallery Publishing.

Sewell, H. (1980) *The Journal of Henry Sewell, 1853–7*, Christchurch: Whitcoulls.

Turnbull, T. (1889) 'Earthquake and architecture', in W.M. Maskell and T.A. Turnbull *Discussion on Earthquakes and Architecture*, Wellington: Lyon and Blair Printers.

Wellington Independent (1848) 18 October.

Wellington Independent (1857) 23 September.

Williams, P. and Chrisman, L. (eds) (1994) *Colonial Discourse and Post-Colonial Theory: a reader*, New York: Columbia University Press.

12 Pacific island migration

Mike Austin

SETTLEMENT

Ever since their re-discovery by Western explorers, Pacific islands and their populations have been the source of much theorizing. Every continent, except the closest (Australia), seems to have been proposed as an origin for the inhabitants, while speculation has continued about whether settlement occurred by planned or accidental voyaging. The allied question and also the subject of debate, is whether return voyages were possible. Indigenous origin myths speak of fleets of planned migration, but these were challenged by Andrew Sharp who proposed that settlement was from one-way voyages due to accidental drift of fishermen or exiles (Sharp 1956). This theory has always had an internal difficulty that for settlement to survive the accidental journey requires the drifting vessel to have on board a fertile couple as well as, in some cases, plants and animals.

Another difficulty with this drift theory has been that the presumed movement and migration of the populations in the Pacific was from west to east which was against the prevailing winds. This, and the widespread presence of the South American sweet potato, led anthropologist Thor Heyerdahl to postulate settlement from the east (Heyerdahl 1968). This theory is not now generally accepted. A solution to the dilemma of settlement from the west was Geoffrey Irwin's hypothesis that journeys of exploration were against the prevailing winds precisely because they could be relied upon for the return journey (Irwin 1992). Exploration, by definition, does not know its destination, but what the navigator does need to know is how to get home. Computer simulations of planned voyages into the Pacific in an easterly direction from source islands seem to concur with evidence of settlement dates given by archaeology and linguistic analyses (Irwin 1992). It is currently thought that settlement of the Pacific was by island hopping through the Indonesian and Melanesian archipelagos and then crossing the relatively open stretch of ocean into Polynesia around 1000 BC. The dispersal of populations to the far-flung corners of the Polynesian triangle occurred within the first millennium AD. However such competing accounts of the settlement of the Pacific might be assessed, what does remain inescapable is the fact that almost every habitable island in the Pacific ocean – a body of water covering one-third of the planet – has been occupied at one time or another.

The controversy over the purposefulness of settlement of this part of the globe was perhaps perpetuated by the view that the water-borne craft indigenous to the region were thought to be incapable of lengthy ocean voyages. Recent stories of survival of up to 150 days in craft without drinking water give credence to the possibility of lengthy ocean journeys. Return voyages undertaken in contemporary times in replica canoes have tended to dispel some of these doubts but the prejudice continues. The speed of the indigenous vessels was, in fact, noted from the beginning of contact but the craft have somehow seldom been taken seriously. It has also been argued that the Oceanic craft are unable to sail to windward, yet their performance in this respect was not necessarily worse than the European sailing ship. There has also been confusion over the nature and evolution of the Oceanic rig (Horridge 1987: 162). The sail of Pacific Island vessels has been seen as one version or another of Western rigs but in fact it operates in an entirely different way. The Oceanic sail is a balanced rig, which does not depend upon a rudder, and direction is essentially established by the fore and aft tilt of the sail – as in a modern windsurfer.

To call the vessel a 'canoe' implies an inferior and decidedly limited voyaging craft. Malinowski for instance thought that the canoe (*waga*) of the Trobriand Islands in Melanesia was inferior to a 'fine European yacht' but was forced to admit that 'to the native his cumbersome, sprawling canoe is a marvelous, almost miraculous achievement and a thing of beauty' (Malinowski 1961: 106). He insists that: 'the canoe is made for a certain use, and with a definite purpose; it is a means to an end, and we, who study native life, must not reverse this relation and make a fetish of the object itself' (Malinowski 1961: 107). Nevertheless most of his illustrations in perhaps his most famous monograph, *Argonauts of the Western Pacific* are of *waga* and he devotes one chapter to the building, and another to sailing of the vessel which he describes as 'gliding over the waves in a manner almost uncanny' (Malinowski 1961: 107). By invoking the Argonauts in the title of his book, Malinowski compares the *kula* voyages undertaken by Trobriand Islanders between the islands of this area of Papua New Guinea with the mythical Greek voyages, but implies somehow that the former adventuring is less significant. Nor was this an isolated bias as even Te Rangi Hiroa (of Maori ancestry) in his book on Polynesian migration had to justify the achievements of the Polynesians by calling them '*Vikings*' (Buck 1954).

Origin myths in the Pacific involve boats and boat imagery: 'a common Rotinese saying asserts that the husband is the "keel" of the house and the wife is its "rudder" or "steering oar"' (Fox 1993: 161). A Polynesian myth says that there was, in the beginning, some debate as to whether a house or a canoe should be built. In the Samoan version of the story a house was built first and thus it was that sennit (coconut fibre) was used in constructing canoes. In a Tongan version of the story it was decided to build the canoe first and when this was done it was turned upside down on poles to provide shelter for the night. From the island of Mangareva there is the story of Rata who rescued his parents by turning his grandparents' house roof upside down – using it as a canoe and then returning it to the house. Certainly, the construction methods and skills and the decorations of these two fundamental artefacts are connected, and it is clear that water and boats affect Oceanic architecture in many ways from structure to construction to detail ornament. In the Pacific, sails become floor mats (and vice versa), old boats are used as storage structures, and both buildings and boats are held together by a technology of weaving and tying – 'Sailors do not nail or peg things, but instead they tie and lash them together, because at sea lashings hold better than nails or pegs' (Handy 1965: 69).

The storage and protection of the boat itself was also important, so that the canoe shed was a significant location on many islands, being the site of ritual and ceremony. In Samoa the canoe shed was constructed by branches bent over and tied together (a ridge pole would obstruct the insertion and removal of the canoe) in a way that is reminiscent of the fanciful origins of the Gothic arch in Western architectural traditions. This canoe shed (*afolau*) is suggested as the source of, and shares its name with, the guest-house (*fale afolau*) both having the same gently curved roof that is, itself, like an upturned canoe (Hiroa 1930: 11). Lewcock and Brans argue the form of the Tana Toraja house on the island of Sulawesi in the Indonesian Archipelago derives from the protection of the canoe by palm leaves (Lewcock and Brans 1975: 107).

Because boats were of paramount importance in Oceania so-called nautical symbolism is found in the architecture of the region. Lewcock and Brans claim that the traditional village layout in West Flores in the Indonesian archipelago is based on the boat. It is also notable that these authors take all their examples of connections between house and boat from the Asia Pacific region (Lewcock and Brans 1975: 113). The boat was represented in buildings in various ways – typically among those who no longer have a nautical tradition such as the Tana Toraja people, or the Polynesians of Easter Island. Boats require particular forms of cooperation and the political grouping called *waka* in Aotearoa/New Zealand derives from those who are descended from the voyagers who arrived in the origin canoes. The word derives from *va* (the space between), which refers to the concept of the bridging by space of emptiness and is comparable to the well-known *ma* of Japan (Refeti 2002: 538). This is an island aesthetic sensibility that Isozaki has suggested is utterly different to that of continental people (Isozaki 1996).

In Oceania the questions of architecture and migration present quite precise difficulties where the movement that is associated with boats and migration cannot be disentangled from the fixity associated with settlement and place.

The architectures of the Pacific are thoroughly imbricated with the technologies, mythologies and aesthetics of movement. Furthermore, Pacific Island buildings are constructed in materials that decay rapidly giving the architecture a shifting and transient quality. Even within fixed settlements, there is movement of young men and women (to neighbouring villages or to men's houses) due to rules of residence revolving around exogamy and the incest taboo. These dimensions of architecture in the Pacific contrast sharply with the fixity associated with Western architecture.

THE HUT

These difficulties might be elaborated by considering the theme of the primitive hut in Western architectural traditions. Nowadays, architecture in the Pacific is popularly associated with the grass hut but, just as the canoe is not a proper boat, the Pacific grass hut is generally not included in the architectural canon. In his comprehensive study of the origins of architecture in the primitive hut, Joseph Rykwert says: 'In the present rethinking of why we build and what we build for, the primitive hut will, I suggest, retain its validity as reminder of the original and therefore essential meaning of all building for people: that is of architecture' (Rykwert 1981: 192). The hut is claimed as the source of all architecture but, at the same time, it is dismissed as mere building. For instance, the structure of the hut is not taken seriously so that it is often not realized that the simple section of the hut collapses if it is constructed with pin joints and alternative construction means such as fixed joints are difficult with 'primitive' technology. Typically, stability in the hut construction is provided by making the supporting posts vertical cantilevers out of the ground. However, the sloping roof of this arrangement still exerts a horizontal force on the tops of the exterior wall posts, a force that is resisted in the European tradition by the addition of plates, lintels, or ties to the top of the posts or, in the extreme sophistication of the Gothic, by flying buttresses. In the Pacific, on the other hand, the ridge is directly supported on posts so that the outward thrust of the rafters found in other architectural traditions is eliminated. These ridge pole supports are so ubiquitous that they are, in many ways, a signifying characteristic of the Pacific hut in its various forms of *vale*, *whare*, *fare*, *fale*, etc.

But if the primitive hut is unstable, what accounts for the longevity of that most famous hut of all? Why does the Parthenon stand up without fixed joints and without lateral support from the ground? In this case, it is the walls and the sheer weight of the structure that holds the building together. However, a good Pacific cyclone or earthquake might succeed in dislodging the keyed connections. The instability of the hut, and the addition of weight to stabilize it, is at the heart of classical architecture with its complex and ambivalent attitude to structure. Weight, in the form of ballast, is also what keeps a single-hulled European boat upright. It is always a source of amazement to multi-hull sailors (and Ocean voyaging Pacific craft were uniquely multi-hulled) that the basis of the boat's stability is also the very weight that would sink the craft if it were overwhelmed. The Pacific sailor, on the other hand, tended to respond to storms by submitting to the sea, which meant lowering all sail (including mast and rigging) and taking to the water alongside the boat which now becomes a life raft. The sea was seen as a refuge rather than an enemy (Emory 1975).

But more importantly we have suggested that the boat is an important source for the Pacific hut and yet Rykwert does not consider this as another possible origin for architecture. He mentions boats in passing and one is even illustrated in discussion of Egypt and Mesopotamia but their role in the story of the origins of architecture is disregarded. It is proposed as inevitable that 'the simple sailor such as Crusoe, when stranded on a desert island, will rehearse the theoretical development of primitive man' (Rykwert 1981: 76) but no mention is made of the lost boat that Crusoe rebuilds on land. Rykwert claims global and pan-historical relevance ('all peoples at all times') and says the primitive hut plays a role in the 'rites practised by a number of peoples: Greeks Romans, Jews, Egyptians, Japanese' (Rykwert 1981: 182).

However, the Japanese temple of Ise gives some difficulties:

> The most curious feature, perhaps, of the construction of Ise is the way in which the roof is carried. The chambers of the shrines are raised on timber piles analogous to the central sacred one. [. . .] The oddest feature is that the roof is not supported on the walls. The rafters do indeed rest on purlins, but the ridge beam is independently carried by two large columns which go directly into the ground.
>
> (Rykwert 1981: 178)

As we have seen, this is typical for a Pacific hut, and Rykwert gives himself a clue as to this other heritage when he points out that worship concentrates on a mirror which 'is kept in a number of silk and wooden containers, on a boat-shaped stand directly over, and also substituting for, the sacred central post' (Rykwert 1981: 177). Ise is not just another example but has a special status in Pacific architecture. It is claimed by Kenzo Tange as the prototype of all Japanese architecture (Tange 1965) and it is a key example for Lewcock and Brans in their arguments for connections between houses and boats.

Further, while Rykwert acknowledges the existence of pile dwellings in South East Asia he sees no reason to make exceptions of these or of Ise, thereby sustaining the general thrust of his narrative. In fact, in his claim for the universal relevance of the hut he goes to a site more primitive than the primitive, to the very centre of Australia to those who supposedly have no building – although he says that Aborigines may have 'degenerated from a higher level of material culture form' (Rykwert 1981: 187–8). Here, he finds evidence of the operation of the hut – if not in the form of an actual building, in the form of a decorative construction.

Earlier in his book Rykwert refers to that other site of the primitive – New Guinea – where he manages to make the many separate cultures appear homogeneous (Rykwert 1981: 150). His source is the anthropological writings of Margaret Mead, in particular her writing about the people she called the Mountain Arapesh, but it might be noted that even in this inland location there are a dozen index references to canoes (Mead 1950). Mead wrote another book about another Papua New Guinea group (the Manus people) about whom she says: 'A lifetime of dwelling on the water has made them perfectly at home there' (Mead 1930: 23). She points out that 'Understanding canoe and sea come just a little later than the understanding of house and fire, which form part of the child's environment from birth' (Mead 1930: 30). Despite this evidence of another more complex narrative, Rykwert persisted with his assertion of pin-jointed, ballasted, and classicized origin for all architectures.

More recently there are signs of a water-borne sensibility within the terrestrial traditions of Western architecture. Even modernism has been claimed to have watery origins beyond the well-known associations with ocean liners. Adolf Vogt in his book *Le Corbusier the Noble Savage*, traces the origin of pilotis (the free-standing posts that have become a signifier of the modern in architecture) to water dwelling architecture from the Asia Pacific area (Vogt 1998). To state the virtues of these buildings over the water in terms of contemporary pre-occupations, we might say that they have advantages of security, climate control, rubbish disposal, and easy access to work. What is more interesting is the floating quality intimately associated with the architecture of the modern movement. In the work of Japanese architects such as Itsuko Hasegawa and Toyo Ito, floating becomes a continuing and important contemporary architectural concern. We have seen that in Oceania the cultures look to the sea and boats as an origin. The architectures that result from such an outlook have some similarities to the so-called 'hi-tech' movement, a particular style of contemporary architecture associated with Great Britain – another island. The technology of this architecture may not be high but it is nautical in origin, using tension and fabric systems (rigging and sails), and it can be characterized by the obsessive jointing and detailing associated with boats.

THE *MANEABA*

The thoroughness with which boat and house, ocean and architecture, movement and fixity are inter-twined in the Pacific might be demonstrated by examining one particular traditional building form – the *maneaba*. Sumet Jumsai puts his argument for what he called 'water-based cultures' and the difference between their architecture and those of 'earth-based cultures' (Jumsai 1989).

His area of concern is, again, South East Asia with references to Indonesia and further east into Polynesia. He includes Japan (specifically Ise temple) in his category of water-based cultures but does point out the climatic disadvantages of a house on stilts at 35 degrees latitude. The building that he sees as paradigmatic of water-based culture is what he calls the maneapa, which he says is a 'Polynesian' word (Jumsai 1989: 45). The orthography of the word is usually '*maneaba*' which is a community building found on the islands of Kiribati formerly known as the Gilbert Islands. Jumsai bases his information on a book by Austin Coates that claims the Gilberts (Kiribati) to be the origin of certain attitudes to food, time, money and space found throughout the Pacific. Kiribati consists of atolls, low islands of dense coral and Coates argues that the cultural attitudes are shaped by the difficulty of growing and storing food on an atoll. Survival demands regular voyaging and Gilbertese are famous navigators known for their knowledge of sea and sky. This knowledge is embodied in the *maneaba*:

> A student of astronomy took the arduous seven year course in the maneapa, (the Austronesian communal meeting hall) without actual reference to the stars. [. . .] Seated in the centre of the maneapa floor, the student learned by heart the names, shapes and positions of the stars and constellations by reference to the divisions in the maneapa roof, which is divided into rectangles by rafters and purlins.
>
> (Coates 1974: 113–14)

An indigenous commentator has said that the *maneaba* was important for locating the stars in direction and elevation because the stars were of significance in navigation as well as prophecy. The position and atmospherics of the constellation of Pleiades for instance were used to 'predict weather conditions and other events even of a world wide nature' (Oma and Coppack no date: 19). The *maneaba* can be seen as a chart of the heavens, somewhat like the stick charts of the nearby Marshall Islands [*ed.* see front cover]. These charts have been described as 'never made to scale' (Haddon and Hornell 1936: 372). Yet, this is to assume that other maps and charts are something other than an abstract representation. The European map too, is full of distortions – produced from the reduction of the earth's curved surface to a flat plane. Furthermore, the European map, preoccupied with grounded object relations, eliminates the surface of the sea with its changeable characteristics as being beyond cartographic description. Even nautical charts remain fixated on the earth (the sea bottom) rather than the visible phenomenon of the waves, winds and currents of the sea's surface. These surface conditions are precisely what the Pacific stick chart indicates. A Polynesian writer Epeli Hau'ofa sums this up when he says there is a world of difference between viewing the Pacific as 'islands in a far sea' and as 'a sea of islands' (Hau'ofa 1999: 31).

The European gridding of the sea was made possible by the technology of the compass and the clock (Deleuze and Guattari 1987: 479). The compass joined with the surveyor's theodolite and chain as the instrument of colonial appropriation and division of space. There have been endless attempts to locate 'primitive' Oceanic compasses and to relate the architecture of the Pacific to the cardinal directions. However, it could be proposed that Pacific people had considerably more than four directions. 'For example, the people of Mangaia in the Cook Islands had names for more than 30 different directions from which the wind blew – actually the names of the holes in the basket in which the winds were confined' (New Zealand Meteorological Service 1976: 5).

Fixed striated directions have, of course, been crucial to Western voyaging. But so dominant did this abstract system of cardinal coordinates become that other systems of navigation and mapping have tended to be dismissed. This bias finds its way into thinking about Pacific architectural formations too. There have also been fruitless attempts to discover cardinal orientations for Polynesian *marae* – which are distinctive configurations of ceremonial spaces and architectural constructions found throughout Polynesia. The sea itself 'a smooth space par excellence' (Deleuze and Guattari 1987: 479) is sometimes referred to as a *marae* when for example the 'canoe was thought to sail on the vast waters of the sea as *marae*' (Tillburg 1994: 82).

The platform that the *maneaba* sits on is also called the *marae*. The *maneaba* in Kiribati have been described as 'gigantic gable roofs, supported on numerous posts and with their eaves resting on mighty blocks of coral limestone standing vertically' (Koch 1986: 178). These limestone blocks are to resist lateral loads because the hard coral of the atoll makes the post as a vertical cantilever impossible.

> The building was the focus of social life, the assembly hall, the dancing lodge, the news-mart of the community. Under that gigantic thatch, every clan had its ordained sitting-place up against the overhang of the eaves. [. . .] The ridge soared sixty feet high, overtopping the coconut palms; the deep eaves fell to less than a man's height from the ground. Within, a man could step fifty full paces clear from end to end, and thirty from side to side. The boles of palm trees made columned aisles down the middle and sides and the place held the cool gloom of a cathedral that whispered with the voices of sea and wind caught up as in a vast sounding box.
>
> (Grimble 1952: 66–7)

The building was (and is) a place of gerontocratic assembly. The seating arrangements within the *maneaba* serve two important purposes according to Henry Lundsgaarde:

> first the *boti* seating position within the *maneaba* is assigned to persons on the basis of their rights, by descent, to occupy a specific location; second *boti* members act as

> one political unit (through its representative) in all matters related to public welfare or community decision-making processes.
>
> (Lundsgaarde 1970: 243–4)

Furthermore, Maude has shown that these seating arrangements reflect the location of the various groups' positions on the atolls (Maude 1980). The building is a microcosm of the island – a palimpsest of territorial and geographical arrangements.

This building was not insubstantial. 'The *maneaba* at Utiroa on Tabiteuea, visited by the Americans in 1841 was, for example, 120 ft. long, 45ft. wide and 40 ft. high' (Koch 1986: 178). The construction of the *Maneaba* was 'attended by numerous restrictions, precautions, injunctions and *tabunea* (magical rites)' (Maude 1980: 15). These rules and injunctions concerned the ratios proportions and procedures of the construction for various categories of the building. 'There are three basic types which differ structurally in the ratio of length to breadth [. . .] each of these types [. . .] is further divided into three subtypes [. . .] producing 9 subtypes each of slightly differing proportions.' (Maude 1980: 7–11).

'Regardless of type, however, the gables of a traditional *maneaba* invariably faced north and south, its length thus facing east and west (west being the side normally facing the lagoon or, on a reef island, the western shore)' (Maude 1980: 7). However, in practice these orientations vary around the atoll and the *maneaba* is oriented towards the shoreline. Because the building is sited on the western shore 'the west (or sea side) is the side of Bakoa, while the east (or land side) is that of the immigrants who brought and perfected the *maneaba* complex (Maude 1980: 16). The building explicitly embodies this opposition between east and west that is coded as a finely balanced opposition between immigrants and indigenous inhabitants and between good and evil – an opposition in which the good dominates the evil (Bakoa) side by the merest amount. This opposition is carried through every aspect of the building's construction from the setting out of its dimensions to the numbers of structural members, to the fixing of the thatch and even to the final laying of the coconut leaf floor mats (which overlap on the floor like waves on the ocean) (Maude 1980: 37).

Some of the precautions specified during construction seem time consuming and tedious. For example, 'When cutting any post end, etc., aloft in the *maneaba* it must not be allowed to fall but should be lowered gently to the floor at the end of a rope' (Maude 1980: 45). These practices have been termed 'superstitions' which is a term of dismissal, but such behaviours make sense among seafarers where they have utterly pragmatic and lifesaving significance. The perils of voyaging and a lifetime on the sea teach the importance of absolutely correct routines, balance and proportions to keep the boat afloat. This attitude can be seen in other Pacific and nautical traditions. For instance in a discussion of Balinese boats we find a similar obsessive preoccupation with position and procedures, where a canoe builder 'was convinced that a ½ centimetre change in the position of the mast makes a difference in the speed' (Horridge 1987: 61–2). This attention to detail is not unknown among contemporary yachtsmen.

Like the canoe, the *maneaba* is tied together with sennit (coconut fibre) in named patterns that are both structural and decorative and there are precise traditions as to how pieces are tied. For instance, the infill framing piece in the gable end is tied to one side of the ridge pole. 'If the vertical rib were to be secured directly underneath the ridge pole (and thereby appearing to give the ridge pole extra support), superstition dictates that such an act would strike right through the heart of a man' (Oma and Coppack no date). This 'superstition' also makes perfect structural (and aesthetic) sense in that were the vertical rib to transfer load from the ridge pole it could stress the light member below and precipitate the collapse of the structure as a whole, because boats work by distributing rather than focusing loads.

While it seems the *maneaba* could be carried conceptually on a sea journey, the seating locations within the *maneaba* repeat those found in the positions in the canoe sailing across the wind. The head of the house always sits on the windward side (which is the east side in the trade wind belt) and any visitor sits on the Bakoa side. The important place for stability and steering is to windward. This is the leader's place on the boat and in the *maneaba*. The leeward side of the boat is a location of great danger to stability as is the leeward Bakoa side of the *maneaba*. This building is a boat.

MIGRATION

Although, today, more by air than sea, movement around the Pacific to the more populated areas, continues. The city of Auckland in Aotearoa/New Zealand prides itself as being 'the largest Polynesian city in the world'. This is the result of a sequence of migration movements dating from the 1950s. The first of these involved the indigenous Maori who, themselves a Polynesian population, migrated to Aotearoa/New Zealand over 1,000 years ago – and, as noted above, the political grouping called *waka* is derived from the descendants of those who voyaged in the origin canoes. Maori populations have traditionally lived in rural areas of the country, but during the 1950s and 1960s large numbers of Maori steadily migrated into the towns and cities. This was followed by a second wave of immigrants from the Polynesian islands of Samoa, Tonga, Niue, Tokelau and Cook Islands. This migration also started in the 1950s and continued through the 1960s and into the 1970s until today there are substantial movements both ways, within, and to and from, Aotearoa/New Zealand and these Polynesian islands.

These patterns of migration, combined with a high birth rate in the immigrant families, produced a bottom heavy population pyramid which, in turn, placed considerable pressure on housing provision (Metge 1964). These urban immigrants initially rented accommodation close to the city centre to be near to work in the downtown areas and on the waterfront. Following this, in the 1970s and 1980s the immigrants tended to move to the outer suburbs where new housing was built on inexpensive land – much of it provided by the State. The housing, even that near the centre of town, almost universally took the form of the single family cottage. This timber framed house is another distant descendant of the European primitive hut, which migrated from England and America over the last two hundred years. However, unlike the Polynesian hut, this house is subdivided into small rooms to accommodate the range of functions of contemporary urban life.

There have been several studies that indicate the lack of fit between these houses and their Polynesian inhabitants (Rosenberg 1970: 13–18). For instance, the large Polynesian families stretch the provisions for cooking and eating, while the separate bedrooms in the house are foreign for those who are accustomed to sleeping communally. Furthermore, the relation between inside and outside is different for Polynesians and Europeans (Pakeha). The Pakeha house in New Zealand is enclosed with every room having a window to allow light and ventilation but also for 'viewing' out. By contrast, Polynesian people are used to living outdoors and traditionally use the interior spaces of the house for sleeping and socializing. The accommodation of Polynesian families in Pakeha houses also raises issues of belief surrounding *tapu* (the origin of the European word taboo). For instance, some activities, such as anything to do with the body and especially the head, are considered *tapu* and are thereby contaminated by *noa* (non *tapu*) activities, such as anything to do with food. Many standard European domestic arrangements, such as washing clothes and food in the same place, are consequently difficult and offensive to Polynesians.

For Maori such difficulties came to a particular point of crisis when a death occurred in the family. Economic and practical factors forced the use of the house for the funeral wake (*tangi*) – an event with numerous *tapu* restrictions. This crisis hinged on the difficulty of returning to the place of tribal origin – the rural meeting house and *marae*. *Marae*, as noted above, are configurations of ceremonial spaces and architectural constructions found throughout Polynesia; in this Maori context the term refers to the outside area of the meeting house and specifically, or properly, the courtyard in front of the house (Austin 1976: 629–32). This community facility is sustained by the *tangi*, the protocols of which are the paradigm for all the activities that occur on the *marae*. During the late 1960s and early 1970s the possibility of constructing urban *marae* was extensively debated. Conservative Maori argued that as the *marae* was tribal in origin it could not be transported out of the tribal districts (Kawharu 1968: 174–86). All sides of the discussion agreed, however, that there was an ongoing need for *marae*, a need that had been expressed many years previously by a Maori leader (Sir Apirana Ngata) when he argued for *marae* as a priority in housing. Ngata said that: 'a cottage would be used only by one man, but a meeting house would be for everyone' (Sutherland 1940: 94–5). The debate on the possibility of an urban *marae* continued and, at one stage, a local Pakeha politician asked a Maori elder if he could explain the purpose of a *marae*. The reply was illuminating:

> That we may rise tall in oratory
> That we may weep for our dead
> That we may pray to God
> That we may have our feasts
> That we may house our guests
> That we may have our meetings
> That we may have our weddings
> That we may have our reunions
> That we may sing
> That we may dance
> And then know
> The richness of life
> And the proud heritage which is truly ours.
> (Tuhoe Elder 1973)

The idea of an urban *marae* came to be widely accepted and many groups set about constructing such complexes. Some tribal *marae* migrated to the cities. In other instances urban interest groups constructed innovative meeting houses, which were supplemented by various other facilities such as preschools, pensioner housing and craft workshops, all of which huddled together to 'keep the *marae* warm' – as the saying goes. Rural *marae* not to be outdone were also reconstructed. Now nearly every university, school and town in the country has a meeting house and *marae* to the point that, in some ways, the *marae* has taken over from the church as a community focus.

This is not yet the case for those communities from Island Polynesia, however, who have brought with them their particular varieties of church to serve as a focus in Aotearoa/New Zealand urban settings. These church buildings do not overtly assert traditional island cultural identity and a common explanation for this downplaying of architectural expression is that these buildings are unsuitable for the colder climate in New Zealand. It is certain that these technical difficulties can be overcome and there is the possibility in future that there will be sufficient confidence to construct buildings associated with particular islands to serve the migrants from that island.

The urban *marae* constructed a new attachment to the canoe. Community affiliations among Maori, when not tribal, tend to turn to the next largest grouping – the *waka*. The *waka*, as has been said, are the canoes from the original (perhaps in part mythical) migration of Maori to Aotearoa/New Zealand but, in any case, represent a confederation of tribes and Maori tend to know which canoe they belong to, even if they are unsure of their tribal affiliations. Historically, Neich points out that in the latter nineteenth century: 'As canoes became obsolete and were replaced by the meeting house as the main vehicle of group pride and prestige, parts of old war canoes were incorporated into the houses' (Neich 2001: 174).

Neich has also proposed that painted *kowhaiwhai* designs on paddles were transposed onto the rafters of the house. 'Through the re-use and replication of these elements of canoes, with their powerful messages of ancestors and genealogical descent much of the symbolism of canoes passed on to meeting houses' (Neich 2001: 175). Hulls of canoes were sometimes used as ridge members and in the meeting houses constructed today the underside of the ridge is rounded like the underside of a canoe. The implication is that the house is conceptually underwater with the rafters like paddles ranged out from the ridge/hull. This suggestion is reinforced by the continued reluctance on the part of Maori to allow any openings in the house other than the entry door and window in spite of the difficulty with contemporary building regulations. Once again, there is a return to the boat as source and direction.

REFERENCES

Austin, M.R. (1976) 'A description of the Maori marae', in Amos Rapoport (ed.) *The Mutual Interaction of People and Their Built Environment: a cross-cultural perspective*, The Hague: Mouton.

Buck, P. (Te Rangi Hiroa) (1954) *Vikings of the Sunrise*, Christchurch: Whitcombe and Tombs.

Coates, A. (1974) *Islands of the South*, London: Heinemann.

Deleuze, G. and Guattari, F. (1987) *A Thousand Plateaus: capitalism and schizophrenia*, trans. B. Massumi, Minneapolis: University of Minnesota Press.

Emory, K. (1975) *Material Culture of the Tuamotu Archipelago*, Pacific Anthropological Records no. 2, Honolulu: Bishop Museum.

Fox, J. (1993) 'Memories of ridge-poles and cross-beams: the categorical foundations of a Rotinese cultural design', in J. Fox (ed.) *Inside Austronesian Houses: perspectives on domestic designs for living*, Canberra: Canberra Department of Anthropology, Australian National University.

Grimble, A. (1952) *A Pattern of Islands*, London: John Murray.

Haddon, A.C. and Hornell, J. (1936) *Canoes of Oceania*, Bishop Museum Special Publications nos 27, 28 and 29, Honolulu: Bishop Museum Press.

Handy, E.S.C. (1965) 'Houses and villages', in E.S.C. Handy, P. Emory, H. Edwin, P.H. Buck and J.A. Wise (eds) *Ancient Hawaiian Civilization*, Rutland: Charles E. Tuttle.

Hau'ofa, E. (1999) 'Our sea of islands', in V. Hereniko and R. Wilson (eds) *Inside Out: literature, cultural politics, and identity in the New Pacific*, Lanham: Rowman and Littlefield.

Heyerdahl, T. (1968) *Sea Routes to Polynesia*, London: Allen & Unwin.

Hiroa, Te R. (P.H. Buck) (1930) *Samoan Material Culture*, Bernice P. Bishop Museum Bulletin 75, Honolulu: Bishop Museum.

Horridge, A. (1987) *Outrigger Canoes of Bali and Madura, Indonesia*, Bishop Museum Special Publication no. 77, Honolulu: Bishop Museum Press.

Irwin, G. (1992) *The Prehistoric Exploration and Colonisation of the Pacific*, Cambridge: Cambridge University Press.

Isozaki, A. (1996) *An Island Aesthetic*, London: Academy Editions.

Jumsai, S. (1989) *Naga: cultural origins in Siam and the West Pacific*, Singapore: Oxford University Press.

Kawharu, I.H. (1968) 'Urban immigrants and tangata whenua', in E. Schwimmer (ed.) *The Maori People in the Nineteen Sixties*, Auckland: Blackwood and Janet Paul.

Koch, G. (1986) *The Material Culture of Kiribati*, Suva: Institute of Pacific Studies, University of the South Pacific.

Lewcock, R. and Brans, G. (1975) 'The boat as an architectural symbol', in P. Oliver (ed.) *Shelter, Sign and Symbol*, London: Barrie and Jenkins.

Lundsgaarde, H.P. (1970) 'Law and politics on Nonouti Island', in T.G. Harding and B.J. Wallace (eds) *Cultures of the Pacific*, New York: Macmillan Publishing.

Malinowski, B. (1961) *Argonauts of the Western Pacific*, New York: Dutton.

Maude, H.E. (1980) *The Gilbertese Maneaba*, Suva: The Institute of Pacific Studies and the Kiribati Extension Centre of the University of the South Pacific.

Mead, M. (1930) *Growing Up in New Guinea*, New York: Mentor Books.

Mead, M. (1950) *Male and Female*, London: Victor Gollancz.

Metge, J. (1964) *A New Maori Migration: rural and urban relations in Northern New Zealand*, London: University of London Athlone Press.

Neich, R. (2001) *Carved Histories: Rotorua Ngati Tarawhai woodcarving*, Auckland: Auckland University Press.

New Zealand Meteorological Service (1976) *Tropical Storms and Hurricanes in the Southwest Pacific*, Wellington: Ministry of Transport.

Oma, T.R.G. and Coppack, M. (no date) 'Gilbert and Ellice Islands', unpublished paper (no place).

Refeti, A.L. (2002) 'Polynesian architecture and its cross-cultural boundaries in New Zealand', in E. Haarhoff, D. Brand and E. Aitken-Rose (eds) *Southern Crossings: Whaka whitiwhiti au Tonga*, Auckland: School of Architecture and Department of Planning, University of Auckland.

Rosenberg, G. (1970) 'House plans for Maori families', *Te Maori* (Summer).

Rykwert, J. (1981) *On Adam's House in Paradise*, Cambridge, Massachusetts: MIT Press.

Sharp, A. (1956) *Ancient Voyagers in the Pacific*, Wellington: Polynesian Society.

Sutherland, I.L.G. (1940) *The Maori People Today: a general survey*, Christchurch: Whitcombe and Tombs.

Tange, K. (1965) *Ise, Prototype of Japanese Architecture*, Cambridge, Massachusetts: MIT Press.

Tuhoe, E. (1973) *South Auckland Courier*, 23 August.

Tillburg, J. van (1994) *Easter Island: archeology, ecology and culture*, London: British Museum Press.

Vogt, A.M. (1998) *Le Corbusier, the Noble Savage: toward an archeology of modernism*, Cambridge, Massachusetts: MIT Press.

Chapter 13: La Frontera's Siamese twins

Mike Davis

The Mexican-US border may not be the epochal marriage of cultures that Brazilian futurist Alfredo Valladão 1996 has in mind, but it is nonetheless a lusty bastard offspring of its two parents. Consider, for example, *La Mona* (Figure 13.1). Five stories tall and buck-naked, 'The Doll' struts her stuff in the dusty Tijuana suburb of Colonia Aeropuerto. Distressingly – to the gringo eye at least – she looks like the Statue of Liberty stripped and teased for a *Playboy* centrefold. In reality, she is the home of Armando Muñoz García and his family. Muñoz is an urban imaginer somewhere on a delirious spectrum between Marcel Duchamp and Las Vegas casino entrepreneur Steve Wynn. 'Give me enough rebar and an oxyacetylene torch,' he boasts, 'and I'll line the border with giant nude Amazons.' In the meantime, he eats in *La Mona*'s belly and curls up to sleep inside her enormous breasts. When asked why he built a house with pubic hair and nipples, he growls back, 'Why not?'

¿Porqué no? is an appropriate slogan for the West Coast's most astounding metropolis. Like Swift's floating sky-city of Laputa in *Gulliver's Travels*, Tijuana seems to defy the ordinary laws of gravity. With an estimated 1.3 million inhabitants (1999), it is now larger than its rich twin, San Diego, as well as San Francisco, Portland and Seattle. Yet, its formal economy and public budget are barely sufficient for a city one-third its size. Tijuana's urban infrastructure has always lagged at least a generation behind current demand. Grassroots audacity, symbolized by *La Mona*, makes up the difference (see Davis 1996). Tijuanenses are consummate *bricoleurs* who have built a culturally vibrant metropolis from the bottom up, largely using recycled materials from the other side of the border.

A dusty rancho in 1900 and a gilded gambling spa for the Los Angeles movie colony during the 1920s, Tijuana became a boom-town during the Vietnam War expansion of the mid-1960s when urban Southern California began to import Mexican labour on a larger scale. Apart from some smaller Mexican border cities, the only city in North America to duplicate its explosive growth – and their population curves are uncannily synchronized – has been Las Vegas. The comparison is richly ironic since Mexican president Lázaro Cárdenas, rather

Figure 13.1 'LA MONA'. (Photograph: Alessandra Moctezuma)

than Bugsy Segal, has claim to be the true father of the glitterdome: it was his 1938 closure of Tijuana's Agua Caliente casino that sent the big gamblers and their Hollywood friends packing to Nevada.[1] Today, each of these instant cities unconsciously vies with the other in the replication of phantasmagoric urbanism.

The Border, however, easily trumps the Strip as surrealist landscape. Spanish offers the useful distinction between *La Línea*, the physical and jurisprudential border with its 230 million individual crossings each year, and *La Frontera*, the distinctive, 2,000-mile-long zone of daily cultural and economic interchange it defines, with an estimated 8 million inhabitants.[2] All borders, of course, are historically specific institutions, and *La Línea*, even in its present Berlin Wall-like configuration, has never been intended to stop labour from migrating *al otro lado*. On the contrary, it functions like a dam, creating a reservoir of labour-power on the Mexican side of the border that can be tapped on demand via the secret aqueduct managed by *polleros*, *iguanas* and *coyotes* (as smugglers of workers and goods are locally known) for the farms of south Texas, the hotels of Las Vegas and the sweatshops of Los Angeles. At the same time, the Border Patrol maintains a dramatic show of force along the border to reassure voters that the threat of alien invasion (a phantom largely created by border militarization itself) is being contained. 'The paradox of US–Mexico integration is that a barricaded border and a borderless economy are being constructed simultaneously' (Andreas 1999a: 12) (Figures 13.2 and 13.3).[3]

Although the escalation of border policing, as Peter Andreas shows in a brilliant study, only seems to promote the growth of more sophisticated and thoroughly criminalized smuggling, its failure as a practical deterrent generates 'perverse consequences that increase pressures for more policing'. 'Perceptual impact and symbolic appeal' are the Border Patrol's real business: 'In other words, this is [. . .] a story about the political success of failing policies' (Andreas 1999a: 12). An increasingly Orwellian but deliberately porous border is the result. 'This bizarre combination of ineffectuality and force at the border,' writes Josiah Heyman, 'determines the niches that undocumented immigrants occupy. In the border area, immigrant peoples are both boundary-defined foreigners and tacit, though bottom of the class structure, insiders' (Heyman 1994: 49 and 56). In the past, and still to a surprising extent today, the absence or nonenforcement of employer sanctions has ensured that only the workers themselves pay the cost of their 'illegality' (in deportation, lost wages, even imprisonment) – a powerful tool for intimidating workers and discouraging unionization.

The emergence of a dynamic *maquiladora* (*maquila* for short) economy employing one million workers, 60 per cent of them women, in partial assembly operations on the border itself has done little to stem the flow of surplus labour northward, since Mexico adds one million more new workers each year than it can actually employ in its formal economy. Indeed, the counterpoint to

Table 13.1 Hypergrowth: Tijuana and Las Vegas

Year	*Tijuana*	*Las Vegas*
1950	65,000	48,283
1960	166,000	127,016
1970	341,000	273,288
1980	462,000	461,816
1990	747,000	784,682
1996	est. 1.2 million	est. 1.1 million
2000	est. 1.3 million	est. 1.3 million

Source: Borderlink 1994, San Diego State University 1994 (economic profile of the San Diego-Tijuana region); Eugene Moehring, Resort City in the Sun Belt: Las Vegas, 1930–1970, Reno, Nevada: 1989; and Las Vegas convention and visitors authority (1990 and 1996 figures).

the explosive growth of the border *maquila* economy has been the drastic decline of Mexico's interior, home-market manufacturing (Cobo 1993; Fussell 1998). In 1970, for example, Mexico had a larger and more advanced consumer electronics industry than either Taiwan or South Korea. But whereas competing Japanese and US multinational investment led to a dramatic increase in technology transfer and local sourcing in both Asian countries, US-owned electronics *maquilas*, Nichola Lowe and Martin Kenney (1999: 1434) have pointed out, 'simply took advantage of Mexico's lower labour costs. As a result, these initial investments did not provide firms in Mexico's interior with the opportunity for establishing joint ventures or purchasing arrangements.' Instead of incorporating indigenous firms into production alliances, the *maquilas* simply drove them into rapid extinction, a situation that has only worsened with the replacement of the US dinosaurs by the highly efficient Japanese *maquilas* with the captive supply chains (Lowe and Kenney 1999: 1434).

If border industrialization, then, sustains only a mirage of national economic development, it nonetheless has dramatically reshaped the culture of La Frontera and the inter-relationships of the dozen or so twin cities that span the border from Matamoros/Brownsville on the Gulf to Tijuana/San Diego on the Pacific.[4] The two largest and most dynamic of these binational metropolises are El Paso/Ciudad Juárez (1.5 million residents and 372 *maquilas*) and San Diego/Tijuana (4.3 million residents and 719 *maquilas*) (Arnaiz *et al.* 1996).[5] Despite some obvious differences, like the more radical abruptness of the socio-economic divide between San Diego and Tijuana, these pairs of *ciudades hermanas* are evolving along similar pathways that have few analogues within any other system of international frontiers.[6]

In both cases, *maquila* industrialization – led by garment and electronics assembly in Ciudad Juárez and television manufacture in 'Tivijuana' (as the locals call it) – has elaborated complex cross-border divisions of labour within larger webs of international trade. Within the framework of the North American Free Trade Agreement (NAFTA), adopted in 1994, Asian capital has played nearly as prominent a role as US investment in modernizing La Frontera. *Mexico Business Monthly* estimated in 1997 that *maquilas* source about 60 per cent of their components from Asia versus 38 per cent from the US and just 2 per cent from Mexico itself (Anon. 1997). Nearly 40,000 Tijuanenses, meanwhile, work for Japanese *keiretsu* or Korean *chaebol*, many of which – like Sanyo and Samsung – have extensive distribution and engineering facilities across the fence in San Diego (Grimes and Richardson 1998: 4 and 7). Although NAFTA is supposed to increase the North American content of *maquila* output dramatically, the US–Mexico border will likely remain Latin America's most dynamic interface with East Asia.

As La Frontera has become a major spoke in the Pacific Rim, old antinomies of development have given way to new paradoxes of integration. Whereas twenty years ago the most striking aspect of the border was the startling juxtaposition of opposites (Third World meets First World), today there is increasing interpenetration, in an almost magical-realist mode, of national temporalities, settlement forms and ecologies. Just as rows of ultra-modern assembly plants now line the south side of the border, so have scrap wood and tar paper shantytowns become an increasingly common sight on the US side of the border. This urban-genetic exchange has only strengthened the distinctiveness of La Frontera as a transcontinental cultural system in its own right.

In Tijuana, Samsung, Sony, Sanyo and Hyundai dominate the *maquila* economy, master-planned industrial parks and postmodern company towns like Ciudad Industrial Nueva and El Florido – little kingdoms of 'unlimited managerial prerogatives' or what Devon Peña calls 'hyper-Toyotism' – directly abut the border on the Mexican side (Peña 1997: 275–6).[7] *Maquila* managers commute to Tijuana's industrial zone every morning from lush San Diego suburbs like Chula Vista, while green-card-carrying Tijuanenses (officially known as 'transmigrants') make the opposite commute by the thousands to work in San Diego's post-industrial economy. Despite the enduring income precipice between the two sides of the border, social indicators no longer always point in one direction. While more than 40 per cent of Tijuana's residents, for example, lack sewer hookups and running water, they can be proud that 90 per cent of their school-age population actually attends school, in contrast to only 84 per cent in far wealthier San Diego (Arnaiz *et al.* 1996).

In El Paso, on the other hand, more than 150 Mexican-style residential *colonias* (population 73,000), with minimal water supply or infrastructure, sprawl along the northern bank of the Rio Grande. Here, persistent poverty on the US side of the border is equalizing residential landscapes to Third World conditions. 'Drinking water', the magazine *BorderLines* explains, 'is hauled in or acquired via shallow, dug wells that quickly become tainted by human waste, pesticide runoff, or heavy metals present in the surrounding soil. The water is kept in open, unsanitary containers – receptacles formerly used in industrial plants are a common method of storage, many still bearing labels that read "not to be used for water". One group of researchers recently discovered a family using old ten-litre pesticide bottles to store water. Scarcity means that water for bathing and cleaning comes from irrigation ditches. Bathroom and kitchen wastes are usually disposed of in septic tanks or open cesspools. Most *colonias* have no regular trash collection. Given this situation, the grim health statistics of *colonias* are unsurprising.' Due to the acute shortage of low-income housing in border counties, 1.5 million poor US residents, Latinos and a few Native Americans, are estimated to be living in shanty *colonias*, principally in New Mexico and Texas (Anon. 1998; Ward 1999).

Maquila industrialization and runaway urbanization have also spawned such terrible environmental problems that the National Toxics Campaign now talks about the border as 'a 2,000-mile-long Love Canal'. The Tijuana River, for example, has until recently discharged 12 million gallons of raw sewage daily on the San Diego side of the border, while the New River, which flushes Mexicali's sewage into California's Imperial Valley, has been described by the US Environmental Protection Agency as carrying 'almost every know viral and bacterial micro-organism fatal to human beings in the Western Hemisphere'.[8] Conversely, US firms are estimated to ship thirty times more hazardous waste southward than Mexican firms send northward, despite NAFTA regulations that outlaw environmental dumping and require toxic by-products of assembly processes to be recycled in the country originating the component or raw material (Reed 1998). Long a refuge for US manufacturers fleeing environmental regulation, the Border risks becoming North America's toxic sink. The danger is aggravated by the fiscal free ride offered to *maquila* capitalists, who pay little or nothing in taxes for supporting infrastructure. Every Mexican border city is forced to practise a triage of shifting scarce civic resources from poor neighbourhoods to industrial parks: for example, clean water for the *maquilas* but none for the *colonias*. When workers or residents protest such conditions, as Heather Williams points out, they are the victims of punctual repression, facing dismissal, arrest, beating, even *desaparición* (Williams 1999: 141).

Some macro-environmental problems, however, cannot be rendered invisible by state violence and, because they impinge directly on corporate profits or US quality of life, have necessitated novel binational initiatives. The siting of so many thirsty *maquilas* along the arid border, for example, has transformed a chronic water shortage on the Mexican side into a genuine emergency: one Samsung plant alone in Tijuana slurps up 5 per cent of the city's annual water supply.[9] Because they share these indivisible ecological problems, the border's Siamese twins are slowly being compelled to integrate and transnationalize their urban infrastructures. In 1998 Mexican and US officials opened up the $440 million International Wastewater Treatment Plant which treats Tijuana's excess sewage on the San Diego side of the border, the first facility of its kind in the world. By 2010, San Diego and Tijuana water agencies are hoping to have constructed a binational aqueduct to the Colorado River. Similarly, El Paso and Ciudad Juárez – blanketed with the same smog – are currently discussing the creation of a unified air quality district (Kelly 1994).

In each case, moreover, binational approaches to local environmental management (and, potentially, to law enforcement) are strengthening the 'New Federalism' in Mexico along lines passionately advocated by the neoliberal opposition party, the PAN, which currently governs several key border states (Shirk 1999). This weakening of ties to the national centre in tandem with the proliferation of so many new cross-border alliances and collaborations is a profound disturbance in the national equilibrium of Mexican politics. Some nationalist writers have compared it to the unsettling influx of US capital and influence into northern Mexico in the years just before the Revolution. Yankee xenophobes, sleepless over the threatened 'take-over' of the Southwest, have their anxious counterparts in the D.F. (Districto Federal), biting their fingernails over the potential secession of El Norte.

The ultimate configuration of national and transnational loyalties will depend on how both sides of the border deal with the new physical hazards and social problems created by President Clinton's unilateral militarization of the border in 1994. In the NAFTA era, capital, like pollution, may flow freely across the border, but labour migration faces unprecedented criminalization and repression. In an attempt to steal the wedge issue of 'uncontrolled immigration' from the Republicans, Clinton (cheered on by California senators Diane Feinstein and Barbara Boxer) massed Border Patrol personnel on the San Diego/Tijuana border ('Operation Gatekeeper') and prodded Congress to double the armed agent force of the Patrol and its parent, the Immigration and Naturalization Agency (Dunn 1996).[10] With help from the Pentagon, surveillance of key border sectors has been automated with seismic sensors that pick up the tiny 'earthquakes' of immigrants' footsteps. Other futuristic border-control gimmicks, including 'an electronic current that stops a fleeing car, a camera that can see into vehicles for hidden passengers, and a computer that checks commuters by voiceprint', are being studied at San Diego's Border Research and Technology Center, which was established in 1995 specifically to support Operation Gatekeeper with cutting-edge military and CIA technologies (Andreas 1999b: 16).

At the same time, the principal battleground of the 'War on Drugs' has been shifted from Colombia and the Andean countries to the Mexican border, where the US military, including elite Marine reconnaissance units, provides covert backup to the Drug Enforcement Administration and the Border Patrol. As Andreas notes, 'The logics of US drug and immigration control are in many ways similar: the foreign supply is defined as the primary source of the problem and deterring the supply through enhanced policing is promoted as the optimal solution' (Andreas 1999a: 5–6).[11] In practice, the distinctions between immigration control and narcotics interdiction, or between policing and low-intensity warfare, have become so blurred that border-dwellers speak routinely of the 'war against drugs *and* immigrants' (Tobar 1996).

It is a war, moreover, with many real casualties. In recent years the highly publicized crackdowns on twin-city borders (nearly one million arrests per year) have forced more immigrants to attempt dangerous crossings on remote stretches of the Rio Grande or through furnace-hot southwestern deserts. By one estimate, nearly 1,600 have died as a result, including a group of ten who perished of thirst in the desert east of San Diego in August 1998 (Eschbach *et al.* 1999: 431;

Seltzer 1998). Others have been killed in increasingly violent encounters with the Border Patrol, or, in the case of Esequiel Hernández, a teenager from the US border community of Redford, Texas in an ambush in 1997 by Marines looking for drug smugglers. Few Americans outside of La Frontera are aware of how entangled federal law enforcement agencies and the military have become in regulating the daily lives of border communities.[12] As one Laredo city councilmember complained after the shooting of Hernández, 'I already feel like we are living under martial law here'. Amnesty International agrees that 'cruel, inhuman or degrading treatment', of US citizens as well as undocumented immigrants, has become disturbingly common, and in a 1999 visit to Tijuana, High Commissioner for Human Rights Mary Robinson (the former president of Ireland) expressed the United Nations' growing concern with the humanitarian crisis on the border (Schiller 1998).

The popular perception of a transnational police state along the border has been reinforced by President Zedillo's sweeping deployment of the Mexican army in open contempt of the constitution to conduct arbitrary searches of civilians and mount highway checkpoints. Mexican law was also violated in 1998 when more than 100 elite 'Special Forces' police were used to herd strikebreakers through picket lines at a Tijuana feeder plant for Hyundai Motors. The government's iron-fisted response to the first strike by a genuinely independent *maquiladora* union may prefigure a violent future for industrial relations along the border. In the neoliberal utopia of the border economy capitalized on Mexico's catastrophic national level of unemployment, real wages bear little or no relationship to workers' productivity or their cost of living. Despite 'a tight labor market, high productivity, and record profits', the *maquilas* 'have yielded successively lower wages for the people who work in them. In real dollar terms, the average wage rate in the *maquiladoras* has declined by a staggering 65 per cent since salary peaks in that sector in 1981' (Williams 1999: 140).[13]

The government's efficiency in suppressing the seeds of labour militancy contrasts, of course, with its famous inability to arrest the notorious border drug barons, supposedly the most wanted men in the hemisphere, as they brazenly lounge at Caliente racetrack or boogie the night away in trendy discos. The two warring cartels based in Ciudad Juárez and Tijuana now control much of North America's drug imports, intercepting the cash flow that formerly returned to Medellín and Cali. They effectively constitute the invisible third government of La Frontera. With Andean-sized drug profits has come Colombian-scale drug violence involving the comprehensive collusion of police and military officials. In 1994, Tijuana (which fifty years earlier had been Al Capone's favourite resort) became the arena of spectacular broad-daylight gunbattles between corrupted police forces allied with competing cartels. In a single two-month period, writes Sebastian Rotella (1998):

> The state police, in league with drug lords, were accused of killing a federal commander in a shoot-out. An assassin had killed the presidential candidate [Luis Donaldo Colosio], whose own campaign guards were suspects in the assassination. The federal police, in league with drug lords, were suspected of killing the city police chief. The federal police had arrested the deputy state attorney general and charged him with corruption.

By 1997 as many as 600 murders annually were being attributed by human rights activists to *narcotraficantes* or their bad cop henchmen (Limón 1998; Rotella 1998).

In September 1998 the drug war produced a slaughter of innocents. A dozen gunmen working for an affiliate of Tijuana's Arellano-Félix cartel forced 21 people from their beds in the Ensenada suburb of El Sauzal, ordered them to lie face down on a concrete patio, and opened fire with automatic weapons. Nineteen of them were killed, including infants, small children and a pregnant woman. The victims were members of the Pai-Pai tribe, one of the Baja California's few remaining pre-Columbian communities. After narrowly escaping extermination in the nineteenth century, the Pai-Pai hid out for decades in a mountain fastness of the Baja California desert before being 'rediscovered' by Sierra Club hikers in the 1950s. The massacre apparently was the climax to a long struggle over the cartel's use of communal Indian lands for marijuana cultivation and clandestine airstrips.[14]

For more upscale carnage, including the assassinations of prosecutors, police chiefs and newspaper editors, the Arellano-Félix syndicate prefers to recruit its gunmen, not from local *colonias*, but from the meaner streets of San Diego's

Figure 13.2
US/MEXICO BORDER AT SAN DIEGO/TIJUANA FROM THE NORTH.
(Photograph: M. Apigian, reproduced with permission)

Figure 13.3
US/MEXICO BORDER AT SAN DIEGO/TIJUANA FROM THE AIR.
(Photograph: M. Apigian, reproduced with permission)

slums. This is the *Clockwork Orange* version of binational urbanism. It was Arellano mercenaries from San Diego's Thirtieth Street gang, armed with automatic weapons, who gunned down Cardinal Posadas Ocampo of Guadalajara in 1993 and then carried out a sensational string of drive-by killings in luxurious San Diego suburbs. The sinister image of an armour-plated Chevy Suburban (many of its parts manufactured in *maquiladoras*) spewing deadly AK-47 fire out of its windows has become a popular icon of the transnational gangsterism celebrated in Border rap as well as traditional *corridos*. Unsolved murders (including those of 171 young female *maquiladora* workers in Ciudad Juárez since 1993) are just part of the day's freight in the brave new world being created by NAFTA (Rotella 1998: chap. 4; Mackler 1999).

NOTES

1 See the fascinating but sadly unpublished history by Vincent de Baca (1991).
2 Up to a fifth of the populations of some northern Mexican states now resides north of the border (*Los Angeles Times*, 31 July 1998).
3 [These images, courtesy of Michelle Apigian, are additions to the original text] (ed.).
4 Daniel Arreola and James Curtis (1993) at the University of Arizona have compared the distinctive spatial organizations of fourteen cities on the Mexican side of the fence.
5 *Maquiladoras* details from Mexico: Secretaria de Comercio y Fomento Industrial, 1998.
6 Cf., Herzog (1990); Martinez (1994); and Kearney and Knopp (1995).
7 'Instead of adapting the Toyotist regime to cross-cultural dynamics, Japanese transnationals with Mexican *maquilas* have integrated their production strategies, in basically unmodified form, into a structure that gives management enormous leeway in the mediation and control of industrial conflicts and the micromanagement of shop-floor struggles. This is what I have called hyper-Toyotism, because it involves a strategy that exaggerates tendencies already found in the historical Japanese context' (Peña 1997: 276).
8 EPA, as paraphrased by Peña (1997: 291).
9 *US Water News Online*, November 1996.
10 Operation Gatekeeper was modelled on El Paso's 1993 Operation Blockade and has been followed by Operation Safeguard in Nogales and Operation Rio Grande in Brownsville.
11 'Moreover the focus on border controls has obscured and drawn attention away from the more complex and politically divisive challenge of curbing the domestic US demand for both imported drugs and migrant labor' (Andreas 1999a: 14).
12 Nor do they recall the ominous precedent of the 1992 Los Angeles riots when the regular military, federal police agencies (including a huge Border Patrol contingent), the national guard and local police occupied inner-city neighbourhoods, often in the most brazen defiance of civil liberties.
13 See also Hinojosa-Ojeda and Robinson (1992) 'Labor issues in a North American free trade area'.
14 Cf. *New York Times*, 26 September 1998; *Los Angeles Times*, 2 October 1998; and *San Diego Union-Tribune*, 12 August 1999.

REFERENCES

Andreas, P. (1999a) 'Sovereigns and smugglers: enforcing the United States-Mexico border in the age of economic integration', unpublished thesis, Cornell University.

Andreas, P. (1999b) 'Borderless economy, barricaded border', *NACLA Report on the Americas* 33 (3): November/December.

Anon. (1997) 'Seeking US suppliers for maquiladoras', *Mexico Business Monthly*, September.

Anon. (1998) 'Colonias: problems and promise', *BorderLines* 6 (1): February.

Arnaiz, R., Bell, G., McGill, W. and Nathanson, C.E. (1996) *Demographic Atlas San Diego Tijuana*, La Jolla, California: University of California, San Diego.

Arreola, D. and Curtis, J. (1993) *The Mexican Border Cities: landscape anatomy and place personality*, Tuscon, Arizona: University of Arizona Press.

Cobo, E.P. (1993) 'The limits of the Mexican maquiladora industry', *Review of Radical Political Economics* 25 (4): 91–108.

Davis, M. (1996) 'Huellas fronterizas', *Grand Street* 56: Dreams (Spring): 23–32.

de Baca, V. (1991) 'Moral renovation of the Californias: Tijuana's political and economic role in American-Mexican relations, 1920–1935', unpublished thesis, University of California, San Diego.

Dunn, T. (1996) *The Militarization of the U.S.-Mexico Border, 1978–1992: low-intensity conflict doctrine comes home*, Austin, Texas: CMAS Books, University of Texas at Austin.

Eschbach, K., Hagan, J., Rodriguez, N., Leon, R.H. and Bailey, S. (1999) 'Death at the border', *International Migration Review* 33 (2): 430–54.

Fussell, E. (1998) 'The gendered geography of production: women and work in Tijuana and Mexico', unpublished thesis, University of Wisconsin.

Grimes, S. and Richardson, T. (1998) 'Regional links to Asia: what does the relationship mean to San Diego and Northern Baja California?', paper presented at San Diego Dialogue Conference (June).

Herzog, L. (1990) *Where North Meets South: cities, space and politics on the U.S-Mexico border*, Austin, Texas: Center for Mexican American Studies, University of Texas at Austin.

Heyman, J. (1994) 'The Mexico-United States border in anthropology: a critique and reformulation', *Journal of Political Economy* 1: 43–65.

Hinojosa-Ojeda, R. and Robinson, S. (1992) 'Labor issues in a North American free trade area', in N. Lustig, B. Bosworth, and R. Lawrence (eds) *North American Free Trade: assessing the impact*, Washington DC: Brookings Institution.

Kearney, M. and Knopp, A. (1995) *Border Cuates: a history of the US-Mexico twin cities*, Austin, Texas: Eakin Press.

Kelly, T. (1994) 'Sewage diplomacy: the political geography of cross-border sewage flows at San Diego-Tijuana', unpublished thesis, Fletcher School.

Limón, M.S. (1998) 'En Tijuana, 600 ejecuciones en un año, denuncian abogados', *Cronica* 11 January.

Lowe, N. and Kenney, M. (1999) 'Foreign investment and the global geography of production: why the Mexican consumer electronics industry failed', *World Development* 27 (8): 1427–43.

Mackler, A.M. (1999) 'Another girl found murdered', *Frontera NorteSur*, January.

Martinez, O. (1994) *Border People: life and society in the US-Mexico borderlands*, Tucson, Arizona: University of Arizona Press.

Peña, D.G. (1997) *The Terror of the Machine: technology, work, gender, and ecology on the U.S.–Mexico border*, Austin, Texas: Center for Mexican American Studies, University of Texas at Austin.

Reed, C. (1998) 'Hazardous waste management on the border', *BorderLines* 6 (5): July.

Rotella, S. (1998) *Twilight on the Line: underworlds and politics at the US-Mexico border*, New York: Norton.

Schiller, D. (1998) 'Mighty border patrol force finds deep ambivalence along the Rio Grande', *New York Times News Service*.

Seltzer, N. (1998) 'Immigration law enforcement and human rights abuses', *BorderLines* 6 (9): November.

Shirk, D. (1999) 'New federalism in Mexico: implications for Baja California and the cross-border region', paper presented at San Diego Dialogue Conference (July).

Tobar, H. (1996) 'New border in Tijuana', *L.A. Weekly*, 15–21 March.

Valladão, A.G.A. (1996) *The Twenty-First Century Will be American*, trans. J. Howe, London: Verso.

Ward, P. (1999) *Colonias and Public Policy in Texas and Mexico: urbanization by stealth*, Austin, Texas: University of Texas Press.

Williams, H. (1999) 'Mobile capital and transborder labor rights mobilization', *Politics and Society* 27 (1) March: 140–1.

Chapter 14: Screening Los Angeles

Architecture, migrancy and mobility

Brian Morris

> To grasp its secret, you should not begin with the city and move inwards towards the screen; you should begin with the screen and move outwards towards the city.
>
> (Baudrillard cited in Friedberg 2002)

INTRODUCTION

In the final chapter of *Ecology of Fear* (1998), which maps and dissects the paranoid imaginary central to Southern California, urban sociologist Mike Davis offers an incisive critique of the iconic film *Blade Runner* (Ridley Scott, 1982). A decade and a half following *Blade Runner*'s release, Davis makes a strong case for the surprisingly 'unprescient' nature of the film's dystopic vision of a future Los Angeles. In particular, the vertical/horizontal architectural forms that structure the integrated urban and social spaces of the film are, for him, simply 'another edition of the core modernist fantasy of the future metropolis [. . .] *ville radieuse* or Gotham City [. . .] [a] monster Manhattan' (1998: 361).[1] As he succinctly puts it, '*Blade Runner* is not so much the future of the city as the ghost of past imaginations' (1998: 361). For Davis, the dystopic cityscape imagined by the film is marked by a curious failure to recognize the particularities of Los Angeles' unique urban and architectural form which, for him, is perhaps better characterized by the low-rise, suburban dystopias found, for instance, in Octavia Butler's LA-based science fiction writing.[2]

Similarly, another urban sociologist, Janet L. Abu-Lughod, has also recently commented on deficiencies in *Blade Runner*'s highly influential and widely disseminated images of a future Los Angeles in her *New York, Chicago, Los Angeles: America's global cities* (1999).[3] Like Davis she queries the film's representation of architectural and urban form, focusing in particular on its representation of ethnicity. For her, the film is a 'lurid and violent "projection" of a variety of anxieties – over environmental pollution, robotic alienation, and "ethnic contamination"' (Abu-Lughod 1999: 378). This last source of anxiety concerning 'ethnic contamination' – or more specifically, the spectre of a cultural 'tide' of Asian migration found in *Blade Runner* – provides a useful starting point for this chapter. As Abu-Lughod observes, one of the most striking features of the film, given its mythic Los Angeles setting and related demographic shifts over recent decades, is the relatively 'muted, if not entirely absent' (1999: 378) presence of Hispanic characters and cultures (the nearest correlate she can find is in the figures of the alienated cyborg labour force central to the film's narrative). Instead, the film's pronounced anxiety over migrancy and its shaping of the city environment finds its primary representation in an 'Asianized' urban underclass who populate the permanently rain-soaked, gloomy and crowded city streets, while those with money and mobility (implicitly coded here as Anglo) have long ago left for more pleasant and ethnically homogeneous 'off-worlds' – the 'gated' communities of the future.

Following on from Davis' and Abu-Lughod's implicit recognition of the power of the cinematic imaginary in framing broader debates about Los Angeles' status as urban exemplar, I am concerned in this chapter with more recent filmic renderings of migrancy in relation to this city. Specifically, I offer a close reading of *The End of Violence* (Wim Wenders, 1997), a more recent Los Angeles-based film. While billed in much of its publicity as a 'suspense-thriller', *The End of Violence* (*TEOV*) resists any singular generic categorization as it also exhibits a similar narrative structure and thematic concerns akin to a number of recent other LA-based films such as *Short Cuts* (Robert Altman, 1993) and *Magnolia* (P.T. Anderson, 1998). Set to differing degrees in an alienated and pre-apocalyptic urban landscape, all these films are marked by complex, interlinked narrative threads involving multiple characters and stories. While not as widely seen as the Altman and Anderson films, *TEOV*'s attention to Los Angeles' contemporary socio-spatial landscape makes it a highly useful lens through which issues of migrancy and ethnicity might be discussed. At the same time, its self-conscious depiction of Los Angeles in terms of what I term an 'architecture of screens' enables an analysis of the ways in which localized and globalized technologies of vision organize relationships for city inhabitants in terms of regimes of migrancy and mobility, visibility and invisibility.

MIGRANCY/MOBILITY (LOS ANGELES)

The migrant experience fundamental to the growth and identity of Los Angeles was, in its earliest mythic incarnations, linked to travelling west and the promised economic and social mobility to be found in the land of sunshine. This contrasts with contemporary demographic trends (see Abu-Lughod 1999; Davis 2000), which underscore claims for Los Angeles' status as a radically multicultural, global city, and which bear witness to a south–north axis of transnational migration as distinct from that previous, national east–west drift. In particular, the more recent history of the city has been profoundly shaped by the forces and effects of global migrations of capital and populations from Latin American and Asia (particularly during the 1980s and 1990s). A steadily growing 'majority-minority' population – combined with the long-term aftershocks of the watershed 1992 uprising – has ensured that the politics of race, ethnicity and migrancy are more central than ever to the production of the city's frequently commented upon 'fragmented, paranoid spatiality' (Davis 1990: 238). Responding to these demographic and political shifts, a number of writers on the phenomena of transnationalism, globalization and urban space have begun to foreground the increasing 'Latinization' of Los Angeles. Davis' *Magical Urbanism* (2000), for instance, is a provocative and persuasive argument for Latin American populations being a key cultural and political urban force 'from below', frequently responsible for reinvigorating an older notion of public space and its uses. However, as he notes:

> The stubbornly binary discourse of American public culture has, however, yet to register the historical significance of this ethnic transformation of the urban landscape. The living color of the contemporary big city, dynamically Asian as well as Latino, is still viewed on an old-fashioned black-and-white screen.
>
> (2000: 8)

Davis' screen metaphor is particularly apt. Hollywood cinema (and television)[4] has largely been unable or unwilling to represent this transnational, migrant population and the complex ways in which it is shaping global, American cities, and this absence is particularly telling in those Los Angeles-based films which mobilize the particularities of the city in a fundamental way.[5]

This chapter provides a close reading of the representations of migrants and migrancy in *TEOV*, a film which to some degree challenges the 'stubborn binary discourse' identified by Davis. At the same time, *TEOV* is doubly marked by its attempt to evade the logic of another crucial binary discourse that intersects with the black/white representational divide identified by Davis. That other discourse consists of the specifically utopian/dystopian narratives of Los Angeles which have been fundamental to the mythic place-meanings of this city (such as those expressed in *Blade Runner*), and which even its best critics such as Davis himself prefer to work within.[6] Against the grain, I argue, *TEOV* marks a notable effort to produce a 'post-utopian/dystopian' Los Angeles film. In *TEOV*, this refusal to work strictly within that dominant mode of representation finds its impetus in the practices of transnational mobility *and* migrancy that shape urban space and sense of place. Los Angeles in this film is represented as a complex virtual space, simultaneously local and global, due largely to the central role of media and communication technologies in the contemporary construction of urban environments and locales.

New media and communication technologies have increasingly redefined our understanding of architecture. As a chorus of critical architectural and media theorists have observed (see, for example, Virilio 1991a, 1991b), urban architecture cannot simply be defined as the geographical agglomeration of buildings and concrete freeways and so on, but is simultaneously comprised of, and cut through by, a history of media representations and technologies such as cinema that provide and structure ways of experiencing and knowing 'the city' as well as particular places such as 'Los Angeles'.

Here, it is useful to flag the rich vein of scholarship in the field of cinema studies exploring the mutually constitutive historical connections between architecture, the city and the cinematic image. Giuliana Bruno (1997), for instance, has provided a genealogy of cinema that places it within the context of the transformed modern (European) city. Her work reminds us that cinema – like architecture – is a profoundly *spatial* form of cultural production (Shiel 2001: 5). For Bruno cinema emerges from the 'shifting perceptual arena and the architectural configurations of modern life' (Bruno 1997: 11) and is described by her as a 'means of travel-dwelling' (1997: 23) due to the kinds of visual, urban mobility it provided its early audiences. In particular, it is the *flâneuse/flâneur* – the simultaneously celebrated and scorned nineteenth-century Parisian streetwalker, stroller through the proto-cinematic spaces of the early arcades, and observer of the urban crowd – who has provided a productive trope for historically linking the experience of the modern city with the dominant modes of spectatorship that accompanied the birth of cinema as a social institution (see Friedberg 1993). However, the relation between architecture and cinema in the context of postmodern, multicultural urban space of Los Angeles is obviously very different to that of the European, modernist city and other American cities like New York. It is not the pedestrianized mobility of the *flâneuse/flâneur* that offers a metaphor for the visual regimes structuring everyday urban experience in Los Angeles: instead, it is necessary to look to the particular postmodern forms and practices of *auto*mobility organized around the freeway and car window in order to understand the broad relationship between vision, urban landscape and experience in this context.

While a number of postmodern theorists have contributed to seminal discussions of Los Angeles' urban space and architecture in the 1980s and 1990s (see, for example, Jameson 1984; Soja 1989), one of the best, early critical 'guides' to the city was Reyner Banham's *Los Angeles: architecture of four ecologies* (1971). In his preface, Banham takes his reader on the original postmodern, freewheeling academic tour of LA (since indirectly emulated to good effect by Fredric Jameson, Mike Davis and Edward Soja), framing it for the reader as an 'historical illumination' by way of the 'rear-view mirror' (Banham 1971: 36). Banham, an Englishman, maps out four key ecologies that shape the city's architecture: surfurbia, the foothills, the flatlands, and autopia – explicitly positioning the automobile as the technology stitching these ecologies together:

> One can most properly begin by learning the local language; and the language of design, architecture, and urbanism in Los Angeles is the language of movement. Mobility outweighs monumentality there to a unique degree [. . .]. So, like earlier generations of English intellectuals who taught themselves Italian in order to read Dante in the original, I learned to drive in order to read Los Angeles in the original.
> (1971: 23)

Contemporary Los Angeles is a city almost entirely constructed around an 'architecture' of structures and practices of mobility. These technologies of the automobile and freeway are also imbricated in practices of visuality. Recent scholarship, often focused on the exemplary but by no means unique Californian urbanscape, has elaborated the symbiotic relationship of the automobile to screen technologies such as cinema and television (see, for example, Baudrillard (1988), Morse (1990), Dimendberg (1995) and Friedberg (2002)). As Friedberg comments, '[s]een through the windshield or car window, Los Angeles unfolds as a narrativised screen space, obeying a spectatorial logic determined by the topography of the freeway and its off-ramp, the boulevard and its alley, the winding hill drive and its rare vista' (2002: 185).[7] Central to the issues focused upon in this chapter is Friedberg's related contention that Los Angeles illustrates a 'key and recurrent theoretical tangle: the tension between the material reality of built space and the dematerialized imaginary that the cinema has always provided' (2002: 186). However, I would argue that it is the broader figure of the 'screen' – in the form of the house window, the automobile windscreen, the television, and more recently the computer monitor – which mediates that tension and offers a useful point of critical intervention where the notion of urban 'architecture' can be legitimately broadened in order to get to grips with the complexity of the experience of the contemporary city.

It is the increasing proliferation of new media technologies, figured in *TEOV* in the form of the extraordinary communicative capabilities of wireless, laptop computers, complex satellite telecommunication networks and so on, that signal a shift in understandings and experiences of architecture and urban space in Los Angeles and an increasing number of 'globalized' cities. Curiously, perhaps, it is the 'old' screen technology of cinema that is being utilized in order to explore and, at one level, critique these dramatic changes within the context of this particular city. Yet, this is not surprising or incongruous given that 'Hollywood' has long been both a source of fascination and loathing for 'outsider' filmmakers like Wenders, as well as a consistent synecdoche for Los Angeles itself. Additionally, Hollywood cinema itself has produced a number of films which are self-consciously concerned with its centrality as the world's image-producing capital, and within this body of reflective narratives there are those that have been concerned with the introduction of competing screen technologies that threaten to, or have indeed, usurped cinema in terms of its centrality as an everyday entertainment medium producing images of the world.[8] Regardless of the fact that cinema may have, to some degree, been 'superseded' in an everyday sense by newer communication mediums, it is still the case as Goggin (2001: 72) comments in his analysis of *TEOV*, that established media institutions continue to fulfil a vital role in terms providing 'a [familiar] language in which new media can be discussed, understood and imagined'. Cinema thus provides a vehicle for mapping the everyday 'cultural imaginary' (Goggin 2001: 72) in which new media is becoming embedded – an everyday imaginary that is itself potentially transformed in the process.

In the sections that follow I analyse important aspects of the shifting contours of that new imaginary through a focus on the two central narrative threads of *TEOV* which involve parallels and intersections between white, male Anglos and migrant characters, who are in different ways defined by their practices of mobility and their relationships to technologies of (in)visibility. Drawing from the aforementioned notion of the simultaneously material and dematerialized mobilities through urban space that organize the experience of contemporary cities, my argument here is that the urban landscape and spaces of Los Angeles now need to be considered and reframed within the historical context of contemporary migrant movements, and the increasing role of *global* flows of bodies and media and communication technologies in the production of 'local' urban space. *TEOV*, while still appearing at one level to once again privilege the urban mobility of white-male protagonists is unusual as a representation of Los Angeles in its self-conscious attention to the presence of that transnational population. It offers an important case study detail precisely because of its unusual foregrounding of the socio-spatial architectures of an urban landscape where local and transnational structures of migrant visibility and invisibility are insistently inscribed upon the text of the city.[9]

SCREENING 'HOME': MIKE MAX/RAMON AND THE MEXICAN GARDENERS

Released in 1997, *TEOV* was the nineteenth of Wim Wender's films. At the time it was only the second of his films shot entirely in the US, and the first in English since *Paris, Texas* (Wim Wenders, 1984). Shot in a combination of Los Angeles locations and studio sets, *TEOV* offers yet another addition to the already enormous number of cinematic representations of Los Angeles, arguably the most 'screened' urban agglomeration in the world. *TEOV*, however, I would argue, belongs to a distinct group of films in which, as Geoffrey Nowell-Smith (2001) puts it, the city acts as a 'conditioning actor on the fiction precisely by its recalcitrance and its inability to be subordinated to the demands of the narrative. The city becomes a protagonist, but unlike the human characters, it is not a fictional one' (Nowell-Smith 2001: 104). While Nowell-Smith's identification of the city as non-fictional is problematic – after all, it is still a representation of the city we are encountering – his attention to the way in which specific urban landscapes almost take on an agency of their own in particular films is instructive.[10] In *TEOV*, the city continually 'leaks' in to the narrative: it is an extra cinematic character or presence that continually foregrounds the naturalized socio-spatial divisions and hierarchies that typify Los Angeles.

One of the two main (and perhaps the best realized) narrative strands of *TEOV* features Mike Max (Bill Pullman), a 'big-shot Hollywood producer' of popular violent films, who is forced to go 'underground' in Los Angeles with a family of Mexican gardeners who rescue him. Max's rescue follows a botched assassination attempt by sinister government forces tracking information leaked to him concerning the development of a high-tech, urban surveillance system. In the first scene of the film to introduce Mike Max, we find him at his coastal house organizing his latest movie deals outdoors via an electronic 'workstation'. This emblematic scene and the sequence that follows neatly encapsulate a number of recent commentaries on the role of information technologies in blurring the boundary between work and home, and between human and machine. Max sits inside a combined executive chair/workstation, a cyborg linked to his laptop, mobile phone and fax machine. This workstation, a materialized structure of informational architecture with its locus in the computer screen, resembles a curious cross between a virtual reality arcade game and the cockpit of a fighter plane, the logical fusion of the two key industries – the military and entertainment – that have historically been at the core of the Southern Californian economy. Max's body, plugged into multiple communication channels, functions here as an agent directing flows of money, people and capital around the world.

Here, Max, as a possible stand-in for an economically privileged, white, Los Angeles subject who lays claim to this (globalizing) city, is presented to us as a 'nomadic' figure in the sense described by Deleuze and Guattari:

> The nomad distributes himself in a smooth space; he occupies, inhabits, holds that space; that is his territorial principle. It is therefore false to define the nomad by movement [. . .]. Whereas the migrant leaves behind a milieu that has become amorphous or hostile, the nomad is one who does not depart, does not want to depart [. . .] and who invents nomadism as a response to this challenge. Of course, the nomad moves, but while seated, and he is only seated while moving.
>
> (1987: 381)

Mobility for this postmodern nomad is portrayed here as an issue of choice, freedom and privilege, and also as a particular inflection of dwelling-in-travel.[11]

A voiceover accompanies the shots of Max sitting outside his luxurious house, his gaze sweeping over a swimming pool to the California coast beyond. Citing the cold war era of his adolescent years, Max describes how:

> [w]hen I was a boy my brother fished, I watched films [. . .]. We suddenly seemed so vulnerable to killer sharks, nuclear submarines, an alien invasion [. . .] the enemy could come from anywhere [. . .] the land, the water, the sky, the Chinese [. . .] you couldn't trust any of them anymore.

One of the shots accompanying this voiceover is that of his laptop screen which features the yet unnamed, Claire (Rosalind Chao), Max's Asian-American personal assistant. In this scene the film juxtaposes the paranoia associated with an older, racialized yet 'invisible' enemy with the electronically present non-Anglo American subject. Yet, while that 'Asian', though now American subject is proximate in one sense, the computer screen also suggests a spatial boundary (and thus a mediated form of interaction between the racial/ethnic groups inhabiting the city).

At the same time, Max's pristine panorama and narrative reverie in the opening sequence as described above is continually interrupted, for example, by intercut shots of anonymous immigrant gardeners raking leaves from the swimming pool's surface, by the noise of their labour in the form of leaf blowers, and by an unseen helicopter. Thus, the screen of his computer does not guarantee Max a singular, immersive environment and insulated 'bubble' for forms of visual 'distraction' persistently intrude. In this case, that 'distraction' is clearly linked to the urban presence of ethnicized migrant labour (a presence which is continually repressed or made invisible). These migrants are, in a sense, insistently figured in the film as personifications of the hidden 'Los Angeles' which demands inclusion in the narrative and is not simply a built environment but also a product of the diverse practices of the various populations who inhabit it. To represent the city and its spaces in this manner raises a critical question as to why the cinema of Los Angeles continues to be one in which the experience of the white, male subject in the city is persistently universalized in order to represent a diverse social demographic.

A pertinent issue here, then, is the film's suggestion of some sort of parallel between the technological apparatus 'inhabited' by Max and the backpack mounted, leaf-blowing machinery that is an extension of the Mexican migrant's body. The film thus represents different social bodies becoming articulated to technologies that allow movement within prescribed spatial economies that are at times invisible to one another. Here, the film attempts to map the post-industrial as a continuation of the industrial without adequate attention to issues of economic hierarchies and the value attached to each kind of labour. However, the ways in which these technologies function as 'transports' or doorways to 'othered' forms of mobility must also be noted. For example, later in the film we frequently see Max with one of these devices as he works with the gardeners. These technological extensions – themselves ethnically coded – transform Max into an invisible subject, and his friends are literally unable to see him, as are the FBI agents who raid an internet café that he visits in order to download the file containing leaked details of the secret surveillance system. Overall, however, the film remains ambivalent about the mobility of the (cyborg)-migrants and the degree of 'freedom' that this entails.

The role of screen technologies in mediating different experiences of place is again played out in the bucolic scenes that take place later in the home of the im/migrant Mexican gardeners (filmed on location in Los Angeles' San Fernando valley). Here, Max's view outside from their/his bedroom window frames a domestic scene that clearly contrasts with his own earlier situation (where he is repeatedly spatially located on the outside of his own marital home, always 'looking in' – and later actually breaking and entering). Max's movement from the house into the yard of the migrant home is figured not simply as a touristic slumming, but the opening of a channel of communication and a passage into an/other space. Zilberg (1998) sees this space as a highly romanticized one. Certainly Ramon's (one of the gardeners) family, as she observes, are depicted as 'salt of the earth, and a God-fearing, simple, although not uncritical, people' (Zilberg 1998: 204). And in her reading, the intercultural encounters of the film are 'ultimately reduced to fanciful rendezvous and to stereotypes – albeit positive and even heroic' (1998: 204).

Zilberg's reading is plausible but I would also suggest that these encounters between Max and Ramon's family do other sorts of spatial and inter-cultural work. Here, it is useful to turn to recent discussions of the increasingly enmeshed realms of architecture and communication technologies. In a discussion of the refiguring of architectural boundaries and interfaces in the postmodern metropolis, Iain Borden (2000) has usefully refined Paul Virilio's (1991a, 1991b) insights into the increasingly virtual nature of architecture and place. Borden is interested in the ways in which everyday urban architecture – sites such as telephone booths plastered with prostitute's cards, entrances to tube stations adorned with advertising – are not just passive structures but are forms of architecture as boundary that become 'a channel of communication along which money surges'(Borden 2000: 240). As Borden comments, it is not simply the case that 'telematics replaces the doorway' as Virilio asserts, but that 'the doorway is being developed in new physical forms and socio-spatial configurations' (2000: 240). In fact, I would suggest that it is not so much doorways but architectural thresholds more broadly that are becoming enmeshed with forms of technology that amplify the function of those portals as communication mediums. Thus, the window/screen with its histories of virtual mobility provides a useful trope for understanding a series of interconnections between the layered visual frameworks that help organize both understandings of Los Angeles, its complex socio-spatial boundaries and subjects' movements, and the (limited) establishment of forms of communications through them. Or, as Heidegger puts it, a boundary 'is not that at which something stops, but [. . .] that from which something *begins its essential unfolding*' (cited in Borden 2000: 240; emphasis in the original). Thus, architecture in this scene in *TEOV* (in the form of a window onto 'the other'), potentially functions here as not just a 'view', but as a threshold through which bodies (like Max's) might migrate and communicate with 'other', contemporaneous urban social spaces.

Additionally, Ramon's family are represented as subjects that are 'at home' (in contrast to many of the non-migrant characters) with this mode of dwelling-in-travel. They provide an image for rethinking contemporary urban space outside of the mobility/migrancy binary – something more akin to outsider-insider figures who are able to negotiate screen architectures. Put another way, the pedagogical and didactic representations of modes of dwelling, migrancy and mobility associated with Ramon's family in *TEOV*, which are ways of inhabiting a globalized yet place-bound territory, provide crucial models for other 'non-migrant' characters in the film. However, the film isn't particularly forceful in alerting us to the fact that the family are not, of course, living in some pre-industrial idyll 'outside' of the city as the scene might suggest, for they also inhabit an urban environment which has screen boundaries that position and contain spatial practices via specific regimes of visibility and invisibility organized according to ethnic hierarchies. These regimes and the urban trajectories they organize have to be negotiated on a daily basis. Such urban spaces are not simply abstract and celebratory 'third spaces' (Soja 1996) outside of the local and the transnational. As Guarnizo and Smith (1998) argue, 'the social construction of "place" is still a process of local meaning-making, territorial specificity, juridical control, and economic development, however complexly articulated these localities become in transnational economic, political, and cultural flows' (Guarnizo and Smith 1998: 12).

TRANSFORMING EVERYDAY (GLOBAL) SPACE: RAY/MATHILDA

Running parallel to this narrative is the story concerning Ray Bering (Gabrielle Byrne), an ex-NASA computer scientist who is developing that same high-tech surveillance system utilizing combinations of satellite and closed-circuit television for the FBI. In an important scene mid-film, Bering and his sinister boss stand looking out over a panoramic vista of the city from the southern side of Mt Hollywood where his boss tells him that the technology he is working on may lead to 'the end of violence'. However, while implementing the system Ray stumbles across footage of the attempted assassination of Max – the system has murderous offensive capabilities – and decides to turn whistleblower. Meanwhile, Ray's boss has arranged for a Salvadoran political refugee rescued by the

American government, Mathilda (and her young daughter), to clean for Ray and keep an eye on him. Mathilda's husband, we are told, was killed by death squads who also tortured her. Her labour in the US also includes sex with Ray, whom she eventually 'betrays', and in the denouement of the film he is assassinated just before he is about to reveal full details of the surveillance system to 'Doc' (Loren Dean), a cop investigating the disappearance of Max.

Like Max, Ray Bering is also almost permanently plugged into screens, in his case in the form of banks of monitors and satellite feeds that dominate his workplace in the iconic Griffith Observatory. As his boss tells him, via a large monitor, while it is easy to look up into space it is a much messier business to look from space down to earth ('you're not in NASA anymore Toto'). Ray is led into the messy world he previously viewed safely from above via the satellite images that he stumbles across of Max's abduction and attempted assassination. Max is carjacked and taken below a spectacular freeway interchange where his two captors argue and hesitate before they are about to kill him (Max, like the Hollywood producer he is, offers them 'a million dollars [. . .] in point not to'). At this moment the camera point of view switches to that of a satellite image of the abduction scene and a computerized crosshair zeroes in on the three figures. While there is initially some confusion and mystery as to what happens next, it is eventually confirmed that the two abductors have been shot by the surveillance weapon and, although targeted, Max managed to escape before being killed. It is at this point that Max takes refuge with the gardeners: tellingly, however, not even the most sophisticated satellite technology can trace him in this invisible economy and urban space in which this im/migrant family dwell and the film thus suggests the coexistence and operation of different regimes of visibility within the same place.

Ray's workplace, where he accidentally witnesses the abuse and murderous capabilities of the new surveillance technology, plays a crucial role in the film in terms of housing what could be described as a classic, 'Orwellian' regime of visibility. As Zilberg (1998) notes, the Griffith Observatory (built in 1934) establishes itself in the film as the architectural locus of the panoptic surveillance of Los Angeles. Inside the Observatory there is a constant feed of panning and zooming shots of city streets and environs caught in the close-up gaze of security cameras. From a vantage point immediately outside of the observatory, the film provides contrasting panoramic shots of a radiant cityscape (and that famous grid of Los Angeles' lights stretching out into an infinite suburban horizon). Undoubtedly, the Observatory's familiarity for many audiences derives from its representation in *Rebel Without a Cause* (Nicholas Ray, 1956).[12] While that film now occupies a central place in terms of film criticism concerning the alienation of youth at this moment in social history, it also needs to be understood in terms of its themes of post-war (auto)mobility *and*, as James Hay (2002) has argued, a concern with images of cinema itself as a disciplinary technology. However, while that disciplinary theme persists in *TEOV*, it is necessarily revised and complicated through an implicit meta-commentary (via the highly self-conscious location of Ray Bering's workplace within the observatory) on the relation of cinema to other urbanized screen technologies that have since augmented or superseded it.[13] In other words, *TEOV* self-consciously alerts us to the 'convergence' of screen (film, television, satellite) architectures and their overlapping roles in envisioning 'Los Angeles' and socially organizing 'the city'. At the same time the ironic tone of this representation exudes a marked ambivalence about the role of (Hollywood) cinema as an agent of cultural normalization that continues to be able to affect all corners of the globe.

In 'An ontology of everyday distraction' (1990), her seminal essay on post-war, American urban environments, Margaret Morse explores the relations between the visual regimes latent in the automobile windscreen and television screen as part of a perceptive mapping of the historical shift in technologized, everyday environments. For Morse, typical realms of contemporary everyday experience – such as the freeway, television and the shopping mall – 'are part of a socio-historical nexus of institutions which grew together into their present-day structure and national scope after World War II' (Morse 1990: 208). Echoing Henri Lefebvre's earlier observation that the everyday is not so much a system in itself, but a 'set of functions which connect and join together systems that might appear to be distinct' (Lefebvre 1987: 9), Morse postulates that the relation between these pervasive contemporary institutions is an interdependent and mutually reinforcing one that allows for 'the exchange of values between different ontological levels and otherwise incommensurable facets of life, for example, between two and three dimensions, between language, images, and the built environment, and between the economic, societal, and symbolic realms of our culture' (Morse 1990: 194). Thus the freeway, according to Morse, is an analogue of the mall and of television; that is, while these cultural forms may not look alike they do 'observe similar principles of construction and operation' (1990: 193).

Her argument, I'd suggest, can be used as basis for further understanding and analysing the interdependent relationship of different historical forms of screen technology in *TEOV* – and their fundamental role in the production of urban space. This screen architecture produces what Morse describes as a '*partially* derealized' contemporary everyday. Such an ontologically unstable environment engenders encounters with otherness at the level of both face-to-face contact *and* through technologically mediated representations. Or, as Morse puts it:

> [t]he late twentieth century has witnessed the growing dominance of a differently constituted kind of space, a *nonspace* of both experience and representation, an *elsewhere* which inhabits the everyday. Nonspace is not mysterious or strange to us,

> but rather the very haunt for creatures of habit [. . .]. This ground is without a locus, a partially derealized realm from which a new quotidian fiction emanates.
>
> (1990: 195–6)

While there may be certain continuities between the everyday of the past and that of the present what *does* distinguish the contemporary everyday is the increasing *virtuality* of experience and its mediation by screen architectures.

But how does this increasing virtuality of experience articulate with modes of dwelling and senses of place in *TEOV*? Recall here Mike Max's narrative and the original architectural 'screen' of the 'home' – windows – which are prominently foregrounded in this film.[14] In the opening sequence of the film referred to above, the windows of Mike Max and Paige's affluent beachside home functions both as a metaphor for the forms of (non)communication and struggle that mark their relationship, as well as a site of contrast in terms of the 'other' domestic settings that appear later in the film. When Paige tells Max she is leaving him (she talks to him via telephone from inside the house while he views her from outside) for 'Guatemala', an imaginary repository of a 'real' life, we are given a sense of the cartoon-like and exoticized sense of place that certain kinds of global communication technologies (and associated visual culture) have produced.

This scene is important in terms of understanding the significance and increasing centrality of the actual migrant-refugee, Mathilda, following Ray's murder toward the conclusion of the film. The final scenes of *TEOV* take place as the sun sets on the Santa Monica Pier that juts out of Los Angeles into the Pacific Ocean. In this scene Mathilda sends her daughter to a lower level of the pier (where Max happens to be fishing) while she tells Ray's boss that she has repaid her debt to the government. The silent Latina as other transforms herself into a subject with agency. (However, this potentially romantic construction of the migrant is tempered by the scars – seen earlier – literally inscribed on the body of Mathilda, and these act as an enduring reminder of the differences between the 'postmodern nomad', such as Max, and the 'migrant-refugee'.) As she backs down the steps, hand shielding her eyes from the sun, two FBI goons ominously appear (one removes a pistol with silencer) and we are poised indefinitely for an assassination that doesn't come.

Meanwhile, on the level of the pier below (observed briefly by Mathilda through a tourist telescope), her daughter provides Max with an impromptu Spanish lesson including the word *cielo* (which means sky and heaven in Spanish), and remarks that 'they are watching over us'. In an intertextual reference to Wenders' Berlin film, *Wings of Desire* (1987), where only children and a few adults could see the legion of angels who watched over the city's population, Mathilda's daughter voices an ambivalence over whether 'they' are benign angels or sinister government authorities. As if in answer to this question, Max's voiceover functions as an attempt at narrative closure as the sun sets and the camera slowly zooms out in a helicopter shot of the receding pier and city:

> Just when you think you had it all figured, in a heartbeat it changes again [. . .]. Thing is, all those years when I was waiting for that sudden attack I became the enemy and when the enemy as expected finally came they set me free [. . .]. Now, when I look out across the ocean I don't expect killer sharks or alien attackers anymore [. . .] I can see China now, and I hope they can see us.

The reference to China here, which echoes the early scene of the film in which Max recounts a general cold war paranoia (while the face of his Asian-American assistant is displayed on his laptop), marks both the film's recognition of the obsolescence of the self/other binary but also a problematic move towards a celebratory globalization narrative. In the context of the discussed opening scene, the idea of 'seeing' China now cannot also fail to resonate with familiar and now established economic discourses regarding that country's potentially vast consumer market and a related softer stance on human rights issues.

Despite this ambiguity, it is the juxtaposed transformation narratives of Mathilda the migrant and Max the nomad which provide the most compelling critical lessons at the film's end. For this closing scene confirms the importance of the dialectic of visibility/invisibility, its constraints and productive potential effects. As the character 'Doc' observes in an earlier scene, 'looking at something can change it'. Technologies of visibility, the film seems to suggest, potentially constitute an act of violence and the end of violence, and are bound up in processes of image production and place-making that are shifting under the influence of the new technologies of mobility and flows of migrants that mark globalization processes. These same processes and the regimes of visibility are an important component of globalization – as well as critical activity – and they not only change places like Los Angeles, but change the nature of place and dwelling itself and audiences' critical understanding of these terms.

THE END OF 'THE CITY' AND THE END OF 'ARCHITECTURE'

> LA has beautiful (if man-made) sunsets.
>
> (Miles cited in Banham 1971: 17)

At the close of *TEOV*, Max has undergone a transformative journey from a successful producer of films that commodify the fear of otherness to a character 'at home' in the multicultural city in a different way:

> [I] turned what you could call a basic fear of strangers into a multi-million dollar enterprise. After all, paranoia is our number one export. Everybody needs an enemy.

> It's only now I've come to understand that there are no enemies or strangers, just a strange world.

The enterprise referred to here is cinema, which as a cultural medium has been particularly vital as a conduit through which variations and revisions of 'the city' are represented and reproduced. However, as James Donald (1995: 92) reminds us, 'the city' as mobilized in discourses from cinema to urban planning is not so much a place but itself a specifically modern 'structure of visibility' which functions as a powerful political tool. *TEOV* interrogates that still dominant modernist discourse of 'the city' by examining its simultaneous efficacy and vulnerability in a postmodern and 'globalized' place, Los Angeles, where its placement was an act of simulation from the start.

Los Angeles has always been distinguished by a paranoid anxiety in relation to cinematic discourses of 'the city'. For instance, as the hegemonic centre of a global cinema and entertainment industry we might also reasonably expect Hollywood/Los Angeles to represent itself as a 'first' global city in a cultural sense. Yet, this isn't the case: Los Angeles is peculiar in that in a cultural sense its self-identity is figured as a cheap type of simulation of the 'real' thing: in this sense it is a 'second-city' always living in the shadow of being found out, and of a resultant catastrophic destruction and disappearance. As Deb Verhoeven (1998) has argued, second cities are marked by a lack of belief in themselves (a fear of relegation to the status of third, fourth city and so on). Second cities live in the grip of the millennial, a fear of imminent disappearance: to guarantee their survival they frequently reproduce spectacular scenes of their own destruction. For as Verhoeven argues, to be a spectator at your own urban destruction is to produce a perverse guarantee of survival. Similarly, as Ackbar Abbas (1997) has demonstrated in relation to Wong Kar Wai's Hong Kong films, anxieties regarding the ephemerality of 'the city' can constitute a 'space of disappearance' which also functions to make visible a 'new' local culture and urban subject whose conditions of being are founded not on a history of dwelling-in-place in the traditional sense, but on structures and patterns of migrancy and mobility and a governing *instability* (in a modernist sense) of place.

Finally, as *TEOV* importantly reminds us, it is a 'new' everyday architecture that functions as a key nexus in terms of contemporary changes in understandings and experiences of place, dwelling and urban space. This is 'architecture' in the sense described by Paul Virilio (1991b), who has repeatedly emphasized the dematerialized aspects of contemporary architecture and its links to the 'space-time of vectors, [in which] the aesthetic of construction is dissimulated in the special effects of communication machines, engines of transfer and transmission' (Virilio 1991b: 64). In *TEOV* this increasingly prolific manifestation of architecture is commented upon through the trope of the screen which functions to demonstrate the important continuities that mark the mediation of urban space through different communication technologies and their associated visual regimes. For Wenders it would appear that these communication technologies have a crucial role to play in potentially refiguring the integrated visual, spatial and material structures central to current identity formations (such as those of the ethnically marked migrant and nomad). Such technologies simultaneously hold out the promise of moments of constructive communication between globalized yet locally segregated urban inhabitants. However, as the relative uniqueness of Wenders' film attests (in terms of its willingness to foreground the nomad/migrant disjuncture as well as the regimes of (in)visibility framing the latter's everyday existence in Los Angeles), a significant shift in the patterns of dominant cinematic representation needs to occur in order to allow an exploration of the consequences and complex political implications of this emergent architecture of place.

ACKNOWLEDGEMENTS

Thanks to my colleagues at RMIT University and the University of Melbourne for their generous and helpful responses to earlier seminar presentations of this chapter.

NOTES

1 Compare this with Dimendberg (1995) who traces representations of the 'centrifugal' urban space of LA organized around the automobile and freeway architecture – as opposed to the 'centripetal' space of New York.

2 In particular, Davis (1998: 362–3) refers to Octavia Butler's *Parable of the Sower* (1993).

3 That dissemination includes subsequent science fiction genre films (see, for example, *The Matrix* (Andy Wachowski and Larry Wachowski, 1999), as well as urban planning documents – for example, Davis (1998: 359) cites a key 1988 strategic document, *L.A. 2000: a city for the future* which refers to the dangers of the '*Blade Runner* scenario' which involves ethnic diversity run amok.

4 See Davis (1998) re the representation (or lack thereof) of Latin Americans in the 1992 riots, even though they were among the populations most affected.

5 This scenario is precisely the one noted by Zilberg (1998) in her analysis of *Falling Down* (Joel Schumacher, 1993) where she contrasts the representations of Latino/Latina migrants in the earlier *El Norte* (1983) with *Falling Down* and a brief commentary on *TEOV*. For a detailed analysis of *Falling Down* and its representation of LA's socio-spatial architecture also see Morris (1999).

6 For example, in *City of Quartz* (1990), Los Angeles is insistently 'sunshine or noir' for Davis, while *Ecology of Fear* (1998) operates around the 'dialectic of ordinary disaster'.
7 Or, as Baudrillard puts it with his typically exaggerated rhetorical flourish: 'The city was here before the freeway system, no doubt, but it looks as though the metropolis has actually been built around the arterial network. It is the same with American reality. It was there before the screen was invented, but everything about the way it is today suggests it was invented with the screen in mind, that is the refraction of a giant screen' (cited in Friedberg 2002: 185).
8 See, for example, *What Ever Happened to Baby Jane* (Aldrich, 1962), an allegory of the decline of Hollywood in which two faded film stars (played by Joan Crawford and Bette Davis) digest the bitter pill of watching their large-screen selves insistently shrunk by the medium of television.
9 See Davis (2000), for a related discussion of the emergence of 'transnational suburbs'. For him this is not simply a metaphor 'but involves radical new social and geographical lifelines that have been forged by the cunning of communities and households judged most "expendable" by the invisible hand of the planetary marketplace' (Davis 2000: 80).
10 I would argue for *TEOV* as a specific 'city film' in the same sense as *Blade Runner* (Ridley Scott, 1982), *Falling Down* (Joel Schumacher, 1992) and the more recent *Mulholland Drive* (David Lynch, 2001). Compare these, for example, with *City of Angels* (Brad Silberling, 1998), (a Los Angeles remake of Wenders' *Wings of Desire* (1987)) a film in which 'the city' merely functions as backdrop.
11 This useful term (albeit used here in quite a different context) is borrowed from Clifford's (1997) exemplary essay/chapter on 'Traveling cultures'.
12 One motivation for Wenders' use of this site can be traced to his admiration for Ray, who was the subject of an earlier Wenders' documentary, *Lightning Over Water* (1980).
13 Los Angeles (like New York with 11 September, 2001), has experienced its own distinct urban traumas such the riots/uprising of 1992. It is notable that television images have been central to many of Los Angeles' social conflagrations and that this medium also closely links (via the trope of mobility) to the city's most distinctive architectural foundation – the street/freeway (e.g. consider the Rodney King beating by LA cops, the Reginald Denny attack at the corner of Florence and Normandy and the still bizarre spectacle of the O.J. Simpson freeway 'chase').
14 See Lynn Spigel's (1997) discussion of the related forms of domestic architecture – the 'window wall'/sliding doors and television – that were a feature of post-war American housing, and which 'mediated the twin goals of separation from and integration into the outside world' (Spigel 1997: 212).

REFERENCES

Abbas, A. (1997) *Hong Kong: culture and the politics of disappearance*, Minneapolis: University of Minnesota Press.

Abu-Lughod, J.L. (1999) *New York, Chicago, Los Angeles: America's global cities*, Minneapolis: University of Minnesota Press

Banham, R. (1971) *Los Angeles: architecture of four ecologies*, London: Penguin Books.

Baudrillard, J. (1988) *America*, trans. C. Turner, London: Verso.

Borden, I. (2000) 'Thick edge: architectural boundaries in the postmodern metropolis', in Iain Borden and Jane Rendell (eds) *Intersections: architectural histories and critical theories*, London: Routledge.

Bruno, G. (1997) 'Site-seeing: architecture and the moving image', *Wide Angle* 19 (4): 8–24.

Clifford, J. (1997) *Routes: travel and translation in the late twentieth century*, Cambridge, Massachusetts: Harvard University Press.

Davis, M. (1990) *City of Quartz: excavating the future in Los Angeles*, London: Verso.

Davis, M. (1998) *Ecology of Fear: Los Angeles and the imagination of disaster*, New York: Vintage.

Davis, M. (2000) *Magical Urbanism: Latinos reinvent the US city*, London: Verso.

Deleuze, G. and Guattari, F. (1987) *A Thousand Plateaus: capitalism and schizophrenia*, trans. B. Massumi, Minneapolis: University of Minnesota Press.

Dimendberg, Edward (1995) 'The will to motorization: cinema, highways, and modernity', *October* 73: 91–137.

Donald, J. (1995) 'The city, the cinema: modern spaces', in C. Jenks (ed.) *Visual culture*, London: Routledge.

Friedberg, A. (1993) *Window Shopping: cinema and the postmodern*, Berkeley: University of California Press.

Friedberg, A. (2002) 'Urban mobility and cinematic visuality: the screens of Los Angeles – endless cinema or private telematics', *Journal of Visual Culture* 1 (2): 184–204.

Goggin, G. (2001) 'The digital family', *Southern Review* 34 (3): 71–86.

Guarnizo, L.E. and Smith, M.P. (1998) 'The locations of transnationalism', in M.P. Smith and L.E. Guarnizo (eds) *Transnationalism From Below*, New Brunswick, New Jersey, Transaction Publishers.

Hay, J. (2002) 'Rethinking the intersection of cinema, genre, and youth', in *Scope: An On-line Journal of Film Studies*, http://www.nottingham.ac.uk/film/journal/ [accessed 1 June 2002].

Jameson, F. (1984) 'Postmodernism, or the cultural logic of late capitalism', *New Left Review* 146: 53–92.

Lefebvre, H. (1987) 'The everyday and everydayness', *Yale French Studies* 73: 7–11.

Morris, B. (1999) 'Warzones of the street', in C. McConville and L. Finch (eds) *Gritty Cities: images of the urban*, Sydney: Pluto Press.

Morse, M. (1990) 'An ontology of everyday distraction: the freeway, the mall, and television', in Patricia Mellencamp (ed.) *Logics of Television: essays in cultural criticism*, Indiana: Indiana University Press.

Nowell-Smith, G. (2001) 'Cities: real and imagined', in M. Shiel and T. Fitzmaurice (eds) *Cinema and the City: film and urban societies in a global context*, Oxford: Blackwell.

Shiel, M. (2001) 'Cinema and the city in history and theory', in M. Shiel and T. Fitzmaurice (eds) *Cinema and the City: film and urban societies in a global context*, Oxford: Blackwell.

Soja, E. (1989) *Postmodern Geographies: the reassertion of space in critical theory*, New York: Verso.

Soja, E. (1996) *Thirdspace: journey to Los Angeles and other real-and-imagined places*, Cambridge, Massachusetts: Blackwell.

Spigel, L. (1997) 'The suburban home companion: television and the neighborhood ideal in post-war America', in C. Brunsdon, J. D'Acci and L. Spigel (eds) *Feminist Television Criticism: a reader*, New York: Oxford University Press.

Verhoeven, D. (1998) 'Melbourne becomes a dead city – again', paper presented at Millennial Encounters: time, millennia and futurity Conference, Melbourne, La Trobe University (9 October).

Virilio, P. (1991a) *The Lost Dimension*, New York: Semiotext(e).

Virilio, P. (1991b) *The Aesthetics of Disappearance*, New York: Semiotext(e).

Zilberg, E. (1998) 'Falling Down in El Norte: a cultural politics and spatial poetics of the reLatinization of Los Angeles', *Wide angle* 20 (3): 183–209.

Chapter 15: By the bitstream of Babylon

Cyberfrontiers and diasporic vistas

Ella Shohat

Like most technological-scientific innovations, cyberspace confronts the cultural critic with a plethora of ambiguities. In a transnational world typified by the global circulation of images and sounds, goods and people, which impact complexly on communal belonging, what do we make out of the new media's promise of shaping *new* identities? Here, I hope to delineate the consequences of the new media for the definition of home and homeland in a world undergoing, simultaneously, intense globalization and immense fragmentation, a world where transnational corporations make sure that 'we're all connected', but where at the same time borders and passports are under surveillance as a reminder that some have more 'connections' than others.

What are some of the political implications of the new media in terms of geographical location, national affiliation, and homeland imaginaries? As I explore the contradictions generated by the new technologies in terms of cyberdiscourse itself, its impact on material struggles over land and labour, its applications for the multiculturalist feminist project, and its import for questions of transnational dislocations, my stance will, perhaps inevitably, be somewhat ambivalent, I will reflect on the metaphorical and metonymic relationships between cybertravel, imperial narratives, national belongings, and diasporic displacements. Throughout, I will perform a delicate balancing act, negotiating between a critique of an ahistorical Eurocentric cyberdiscourse linked to transnational globalization, on one hand, and an examination of some intriguing possibilities opened up for diasporic communities and for feminist trans-national multicultural practices, on the other. My emphasis, overall, will move from a qualified pessimism concerning overall structures toward a qualified optimism concerning specific uses of cyberspace. I will be moving from a critique of an overly celebratory and implicitly Eurocentric cyberdiscourse, toward an examination of alternative, diasporic cyberpractices, always calling attention to the dissonances of the national and transnational as mediated by cyberspace.

CYBERLAND AND THE TRAVELLING GAZE

The contemporary futurist euphoria of cyberdiscourse clearly updates and extrapolates Marshal McLuhan's 'global village'. The digitized world, within this perspective, will facilitate neighbourhoods and cities free of geographic limits on streetwalkers, border-crossers, and transcontinental *flâneurs*. The migrating homesteader, or 'armchair traveller', sits in front of the computer screen hut makes gigantic leaps from cybersite to cybersite. But is it really possible to historically detach the facility of movement in cyberspace from the imperial culture of travel? The colonial exhibition and the ethnographic camera had already enabled the secret pleasures of imperial voyeurism. Does cybertravel continue to authorize the pleasures of predatory glimpses of otherized cultures, mapping the globe as a disciplinary space of knowledge? And does the interactivity of cyberspace promise to facilitate such knowledge differently? After all, isn't this how digitized communication defies a unilateral gaze, by allowing for dialogues from in and from multiple sites, diverse in their geography, culture, and politics?

Interactive cyberspace might potentially create democratic zones, but cyberdiscourse remains trapped within an imperial imaginary and corporate Big Brotherism. Behind Net politics one detects a pioneer settler philosophy of self-reliance and direct action. Safety and freedom of mobility in cyberspace are once again relayed in Eurocentric masculinist terms. The same cyberdiscourse that lauds the shrinking world thanks to instant communications, also mobilizes archaic, allochronic discourses about the Stone Age 'backwaters' of the globe. Cyberdiscourse is rich in imperial metaphors figuring the early days of cyberspace as the 'frontier' or 'Wild West'. The fledgling early computers were compared to 'isolated mountain valleys ruled by programmer-kings' and 'savage' computer interfaces, in a 'hitherto-unimagined territory opening up for exploration', a 'tough territory to travel', given the 'Internet's Khyber Passes', and the 'dangers of an uncontrolled cyber territory'. But the Net, we are told, lacks a 'Banana-republic-like center of authority'.[1] The exciting brave new world of cybernetics comes to us shaped and textualized, then, by a tired rhetoric of historically suspect metaphors. While cyberspace seems to transcend the gravity of geographic location, the metaphors remain grounded in specific third world sites. The Khyber Pass associated with British colonialism in Asia, stands in for tough and dangerous roads, while banana republics, associated with unpredictable Latin American coups, signify authoritarian takeover. As in imperial literature and film, the cyberfrontier narrative is focalized through the civilized explorer who gradually masters dangers in the terrain of the mysterious, the savage, and the despotic.

The problem with this cyberdiscourse is not only that it deploys imperial tropes and a modernizing narrative of progress historically linked to the dispossession of indigenous peoples, but also that the technologies themselves are embedded in the history of the military staking out of geographical territories and spheres of influence. The politics of the new media, in this sense, are imbricated in the politics of transnational economics. Since cybertravel takes place across open digitized frontiers, for example, it is necessary to erect virtual means to protect acquired 'territories' from individual or institutional break-ins into a computer system. Robinson Crusoe's fortress mentality and the frontiers' fenced landscape reappear in connection with protecting military, state, and corporate transnational information. Cyberdiscourse evokes the good-fences-make-good-neighbours ethos, where the fence was seen as the fixed boundary between civilization and savagery, where communities without walls seemed vulnerable to perpetual invasion, while lacking legitimate territorial claims.[2] Thus, the intertwined frontier tropes of sanctuary homes and free movement are transplanted into cyberland. Passwords, which open the gates into shared public space and fenced-off 'private houses', become the passport to the Web, permitting entry for some voyagers but not for others. Therefore, even cyberenthusiasts predict a future of power struggles over cyberspace, network topology, connectivity, and access (though problematically anticipated as substituting for the geographic battles over borders and chunks of territory that have been fought over in the past) (Mitchell 1995: 151).

Yet cyberfrontier discourse, like frontier imagination as a whole, implicitly prolongs the literal or metaphorical annihilation of cultures that stood in the way of progress. In his apologia for the new technologies, Lanham, for example, points that the 'shift from print to the computer does not mean the end of literacy'; rather, 'what will be lost is not literacy itself but the literacy of the print, for electronic technology offers us a new kind of book and new ways to write and read' (Lanham 1993: x). However, the content that Lanham and others imagine for the new technologies remains explicitly Eurocentric:

> Unlike most humanities discussing technology, I argue an optimistic thesis. I think electronic expression has come not to destroy the Western Arts but to fulfill them. And I think too that the instructional practices built upon the electronic word will not repudiate the deepest and most fundamental currents of Western education and discourse but redeem them.
>
> (Lanham 1993: xiii)

In Lanham's figural, biblical language, the 'old testament' of the book is fulfilled by the 'new testament' of hypertext.

Cybernetic metaphors cannot be seen as merely old language intended to facilitate understanding of the new media, which are complex, nonlinear, and not geographically bound. Nor is it simply a matter of the inadequacy of linear language superimposed on the multiply interwoven spatiotemporality of a new medium. The same discourse that carries old colonial tropes of voyages of discovery and exploration is also linked to the new world order of late capitalism and transnational arrangements that perpetuate and even exacerbate the unequal distribution of resources, labour, and power according to stratifications of gender, race, class, and nation. In this sense the critique of globalization as well as of 'scattered' or 'dispersed hegemonies' is amply relevant to the material structures of cybertransnationalism.[3]

THE END OF GEOGRAPHY?

Cyber travel metaphors, furthermore, implicitly render physical travel across national borders as obsolete and substitutable. In fact, the new cyberworld is eloquently charted by William J. Mitchell:

> Click, click through cyberspace; this is the new architectural promenade [. . .]. This will be a city unrooted to any definite spot on the surface of the earth, shaped by connectivity and bandwidth constraints rather than by accessibility and land values, largely asynchronous in its operation, and inhabited by disembodied and fragmented subjects who exist as collections of aliases and agents. Its place will be constructed virtually by software instead of physically from stones and timbers, and they will be connected by logical linkages rather than by doors, passageways, and streets.
>
> (Mitchell 1995: 24)

It is, indeed, indisputable that such technology displaces the familiar sorts of geographical neighbouring and physical connections that have provided access to the places where people lived, worked, worshipped, and entertained themselves. And when what is at stake is largely libraries, news, music, films, and audiovisual commercial communication across the globe, all of which can be cybernetically mediated, physical travel does seem to be superfluous. Travel would seem, in this sense, to be an outmoded mobilization of privilege, replaceable by an even more comfortable and privileged mode of travel. However, the 'anti-spatial' and 'indeterminate' locations of cyberspace seem to be conflated with the ways in which material geography and history shape complex production, consumption, and usage of technology.

In many recent cybercelebratory writings, cybergeography is imagined virtually as a flight from the gravity of geography. Cyberspace, according to writers such as Mitchell, subverts the idea that 'geography is destiny': 'the Net's despatialization of interactions destroys the geocode's key. There is no such thing as a better address, and you cannot attempt to define yourself by being seen in the right places in the right company' (Mitchell 1995: 10).

But such narratives of geocode liberation detach cyberusers from their gendered, classed, sexed, raced, and nationed locations. (In fact, there are many battles over domain names on the Internet, and some even argue to increase the number of domains in order to accommodate different statuses). Where cyber-combat zones and leisure clubs still exist, where hate groups and 'minorities' can both maintain their private cyberspaces as well as interact in the public sphere of the Internet, we cannot speak of total despatialization. Rather than celebrate the destruction of the geocode, I would argue for examining the ways in which the geocode gets to be recodified. The literal and metaphorical spaces of belongings are now carried over into the conflictual cyberzones, while forging intricate relations between cyberspatiotemporality and the material corporeality of its users.

One senses in the contemporary air a desire for a (bearable) lightness of geographical being. A facile declaration of the end of the physical in an era that also celebrates globalization points to a deep connection between such parallel intellectual currents. Having absorbed the postmodern claim of the 'end of history', are we now witnessing an 'end of geography'? But just as one might ask of a certain postmodernism exactly *whose* history was coming to an end, we may also ask, whose geography is coming to an end? The portrayal of the complex architecture of cyberspace as a leisure retreat or corporate energy field raises the question: for whom? Who will be allowed to walk or to jog inside it? And in what ways? In what company? In which material contexts? And for what purposes? What does one then make of this crisscrossing of bits within asymmetrical power relations?

In the Iranian-American film *The Suitors* (Ghasem Ebrahimian, 1983) the Iranian woman who emigrates to the US with her husband (who is murdered by the police, who assume that all Middle Easterners are terrorists), finds herself passportless when, at the end of the film, she tries to escape from her suitors to Europe. She packs herself into a huge suitcase in order to smuggle herself outside the US, passing through the baggage scanning lasers of JFK. Such images vividly illustrate that access to national passports and geographic location still do matter in the age of transnational globalization and supposedly disembodied and fragmented cybersubjects. While people with access to the new multidirectional media cross oceans with a click, recent immigrants and refugees – such as Chinese, Egyptians, and Mexicans – who attempt to cross by boat, plane, or foot are bound by their homeland passports or by their lack of any passport. Does despatialization mean that the future cybernation will have no place for 'Proposition 187'? To put it bluntly, does the virtual voyage mean that immigrants and refugees trying to cross borders would no longer have any reason to do so?

While we become euphoric about the enhanced communications enabled by cybertechnologies, we often forget that the same technologies can be used for repressive purposes. In the context of strict immigration laws and abusive detention centres in places such as New York, New Jersey, Florida, and California, the cyberspace 'travelling' of information is clearly used against the travelling bodies of refugees, immigrants, and border-crossers. The digital world's 'wireless bodynet', the space of the cyber *flâneur*, is also used against such border-crossers as the 'illegal aliens' whose physical bodies are under surveillance by a digitized panopticon. The very same apparatuses that empower Chiapas revolutionaries to communicate with a PCS at the same time allow digital surveillance to keep 'infiltrators' from crossing to what was once their own homeland. Euphoric new media texts, giving the futurist sense of worldwide wandering disencumbered of geography and history, in other words, shape what I would call 'cybermetaphysics', where the struggles against racism, anti-Semitism, sexism, homophobia, and classism all seem strangely passé.

FROM CYBERMETAPHYSICS TO MULTICULTURAL FEMINISM

Cyberenthusiasts anticipate that territorial borders and physical travel would gradually become meaningless. One gets the impression that the new media will generate new communities where geographical boundedness will be obsolete. Such projections are seductive if not articulated in a historicized fashion. Within such a vision of the cyberfuture, history itself becomes 'history', over. That is, 'history' in the sense of contested visions of such issues as colonialism and sexuality, becomes a matter of an irrelevant past, rather than something that shapes our perception of contemporary identities, and with even larger implications for the coming cyberyears. One detects in this notion of the end of history a sense of anxiety about contemporary identity politics, and the presumably unacceptable demands made by people of colour, women, and gays/lesbians. In a future cyberworld where 'nobody knows you are a dog' – that is, nobody knows your real identity – but where anyone can open a homepage – that is create his or her identity – contemporary categories defined by gender, sexuality, race, ethnicity, and nationality are eagerly, and prematurely, dismissed as no longer relevant. In a society negotiating between the so-called contract with America, on the one hand and identity politics on the other, one discerns a desire for a futurist paradise of gender and ethnic tabula rasa(s) interacting fluidly in an infinite oceanic flow of self and community. Such facile colour-blind utopias, however, escape the haunting history of the tabula rasa, of whiteness and heteromasculinity, the fact that subject invisibility is historically associated with Anglo-American heteromasculine privilege.

Futuristic cyberdiscourse implies a transcendence of nationally and regionally bound identities, eroded in favour of new identities shaped by terminal interactions. But there are political traps embedded in the discourse of new identities. To begin with, virtual communication among strangers *is* still grounded in national languages and ethnic identity, since it has to be performed in a globally empowered lingua franca – English. Speakers of languages such as Arabic, Hebrew, or Chinese have to use the Latin script in e-mail, even when they wish to communicate in their own language – a very difficult task that most adhere to only partially. Arabic-speakers on the Net must write English and not Arabic, and even words used in specific dialects – Tunisian, Lebanese, Moroccan – are typed and clicked in Latin script. Even for Middle Easterners, English is the 'open sesame' to a thousand and one bytes. To navigate the Net one must be literate in English. My illiterate grandmother, who speaks only the Iraqi dialect of Arabic, even if taught to click, won't be able to communicate unless oral cybercommunications are popularized. (I hope Masouda, who is still in the Middle East, will still be there in the age of oral/image cybercommunications, since she does not trust airplanes).

Recently I attended a lecture on the new media for educators, offered by some whiz kids, envoys from the cyberfuture. This polished, well-documented performance of the magic available to us somehow did not leave me with a happy feeling of a brave new world. Searching for an example of a nonviable CD-ROM pedagogical project, the whiz kid cited what he called the 'ridiculous' idea of translating Chinese literature into Spanish. But only a Eurocentric perspective would find the prospect of translation and communication between one billion or so Chinese-speakers and five hundred million Spanish-speakers a laughable idea. This prevailing post-Babel desire for homogeneity in the 'world of the future' clearly suggests that non-Anglo subjectivities might not feel completely at home in cyberland. Given such national, racial, class, and gender fissures, I am concerned about the implicit dismissal of multicultural feminist struggle as, so to speak, ancient history.

Within this context, we have to question the prediction that the new media will create new identities, 'New Adam' discourses of self-shaping elide the histories of the eliminated. Just as the 'discoverers' of 'virgin lands' did not create being from nothingness and still carried their Old World cultural baggage, the 'new frontier' of virtual voyages, unless challenged, might merely extend a Eurocentric vision of history, geography, and identity. The new media, like all technologies, are embedded in ambient political struggle. Our role as cultural critics, activists, and educators is to prevent the erasure of critical perspectives on history, and to support a polycentric multicultural project of transforming global and local power relations.[4] Cyberhomes in this critical perspective will not be simply castles for Eurocentric thought and transnational megapower, but part of a continuous terrain of competing discourses, where the battles over resources that rage outside cyberspace continue, even if in a fragmented fashion, inside it as well.

The idea that cyberspace would make everyone 'at home in the world', furthermore, has to be articulated in the context of cybercombat zones and imaginary homes, especially for those communities literally shorn of homes and/or homelands. While computer networks do radically redefine our notions of place, community, and urban life, one cannot separate this fact from the ways in which cybercommunities are entangled in unequal material realities. Cybernetics itself does not transform existing local and global power relations: it extends them into a new space and inflects and shapes them through its diverse formats, even when they are interactive. As with the history of previous technologies, the democratization associated with cyberspace can still be limited to those who are economically, culturally, sexually, and racially at home in the world, a tiny privileged transnational jet-set elite, now cyberized and online. Access to the Net, for example, is not universal and uniform. Apart from the fact that one's access is determined by one's class and national location, it is also determined by governments who restrict access to it physically (by, for example, creating locally controlled computer centres) institutionally (by locating these centres within specific institutions such as the military, intelligence, or the university), and economically (by driving the cost of linkage and electronic mail so high that only the elites can afford to hook up). As a result of this multifaceted unequal access, the decentring of the new media does not exactly materialize for all sites, nor does it materialize in the same ways for all sites.

Communities invisible in the 'old media' have begun to relocate their struggles over land and resources to online technologies. Even histories of dispossession gradually find their way to notices on the Net board, where activist exchanges, and even racist and antiracist battles, continue in cyberspace. Thus, in the Americas, as the homeland of diverse indigenous people who became refugees in their own homeland, the new media are used to recuperate the symbolic space of Pindorama, Land of the Condor, and Turtle Island. Such virtual spaces come to stand for an imaginary homeland. In this sense the notion of an originary and stable home, encapsulated in phrases such as 'home sweet home', 'my home, my castle', and 'no place like home', is cybernetically redefined for dispossessed nations not simply as a physical location but as a relational network of dialogic interactions.

Permeating cyberdiscourse, colonial metaphors evoke a corporeally violent history and brutal policies toward racialized communities. Such metaphors can also be seen as prefiguring transnationals' digitized expansionism in and outside cyberland. The fact that cybercartography – like the colonial mappings of the Americas – relies on old territorialized metaphors points to an envisioning of a future cyberworld that would still be implicated in transnational powers. Computer corporations such as IBM and Apple create a discourse in their own image. Just as cybercommunications transcend a specific geographic home and a single national homeland, transnationals have long since shaped mobile locations for their digitized production of digital technologies. (In fact, many US companies have moved their operations outside the US to avoid taxes and to profit from the international division of labour.) Cheap labour in places such as Taiwan determines at which site transnationals choose to produce their hardware and software. In this sense, transnationals still reproduce a world where cyber-privileges are constructed not so much on the backs but, rather, on the fingers and eyes of largely female third world workers.[5]

Although the new technologies were largely developed by and for the military, they have at the same time become the site of activism and grassroots organizing. *Cyber-* in this sense becomes an embattled space for becoming 'at home' in the world. Indeed, coming years might witness an ever-growing use of the Net for transnational labour organizing; technologies can thus be hijacked for jujitsu purposes, ones quite different from those initially intended (see Carillo 1998). And if the Net has been used to promote militias and neo-Nazi organizing, it has also been used for antiracist and antihomophobic mobilizations. IBM workers, Chiapas revolutionaries, South African labour organizing, women's antiviolence networking in the US, and human rights groups in Palestine have used the new media for internal and external communication. The Net has helped Palestinian and Israeli Human Rights advocates, for example, to inform the world about abuses by both Israeli and Palestinian authorities, allowing for a certain democratic human rights forum, as well as for fostering a transcommunity feeling of solidarity. When counterhegemonic information still travels across national, cultural, and political borders, we cannot say that a whole new world is simply transformed; rather a new terrain has been opened for what used to be called *'a luta continua'*.

THE GRAVITY OF HISTORY: TRANSNATIONALITY AND THE EXILED NATION

Clicking on an icon to open a file filled with messages from around the world has provoked celebratory ideas of the new global village. Cyberdiscourse projects a future utopia where there will be no 'remote places' where one would feel 'far from the centre of things', since the digitized future will be decentred. For those who, already since the 1960s and 1970s, have engaged in debates about centre and periphery, this digitized decentring of fluid spaces should sound like good news. And for those engaged in postcolonial debates on hybrid diasporic identities, it might sound like a relief to imagine a future free of the gravity of geographies of identity. Postcolonial writings on the hybrid and the diasporic have performed a double-edged critique of colonial discourse and of third world nationalism.[6] In nationalist discourses, the tropes of home and homeland were often represented as the site of fixity as opposed to the suspect instability and mobility of the nomadic. And while colonial discourse privileged the figure of the voyager, the explorer, as the dynamic centre of the text/discourse who teleologically settles on the range, postcolonial theory has privileged the figure of the traveller, the diasporic, the hybrid, the exile as a destabilizer of fixed centres. Since the very definition of house, home, and homeland requires a boundary, whether that is a fence, a wall, or a border, the metaphors of fluidity in diaspora and postcolonial discourses express the critique of a fixed notion of identity. If the concept of the third world was about generating an intellectual and political home for colonized nations, the postcolonial, I would argue, is about generating a home for displacements in the wake of such decolonization. And while the third worldist discourse suppressed diversity, conflicts, and 'minority' perspectives within 'the nation' in order to chart a homogeneous anticolonial master narrative, the postcolonial has tended to privilege diasporic, migrant, nomadic identities, where access to power among those wandering, and their relation to their nation-state of origin and destination, have been obscured.

Cyberspace's nonlinear stream seems to make a good analogue for the poststructuralist sense of the fluid slippages of identity. And the cyberwritings' emphasis on decentring seems to overlap with a certain postcolonial imaging of fluid dwellings and moving homelands, where no home is presumably central or marginal. It might even seem as though diasporas (demographically decentred by definition), peripheralized nation-states, and marginalized communities would all have a natural affinity and concrete interest in the new media. This enthusiasm for the cyberdream, I have tried to argue, must be accompanied by a number of caveats. But it is still worth contemplating the potentialities of cyberspace. Despite the political ambiguities of the new technologies, they open up intriguing transnational possibilities for multicultural feminist practices as well as for the agency of displaced communities.

Cybertransnationalism on one level would seem to transcend some of the pitfalls of nationalism, especially for those minority communities displaced in the wake of postcolonial and colonial partitions. In the cyberfuture, feeling at home in the world might mean that digital technologies will exist in the service of currently marginalized communities. In a virtual world of communication where sound, image, and text can synchronously cross distances in less than a second, upper-middle-class diasporic communities split by circumstances might be able to perform a ritualistic get-together at the computer dinner table or in the computer livingroom or diwan. One can even imagine a digital linking of displaced communities of migrating computer bits through global networks, where the new media allow for new virtual communities of people whose sense of national and geographical homeland is fragmented and fractured. The new media can become the imperfect means by which dislocated people who lost their geographic home retain their home imaginary, while also struggling for a literal and metaphorical place in new countries such as the US and Britain, whose foreign policies have concretely affected their lives. Each interaction, however, is layered by a distance at once temporal and spatial, each situated, produced, and received in precise historical and geographical circumstances. Although cyberspace's multisitedness would seem to favour a dispersed existence, such communities are not suddenly extracted out of geography and history. Digitally mediated environments, with their information highways and *infobahns*, furthermore, do not necessarily shed the narrative of searching for a national home, in both its liberatory and repressive senses. Cyberspace, in fact, can permit a new mode of fetishizing 'our' lost homeland. Yet, even in this act of logging in nostalgia for ancestral homes, virtual communities reshape and alter the diasporic subjects. Thus interactive networks of links, cementing dispersed communities, also enact a virtual performance of what constitutes the nation.

Cyberspace allows for diverse forms of diasporic linking and interacting: temporal links that bring together the clashing historical perspectives of contesting communities, spatial and geographical links between different parts of the world. In this way downloaded images, sounds, and texts enable critical communities to pass on their perspective, and identifications, and their affiliations. Interactive media disperse the hegemony of nation-states through virtual proximity, enabling exilic communities to share, teach, and inform beyond the often unbearable familial devastations. Whereas cyberspace allows for the creation of interactive communities of strangers, it can also empower the diasporized to overcome the estrangement of displacement. The digital undermining of territoriality can thus operate simultaneously with the virtual reterritorialization of immigrants and refugees'.[7] This is not to suggest that such virtual transnational gatherings of the 'nation' are necessarily oppositional. It is, rather, to say that such virtual spaces can become, in specific contexts, important for critical practices.

The implicit promise that terminal identities will eventually transcend geographies of national identity raises interesting questions for displaced and diasporic communities whose very existence already transcends the boundaries of the nation-state. The case of Gawat Izzawi – Izzawi's Cyber Café – of which I am a member, illustrates some of the political issues at stake. An exilic e-mail community from Iraq, the original site of the Babylon of this title, is composed of strangers of Iraqi origins who met largely through notices on the Net board. 'Gawat Izzawi' refers to an actual popular café in Baghdad, about which many popular songs were written. The electronic-mail café name functions as a chronotope, expressing nostalgia for both a place and a period, since Iraqis from diverse religious backgrounds and ethnic communities used to socialize in the physical Gawat Izzawi. Exilic nostalgia is freely exercised in the 'private' public space of the electronic Gawat Izzawi, a community of intimate strangers.[8] Gawatt Izzawi points to the cyberintimacy of people who have never met but who have developed an Arablish language (Arabic and English) and a set of references that draw on Iraq, the Arab world, and the traces of their dislocations. Baghdad of the historical Gawat Izzawi is an emotional site for all of us who became refugees and exiles. This evocation of a multicultural past extends into cyberspace a certain reading of Baghdad as multicultural, in a doubly temporal desire for both a lost past and a hopeful future. Multicultural Iraq, prior to its multiple exoduses over the past fifty years, included Sunnis, Shiites, Jews, Assyrians, Assyrian Christians, Caldian Christians, Kurds, Turkomani, and Persians, with diverse dialects and languages, ethnicities, religions, and political affiliations. But that multicultural fact was never transformed into a multicultural *project*; it was always threatened by the ideology of the 'Nation' as embodied by Sunni Muslim hegemony.[9]

The nation-state ejected its Iraqi Jews several years after the partition of Palestine and the establishment of the State of Israel, while the Kurds in the north remain stateless, and the Shiites in the south oppressed. A kind of 'return to the future', where history reconfigures a desired future, was evoked when one of the members e-mailed me: 'Ahlan Habiba [Welcome Habiba], looking forward to sharing with you a piece of Iraq that was lost.'[10] Not coincidentally, she also wrote that she was Assyrian, one of the Christian minorities in Iraq – where Babylonian Jews and Assyrians pre-dated the Arab conquest of Mesopotamia, but who over the centuries became Arabized. My family and community were exiled by the erection of two mutually exclusive national narratives: Jewish and Arab, which on both ends allowed no room for Arab-Jews, that is those Jews who were Arab in language and culture but Jewish in religion. In other words, the Arab national narrative became difficult for Arab-Jews, especially since Arab nationalism reproduced the Zionist master narrative of 'Arab' versus 'Jew'.

Within the context of postcolonial displacements, nation-based cyberspaces fill in a certain vacuum within the dominant old media. The experiences of marginalized communities can be narrated despite their invisibility and lack of access to transnational storytellers such as CNN, the Associated Press, Reuters, ABC, BBC, and Hollywood. The new media allow for multisited clashing perspectives to combat and convince. Middle Easterners and North Africans in the US have used the Net to put themselves on the cybermap.[11] At this historical conjuncture, watching television and surfing the Net give totally different impressions of the 'American' environment we live in. In the case of Middle Easterners, their media invisibility in the US is challenged by their presence on the Net. The Net in this sense challenges the otherizing of Middle Eastern and North African cultures as something that presumably belongs *only* 'over there', thus challenging the exclusion of these communities from the US multicultural debate.

The desire for a multicultural Iraqi nation is channelled through cyberspace, which in this sense provides an imaginary home. For Arab-Jews, abruptly disconnected from the Arab world, relocation to the US, Brazil, Canada, and Europe requires a medium whereby such dialogic interactions can be enabled and revitalized. The Net intensifies this process, mediating between diverse regional communities that otherwise wouldn't meet because of both physical and ideological borders. Therefore, Iraqis, Iranians, Moroccans, and Egyptians who grew up in Israel and never had the possibility of meeting the peoples inhabiting their countries of origin now engage via the Net. If the postmodern Babylon of the Iraqi diaspora throughout Amman, London, New York, Chicago, Ramat Gan, Toronto, Paris, and Berlin is sometimes traceable on the Net, Iraqis in Iraq itself are largely absent.[12] 'All you need,' the promotional brochures inform us, is 'access to a computer.' That is exactly why such communication is not allowed in a dictatorship such as Iraq [pre-2003], while Iraqis in the diaspora, some of them victims of the Gulf War's digitized warfare, do maintain a sense of community, thanks to electronic mail, and 'run into' people from their own community on the Internet. For the millions of displaced Iraqis, cybertravel across national borders becomes a travel of recuperation and reconfigurations as well. Religious and ethnic 'minorities' have had to play the role of historical narrators, telling of massacres and violence, rewriting the official national Iraqi history. Virtual travel in cyberspace, where personal identities might be masked but where ethnic, religious, and gender identities are revealed, creates dialogical networks for people, even if they come from the opposite ends of the political spectrum of the nation. In fact, the very act of computer communication for exilic Iraqis is an act of imagining a democratic home, since PCs were not permitted in Iraq. (If you tried to e-mail Baghdad, you can be sure that you would have reached the Ba'ath party and that the Muhabarat – security services – were watching.) The nostalgia associated with exile and diaspora is dialogically reshaped through explicit and implicit contestation of who and what constitute the nation. In the case of women, in particular, virtual cafés or clubs permit a partially disembodied dialogue, subverting a masculinist history where women – with the exception of dancers, singers, and prostitutes – were formerly not welcome in the café, their bodies seen as transgressive of male public space. That many female members of the Iraqi cybercafé ended up developing parallel channels of communications alongside the official one only testifies to the ways the 'nation' is contested and reinvented within the transnational cyberspace.

Since cyberspace can maintain a long-distance sense of community or, better, of overlapping interactive communities, current nationalist and ethnic pressures of committing oneself to one or two geographies of identity are challenged by a quintessentially postmodern technology. The increasingly popular usage of e-mail and the Net already allows geographically dispersed communities to interact beyond the literal and metaphorical boundaries of nation-states. Such communications, especially for exilic communities, produce a simultaneous rejection of the 'nation' while also forging a kind of cyberhomeland shaped by and from the palimpsest of geographical, national, and transnational dialogics. Cyberspace can potentially facilitate a discussion of community identities – not in isolation, but in relation. Cyberspace in this sense is a negotiated site of multiple community positionings within diverse temporalities. Each positioning of communities in relation generates a different sense of affiliation. Like diasporic deterritorialization's crucial role in shifting and redefining hybrid identities in diverse contexts, cyberspace becomes a process where, without physical travel, communities might experience the liminal borders of their subjectivity. The very nature of cyberspace, in a sense, forces a rearticulation of the idea of homeland, as subject constructions become multiple with overlapping and contradictory identifications and affiliations.

I have tried here to communicate a sense of both the possibilities and the limitations of the new media technologies, displaying a kind of optimism of the local in terms of the uses to which these technologies can be put, and a pessimism of the global in terms of larger overriding structures. The new media, I have tried to suggest, have significant implications for charting diasporic movements across national borders, and perhaps for envisioning a creative navigation of diverse cultures and historical points of view, and of conflictual claims to homes.

NOTES

1 'There are few *Khyber Passes* on the Internet [. . .] and there is no effective way to gain control of it. Unlike *Banana Republics*, it does not have a clear center of authority to take over in a coup. The *uncontrolled territory* has its dangers' (Mitchell 1995: 150; emphasis added).

'The early days of cyberspace were like those of the *Western frontiers*. Parallel, breakneck development of the Internet and of consumer computing devices and software quickly created an astonishing new condition: a vast, *hitherto-unimagined territory began to open up for exploration*. Early computers had been like *isolated mountain valleys* ruled by programmer-*kings*; the archaic digital world was a far-flung range in which narrow, unreliable trails provided only tenuous connections [. . .]. An occasional floppy disk would migrate from one to the other, *bringing the makings of colonies* [. . .]. Cyberspace is still *tough territory to travel*' (Mitchell 1995: 109–10; in a section entitled 'Wild West/electronic frontier'; emphasis added).

'Cyberspace is a *frontier region*, populated by few hardy technologies who can tolerate the austerity of its *savage* computer interfaces [. . .] the general lack of useful maps or metaphors' (Kapor and Barlow 1990; emphasis added).

2 But in other instances fences can be a witness to dispossession: the sabra-cactus plant, whose Arabic etymology (s.b.r.) means patience, were originally planted to mark borders, and they remained, even after the Euro-Israeli settling of the destroyed villages, as a reminder of an absence.

3 'Scattered hegemonies' is Inderpal Grewal and Caren Kaplan's term (1994), see their edited *Scattered Hegemonies: postmodernity and transnational feminist politics*; 'dispersed hegemonies' is Arjun Appadurai's phrase, see 'Disjunction and difference in the global cultural economy' (1990).

4 On polycentric multiculturalism, see Shohat and Stam (1994).

5 It is not only imperial ideologies that travel in cyberspace. The transnational shipment of hardware and software allows corporations to dump old technologies on the third world and on minoritarian communities in the first world. New technologies are celebrated also for minimizing 'travel' to work. Although certain types of office jobs and business can be performed from

anywhere via cyberspace, other jobs still require a delimited physical location. While the garment industry uses cybercommunication to save time and money, the Chinese and Chicana workers in the sweatshops labour on the assembly line.

6 In this sense, the 'postcolonial' is actually a post-third worldist critique, moving beyond the ideology of third worldism, rather than colonialism. On my critique of the 'postcolonial', see my 'Notes on the post-colonial' (1992), and 'Post-third-worldist culture: gender, nation and the cinema' (1997).

7 For a complex analysis of 'de/territorialization' in contemporary intellectual thought, see Caren Kaplan (1995), *Questions of Travel: postmodern discourse of displacement*.

8 For an elaborate discussion of exilic nostalgia, see Hamid Naficy (1993), *The Making of Exile Cultures: Iranian television in Los Angeles*.

9 On the distinction between the multicultural fact and the multicultural political project see Shohat and Stam (1994).

10 Habiba is my Arabic name, that was not officially registered on my Israeli ID card because of fears of antagonism and racism from Euro-Israel. See my (1998) 'Sephardim in Israel: Zionism from the standpoint of its Jewish victims'.

11 Despite the growing numbers of immigrants, refugees, and exiles from the Middle East/North Africa in the US, Middle Easterners tend to be absent from the public sphere even in debates on 'ethnic identities'. Although this presence dates back to the late nineteenth century, the waves of immigration from the Middle East have been rendered invisible, while more recent ones are often associated with terrorist infiltrations.

12 In a country where communications are government-controlled, access to computers is out of the question, especially in a post-Gulf War Iraq, where food and medicine are rare commodities. Given the difficulty of establishing communication with Iraq, and given the American media invisibility of Arab culture, e-mail information becomes even more precious.

REFERENCES

Appadurai, A. (1990) 'Disjunction and difference in the global cultural economy', *Public Culture*, 2 (2) (Spring): 1–24.

Carillo, T. (1998) 'Cross-border talk: transnational perspectives on labor, race and sexuality', in E. Shohat (ed.) *Talking Visions: multicultural feminism in a transnational age*, Cambridge, Massachusetts: MIT Press.

Grewal, I. and Kaplan, C. (eds) (1994) *Scattered Hegemonies: postmodernity and transnational feminist politics*, Minneapolis: University of Minnesota Press.

Kaplan, C. (1995) *Questions of Travel: postmodern discourse of displacement*, Durham, North Carolina: Duke University Press.

Kapor, M. and Barlow, J.P. (1990) 'Across the electronic frontier', paper presented at Electronic Frontier Foundation, Washington DC, 10 July.

Lanham, R.A. (1993) *The Electronic Word: democracy, technology and the arts*, Chicago: University of Chicago Press.

Mitchell, W.J. (1995) *City of Bits: space, place and the infobahn*, Cambridge, Massachusetts: MIT Press.

Naficy, H. (1993) *The Making of Exile Cultures: Iranian television in Los Angeles*, Minneapolis: University of Minnesota Press.

Shohat, E. (1988) 'Sephardim in Israel: Zionism from the standpoint of its Jewish victims', *Social Text* (Fall): 1–35.

Shohat, E. (1992) 'Notes on the post-colonial', *Social Text* (Spring): 99–113.

Shohat, E. (1997) 'Post-third-worldist culture: gender, nation and the cinema', in M.J. Alexander and C.T. Mohanty (eds) *Feminist Genealogies, Colonial Legacies, Democratic Futures*, New York: Routledge.

Shohat, E. and Stam, R. (1994) *Unthinking Eurocentrism; multiculturalism and the media*, London and New York: Routledge.

Index